Wearing the Breeches
Gender on the Antebellum Stage

Elizabeth Reitz Mullenix

St. Martin's Press
New York

WEARING THE BREECHES
Copyright © Elizabeth Reitz Mullenix, 2000. All rights reserved. Printed in the United States of America. No part of this book may be used or reproduced in any manner whatsoever without written permission except in the case of brief quotations embodied in critical articles or reviews. For information, address St. Martin's Press, 175 Fifth Avenue, New York, N.Y. 10010.

ISBN 0-312-22349-8

Library of Congress Cataloging-in-Publication Data

Reitz Mullenix, Elizabeth.
　Wearing the breeches : gender on the antebellum stage / by Elizabeth Reitz Mullenix.
　　p.　cm.
　Includes bibliographical references and index.
　ISBN 0-312-22349-8
　1. Breeches parts.　2. Male impersonators.　3. Impersonation. 4. Theater—United States—History—19th century.　I. Title.

PN2071.I47 R45　2000
792'.082'0973—dc21   99-059917
                                                                                                  CIP

Design by Letra Libre, Inc.

First edition: June 2000
10　9　8　7　6　5　4　3　2　1

*To my parents,
Ann Leonard Reitz
& Bartley L. Reitz*

Contents

Acknowledgments		vi
Illustrations		ix
Introduction		1
Chapter 1	American Breeches Performance: 1800–1869	19
Chapter 2	Breeches, Bloomers, and "Biddy in the Kitchen": Breeches Performance as Feminist Politic	71
Chapter 3	Mapping the Bo[d]y Female: Immaturity, Femininity, and the Antebellum Actress-as-Boy	127
Chapter 4	Acting Between the Spheres: Charlotte Cushman as Androgyne	185
Chapter 5	The Decline of Breeches Performance	231
Conclusion	"A Doublet and Hose in My Disposition": Feminism, Lesbianism, and Late Century Breeches Performance	281
Notes		301
Appendix		354
Bibliography		357
Index		368

Acknowledgments

WHILE THE FASCINATING WOMEN WHOSE LIVES comprise this study made my job as a writer/researcher an eminently pleasant one, this work could not have been completed without the help of the following individuals and institutions. I gratefully acknowledge the staff at the University of Illinois Graduate Library, the Harvard Theatre Collection, the Schlessinger Library, the American Jewish Archives at Hebrew Union College, and Illinois State University's Milner Library and Office of Research in Arts Technology; I especially wish to thank librarians, curators, and computer experts William Ogg, Annette Fern, Heather Ahlstrom, Dorothy Smith, Steve Meckstroth, Steve Gossard, and Peter Guither. The Huntington Library, Columbia University, and the University of Rochester must also be recognized for their willingness to share archival material on Cushman through the mail. I would also like to thank the editors and staff at St. Martin's Press, specifically Michael Flamini, Rick Delaney, Mara Nelson, and Karin Bolender.

In the first stages of this project—when this book was still a dissertation—R. B. Graves, Sonya Michel, Michel Shapiro, and Peter Davis all contributed sound advice and challenging feedback. Bob Graves deserves special recognition for his continued support as this dissertation evolved into a book; his sustained and generous mentorship has been invaluable to me. I would also like to thank my colleagues at Illinois State University for their willingness to listen to my ideas and answer certain questions (Dan Wilhelm's expertise in costume history was particularly helpful), and for their encouragement in the final stages of writing. I would especially like to thank my friend and Chairperson, Fergus "Tad" Currie, for his support during this process, for repeatedly lightening my load, and for honoring my requests for more time to write. To Shari Zeck, John Poole, Lori Adams, and Alvin Goldfarb, I am also especially grateful; their friendship, intellectual stimulation, and much needed moral support were generously given. Rosemary Stockle and Nancy Eller must also be thanked for regularly helping to lighten my workload and for their uplifting humor. Two generous grants from the College of Fine Arts at Illinois State University provided significant funds that helped to subsidize new research and materials. My wonderful, spirited students at I.S.U. (both graduate and undergraduate) must be recognized for making my day on a regular basis and for inspiring me to be as passionate about my research as they are about their art. In particular, I am indebted to my former teaching assistant Heather MacMahon, my research assistants Kris Dallman and Marcie Schwalm, and former M.A. student Michelle Sullivan for their hard work on my behalf and for their intellectual companionship. I also wish to acknowledge my teacher, the late George B. Bryan, for getting me started; this book is, in part, the product of his rich instruction.

Portions of this book have appeared elsewhere: chapter 4 was published in altered form in 1996 in *Theatre Survey* and sections of the conclusion were part of an article that appeared in 1995 in *Theatre History Studies*. I am grateful to the editors of these journals, Gary Jay Williams and Robert A. Schanke, for allowing me permission to reprint.

Finally, I wish to thank my family and friends (some of them mentioned above) for their love and assistance throughout this six year process. I am extremely grateful for the support of my dear friends Ann Haugo and Shari Zeck, whose warm encouragement and keen insight into feminist scholarship continue to nourish mind, body, and soul, and to Kim Marshall, who, because of her exceptional strength of character and her bounteous optimism, repeatedly reminds me that balancing motherhood and a demanding professional career is an act that can be done with dignity. As professors, feminists, and nineteenth-century scholars, my mother, Dr. Ann Leonard Reitz, and my sister, Dr. Caroline W. Reitz, have functioned as excellent role models; they inspire me with their challenging, witty ideas, their devotion to women's issues and to literature, and their excellent guidance on all fronts. Likewise, my father Bartley L. Reitz has also served as a significant role model, for his foundational teachings about high standards and perseverance helped me to stay focused on this book when other things seemed more attractive (like sleep). My precious sons Tom and Charles Reitz Mullenix not only gave me direct insight into the mysteries of "boy culture," but also served, and continue to serve, as constant sources of joy. My deepest love and thanks go to my husband Robert Mullenix, without whose devotion, dogged and enthusiastic support, artistic insight, intellectual camaraderie, and unbounded patience this work could not have been possible.

Illustrations

Fig. 1.1:	Peg Woffington as Sir Harry Wildair	33
Fig. 1.2:	Clara Fisher as Richard III	49
Fig. 1.3:	Mrs. Henry Lewis as William Tell	55
Fig. 2.1:	Amelia Bloomer in her pantaloons	81
Fig. 2.2:	Adah Isaacs Menken as William the Sailor	88
Fig. 3.1:	Charlotte Cushman as Romeo	132
Fig. 3.2:	Ellen Tree as Ion	168
Fig. 4.1:	Charlotte Cushman as Romeo with Susan Cushman as Juliet	193
Fig. 5.1:	Adah Isaacs Menken as the French Spy	243
Fig. 5.2:	Adah Isaacs Menken in fleshlings	244
Fig. 5.3:	Leo Hudson as Mazeppa	256

INTRODUCTION

ON THE 23RD OF FEBRUARY, 1663, SAMUEL PEPYS wrote in his diary, "To the Duke's House . . . being most pleased to see the little girl dance in boy's apparel, she having very fine legs."[1] Entries such as this peppered Pepys' diary as he chronicled his repeated trips to the theatre during the first decade of the Restoration. Indeed, the author of this famous journal continually delighted in the novel presence of the actress on the English stage, remarking upon her physical attributes as frequently as he did her histrionic abilities. Roughly 80 years after Pepys wrote of his visit to the Duke's House (the Lincoln's Inn Fields Theatre), another actress made theatrical history and delighted English audiences by "wearing the breeches"—which by this time had become a popular practice in English theatres. According to legend, one night after the celebrated eighteenth-century actress Peg Woffington performed the role of Sir Harry Wildair from George Farquhar's *The Constant Couple,* she rushed into the Green Room of the Drury Lane—exuberated by the success of her impersonation—and announced, "By God, half the audience thinks me to be a man." Woffington's rival, actress Kitty Clive, immediately retorted, "By God madam, the other half knows you to be a woman."[2] Both of these anecdotes—which together foreground the sexual objectification of the female transvestite onstage and link her theatrical transgressions to illicit practices offstage—are illustrative of the history that surrounds breeches performance; whether "fact," like the excerpt from Pepys' diary, or "fiction," like the hackneyed and seemingly apocryphal tale from the Green Room, the breeches actress is remembered primarily for her sexual appeal.

Recent studies about cross-dressing however, as evidenced by the proliferation of essays and book-length investigations by feminist scholars, theatre historians, and gender theoreticians in the

1980s and 1990s, suggest that there was more to the breeches performer than what—quite literally—met the eye. Indeed, current post-structuralist paradigms that emphasize the instability of identity and the disruption of established and "naturalized" ideologies are fortified by alternative conceptual ideas, such as transvestism, that challenge both constructed notions of gendered behavior and hegemonic institutions. For this reason, studies of cross-dressed performance have become attractive to theatre historians, critics, and theorists who are seeking new insights into traditional avenues of representation. Contemporary feminist scholars are especially interested in theatrical cross-dressing as a way of exposing the performative nature of gender; many of their studies also focus on the cross-dressed actress specifically, exploring the ways in which her portrayals of masculinity suggest both a subversive desire to transcend the limitations of gender and to appropriate male power.

Despite academia's current fascination with cross-dressing, a paucity of historical analysis exists regarding perhaps the most celebrated of all theatrical transvestites: the nineteenth-century American breeches actress. Established as a convention during the English Restoration, breeches performance gave women the opportunity to play men's roles (in tight-fitting knee-length breeches) in a variety of theatrical genres. Throughout the seventeenth, eighteenth, and nineteenth centuries, women frequently appeared as boys, romantic male leads, and Shakespearean tragic heroes on the English-speaking stage. The popularity of this convention reached its peak in America during the first half of the nineteenth century, as actresses regularly donned doublets and hose, tunics and tights in theatres throughout the country. Indeed, the majority of American actresses who experienced substantial stage careers played at least one breeches role at some point during their careers and many established their reputations by performing such parts. Regardless of the American breeches performer's ubiquitous appeal, however, many histories of the theatre make no mention of this convention, and those that do, discuss stars such as Charlotte Cushman (1816–1876), the most famous American breeches performer, whose experience was extraordinary and therefore not entirely representative.

Furthermore, as the above anecdotes imply, the history that has been written about the breeches performer—beginning with her appearance on the seventeenth-century English stage—consists largely of a discussion of the actress as a sexual object. Traditional explanations for the popularity of the practice are based on the conjecture that the breeches actress served only to titillate a predominantly male audience, that her performance, no matter what the context, was seldom more than a cleverly disguised leg show. Such assumptions have been cultivated and sustained by commentators past and present. "[A] pair of handsome legs has oftener been the instigation to 'get up' Romeo than any impression of intellectual capacity to do justice to the part," bemoaned the "Lady Correspondent" from *Porter's Spirit of the Times* in 1858.[3] Similarly, contemporary feminist theatre historians have also written about the breeches performer as a "sexual commodity." In her book, *Actresses as Working Women: Their Social Identity in Victorian Culture,* Tracy C. Davis observes of English actresses, "The exposure of legs has a long stage tradition, and the effect of this ploy on box office receipts suggests that its sexual power, first discovered in the reign of Charles II, did not wane under Victoria."[4] This association between the breeches performer and her lower limbs is the most salient historical explanation for the longevity and popularity enjoyed by this theatrical convention.

Barnard Hewitt suggests other reasons for the popularity of the breeches performer in his attempt to understand the convention's singular position as "a phenomenon of the nineteenth-century [American] theatre."[5] In addition to the audiences' fascination with "the female form," these reasons include an equally powerful lust for novelty in a century that sported a relatively static standard repertoire, and a theatrical climate largely antithetical to native playwriting until the first American Copyright Law was established in 1856. It is Hewitt's final theory regarding the popularity of breeches, however, that is the most compelling and that inspired this study. Hewitt collectively attributes the success of cross-dressed female performance to an interest in variety entertainment, sex appeal, and women's rights. "Feminism was on the march and some of its first victories were in the theatre."[6]

This book elucidates Hewitt's somewhat cryptic remark and strives to prove that breeches performance was not just a leg show. Through a gendered historical analysis of the American stage from 1800 to 1869, traditional treatments of the cross-dressed actress are revised and explained. Certainly, the breeches performer was occasionally objectified by the press, yet she seldom invited such perceptions; nor were these critical observations rendered innocently. Rather, discourses of containment (of which sexual objectification was one) were instituted in order to mitigate fears of female usurpation and "petticoat government." In an effort to reinforce dominant gender ideology, critics repeatedly feminized, infantilized, and sexualized the cross-dressed actress in a deliberate attempt to show that her disguise was translucent, that no matter how skilled she was in "wearing the breeches," her femininity was indelible. Such recuperative critical strategies became necessary as more and more actresses began to assume male lines of business, and threats of female revolution became increasingly palpable for the male critic. By self-consciously dissolving gender boundaries through their attempt to pass as men both on and off stage, actresses contributed to these critical anxieties. Indeed, the breeches performer, who generally thought of herself as a serious artist, often betrayed a feminist politic behind her male mask, evidenced by her adoption of "male" societal roles beyond the footlights and her aggressive desire to compete with her male colleagues. While such insurgencies were often contained, select performers were able to use their male personas to liberate themselves from the domestic sphere and to brave new territory for American women.

Despite the copious amount of material generated in the last decade about transvestism in general, cross-dressed female performance remains relatively unexplored, and the scholarship that does exist betrays a marked patriarchal bias. Indeed, the major texts, dissertations, and articles that include discussions of the breeches performer or the male impersonator largely reinforce images of women that were constructed in the nineteenth century (or earlier), and do not expose the oppressive ideologies or clandestine operations of gender that more recent feminist histories seek to unveil. Rather, antiquated perceptions of women as angelic and lascivious pervade traditional scholarship surrounding the cross-dressed actress.

Before reviewing the previous literature about female theatrical transvestism, however, I must pause and briefly discuss my use of terms such as "breeches performance," "male impersonator," and "transvestite," which are often used interchangeably by scholars who study cross-dressed female performance. For example, actresses such as Woffington and Cushman are frequently described as male impersonators although they played what are most commonly called breeches roles, and many historians who write about cross-dressing seem to perceive the breeches performer—an actress who played a male character role—as a prototype for the male impersonator, which is the term I will use to designate what Laurence Senelick refers to as the "flash young spark," the variety performer who dressed in contemporary fashionable men's wear and inhabited the American concert-saloons, vaudeville stages, and English music halls in the late nineteenth and early twentieth centuries.

Although some historians suggest that only dashing young heroes in romantic comedies could qualify as breeches parts and that more serious dramatic roles such as Hamlet, Romeo, and Claude Melnotte were not actually breeches roles,[7] this argument is considerably weakened by actual evidence from the period. In the nineteenth century, the term "breeches" is used by contemporary playwrights, managers, and historians to discuss the female theatrical transvestite in serious, comic, and melodramatic roles. For example, in 1844, William E. Burton wrote a letter to the London theatre manager Benjamin Webster regarding Cushman; in this epistle he declared her to be "undoubtedly the best breeches figure in America."[8] Similarly, in a letter to William Dunlap dated 1832, playwright Mordecai Noah writes, "In the year 1812, while in Charleston, Mr. Young requested me to write a piece for his wife's benefit. You remember her, no doubt; remarkable as she was for her personal beauty and amiable deportment, it would have been very ungallant to have refused, particularly as he requested that it should be a 'breeches part,' to use a green-room term, though she was equally attractive in every character."[9] The role that Noah wrote for Mrs. Young was that of the "fearless, intrepid, and quick-witted boy" Justin in *Paul and Alexis, or The Orphans of the Rhine*, later retitled *The Wandering Boys*.[10] Certainly Justin is not a dashing romantic hero such as Wildair, nor does this melodrama resemble a romantic comedy. Furthermore, Cushman's male repertoire, referred to by Burton, included tragic adult roles, melodramatic boys, and romantic heroes. Based on this nineteenth-century usage, therefore, I will use the terms "breeches role" or "breeches part" to designate any role written for men and played by women, regardless of the age of the character or the genre.

The breeches role also needs to be distinguished from the disguise role, an impersonation especially popular in the Restoration in which the character in question is female but must assume male garb during the course of the play in order to work out some machination, as Rosalind does to educate and test Orlando in Shakespeare's *As You Like It*.[11] In addition to the breeches performer, the disguise-role actress and the male impersonator, England's principal boy—the juvenile romantic lead of the British Pantomime—serves as another example of cross-dressed female performance popular since the mid-nineteenth century (and still performed today).

All of these performers are also often described by contemporary scholars as transvestites, and while such broad usage is generally accepted, Marjorie Garber suggests a much more specific definition for the transvestite (and one that I will adopt in my discussion of the actress-as-boy in chapter 3). According to Garber, who unfortunately gives the breeches actress short shift in her extensive discussion of cross-dressing, the transvestite serves a very particular function within society; "the appearance of the transvestite in a cultural representation signals a category crisis."[12] She further explains that the transvestite always signifies underlying tensions between two conflicting concepts, ideas, individuals, and/or political institutions (e.g., youth and age, male and female, middle- and working-class, Caucasian and African American). For Garber, the transvestite inhabits a "space of possibility" between male and female and therefore renders these poles unstable. Such a theory is extremely useful for highlighting the subversive nature of nineteenth-century breeches performance, which took place in an age of rigid separate spheres where strict gendered codes of behavior were cultivated and where True Women eschewed all masculine proclivities for the sacred virtues of domesticity.[13]

Although many terms have been used to identify the cross-dressed actress, it is only recently that scholars have endowed such terms with theoretical content and have begun to read her performances semiotically. While Garber explores the transvestite's signifying potential and transgressive power, most historical treatments of the breeches performer reveal the same binary thinking that controlled nineteenth-century observations. The cross-dressed actress is remembered as either a sexual object or an innocuous "pretty little woman." The breeches actress never achieves a convincing illusion of masculinity, according to this traditional school, but ultimately *plays herself* or reproduces prescribed images of Woman as madonna/whore, feminine/sexual created by male playwrights and maintained (through popular and financial support) by male audience members and managers.[14] Such readings are most apparent in treatments of the actress written before the 1980s. Included in this group are American theatre historians (who mention the breeches performer in conjunction with other nineteenth-century theatrical conventions) such as William Dunlap and Joseph Ireland; authors like Rosamond Gilder who write specifically about women onstage; and scholars like Charlene Edwards whose 1957 dissertation is the only previous full-length investigation of this subject.[15] Most of the historians in this category published in the nineteenth or early to mid-twentieth century; however some recent studies also reinforce traditional bifacial conceptions of the breeches performer or repeat long-held claims that actresses "played up the possibility of titillating the predominantly male audience by displaying shapely bodies and legs."[16] Despite the fact that some of the work that emerges from this school is quite valuable (Edward's dissertation, for example, is a rich source of names and dates), most of the material is governed by reductive views of the cross-dressed actress, views that definitively cast her within the madonna/whore binary.[17]

These historians argue that sexual showcasing contributed significantly to the convention's popularity. As Hewitt explains, "In a day when a glimpse of a female ankle was titillating, the sight of a considerable portion of a woman's legs—though by later standards the costumes were modest—was certainly an attraction for men."[18] Edwards also upholds this traditional view of the eroticized cross-dressed performer yet, unlike Hewitt, she offers no feminist alternatives to counter such explanations. She posits sexual allure as one of the three main reasons (the others are novelty and utility—more male roles than female roles in the standard repertoire) that the convention endured on the English-speaking stage. According to Edwards, "The breeches actress . . . has from the very beginning been a sex (sexual or 'sexy') institution of the theatre. A predominantly male audience might require a 'male' play, but a female dressed as a male gave the play a duel value, that of sex and of male adventure. . . . Present-day audiences have little need for the breeches figure with the prevalence of 'cheese-cake,' the deliberate display of the female figure for sex projection."[19] The breeches performer's primary function, Edwards suggests, was to cater to male sexual desires; once burlesque and other forms of erotica emerged in the later half of the nineteenth century, the breeches performer became obsolete, as male appetites feasted on richer fare. This implies that other requirements that were commonly considered crucial to ensure any actor's success, such as talent, versatility, agility, and a powerful voice, were secondary to what one twentieth-century critic calls the "essential asset" of the breeches performer: "a good pair of legs."[20]

Another stereotype that is perpetuated by past histories is the image of the breeches performer as boyish. Because actresses often played boys throughout the eighteenth and nineteenth centuries, certain historians conclude that the cross-dressed actress was somehow equivalent to the juvenile whom she impersonated. Edwards explains that "the boyish-looking actress lent herself in talent and appearance to a succession of boyish types that began to emerge in drama."[21] This affinity between breeches performers and adolescence implies that the actress was, like the boy, socially, emotionally, and intellectually (perhaps even physically) immature, that she lacked the privilege and legitimacy that accompanies both manhood and adult life. Actresses played boys, Edwards suggests, because they were similar to them "in talent and appearance"—an argument that, like the associations made between the breeches performer, femininity and sexual appeal, limits the potential of the cross-dressed actress as a serious artist or as a feminist agent. Indeed, nineteenth-century critics employed similar ideologic strategies equating the breeches actress to the boy in order to undermine the potential power of women who "wore the breeches." Rather than deconstructing the politics behind such gendered tactics, however, traditional historians simply reproduce the recuperative stereotype.[22]

More recently, scholars have begun to challenge traditional models through more gendered analyses. Laurence Senelick's 1992 study *Gender in Performance: The Presentation of Difference in the Performing Arts* and Lesley Ferris's 1993 book *Crossing the Stage: Controversies on Cross-Dressing* are perhaps emblematic of the new directions being undertaken by contemporary historians and theorists. Although the topic of nineteenth-century American breeches performance is not undertaken specifically in any of the essays appearing in these anthologies, many innovative theories concerning the cross-dressed performer (both male and female) are explored. In Ferris's study, several authors move the discourse concerning cross-dressed actresses (the text includes detailed discussions of eighteenth-century breeches actresses, principal boys, male impersonators, and transvestite travesty dancers in opera) away from stereotypes and outline instead the ways in which performers subverted hegemonic institutions and categories. According to these scholars, cross-dressed theatrical women questioned rigid gender boundaries and artificial constructions of femininity and masculinity by foregrounding the performative nature of gender. Not only are the categories of male and female destabilized by drag performances, but the notion of one's ability to posses a fixed identity is also challenged. Additionally, some scholars argue that cross-dressed actresses often took their roles seriously and approached male characters with an aim to pass rather than to present a male grotesque onstage similar to the debased images of women presented by female impersonators or the Pantomime's

Dame. Conversely, others explain that by impersonating men onstage, the female theatrical transvestite sought to parody and critique masculinity. In either case, contemporary critics perceive the assumption of male dress onstage as an attempt by women to appropriate male power, to claim a subject position, and to open up new spaces of possibility for women in general. Furthermore, those studies that do discuss feminine, sexual, and boyish stereotypes do so with an aim to expose the workings of a male theatrical hegemony concerned with preserving masculine and feminine binaries by reinforcing dominant gender ideology and constructing specific discourses of containment.[23]

Additional recent material on the cross-dressed female performer reflects many of the gender and performance theories posited by the authors who contributed to Senelick and Ferris's studies. Both Anne Russell and Faye Dudden, for example, relate the notion of destabilizing gender polarities and performing gender to the breeches actress.[24] Many current discussions of cross-dressing have also drawn upon the methodological strategies of gay and lesbian studies, as historians employ queer theory to explore transvestism's power to disrupt readings of both gender and sexual identity. Beth H. Friedman-Romell and Kristina Straub's treatment of eighteenth-century drag performances by both men and women are representative of this approach, as are Denise A. Walen, Noreen Barnes-McLain, and Lee Allan Morrow's treatment of cross-dressing in Robert A. Schanke and Kim Marra's anthology *Passing Performances: Queer Readings of Leading Players in American Theatre History*.[25] Lisa Merrill's new biography of Cushman also investigates performance and cross-dressing through the use of queer theory, and argues that Cushman transgresses both gender boundaries and heterosexist notions of desire in her "sapphic" performances of Romeo.[26]

While the above studies do indeed advance the dialogue on female theatrical cross-dressing beyond a reinscription of stereotypes, few scholars have considered the case of the breeches player in particular. Investigations of Cushman's career often include discussions of breeches performance (Merrill and Dudden's book or Russell's article), as do biographies of Adah Isaacs Menken and Lydia Thompson. While some of these studies are exceptional in interweaving feminist/gender theory, contextual information, and readings of performance (Renee Sentilles' dissertation—and forthcoming book—is a postmodern biography, an excellent study of Menken as constructor and performer of identity in antebellum America), no previous full-length study exists that applies such an approach to the convention of breeches performance on the nineteenth-century American stage (although other forms of popular/novelty entertainment such as burlesque and minstrelsy have enjoyed recent scholarly attention).[27] This study is a response to this gap within cross-dressing studies and an attempt to position the history of this phenomena within a materialist discourse.

Many breeches performers were regarded as suspect by various individuals (critics, managers, or fellow actors) on specific occasions because their performance seemed to suggest that they were not proper ladies, that they exhibited a subtextual agenda—a feminist message that had little to do with novelty or sexual objectification. Because this study deals with many minor actresses who generated little extant personal documentation, it is often difficult to glean whether such an agenda was consciously adopted by these women. I will argue, however, that regardless of whether these performers were articulating a self-conscious and deliberate political position, the adoption of male roles might still have been viewed as political (feminist, subversive, and/or rebellious) to nineteenth-century audience members and critics when placed within the context of antebellum American culture with its rigid doctrine of separate spheres, the cult of True Womanhood (which dictated that women were to be virtuous, devout, domestic, and subservient), and the dress reform movement.[28]

By calling certain breeches performances political, I also mean to imply that for a number of reasons (which were both initiated by the actress and generated by more general cultural paradigms), select actresses were in some way advocating societal change and challenging long-established gender codes. Such messages, which were sometimes quite obvious and other times more subtle, were considered threatening, for in the nineteenth century women were simply not allowed to enjoy male privileges or "wear the breeches." The actress's serious attempts at cross-dressing (or "drag," which is deliberately performative) identified the construction of gender and thereby threatened both the status quo, by questioning the legitimacy of social asymmetry (men as public and women as private individuals), and the institutions that perpetuated such separate spheres. Through her performance the breeches actress asks: if women can *perform* both masculinity and femininity, then what is gender but an artificially created discourse?

This desire to expose a patriarchal script behind the establishment, operation, and maintenance of gender and to analyze, as feminist historian Joan Scott says, "the ways in which politics construct gender and gender constructs politics," speaks to my materialist methodological approach, an approach that has been shaped by women's history and feminist theory.[29] A study of theatrical transvestism invites theories about gender performance as well as gender construction since, as Judith Butler argues, "the various acts of gender creates the idea of gender." For Butler, gender is not an essential characteristic but a series of stylized acts "both conditioned and circumscribed by historical convention." Indeed, the body "is a historical situation . . . a manner of doing, dramatizing, and *reproducing* a historical situation."[30] Sandra Gilbert and Susan Gubar have also contributed to my thinking about cross-dressed performance, particularly with respect to their notion of male clothing as a "freedom suit" for women, a sartorial sign that signifies power within the public sphere. Through cross-dressing, women can appropriate male power and remark upon the inequity of existing gender prescriptions in addition to claiming a liminal and simultaneously powerful place where new alternatives for women can be imagined.[31] Yet, as I have implied above, exposing gender constructions is subversive, and subversions require containment. Scott and Carroll Smith-Rosenberg both substantiate this idea, as does Straub who discusses the institutionalization of containment strategies.

Wearing the Breeches is therefore a materialist feminist study focusing specifically on American breeches performers during the first half of the nineteenth century. Not all the subjects of this history were native to North America however; some of the actresses considered in this book were born in England and others were foreign stars who regularly toured America or who lived in America for extended periods. Because 1800–1869 is a rather extensive time span, I do not chronicle every single breeches performance that occurred during these years or every player (which is Edwards's approach), but concentrate instead on trends that occurred in breeches performance as a genre. I discuss how the convention, the actresses, the costumes, and the critical reception changed and was influenced by nineteenth-century American culture and gender ideology.

I have chosen to cover the years 1800 to 1869 because this time frame allows for an investigation of the events that preceded and followed the convention's peak on the American stage in terms of the practice's critical acceptance and its audience appeal. Breeches performance can be seen as changing from a practice employed out of necessity (stock companies were always in need of more male players to satisfy the requirements of a dramatic repertoire that featured many more male roles than female roles) in the beginning of the century to a successful type of entertainment independent of utilitarian demands as the century progressed. I have chosen to end the study in 1869 because this year marks the institutionalization of Thompsonian burlesque, which, I argue in chapter 5, changed the performance climate with regard to breeches, altered critical perceptions of the cross-dressed actress, and contributed to the convention's ultimate erasure from the American theatre.

Furthermore, this study investigates the phenomenon of breeches specifically as it thrived upon the New York City stage. I have chosen to discuss major and minor actresses who worked in New York as this was considered a major theatrical center in the early nineteenth century and gradually became the nucleus of American theatre as the century progressed. However, because many of the principal breeches performers toured regularly throughout the first half of the nineteenth century, I occasionally discuss performances that occurred in other major theatrical cities such as Boston, Philadelphia, and New Orleans. The actresses who constitute my database are both major stars and minor players who performed a variety of "legitimate" and "illegitimate" dramatic roles. Before I continue, I must note that although I find the terms "legitimate" and "illegitimate" informative as ways to signify different types of entertainment (a specific usage that began in seventeenth-century England with the institutionalization of patent theatres in London), employing such terms invites pejorative associations that I wish to avoid, since I regard "illegitimate" forms as significant cultural texts and scrutinize such performance throughout this study. Therefore, I will refer to roles within the nineteenth-century standard American repertoire as traditional (although I realize that there are also inherent problems with this term as well)—which included, for the breeches actress, largely Shakespearean roles but also "regular" comedy, tragedy, farce, and melodrama—and will term breeches parts in equestrian melodrama, extravaganza, and burlesque as popular.

Thus the actresses under analysis here performed traditional and popular *dramatic* roles (as opposed to opera) and were generally European, white, lower to middle-class women who began performing either as children or as young adults in New York's resident stock companies. While I lament the white Eurocentricism of this study, I have found evidence of breeches performance at only one antebellum theatre that featured actors and playwrights of color, the African Theatre, which operated in New York from 1821 to 1824. The repertory of the African Theatre, formerly referred to by theatre historians as the African Grove Theatre, contained at least three plays that often contained breeches parts: *Douglas, Richard III,* and *Tom and Jerry,* but I have discovered only three accounts of breeches performance and no critical information about these actresses (a Miss Johnson and a Miss S. Welch who performed dramatic roles, and a Miss Shaw who danced "a sailor's hornpipe in character"), an occurrence that speaks to the racial hostility and prejudice that pervaded American practice—both theatrical and critical—in the Northern states as well as the South prior to the Civil War.[32]

This book is divided into five subsequent chapters and a conclusion; a configuration that allows me to chart breeches performance chronologically, conceptually, and ideologically. Chapter 1 places the convention in historical context and outlines the origins, patterns, trends, and themes that surrounded, and therefore helped to define, breeches performance. Included in this chapter is a survey of roles that were popular in each decade, an introduction to the representative actresses who played these parts, and an examination of how these performances were perceived by critics and audience members. In addition, the societal threat generated by the cross-dressed actress, the woman who claimed male privilege in the public sphere, is investigated with an aim both to outline the proliferation of this threat throughout the early and mid century and to interpret theatrical subversions within the larger context of the burgeoning women's rights movement. A brief summary of the various discourses of containment used to counter and control these transgressions is also introduced.

Chapter 2 moves the discussion of "wearing the breeches" into a theatrical context and foregrounds the ways in which women used cross-dressed performance (both onstage and offstage) to communicate a feminist politic. Because trousers took on symbolic significance during the first half of the nineteenth century, male critics and authors frequently associated expressions of male power with male dress. Even women who wore the broad-shouldered "Bishop sleeve"—a popular women's fashion—were thought to be "unnatural and masculine," and those who abandoned the whalebone corset for looser dresses and pantaloons were condemned for their suspected attempts to usurp male prerogative, just as minor actress Sarah Timm's display of courage during a Bowery riot in 1844 was explained by a critic for the *Spirit of the Times* as the direct result of her "so often wearing the breeches and personating the man." As the women's rights movement gained notoriety, such associations between male power and female cross-dressing engendered more palpable critical anxiety, and actresses who played tragic breeches roles were castigated by the press. On certain occasions, breeches performance became directly political, as is evidenced by one actress's decision to rival her male colleague by playing Count Belino (her first male role) on her benefit night. In wearing Belino's sword and breeches, Mrs. Sharpe briefly claimed a subject position and exposed specific unequal distributions of power within the New York theatre. Moreover, her performance raised questions about how such distributions of power are instituted and maintained.

Vitriolic reviews of breeches performers in serious male roles imply a deliberate critical struggle to contain the threat of the usurping cross-dresser. Worries about female revolution were mitigated, however, through certain discourses of containment. Straub's theory of the ways in which subversive actions are recuperated through discourse proves a valuable tool in deconstructing nineteenth-century critical rhetoric regarding the breeches performer. For example, the public's fascination with women who played young male roles—the subject undertaken in chapter 3—is understood by exposing the reductive associations between femininity and immaturity perpetuated throughout the first half of the nineteenth century. Critics drew upon established social and cultural parallels between women and children (which were themselves political constructs) in assembling their own corrective discourses. Likewise, the dramatic boy who was too bold, too much the young warrior (such as Norval, Romeo, and Ion) was refashioned to resemble the actress who played him. As the *New York Mirror* critic put it, "[Ellen Tree] becomes not Ion, but Ion becomes Ellen Tree."

Gendered analyses of nineteenth-century melodramas also deconstruct power relationships and expose discourses of containment meant to infantilize and feminize the breeches performer. Countless examples of virtue in peril and True "Boyhood" can be found in the melodramatic scripts that furnished breeches actresses with their most popular vehicles throughout the early and mid-nineteenth century. Upon visiting the theatre, predominantly male audiences could regularly witness the actress-as-boy being delivered or protected by a male savior. Costumes, dialogue, and stage blocking reinforced themes of dominance and submission that existed in the dramatic texts as cross-dressed boy actresses fell to their knees in supplication before male heroes or gestured wildly to communicate ideas that they, being "dumb" (literally, as they played mute characters, and figuratively, as women within Victorian society), could not articulate—messages that could only be decoded by a male translator.

Recuperative critical and dramatic constructions were challenged, however, by Cushman, who proved to be no "ordinary trespasser" and whose experiences as "androgyne" are considered in chapter 4. While many recent accounts exist that detail Cushman's career and her interpretation of Romeo, this study is the first to discuss in detail her double image, her androgyny. Because Cushman was perceived as both male and female, she was able to cross boundaries, act between social spheres, and expose the contingency of gender prescriptions; she shattered notions of True Womanhood and offered Victorian women new alternatives. Indeed, her androgynous persona became a symbol of transcendence in an age of irrefutable gender binaries. For nineteenth-century viewers, Cushman's androgyny functioned as a critical metaphor: spectators could both delight in her transformations and still categorize her as female. For contemporary students of cross-dressing, Cushman's androgyny serves as a theoretical paradox, a model that serves to enhance current discussions of gender performativity, and that contributes to the deconstruction of hegemonic ideologies.

The conceptual possibilities that Cushman's androgyny suggested, however, were countered by the unprecedented critical preoccupation with the female body during the 1860s—a topic considered in chapter 5. Expansive protofeminist messages about the malleability of supposedly indelible gender roles/traits were subverted as critics continually reminded audiences that the cross-dresser was a woman. Opportunities for "passing" decreased as benefits were eliminated, serious breeches roles (with the exception of boy roles) almost disappeared from the American repertoire, and the fleshling suit (or fleshlings—a tight-fitting body stocking that suggested nudity) became the genre's defining feature. Feminist expressions by actresses such as Adah Isaacs Menken (1835/36–1868) were undermined by the sexualizing rhetoric that defined the craze for equestrian melodrama, just as the notorious burlesque performer Lydia Thompson's parodies of masculinity were overshadowed by the anti-burlesque hysteria generated by critics such as Olive Logan. Although it was the burlesque performer who was on trial, all cross-dressed actresses were implicated in the crimes associated with the leg business and all were found guilty—a judgment that largely eradicated the convention on the nineteenth-century stage except for lingering displays of transvestism in burlesque performance. As the conclusion makes clear, breeches performance received its final blows in the late nineteenth century as critical juxtapositions between lesbianism, feminism, and cross-dressing emerged in the press.

The history of the breeches performer reveals much more than a shapely thigh. Rather, this convention's existence within the annals of nineteenth-century theatre history is marked by a delicate balance between female subversion and hegemonic containment. The cross-dressed actress can be read not simply as a sexual body, an object of desire within the closed economy of the male gaze, but as an acting subject who disrupted fixed notions of nineteenth-century femininity and female performance. Despite critical representations of her as a sexual object or as a feminized boy, the breeches performer occasionally seized center stage and proved that she, too, could, as Juliet's Nurse urged, "stand up and be a man."

CHAPTER 1 ✥

AMERICAN BREECHES PERFORMANCE
1800–1869

Her performance of [Romeo] has everywhere received the highest encomiums, and it seems to be conceded that she has almost made it her own. We think her eminent in the personation, and well deserving the high praise that has been bestowed upon her.

—The Spirit of the Times, 1850

Romeo requires a man, to feel his passion, and to express his despair. A woman, in attempting it, 'unsexes' herself to no purpose, except to destroy all interest in the play . . . and sets up a monstrous anomaly.

—George Vandenhoff, 1860

ON MARCH 20, 1807, WILLIAM WIZARD'S COLUMN on the theatre appeared, as usual, in the weekly periodical *Salmagundi*. Wizard's entry, located under the rubric "Theatrics," concerned a recent production of *Othello* that he had seen in Philadelphia with his friend and constant theatrical companion, Snivers. Wizard (otherwise known as Washington Irving) recalls an invigorating conversation that he had with Snivers regarding Desdemona's wish that heaven had made her a man like Othello; both conclude that this sentiment proves Desdemona's secret desire to dominate an unfortunate and subjugated Othello. Wizard opines:

> I think it was a very *foolish,* and therefore *natural* wish for a young lady to make before a man she wished to marry. It was, moreover, an indication of the violent inclination she felt to wear *the breeches,* which was afterwards, in all probability, gratified, if we may judge from the title of 'our captain's captain,' given her by Cassio, a phrase which, in my opinion, indicates that Othello was, at that time, most ignominiously *hen-pecked.*[1]

Wizard's remark is telling, for it contains in microcosm many of the ideals and concerns that were circulated during the first half of the nineteenth century about women and their designated "natural" position within American society. "Wearing the breeches" was a phrase that appeared frequently in many nineteenth-century periodicals and newspaper columns, yet this expression was by no means confined to the "Theatrics" section, nor did it always refer to actresses who played male theatrical roles. Nineteenth-century women were generally regarded as suspect if they, like Desdemona, in any way tried to "wear the breeches"—a figure of speech that obviously connoted far more than the adoption of an unorthodox style of dress.

Throughout the nineteenth century, an era in American history that was in many ways defined according to strict gender binaries, breeches were emblematic of masculine privilege; they signified male power, which was acted out in a very public sphere. Described by one critic as an "appendage to manhood,"[2] breeches were to masculinity and public life what the petticoat was to femininity and domesticity.[3] Women who donned male attire (both onstage and off) were thought to be stepping out of their proper environment in order to claim an undeserved male advantage. That such usurpation was perceived as threatening to nineteenth-century male critics is evidenced in sundry articles and letters, journalistic pulpits from which women were admonished to eschew completely *all* the trappings of manhood. An aptly named contributor to *Salmagundi,*

Roderick Worry, expressed such concern in a letter to Anthony Evergreen, a regular columnist for the journal. He writes:

> Dear Anthony,
>
> Going down Broadway this morning in a great hurry I ran full against an object which at first put me to a prodigious non plus. Observing it to be dressed in a man's hat, a cloth overcoat, and spatterdashes, I framed my apology accordingly, exclaiming "my dear *sir,* I ask ten thousand pardons—I assure you, *sir,* it was entirely accidental—pray excuse me *sir,* &c." At every one of these excuses, the thing answered me with a downright laugh; at which, I was not a little surprised until, on resorting to my pocket glass I discovered that it was no other than my old acquaintance Clarinda Trollop—I was never more chagrined in my life, for being an old bachelor I like to appear as young as possible, and am always boasting of the goodness of my eyes. I beg of you, Mr. Evergreen, if you have any feeling for your contemporaries, to discourage this hermaphrodite mode of dress; for really, if the fashion take, we poor bachelors will be utterly at a loss to distinguish a woman from a man. Pray let me know your opinion, sir, whether a lady who wears a man's hat and spatterdashes before marriage, may not be apt to usurp some other article of dress afterwards.[4]

The author's fear that women would soon "wear the breeches" seemed relatively widespread, yet certain critics who wrote about breeches performers, throughout the first half of the century, surprisingly did not share Roderick's worry. Rather, critics often praised the breeches performer's seeming ability to appear "natural" in male disguise and celebrated her cross-dressed efforts in general. Although nineteenth-century criticism followed certain patterns and trends, critical responses to the breeches performer were sometimes as mercurial as the actresses themselves. A brief historical overview of this convention, beginning with its origins in the English Restoration, precedes a survey and critical assessment of breeches performance in the early and mid-nineteenth century; this survey proves beneficial in mapping out the multiple routes that critical expression traveled as women went from exclusively playing boys in the early years of the century to attempting serious renditions of Hamlet in the 1830s and burlesqued romantic heroes in the 1860s. Through outlining both the roles that were popular in each decade and the actresses that played these parts, the esoteric and subtextual workings of gender behind dramatic criticism begin to emerge and the real woman becomes discernable from the Man (or in many cases "Woman") being enacted on the boards.

VIEWING AND REVIEWING

Antebellum dramatic critics, the overwhelming majority of whom were male,[5] saw their role as twofold prior to midcentury: they were at once the watchdogs of society and the moral protectors of the stage. Although critics felt that the drama should epitomize societal virtue, the stage was nevertheless thought to be in need of constant reform. Because the managers and actors did not always see that reforms were carried out or that high standards were imposed and maintained, theatre critics felt that it was their job to establish a sort of moral, technical, and literary quality control. Despite this noble goal, however, dramatic criticism was, in fact, often a simple soapbox for extreme opinions; many reviews were comprised of unwarranted excoriations or blatant and undeserved puffs. As one editor remarked, "A newspaper criticism is generally either a puff or a libel—either an extravagant eulogy or a violent attack."[6]

The "paid puff" became an established practice in the American theatre by the 1820s, much to the dismay of many reputable critics. To secure a puff, or favorable review, theatre managers would provide critics with certain benefits such as season tickets or free refreshments. The notorious Cold Cut Room at the Bowery Theatre (supplied with paper, pens, food, and drink) is a good example of the types of arrangements that were made in order to ensure good press. As publicity techniques were sophisticated, puffing became increasingly unnecessary—an event that was celebrated by the more serious critics who had always looked upon this practice with disdain. Walt Whitman, a vocal enemy of the puff, claimed that this phenomenon was so ubiquitous that five-sixths of all theatrical criticism was written before the show. Yet notwithstanding certain "manifestly unjust" practices, a great many periodicals in the nineteenth century devoted a sizable portion of their papers to dramatic criticism and many critics claimed to abstain from puffing.[7] Reviewers tried to establish critical standards for the theatre in the early decades of the century, prescriptions usually based upon Hamlet's advice to the players "to hold, as 'twere, the mirror up to nature." Although one could argue that "natural" acting had been regarded as a desirable goal since antiquity, nineteenth-century critics cultivated a special awareness of this quality because of their familiarity with and dedication to the neoclassical doctrine of verisimilitude. Managers, producers, and dramatic critics regarded verisimilitude—the representation or expression of truth—as a crucial component of successful theatrical productions. In order to achieve verisimilitude, the performance must display the simultaneous appearance of reality, generality, and morality. The actor or actress was charged not simply to present man (or woman) as s/he was, but as s/he should be.[8]

In addition to using the mirror as a metaphor, dramatic reviewers also championed moral didacticism as an important critical tool. Although naturalness of style was important, critics agreed that "truth" must sometimes surrender its prerogative to propriety. As an early contributor to the *Polyanthos* explains,

> While we express an ardent desire for the prosperity of the theatre, as a school of nature, as a mirror in which mankind are seen, we wish to check what too often exists, a propensity to that kind of wit, which savours of indelicacy. All that is written should not be spoken. Cannot the manager erase? Why then must innocence blush, and modesty hide her face? The exhibitions of the stage, though they borrow the sublimity of love, the strength of Hercules, and the beauty of Venus, should never forsake the chastity and refinement of Diana.[9]

By applying a high ethical standard to both the performers and the plays, critics felt that they were furthering their goals both as societal watchdogs and as theatrical guardians; they were ultimately helping to reform the theatre (and society) and to redeem the drama's name among puritanical and censorious circles. "While the critics defended the actors as a class no more immoral than the rest of mankind, they often censured particular conduct upon the stage when it threatened an evil effect," concludes Vincent Angotti in his dissertation on dramatic criticism. "Most criticism of the stage is technical in outlook, but occasionally a reviewer would speak out against what was considered a common transgression and a serious moral detriment."[10] Nevertheless, morality and the mirror worked well together as critical approaches in many respects. Ideologically, because early nineteenth-century American critics were working under the precept of verisimilitude (the moral ideal reflected in human nature), an increased proximity to "natural" representations onstage would, in theory, result in increased depictions of morality.

Problems occurred, however, when such moral messages became significantly more important than the mirror—a battle waged particularly over melodrama. Critics agreed that the theatre should both reflect nature and teach a lesson, yet most were disdainful of melodrama, which too often sacrificed "realism" to didacticism. This genre, which grew increasingly popular as romanticism became paradigmatic in America, was condemned by critics for its presentation of two-dimensional characters, its heavy reliance on spectacle, and its mechanical plot structures. Regardless, however, of critical efforts to undermine the popularity of the genre, melodrama became the order of the day, forcing even the most distinguished man of letters to capitulate in order to remain financially solvent. William Dunlap, a successful playwright, painter, theatre historian, and manager of New York's Park Theatre, exemplifies this defeat. Although Dunlap was resolved to reform the theatre, he was forced to translate and produce many of Kotzebue's melodramas in order to keep his theatre operating; he even transformed his own tragedies into spectacles, as his blank verse epic *Andre* became the spirited yet maudlin melodrama *The Glory of Columbia—Her Yeomanry!*

In the first few decades of the nineteenth century, therefore, dramatic criticism was dominated by a preoccupation with verisimilitude and "natural" acting. In addition, critics championed a didactic evaluation of both players and dramatic literature and rejected melodrama as unworthy of critical consideration. These three primary critical features often proved unsatisfactory or problematic, however, when used to evaluate the convention of breeches during the first half of the nineteenth century. For example, determining an actress's supposed "naturalness" or truthfulness became difficult for critics when the performer under their scrutiny appeared in cross-dress, for she attempted to "truthfully" portray something she could never "realistically" become. Because her sexed body stood in opposition to the gender that she performed, the breeches actress was often reported to be unnatural (the reverse of the image in the mirror) even if her performance was technically impeccable, her character convincing, and her protean talents undeniable. Contrarily, quite a few popular actresses who played leading male roles were described as seeming extremely natural even though it was evident that they were women in male masquerade.

Such critical discrepancies between natural and unnatural performance qualities can be explained through an investigation of dramatic genre. While there were definite exceptions to this pattern, nineteenth-century critics were much more likely to label a breeches performer "natural" if she portrayed a melodramatic, romantic and/or farcical character. Because the cross-dressed actress who played these roles often displayed traits that were thought indicative of nineteenth-century womanhood (helplessness, melancholy, foolishness, sentimentality), she could still legitimately hold her mirror up to nature. Moreover, since her performance actually reinforced dominant gender ideology, the breeches actress who played the melodramatic male lead could thrive unhindered by critical aspersions. Conversely, women who played serious or tragic male roles, roles that presented unequivocally "masculine" images, were thought to be unnatural as they attempted to appropriate male behavior and dress, in turn smashing the mirror—or at least presenting a reflection that confused, distorted, and therefore contested the assumed naturalness of nineteenth-century gender binaries. It was these serious or tragic performances that generally appeared most threatening to critics who feared that actresses, who sought to play masculine heroes such as Norval and Richard III, were aiming to wear their breeches in a more figurative sense. Such portrayals were morally offensive to critics who neither recognized the image in the mirror nor believed that the performer was attempting to operate within the bounds of verisimilitude, since a woman could never depict the tragic hero as he *should* be.

Critical contempt for the genre of melodrama also contributed to the dramatic license (or freedom from vitriol) experienced by melodramatic female performers in male dress. The melodrama was generally deemed unworthy of critical praise and devoid of true moral influence, a genre "signifying nothing," and because of melodrama's critical insignificance, the breeches performer who assumed a leading male part within this genre did not seem to present a critical threat since the vehicle itself was dismissed as influential in any way. David Grimstead argues that the "intended guardians of the stage could only denounce 'the sickening degradation' which marked drama's retreat 'from the solid to the shell; from the substantial to the ephemeral; from the giant to the dwarf.'"[11]

This genre-based prejudice is evident from the paucity of play reviews written about melodramas. Theatrical commentaries were largely composed of remarks about an actor's physical presentation and/or interpretation of a specific—usually classical—role, while melodramatic performers, playwrights and plays (the bulk of the theatre's repertories) were often ignored.[12] This critical trend proves lamentable for the historian of breeches, since the majority of theatrical women who cross-dressed during the first half of the nineteenth century played male roles in such "mediocre" (frequently melodramatic) vehicles. Although the breeches performer did play classical roles, these parts were often reserved for benefit nights, at least until the 1830s when actresses began to attempt such characters with more frequency.

Critical precepts began to change, however, as the century progressed and as a group of professional critics began to emerge by midcentury. This transformation was marked by a dismissal of didacticism in exchange for a much lighter, less judicial approach. The nature of the newspaper market was profoundly altered by the great number of immigrants who arrived in New York City during the 1850s, for newcomers introduced fresh ideas and innovative writing techniques. Many of the young journalists who worked in New York at this time had a strong disregard for traditional critical practice. Older guiding principals (morality and the mirror) were exchanged for new critical techniques such as the French "feuilleton," an approach to writing that was characterized by its wit and levity—the art of writing "brilliantly about trifles."[13] Midcentury critics jettisoned the antiquated sentiments held by their predecessors along with their writing style; in short, critics became less concerned with "formal principals of aesthetics," with policing the public, and more interested in the impressions formulated as a result of their own specific artistic interests.[14] Yet, artistic tastes still reflected larger societal notions about gender, and the serious or tragic breeches performer rarely benefited from this more cavalier critical style. Melodramatic and comic actresses were still reviewed more magnanimously, the only difference being the increased tendency toward sexualization as popular forms of entertainment began to draw the majority of breeches actresses away from standard repertories and mainstream theatres. Critics became increasingly preoccupied with the erotic display of the female form as more and more women began to don their tunics and tights upon variety and burlesque stages after midcentury.

※ ※ ※

Early-nineteenth-century dramatic critics based their reflections on the theatre upon neoclassical aesthetic principals and often modeled their reviews after essays by Samuel Johnson, Charles Lamb, Samuel Coleridge, and others.[15] Yet authors such as Johnson had more to offer these critics than simply a model upon which to base their own writing. Johnson's now hackneyed verse, "the drama's laws the drama's patron's give," describing the audience's ultimate prerogative in the theatre, was repeatedly invoked by acrimonious writers, whose attempts to reform both the drama and the theatre fell upon the deaf ears of the so-called uncultured masses. The nineteenth-century audience member, who also proved highly influential in determining the success or failure of an actor or play, often disagreed with the dramatic critic and sometimes held radically different views regarding both the drama and the performance. A critic for the *Ladies' Port Folio* exemplifies this disparity between critical and popular sentiment (specifically regarding the breeches performer) in a review he wrote about Mary Barnes's Hamlet in Boston in 1820. Dismayed by the favorable reception given to Barnes by the audience, the critic bitterly exclaimed, "It may perhaps pass off for a night or so, as a gag upon the multitude, and be the means of producing in these 'hard times,' a comfortable emolument; yet even then though it 'may make the unskillful laugh, it cannot but make the judicious grieve; the applause of one of which is worth that of the whole theatre of others.'"[16]

Historians concur that, prior to midcentury, this congregation of "others" was indeed heterogeneous. Theatre scholars generally describe the antebellum theatre as being divided into three markedly classed areas: the boxes, which housed the "fashionables" and where the few respectable women (always escorted by men) would sit; the pit, which generally accommodated middle-class working men and professionals and seldom women; and the gallery, which was populated by working-class women and people of color. Many theatre historians have extended this class-based configuration of the audience to characterize entire theatres. For example, the three New York theatres active in the first few decades of the nineteenth century are often described in terms of the class of spectators that patronized them. Many claim, based on the observations of Frances Trollope, that the Park attracted an elite audience, the Bowery sported a more "democratic" assembly, and the Chatham housed lower-class patrons—a conclusion that would significantly affect the ways in which consensus may have been formulated regarding the cross-dressed actress. Yet this somewhat limited analysis has been revised in a recent study by Rosemarie K. Bank, who argues that such casting of New York theatres was more about competitive self-fashioning than about the economic character of a specific audience. While the managers of the Park and Bowery, for example, perpetuated notions of their theatres as respectively elite and nationalistic, there was—as Bank makes clear—more similarity than difference:

> Their ticket prices were nearly the same, each had the sort of financial success that indicates patrons in all parts of the house, and each experienced the same slumps in attendance. The repertories

of both theatres are similar.... Both theatres alternated star visits with company vehicles run as long as public interest could sustain them, and both theatres offered similar settings for audiences, the Bowery's auditorium consistently newer and frequently refurbished (assisted by fires).[17]

Contemporary sources seem to indicate that theatre attendees were predominantly male during the first half of the century, although Bank's research suggests that women may have been figuratively erased from the antebellum audience by newspapers in an attempt to "gentrify" the American playhouse, when in fact they regularly attended the theatre. Walt Whitman describes the Bowery pitties as "well-dress'd, full-blooded young and middle-aged men" who inhabited a space where there was "no dainty kid-glove business, but electric force and muscle from perhaps 2,000 full-sinew'd men...."[18] Similarly, Barnaby Bangbar, the editor of an early theatrical periodical published in Philadelphia, reports upon "the recent flashing of a fashionable custom," which included banning women from the theatres on the first night a play was to open.[19] Furthermore, Robert Allen implies that the theatre during the 1820s and 1830s was a male institution, and "women onstage and in the audience continued to be problematic and, at times, controversial throughout the first half of the century."[20]

A portion of the women that did occupy this *public* space were appropriately termed "public women," a euphemism for prostitutes and a seeming oxymoron in nineteenth-century America. That prostitutes inhabited "the guilty third tier" of most nineteenth-century theatres is a historical assumption that Bank debunks as both classist and racist since antebellum historians, as she points out, have conflated both working-class women (such as the Bowery G'hal) and people of color—collective inhabitants of the gallery—with prostitution.[21] Certainly prostitutes did attend the theatre (and, in certain establishments, entered through separate doors) and worked the house while the other "public women" in the theatre—the actresses—earned their wages on the boards. Indeed, many working-class women who embraced a professional life onstage were often erroneously stigmatized as prostitutes (like the unescorted female patrons in the gallery), thus causing many elite patrons to approach the theatre with trepidation.

The early nineteenth-century audience may not have had a great deal of control over such paratheatricals in the house, but they certainly exerted an influence over the performances on stage. Famous for their boisterous, uninhibited behavior, nineteenth-century spectators cultivated a highly interactive atmosphere in which they exercised control over both the musicians in the orchestra pit and the players onstage. Favorite songs and scenes were called for again and again, while actors and actresses who failed to please were banished unmercifully to the wings. As Grimstead explains, "the theatregoing public of the period was peculiarly able to insure that no shading in the presentation deviated from its standards. This closeness of audience control made the drama more than any art form, the theatre as much as any social institution, immediately sensitive to public opinion."[22] This necessary dependence upon public opinion plays a crucial part in evaluating the popularity of the breeches performer, for it allows the historian another measure by which to assess her reception. Many critics condemned the cross-dressed actress whose popularity with the audience remained unchallenged. What appeared "monstrous" and "unnatural" to the dramatic reviewer perhaps enchanted the spectators, and, in turn, a performer who captivated the critics possibly alienated the multitude.

Audience control over both the players and the performances continued unabated until 1849 when "a fundamental social reordering" among theatre audiences took place due to New York's Astor Place Riot—an event that many historians consider a watershed in American theatre history.[23] On May 9, lower and middle-class theatregoers, in support of their working-class hero, actor Edwin Forrest (1806–1872), created a riot in and around the Astor Place theatre where the English actor William Charles Macready (1793–1873) was performing. The crowd was reacting against the negative press that Forrest received (supposedly instigated by Macready) during his 1845 tour of London. Although Macready claimed he had nothing to do with Forrest's unfavorable reviews, the American actor fostered resentment. Forrest had displayed his hostility for Macready by unleashing an undeserved hiss during one of Macready's performances in Edinburgh. The battle between the two actors grew increasingly antagonistic, escalating into a violent and bitter class debate between Forrest's loyal followers (many of whom were members of New York's Know-Nothing Party) and the "elite" admirers of Macready. This conflict ultimately culminated in the riot that cost at least 22 people their lives (144 suffered injuries) and that proved an instigator for the gradual transformation of the America audience.[24] After the Astor Place Riot, audiences gradually changed from a heterogeneous and powerful collection of individuals with varying tastes and class backgrounds into more homogeneous assemblies that frequented specific theatres to enjoy specific types of entertainment—a bifurcation of cultural expression that, as Lawrence Levine suggests, culminated in a "chasm" between highbrow or "serious" entertainment and lowbrow or "popular" entertainment.[25] This division ultimately altered perceptions of the breeches performer held by both the audience member and the critic, as the convention became dominated by burlesque and extravaganza players in the 1850s and 1860s, and celebrated breeches performers such as Cushman abdicated their authority to Thompson and her British Blondes.

ORIGINS

In his oft cited book *All the King's Ladies*, J. H. Wilson introduces several revealing statistics about breeches performance during the Restoration. Between 1660 and 1700, of the 375 plays initially produced in London theatres, 89 contained disguise roles or "roles for actresses 'in Boy's Clothes' or in 'Man's Clothes'," 14 contained breeches parts, and three plays were acted entirely by women playing both male and female roles. "Almost every actress appeared at one time or another 'dressed like a man'—as a youth, a page, a gentleman, a soldier, a shepherd, or what you will—and some became famous for their elegant appearance in breeches or pantaloons."[26] The large discrepancy between disguise roles and actual breeches roles outlined here is telling. In the 116 plays in which women donned male apparel, 89 of them facilitated taking it off again—

thus further contributing to the image of the cross-dressed actress (in this case the disguise-role performer) as sexual object. Elizabeth Howe, in her book *The First English Actresses: Women and Drama 1660–1700*, argues that although the actress was objectified and never truly succeeded in passing as a man, it was the drama and the male managers that contributed to her exploitation. Indeed, no evidence exists to suggest that early English actresses were actively complicit in their own objectification and commodification as some twentieth-century critics have implied.[27] Howe—who also conflates the terms disguise role and breeches role—explains, "Breeches roles seem to have been designed to show off the female body—there was no question of the actress truly impersonating a man." According to Howe, Restoration prologues and epilogues were crafted to highlight the "erotic effect of the transvestite convention," and the frequent use of disguise roles provided numerous opportunities for exposing a woman's body as she would have to reveal her "true" sex again at the end of the play.[28]

The first actual breeches role on the English stage was performed in 1670 by Nell Gwynn (then a member of the King's Men under Thomas Killigrew at the Theatre Royal), who put on men's clothes in order to present the prologue to John Dryden's *Almanzor and Almahide, or The Conquest of Granada by the Spaniards.* Gwynn and other Restoration and eighteenth-century actresses such as Susan Verbruggen (Mrs. Mountford), Kitty Clive, Charlotte Charke—an infamous cross-dresser on and offstage—and Peg Woffington popularized the convention of breeches. They played boy roles (pages and princes) and romantic heroes such as Sir Harry Wildair from Farquhar's *The Constant Couple,* Captain Macheath from John Gay's *The Beggar's Opera,* and Marplot from Susannah Centlivre's *The Busy Body.*

In addition to the popular demand for erotic display, eighteenth-century English audiences—whose commitment to neoclassicism had increased since the Restoration—also desired verisimilitude. Paradoxically, breeches performers were seemingly praised for their duel ability to flaunt a tight-encased leg *and* to present an illusion of masculinity. This tension was perhaps best embodied by Woffington, who was supposedly simultaneously sexually

Fig. 1.1: Peg Woffington as Sir Harry Wildair. University of Illinois, Theatrical Print Collection.

alluring and convincingly masculine—compelling as both a man and a woman as theatrical lore via the "Greenroom Brawl" suggests. Straub also remarks upon this sanctioned "double appeal" in her discussion of eighteenth-century actress Charlotte Charke. The breeches actress, Straub explains, could indulge in her performance of masculinity onstage because her life offstage was governed by a heterosexual narrative that reified her position as a sexually titillating performer. As long as masculine masquerades were countered with frequent reports of an actress's feminine "performance" beyond the footlights, "ambiguous appeal" could remain playful and anxieties concerning unwarranted trespasses could be abated.[29]

Perhaps because of this double appeal, Woffington enjoyed an unprecedented success as Sir Harry, which she first performed at the Smock Alley Theatre in Dublin in April, 1740, and in London on November 21, 1740 (see figure 1.1). This role established her reputation in London and rendered male portrayals far less popular.[30] Woffington continued to play Wildair throughout the 1740s and 1750s at both Drury Lane and Covent Garden with great success, and would undoubtedly have been familiar to the members of one of the first troupes to play in America—the Hallams.[31] During this period the Hallams were performing at a variety of theatres in London both permanent and temporary. In the years leading up to their departure for America, they played at their New Theatre in 1744 and at the New Wells in Goodman's Fields on Lemon Street during the seasons of 1744–45 and 1745–46, in addition to touring the provinces and being regular booth occupants at Bartholemew Fair. Certainly, they must have been aware not only of the precedent for breeches performance (boys and comic romantic heroes) begun almost a century before, but also of Woffington's fame in London during this time. Furthermore, the Hallams were also aware of Charke's career, as she is recorded to have played with them at Goodman's Fields in 1745. Philip Highfill Jr. provides evidence of their association, stating that on November 4th, "*The Provok'd Husband* was offered with the Hallam's old acquaintance of the booths, Colly Cibber's transvestite daughter Charlotte Charke ('her first appearance here'), as Lady Townley and Lewis Hallam as Moody."[32] Although Charke did not play a breeches role during this engagement, she had already established her reputation in roles such as Macheath, Marplot, Captain Plume in Farquhar's *The Recruiting Officer*, and Mr. Hen in Henry Fielding's controversial political satire *The Historical Register for the Year 1736; to which is added a Very Merry Tragedy, called Eurydice Hiss'd or a Word to the Wise*—a play that proved to be a catalyst for the Licensing Act of 1737.

The Hallam troupe, headed by Lewis Hallam, sailed to America in the summer of 1752, taking with them a repertoire of plays that included at least nine male roles that were sometimes played by women.[33] However, of the four adult women in the original Hallam company (Mrs. Lewis Hallam, Mrs. Rigby, Mrs. Clarkson, and Miss Palmer), none of them are known to have played a single breeches role in America.[34] The only member of the Company of Comedians from London, as they were called, who occasionally took on a breeches role was Nancy (Anne) Hallam, daughter of William Hallam and Anne Parker and niece to Lewis. Nancy seems to have been the first woman in America to play a breeches role and probably made her cross-dressed debut as the Duke of York in *Richard III* on February 7, 1758. While this performance date is uncertain, since her first documented appearance in a breeches part occurred on June 29, 1759 (also as the Duke), it is recorded that the Comedians, who were now under the leadership of David Douglass, did in fact perform *Richard III* in February of 1758, apparently with the same cast. While Nancy is often referred to as a child and player of children's roles, she must have been in her mid to late teens by the time she was performing with Douglass's company. Neither Highfill nor George Seilhamer states whether or not she came across with the others on the *Charming Sally* in 1752, but as there is no other record of her arrival we can assume that she did.[35] We can also assume that she was well over six years of age when she made the voyage because her cousin Isabella,[36] being only six years of age in 1752, was "too young to stand the arduous passage to Virginia" and therefore was left in the care of her Aunt and Uncle, Ann and John Barrington.[37] Therefore Nancy Hallam, probably nine or ten in 1752, was at least 16 when she began performing breeches roles in the Colonies, an age when many women were already mothers.

Edwards states that the first breeches performance was given by a Mrs. Wall on February 25, 1768. However, in addition to the role played by Nancy Hallam, I have found mention of six other occasions on which women played breeches roles previous to Mrs. Wall's debut. An examination of Appendix 1 reveals not only the names of these early breeches performers and the dates on which they played, but specific patterns in colonial breeches performance such as the tendency for women to play boy's roles. In his *History of the American Theatre Before the Revolution,* Seilhamer records that boy's roles such as the Duke of York and the Prince of Wales were originally played by the two young male actors in the troupe during the 1753–1754 season, Master Lewis Hallam and Adam Hallam.[38] It seems that the tradition for breeches in America began when there were no young men left in the troupes to enact the princes and pages. The lack of adolescent male players within a company provided a chance for women to play boy roles. The only other opportunity seems to have been the benefit, for it was here that women began to expand upon their juvenile impersonations and play leading male adults. Indeed, benefit performances, which were granted to actors and actresses at the end of a theatrical season (usually in June) and for which the performer received all the proceeds minus the house expenses, were considered a privilege because such events marked the only time a player could choose his or her own role. Women often selected a principal male character for their benefit night, such as Wildair, Hamlet, and Captain Flash.

Early performance reports, found in Seilhamer's study, support this theory regarding the origins of breeches performance in America. All records previous to 1758 show that Adam and young Lewis Hallam were playing all the juvenile roles. In 1754, the Hallam troupe dissolved due to the death of Lewis Hallam, Sr., and was reorganized in 1758 under David Douglass who, together with his new wife, the former Mrs. Lewis Hallam, acquired all of the company's choice roles. Lewis Jr. was at this time 18 years of age and was now also playing leading male roles, leaving the juvenile characters to Adam and Nancy, who presumably began to play Fleance and the Duke of York that same year. Formal documentation proves that Nancy performed the Duke on June 29, 1759, with Adam playing Prince Edward; Adam was also Donaldbane to Nancy's Fleance. In 1760, the company moved to Annapolis where Adam continued to play his established line, but Nancy's name does not appear in company listings for this year. In 1761 Nancy's parts were recorded as having been played by "a young master," while Adam began to undertake more sophisticated roles like Benvolio in *Romeo and Juliet* in addition to his boy parts. Indeed, there is no mention of another breeches performer until Miss Dowthwaite appears at the Southwark Theatre in 1766 as the Duke of York. This gap of seven years during which no breeches performances are documented is probably due to the fact that there were again two young male actors—Adam and the "young master"—playing the boy roles. The first adult breeches role was not undertaken until Maria Storer played Flash in 1768—surprisingly not on a benefit night. In addition to Storer, the other popular breeches performer to specialize in leading male roles in the eighteenth century was Mrs. Osborne, who was the first American female Wildair, Macheath, and Prince Hal in *Henry IV, Part 1,* and who performed mainly in the Southern colonies. Both of these actresses were regularly playing breeches roles long before Miss Harding, the actress who Edwards claims is the "first to merit the status of a breeches actress," begins her career in the 1790s.[39]

American breeches performance in the eighteenth century differed from the English convention in that colonial actresses were apparently not critically celebrated for their sexual charms—a discrepancy that is not surprising considering the contrast between New World puritanism and English preoccupations with female display onstage initiated during the Restoration. According to Seilhamer, early cross-dressed women were described in both feminine and boyish terms but did not turn critical heads simply by displaying a naked limb (although this feature certainly could have contributed to the endurance of the convention). An early description of Harding (from the 1790s) as Edward in *Everyone Has His Fault* exemplifies this absence of objectifying rhetoric. As Edward, Harding was reported to be "petite in figure, with a round face, sparkling eyes, and an arch and sprightly expression of feature."[40] Critical focus seems to have concentrated on physical size and facial expression in addition to manner and characterization, as is demonstrated by a reporter from the *Philadelphia Gazette* who commends Harding on her ability to communicate "the impertinence of a rude boy, better fed than taught."[41] Because the American breeches performer was fulfilling a specific duty within the early acting companies in taking on juvenile roles, she was perhaps spared some of the sexual showcasing experienced by her English sisters.

Close examination of the early history of the convention of breeches on the American stage yields significant results. While the tradition for breeches performance in the eighteenth century may have seemed far from prodigious due to its juvenile associations, cross-dressed female performance did not merely serve as a prototype for the burlesqued leg shows of the later nineteenth century, as some historians seem to imply. Indeed, a review of the origins of the breeches convention in America suggests a much more pragmatic beginning. Actresses either played boys out of necessity when "masters" were scarce or chose more challenging male roles for their benefit nights. Yet although many actresses donned the base apparel of the page for practical purposes, women such as Storer and Osborne expanded this boyish repertoire in a marked attempt to create a more profound masculine impression. In deliberately selecting roles like Macheath and Wildair, the early American breeches performer both continued a tradition that had begun upon the late Restoration stage and served to prove that she could compete with male company members, whose lines of business were as firmly established as their superior position within society.

BREECHES PERFORMANCE: 1800–1869

During the early years of the nineteenth century, the tradition for breeches in America continued as it had existed during the second half of the eighteenth century: women infrequently played minor boy parts in Shakespearean drama, melodrama, and farcical afterpieces, and occasionally sported serious male roles on a benefit night (often their husband's). As in the eighteenth century, an actress would usually not appear in a boy's role if the company already possessed a young male actor who could portray the character. If a drama contained two boy's roles, such as the Princes in *Richard III*, one role would generally be played by the company's boy actor and the other by an actress (unless the company had two boy actors, which was rare). For example, William Dunlap's company at the Park Theatre in 1801–1802 included a Master Stockwell who played many roles that were regularly assumed by women after 1810, such as Tom Thumb, Fleance, the Duke of York, Patrick in *The Poor Soldier*, and the Boy in *Pizarro*.

Although critics were relatively supportive of women playing boy roles in the early nineteenth century, detailed reviews of their performances were uncommon. Notices of their appearance within the dramatis personae, however, were standard, as daily newspapers would frequently include the cast lists for afternoon and evening performances in sections of the paper entitled "Theatrics," "Entertainment," or "Recreation." One of the first New York notices to feature a breeches performer in the nineteenth century occurred in the *New York Evening Post* on December 10, 1801. Mrs. Hodgkinson was listed in the dramatis personae as Theodore in *Abbe de Leppe or The Dumb Made Eloquent* (also called *Deaf and Dumb*). Interestingly, the words "deaf and dumb" appear next to the actress's name, thus drawing attention to the character's physical handicap. Such descriptive phrases were regularly found beside the breeches performer's name when she played boy roles, but were curiously absent from lists of male actors playing male roles in the early years of the century. Moreover, this descriptive text always signaled a physical impediment of some kind, as is demonstrated in the case of Theodore and as is also seen in a listing for a play entitled *The Blind Boy*, which appeared in the *Evening Post* on March 30, 1803. This play, which was described as a comedy in five acts, featured Pedro as its principal character, a blind boy played by a Mrs. Johnson. Like Mrs. Hodgkinson in the *Abbe*, the listing in the dramatis personae included the character's name followed by a specification of his handicap—"Pedro (the Blind Boy)"—making it quite obvious that if a woman was to play a male character, it would be at a physical disadvantage. Similarly, on June 23, 1812, a notice appeared announcing *The Peasant Boy*, which was to be performed especially for Mrs. Oldmixon's benefit. Mrs. Darley was to play the peasant boy and again the character name, Julian, was followed by the phrase, "the Peasant Boy," which implied that this time the character's misfortune was material rather than physical.[42]

While it is possible that these phrases were inserted by newspaper editors or dramatic critics only to aid the potential audience member (or to win sympathy for the character), it is curious that such descriptive measures were selectively administered. One possible explanation for this practice may lie in the physical arrangement of the cast lists themselves. Nineteenth-century playwrights and/or dramatic critics continued a tradition that dated back to the sixteenth century in listing women last in the dramatis personae. Actresses' names retained this placement within cast lists that were featured in periodicals, newspapers, posters, and programs. Such a practice reinforced the social, physical, and intellectual polarization of men and women dictated by the doctrine of separate spheres that governed nineteenth-century American thought. Often the women were listed in a separate column beside or, most often, below the male actors and character names. Because this type of display was standard, to see a woman's name among the male actors in the "first" or "higher" column would be startling and perhaps unsettling, possibly signifying Woman's symbolic entrance into a masculine physical space—something that the breeches performer was doing on many different levels. By foregrounding the physical handicap of the male characters who were played by these women, critics minimized the actresses' potential influence (as women assuming male roles or "wearing the breeches") and made it clear to theatregoers that although these performers were playing male parts, these characters were not "real" men but physically or socially inferior boys.

Besides dumb and blind boy parts, the most popular breeches roles adopted by actresses in the first two decades of the nineteenth century included: Little Pickle in the farcical afterpiece *Little Pickle; or The Spoiled Child*, Aladdin, Myrtillo in *The Broken Sword* by W. Diamond, and Norval in John Home's *Douglas*. Although they were sizable roles and therefore likely to be coveted by actresses, these parts (with the exception of Norval) all tended to support dominant gender ideology rather than allow the breeches actress any significant exploration of manhood or masculinity. Melodramatic and farcical boys were often weak, passive, and morally superior, which perhaps explains why actresses who performed these types of roles were generally reviewed favorably (albeit infrequently). For example, the dramatic critic for the *Evening Post* (in a rare review of an early breeches performance) stated that, "Mrs. Hodgekinson in her attempts to exhibit the *joyful* emotions of *Theodore*, succeeded, and so far did herself credit."[43] Although Mrs. Hodgekinson played an occasional breeches role and received relatively constructive criticism from this reviewer, two women stand out as being perhaps the most popular and critically celebrated breeches performers in the early nineteenth century: Mrs. Jones, who was a favorite of audiences during the century's first decade, and Mary Barnes, who held sway in the teens. While both of these women regularly played female roles in addition to their male roles, they were known for their penchant to don the breeches and were among the first to build their careers upon this reputation.

Born in England, Mrs. Jones, whose maiden name was Granger, played for three seasons in Philadelphia upon her arrival in America. After leaving Philadelphia because of her reported inability to collect enough money at her benefit performances to make a living, Jones went to Boston where she played a few seasons with the popular Mr. Powell. In 1806, she moved to New York after her husband abandoned her and left her to raise four children. A biography of Jones printed in the *Thespian Monitor* states that "domestick disquiet entered their dwelling, which ended in her husband's leaving her and her four children and accepting an engagement at Charleston, where he performed one season and where he died in August 1860."[44] Christine Stansell points out that abandonment was a common problem faced by women in the early nineteenth century and significantly contributed both to city poverty levels and to women's need to work outside the home. "Women, one New York charity noted in 1818, were generally more vulnerable to impoverishment than men, being 'more exposed to a sudden reverse of circumstances.' . . . As much as they could, these women tried to hold together disintegrating family economies."[45] In an attempt to avoid complete indigence, Mrs. Jones, now the sole breadwinner in her family, established herself as an actress in New York, which was rapidly becoming the theatrical center of America.

Her principal success came from enacting the title role in the farcical afterpiece *Little Pickle,* which George Odell says was "of doubtful authorship—Bickerstaffe, Hoare, or another."[46] This play, which made its entrance into the regular American repertoire in 1795, is unusual, for it includes both a breeches role and a disguise role—a fact that has confused some historians who mistake Little Pickle for a disguise role. Little Pickle, a mischievous boy, was almost always played by a woman, as was Little Pickle's sister, Miss Pickle, who disguises herself as a boy. Critics spoke extremely favorably of Jones as Little Pickle, declaring that she had "outshown herself." John Howard Payne, later a celebrated "infant prodigy" (despite the fact that he debuted at the age of 17), reviewed her performance in his theatrical journal the *Thespian Mirror.* On December 28, 1805, he writes, "*The Spoil'd Child,* as the after-piece, gratified us with *Little Pickle* by Mrs. Jones.... We can say nothing of the particular beauties of her performance, where the whole was indescribably charming."[47] The following Wednesday, the play was reviewed and once again Payne spoke favorably of Jones: "The charming trifle of the *Spoil'd Child* was successfully repeated. We have before spoken of Mrs. Jones' *Little Pickle,* which probably could not be equalled on the American stage. Her songs, particularly that of 'Polldangit, how d'ye do,' were encored."[48]

Little Pickle, described by Odell as a "romp" and a "favorite of ingenues,"[49] was an afterpiece—as many early breeches vehicles were—meaning that it was performed after the main feature, which was also preceded by a curtain-raiser. Such an arrangement of the evening's entertainment bill required audiences to sit in the theatre for several hours before an afterpiece began. Because audience members had already experienced a rather full evening of theatre before the afterpiece was presented, it is likely that a sizable portion of the audience may have either left the theatre early, therefore missing the play entirely, or have become intoxicated (as there were bars in most theatres until the 1840s), restless, and perhaps obstreperous. A predominantly male audience in such a state of mind may well have stayed to watch a woman display herself in breeches, yet critical indications that Jones or any breeches actress during this period were sexually objectified are extremely rare. Most of the commentary casts them as feminine and as boyish but not as sexually titillating.

The most celebrated breeches star during the second decade of the century was Mary Greenhill Barnes (1780–1864). She was renowned for her Aladdin and for originating the melodramatic role of Myrtillo; both of these portrayals were received enthusiastically by critics and audiences. Barnes also appeared in many other standard breeches roles such as Albert in *William Tell*, Cherubino in *The Marriage of Figaro*, Colin in *Nature and Philosophy*, Edmund ("the Blind Boy") in *The Blind Boy*, and Julian ("the Peasant Boy") in *The Peasant Boy*. Additionally she attempted serious roles for her benefit nights, such as Hamlet, Romeo, and Young Norval. Barnes was born in London, made her stage debut at the Haymarket in 1811, and her American debut as Juliet at the Park in 1816, along with her husband John who played Romeo. She acted periodically at the Park until 1831, at which time she became one of the leading actresses at the Richmond Hill Theatre in New York City, then under the management of her husband. A good example of an actress who successfully competed with contemporary male actors, Barnes is reported to have made more money, on occasion, than the famed Thomas A. Cooper, who was one of the first actors to receive star status in America. Theatrical manager William Wood reports that in December of 1824, Barnes played with Cooper for seven nights in Baltimore and brought in $658 for her benefit, while Cooper only made $372.[50]

The critical response to Barnes's career provides an excellent example of the ways in which literary men would alter their opinions based on the genre in which a breeches performer appeared. Barnes's melodramatic and comic male performances were lauded or ignored (either way regarded as nonthreatening or insubstantial) while her serious roles such as Norval and Hamlet were castigated. The *American Monthly Magazine* section on the theatre, the "Thespian Register," often reports on Barnes in a manner that exemplifies this idea. Her Aladdin was "played with great spirit and naivete,"[51] and as Myrtillo in *The Broken Sword* she was described as "irresistibly charming. Her appearance was lovely, her action easy, appropriate and eloquent." In addition, while playing in a melodramatic opera entitled *Frederick the Great,* the critic described her as natural. "We could not but remark," he writes, "that Mrs. Barnes appeared more at home in the dress of an officer, than in the proper apparel of her sex. She discovered more ease and grace, in the assumed garb, and her voice was much more *natural* in it."[52] Roles such as Myrtillo—a Count's young son, also dumb, who must be rescued by the hero after suffering torture at the hands of the villain—were considered innocuous and praised, while her Norval and her Hamlet were condemned, perhaps because these roles were considered more masculine by nineteenth-century standards, and by playing them Barnes was encroaching into male territory (in both a literal and metaphoric sense). As the *American Monthly* critic admonishes, "When Mrs. B. puts off her bonnet and her slipper for the hat and boot of Myrtillo we are delighted, but the helmet and shield and the claymore we would advise her to decline."[53]

Norval was an extremely popular vehicle for actresses to use for their benefits because he was a young warrior: he was brave, bellicose, honorable, and heroic—qualities that the usual fare of melodramatic/farcical boy and female parts did not feature. Benefit nights were often the only opportunity women had in the early days of the nineteenth century to play more momentous roles like Norval, and, as Odell points out, most "ladies felt privileged to undertake these freaks on such occasions."[54] Many considered the benefit a test of the audience's true opinion of the performer. If the audience considered the actress's previous work a valuable contribution to the stage, they would reward her by attending her benefit at the end of the theatrical season. In addition, actors and actresses often depended upon their benefit night to make up for their insufficient salary (and to help them live through the summer), thus establishing this practice as a necessity rather than simply a gratuity. As a correspondent for the *Mirror of Taste and Dramatic Censor* explains, however, public recognition was often more important than profit:

> The benefit is a sort of *test* of the opinion entertained by the public of the performer's *merit,* and is in fact, a portion of his compensation, made wholly distinct from his fixt salary, in order that so much of it at least may be measured by the general estimate of his services, and the *value set upon his acting by the public.* This is the true reason, why actors feel so much about their benefit; for, upon an average, very little profit accrues to them after paying their expenses, even when the house is what they call a middling one.[55]

Regardless of their importance, however, benefits were not often reviewed by the critics since regular rules of play were thought to be suspended upon these occasions. One critic explained, "we consider *benefit* performances in some measure exempt from criticism."[56] Many critics considered the benefit a sort of theatrical limbo where actors and actresses could make unusual choices and where they were forgiven any transgressions.[57] For the historian of breeches performance, the prospect that benefits were both critically neglected and/or judged according to different standards is especially troublesome, as it is, therefore, often difficult to assess both how the cross-dressed actress was received in more substantial—and often more "masculine"—roles and if these actresses were taken seriously by the spectators even when their efforts were dismissed by the critics.

However, as the century progressed an increasing number of women began to undertake leading male characters in serious dramas and/or tragedies on occasions other than their benefits. Furthermore, the repertoire of the breeches performer was additionally expanded through actresses' adoption of male leads in two theatrical forms that gained repute in the 1820s: equestrian melodrama and multiple-role dramas. Multiple-role dramas or protean comedies, as they were called, allowed the principal actress to play many different parts—both male and female. It is often difficult to assess public opinion concerning breeches performers in these roles, however, because such vehicles were thought to be unworthy of critical attention. Critics mentioned melodramatic and farcical plays, but usually only to report on their performance times and places; players were often ignored completely. For example, the critic for the

Albion writes in 1827, "The active manager of this house [the Bowery] has joined forces with the proprietor of the La Fayette [sic] and opened a campaign on Thursday with horse and foot. *El Hyder* has been got up at much expense and great magnificence."[58] Harry Clifton, the principle character in *El Hyder*, was generally played by women, but due to the brevity of the above notice (and these cursory reports were standard) it is difficult to determine just whose "foot" tread upon the Bowery boards.

Dumb and blind boy roles continued to draw crowds throughout the twenties, as did Aladdin, Little Pickle, Albert, Colin, and other breeches roles that had been favored during the first two decades of the century. Yet, although the convention was becoming increasingly popular with audiences (a fact that was evidenced by the frequency with which actresses began to play cross-dressed roles), breeches performers in leading parts (despite the genre) were often slighted by critics. Indeed, dramatic reviewers were often more eager to discuss supporting cast members than they were leading breeches actresses. In a typical review, one critic described Mrs. G. Barrett's performance as Florio (the leading role) in *The Forest of Bondy* as having been played "with great effect." Rather than elaborate on her efforts or describe why she was so impressive, the critic turns his attention to a relatively minor player. He explains, "The 'Dog' who is a prominent personage in this drama, is a very gentlemanly and accomplished actor.—He has paid great attention to his part, and seems to be familiar with all the business of the stage."[59] Not surprisingly, the canine role accrued more positive critical attention than the leading actress in this instance. Moreover, traditional gender traits were ascribed to the "gentlemanly" four-legged supporting actor, therefore reiterating the importance of imposing binary gender characteristics on dramatic representations—even if the agents were not human.

The practice of categorizing roles (or determining the leading player from the supporting or minor thespian—regardless of his/her/its genus) is the result of the continued use of theatrical lines of business. During the 1820s, critics began to refer to lines of business as spheres. If actresses or actors were doing well in their particular line, they were said to be in their proper sphere, just as it was considered appropriate and natural for women in the nineteenth century to inhabit only the domestic or private sphere and men the public sphere. When women did take on male responsibilities, they not only transgressed beyond their proper societal position but were denied categorization as women. As one female correspondent acknowledged in an article entitled "Woman's Sphere," "Woman has her sphere; and in her desire to act the man, she ceases to be a woman."[60] Similarly, by playing a male role, an actress stepped outside her sphere socially, theatrically, and ideologically. Many papers and periodicals such as the *New York Mirror and Ladies' Literary Gazette,* a regular purveyor of theatrical news, used this term to describe both a woman's domestic environment and an actress's theatrical line of business in *feminine* parts. A woman's place, therefore, was clearly defined in the 1820s—both behind and beyond the footlights. The critic for the *Mirror* exemplifies this, stating, "Miss Clementina was represented with proper spirit by Mrs. Walstein. This is the sphere in which she should move."[61] A review of a female Richard III in 1836 provides another example of this critical practice. Moved by this actress's rendition of Gloucester, the critic allows that the "power and truth with which she personates the most arduous tragic characters has excited the wonder of every one who has seen her, and half inclines us to forgive her stepping out of that sphere in which nature has qualified her so well for almost unrivalled success."[62] As this review demonstrates, critical use of the word "sphere" to indicate both an actress's proper line of business and a woman's proper societal place was employed repeatedly during the first half of the century.

The most celebrated breeches actress of the 1820s was Clara Fisher (1811–1898), who dazzled New York audiences despite her tendency to act outside her "sphere." Fisher played a significant part in the history of nineteenth-century American breeches performance because she, more than any other actress during the 1820s, expanded the repertoire of the breeches actress to include more roles from serious dramas and tragedies. Along with melodramatic boy parts and traditional female ingenue roles, Fisher played Richard III, Shylock, and Ion, characters who had always been exclusively reserved for actors. By enacting these characters during regular runs and not simply on benefit nights, she set a precedent that many women (including Cushman, who was to be her future student) were to follow especially in the 1830s and 1840s, the peak of serious or traditional breeches performance in America.

Fisher was considered an "infant prodigy" or child star—a theatrical convention that significantly contributed to the popularity of breeches performance in the twenties. Because the nineteenth-century American theatre was in many respects a showcase for novelty entertainment, child stars flourished. Canine stars (such as our "gentlemanly and accomplished" Dog), minstrel parodies, and precocious children shared the stage with the cross-dressed Norval and Hamlet and garnered copious praise from audiences eager to embrace any innovation that would alleviate the tedium of the standard repertoire. Odell remarks that the child star, "so . . . desirable in 1820, would seem more fitted to Lyceum platforms than to the stage of a theatre; but from the days of Master Betty . . . the public eagerly ate from the hand of the *infant phenomena.*"[63] The craze to see children act in tragic adult roles began in London with the performances of William Henry West (1791–1874) or "Master" Betty, who was rumored to be so popular that Parliament was once adjourned so that its members could witness the Young Roscius. In America, audiences flocked instead to see young John Howard Payne at the Park in 1809. Interestingly, Payne made his reputation in roles that were rapidly becoming the property of the breeches performer, such as Romeo and Norval. Payne's fame proved ephemeral, however, and unlike Fisher, he shortly left the stage to pursue a playwriting career.

Fisher made her debut at the Park Theatre in 1827. Like most of the early stars of the American stage, she, too, was born in England; yet unlike most English visitors, she made her reputation charming Drury Lane audiences with her novelty performances of Richard III (see figure 1.2). Although she played many male adult roles as a young girl both in London and in the provinces, by the time she appeared in such roles before New York audiences, she was 16. Although past the age when many American women were already mothers, she was still referred to constantly as a child star. From 1828 to 1834, Fisher performed regularly in New York in

Fig. 1.2: Clara Fisher as Richard III. University of Illinois, Theatrical Print Collection.

addition to making extensive tours throughout the country. In 1834 she married the renowned conductor and musical coach James G. Maeder and retired from the stage shortly after giving birth to their son Frederick. Fisher's fame can be attributed not only to the phenomenal success that she experienced in New York in the late 1820s, but also to her profound influence on Cushman's career; Fisher's student eventually surpassed her teacher to become America's most celebrated breeches performer in the 1840s and 1850s.

Anticipating Fisher's arrival, New York critics prepared audiences for her debut. Although much of the press surrounding Fisher's imminent engagement was favorable, one reporter, in particular, condemned the actress for her bold attempts to portray men in serious drama and tragedy. The *Albion's* critic proclaimed,

> Her proper line is romps and hoydens, but a perverse ambition, or a mistaken confidence, has often led her to come out in Richard, Ollapod, Shylock, Pangloss &c to the immense disgust of all rational players, and to the great injury of her own theatrical consideration, though no doubt to the gratification of the people who generally haunt the shilling Galleries. It is to be hoped that Miss Fisher will hereafter perform those characters only for which nature and education have fitted her and which she plays so admirably well.[64]

Such remarks are reminiscent of the types of reviews Barnes received a decade earlier, which suggests that the same critical trends were still operative. After actually witnessing her perform, however, this same critic revised his opinion somewhat, admitting that Fisher's theatrical powers had "expanded and matured" after her arrival in America. Although he acknowledged that the afterpiece that she acted in (a protean drama entitled *Old and Young* in which she played both male and female roles) was fatuous, she nevertheless won him over by her "dexterity, judgement, and nature." He continued approvingly, "Many a year has past away without our witnessing a success so merited and so complete. The approbation of the audience was unmeasured, and if we wanted any evidence of the justness of this eulogy, we might find it in that approbation."[65] This warm praise must be tempered with the knowledge that Fisher's successful vehicle was a farcical afterpiece and not a serious role. When the actress attempted more substantial parts like Goldfinch in *The Road to Ruin* or Norval, however, she was condemned for displaying her talent "at the expense of a great deal of good taste and delicate feeling." Yet it seemed that only the critic's "delicate feeling" was offended by Fisher's unorthodox choices, for local audiences repeatedly flocked to see her performances. Despite her histrionic skill and unprecedented local celebrity, however, Fisher's decision to wear the "masculine" hero's breeches was systematically met with critical scorn: "No excellence of acting can make up for the indiscretion of the selection."[66]

Fisher was so influential in boosting the popularity of breeches in America that some historians have mistakenly credited her (along with other infant prodigies) with originating the convention.[67] Her success did encourage many actresses, who normally would have remained safely within their dramatic "sphere," to branch out and explore challenging male roles. Mrs. Sharpe, a favorite stock actress at the Park during Fisher's residency there, proves a good example of this phenomenon as she discarded her standard line for breeches. Assuming the role of Count Belino from *The Devil's Bridge* on her benefit, Sharpe shocked New York critics who regarded her undertaking as subversive, her performance as absurd. This opera was presently in vogue in New York and was also playing at another theatre concurrently, with a Mr. Pearlman in the leading role of the Count. It was not simply Sharpe's rejection of her traditional repertoire of feminine parts that offended the critics on this occasion, but her desire to compete directly with a male colleague. Sharpe's experience thus provides an important example, not only of Fisher's influence on breeches performance, but of the potential power the cross-dressed actress had to threaten New York's theatrical hegemony during the 1820s.

In the 1830s, the convention of breeches performance continued to grow, perhaps even reaching its peak both in terms of its popular and critical reception and in terms of the regularity with which actresses assumed male roles. New characters and plays were added to the breeches repertoire (although actresses continued to play boys) such as Romeo, Othello, Virginius, Paul in *The Pet of the Petticoats*, Thalaba in *Thalaba the Destroyer*, Peter Wilkins, and numerous fairy roles including Oberon and Puck. One of the influences behind the boom in breeches performance in the 1830s was the burgeoning career of Cushman, who began acting professionally in New York in 1836. This principle player in American breeches performance history, however, was joined by a relatively large supporting cast that included Fisher and Barnes (who both remained popular into the 1830s), Ellen Tree (1806–1880), Eliza Trewar Shaw-Hamblin (1817–1873), Mrs. Henry Lewis (?–1873), Celeste (1814–1882), and Alexina Fisher (1822–1887).

Although women who played men's roles were still reviewed by the press as mere feminine boys, actresses such as Barnes, Hamblin, Lewis, and Cushman were recognized as serious artists with the potential to distinguish themselves by undertaking more weighty roles. Indeed, during the 1830s, critics frequently printed favorable reports of cross-dressed actresses *regardless* of the genre in which they performed. While a young Cushman was being praised for passing as Romeo, for example, other actresses were playing boy roles that were perceived as heroic and powerful as opposed to weak, beautiful, and delicate. The *Mirror* critic describes one actress's rendition of Telemachus, in the play of the same name, based on the Greek myth: "Miss Nelson as Telemachus looked well the youthful hero; and if we were to say in what part of her performance she was most effective, it would be in the combat with Eblis. . . . From the beautiful we again change to the terrible, and Telemachus descends to the infernal regions. He combats with Eblis, conquers, and his trials end."[68] Nelson is indeed described as youthful and beautiful but added to this is a depiction of her as heroic, terrible, and triumphant. Moreover this criticism is free from both disclaimers and pejorative statements meant to temper the success of the breeches performer, like those inserted into reports of Fisher's acting.

Surprisingly, this brief sabbatical from harsh criticism was enjoyed by women who played men as well as by those who played boys. While there are numerous examples of such positive criticism during this brief age of journalistic benevolence, one report stands out as particularly eulogistic. In May of 1836, the Boston theatrical correspondent for New York's *Spirit of the Times* sent a celebratory and detailed review to his editor that described Lewis's engagement at Boston's Tremont Street Theatre. Because the critic was an out-of-town correspondent, it is extremely unlikely that this report was a puff, since neither the editor of the *Spirit* nor the manager of the Tremont had anything to gain through false publicity in New York. In a review that is singular in its unconditional praise for the tragic breeches performer, the correspondent writes:

The principal attraction, at the Tremont for the last fortnight, has been the extraordinary performances of MRS. LEWIS of some of the most arduous of Shakespeare's male characters. At that lady's benefit, she advertised to play the part of *Richard* and although it is now the 'fag end' of the season, the house was very well filled. The people who had been accustomed to see Mrs. Lewis, in the quiet unassuming walks of her profession, felt deeply excited by the novelty, and made up their minds to be disappointed; but her first step and look as she appeared as the 'crook'd back tyrant' suddenly changed the current of their thoughts. Her figure is commanding;—and she has a brilliant eye, and expressive face. Her declamation was full of power and energy; the opening soliloquy was well delivered, and indeed throughout the piece, her 'points' indicated a nice conception, and correct judgement. The 'wooing scene' with Lady Anne was admirably well done, and the 'tent scene' likewise. 'Give me a horse—bind up my wounds,' elicited loud and continued plaudits. The final scene in which it was anticipated her powers would fail, was also very effective, and the fight with Richmond was admirably done. . . . She appeared twice as *Othello* and last Friday night as Shylock, with equal success. She looked the jealous Moor excellently,—this character does not call so fully into requisition the physical as the mental faculties: we discovered much to praise in the portrait represented—genius and the power of thought were alike perceptible . . . [69]

Not only did Lewis enact male roles that were highly unusual pieces for adult breeches performers to play, but she did so without inviting critical disdain. She seemed to pass as a man and was described with adjectives that were heretofore only employed in reviews of male actors. (However, critics did note that Othello was more of a mental role than a physical one, thus suggesting that a woman might render it more successfully than a role that required repeated displays of physical prowess.) During this run, Lewis also found favor with the critics for her portrayal of Virginius and William Tell, neither of which had ever been assumed by an American actress before. Moreover, although Tell had always fallen within masculine lines of business, Albert, Tell's son, was a standard breeches role. Thus by playing the father and not the son,

Lewis broke with previous trends in breeches performance (transcending her proper sphere in more ways than one) and succeeded in her efforts to gain esteem in the most masculine roles currently within the American repertoire (see figure 1.3).

Lewis was not alone in gaining victory over critics and audiences. Actresses such as Cushman and Shaw-Hamblin (who were both box office favorites during the 1830s) were reviewed enthusiastically as Norval and Romeo, while Ellen Tree "drew a tremendous house"[70] with her Ion—although her depiction of the young warrior was feminized by critics. Many events may have contributed to this apotheosis in breeches popularity and critical acceptance. Isolated performers generated enthusiasm about the convention during the 1830s, as was illustrated by Fisher's fame in the late 1820s/early 1830s, Cushman's early career in New York (1837–40), and Tree's tour in 1837–38. Because these women were so celebrated by audiences, critics may have found it unstrategic to defame them in their columns—especially if "relationships" (like those forged within the spacious surroundings of the Bowery's Cold Cut Room) had been established between editors, journalists, and theatre managers. In addition, as Alexander Saxton points out, a mass audience with an increased interest in novelty entertainment blossomed during the Jacksonian era, evidenced by the fact that theatres like the Bowery were rebuilt to accommodate up to three thousand patrons.[71] This enlarged popular audience may also help to explain the greater interest in breeches performance.

Moreover, Jacksonian ideology may have benefited the breeches performer in ways other than through simply cultivating a mass audience who was interested in any alternative theatric that would spice up the standard repertoire. Rather, the machismo of the Jacksonian era perhaps fortified the cross-dresser's appeal, as efforts to appear manly were celebrated regardless of the vehicle. As Mark C. Carnes and Clyde Griffen point out, Jackson acted as a "cultural symbol" of masculinity during the 1830s, an embodiment for antebellum men of "the manliness ethos."[72] Indeed, ubiquitous popular images of "Old Hickory," the self-made, independent child of the frontier, may have influenced New York dramatic critics as well, who were possibly inspired to view the breeches performer not as a

Fig. 1.3: Mrs. Henry Lewis as William Tell. Harvard Theatre Collection, The Houghton Library, Fredric Woodbridge Wilson, Curator.

usurping woman trying to escape the duties of domesticity but rather as an individual seeking only to better herself through the adoption of a superior (masculine) persona. Indeed, popular images of rugged masculinity, which were perpetuated by Jackson's presidency and which contributed to Forrest's career, may have influenced Lewis's popularity in the 1830s as well.[73]

Yet, by the end of the decade, critical magnanimity began to wane and many actresses were once again admonished to remove their whiskers, hang up their trousers, and avoid "such freaks." Shaw-Hamblin, who had been praised as Norval,[74] was mocked by the *Spirit* critic for playing Hamlet on her benefit—a practice that was, by this time, considered ordinary. He wrote, "Mrs. Shaw played *Hamlet!* for her benefit last Tuesday! 'Think of that, Master Brook!' We 'should'nt be surprised' if Barry went on in his wife's bib and tucker for *Ophelia*. How poor Mrs. Shaw must have been frightened at the Ghost!"[75] Adult breeches performers in serious roles were generally judged most harshly; indeed only an 11-year-old Jean Davenport (1829–1903) could gain critical approval during the last years of the 1830s—no doubt because her status as a child star rendered her performance of serious roles somewhat innocuous. Her Richard III was "played in a style of classic elegance that made us readily participate with a delighted audience, in their admiration of the wonderful portraiture," the *Spirit* critic allowed. This praise was immediately tempered, however, as she was described not as masculine or powerful but as "some sort of fairy being to whom nature had denied the full proportions of manhood.... It was difficult to believe there was not some optical deception, some lessening operation in the organ of vision, that gave her the appearance of BOOTH, looked at through the wrong end of a powerfully diminishing opera glass."[76] Davenport was praised because her stature as a child immediately removed the subversiveness involved in masterfully presenting the illusion of masculinity. She proved enchanting as long as she remained on the "wrong end" of the opera glass.

Significantly, this critical shift from approval back to censure for women who attempted serious male roles paralleled public opinion toward women's social involvement in the 1830s. Historians have noted that during this decade women enjoyed certain freedoms that were denied to them shortly afterward—or at least became increasingly suspect. Mary Ryan argues that during the 1830s women did not always linger by the hearth but worked in factories and engaged in religious revivals and public speaking ventures. Similarly, Smith-Rosenberg and Sara Evans discuss this decade as an "age of association," in which women became actively involved in organizations like the American Female Moral Reform Society and, by doing so, carved out a public space for themselves between the spheres.[77] Female education was encouraged by women such as Emma Willard and Catherine Beecher, who argued that institutions of learning would act as conduits through which women's moral superiority might flow; armed with a higher education women might successfully reform societal ills. Associations like the Moral Reform Society, together with temperance and abolitionist organizations, encouraged women to use their moral influence to affect change in the public sphere. Evans points out the sophistication with which women were beginning to learn to exercise their voice within society by the end of the 1830s. She explains that by 1837 a national convention of antislavery women met in New York; their congregation reflected the extensive network of female antislavery societies that had sprung up throughout the 1830s. In addition to organizing for various causes, thousands of women participated in petition campaigns and "exercised their one political right. As they did so they learned the mechanics of the political system and methods of political discourse and persuasion."[78]

Although the women's movement was still in its early stages in the 1830s, voices advocating reform could be heard as figures such as Sarah and Angelina Grimké spoke publicly about women's equality on their tour of female antislavery societies in 1836–37, and Elizabeth Cady Stanton and Lucretia Mott began a dialogue regarding women's rights in 1839 that resulted in the first women's right's conference nine years later. The increasing involvement of women in public life raised certain questions about women's proper position within society. As this debate—which came to be known as the "Woman Question" by Victorians—became more heated, male journalists and religious figures began to see women's growing participation in public activities as unnatural, fearing that women might abandon their private sphere entirely, thus upsetting the balance of society and threatening the harmony, perhaps even the existence, of familial life.

In her book, *Women in Public,* Ryan argues that women who did engage in public activities did so at a cost. Although gender boundaries were well articulated, they often had to be policed. Women who spoke out about inequality, such as the radical Scottish reformer Fanny Wright, were criticized by the press as unnatural "lady men." Similarly, the press undermined women's efforts within the abolitionist movement, tarnishing their reputations "with sexual innuendos" as well as charges of "gender impropriety."[79] As indicated by the demeaning, sometimes vitriolic reviews concerning breeches performers at the end of the decade, it seems that abolitionists and public speakers were not the only women who were excoriated by the press for boundary crossing.

Growing suspicions about societal transgression (a fear that women involved in public work and reform movements would become too masculine) proliferated during the 1840s and 1850s as the women's movement burgeoned. A newspaper article from 1852 exemplifies such suspicions as a columnist for the *New York Herald* tried to determine what kind of woman would fight for equality. He alleges,

> Some of them are old maids, whose personal charms were never very attractive, and who have been sadly slighted by the masculine gender in general; some of them women who have been badly mated ... and they are therefore down upon the whole of the opposite sex; some, having so much of the virago in their disposition, that nature appears to have made a mistake in their gender—mannish women, like hens that crow ... Of the male sex who attend [women's rights] conventions for the purpose of taking part in them, the majority are hen-pecked husbands, and all of them ought to wear petticoats.[80]

Such critical associations between women's efforts to liberate themselves (if only in very minor ways), loss of gender identity, and cross-dressing were especially apparent within the pages of dramatic periodicals. The convention of breeches suffered from these mounting critical anxieties regarding the dangerous societal ramifications of women's involvement in the public sphere, yet specific actresses were able to transcend negative critical treatment. Cushman proved the major exception to critical patterns established in the 1840s and 1850s as her performances were largely exempt from harsh critiques. The patterns and trends in breeches performance throughout the 1840s and the 1850s were dominated both by her triumphs and by the rise of popular breeches performance in spectacular melodrama, burlesque, and extravaganza.

Although Cushman's career is relatively well documented, evidence about her early work in the 1840s is difficult to find, since New York theatrical reviews from this period are terse and infrequent—a phenomenon that may well be connected to the theatrical recession engendered by the Panic of 1837. As a foreign correspondent implies in 1840, "In the whole history of the stage, theatricals, both in this country and the Unites States, were probably never known to be at so low an ebb as they are at this moment."[81] Another factor that contributed to the sparsity of reviews on breeches performers in the beginning of the 1840s was the *Spirit*'s exclusive focus on the Park Theatre. Because many breeches performances were housed at the Bowery during this period, reviews about cross-dressed actresses were infrequent until 1843 when the *Spirit* began to report on Bowery theatricals on a regular basis, a change that occurred largely because Bowery attendance had increased due to lowered ticket prices.

In the late 1830s, theatrical reviews noted that Cushman was a capable and versatile actress and popular with audiences, but it was not until the next decade that she received any significant critical attention. Cushman's early career was spent as a utility actress at both the Park (where she was under contract from August 26, 1837, to August 12, 1840) and at Burton's Theatre in Philadelphia. Having a utility position within a resident stock company facilitated breeches performances because actresses were regarded as universal substitutes, filling in if someone became ill or if there were not enough actors in the company to play all the male parts—especially in the "juvenile lead" lines. During residencies in New York and Philadelphia, Cushman played over 30 breeches roles in a variety of dramatic genres.

In addition to her work as a utility actress or "walking lady," Cushman also briefly acted as manager for the Walnut Street Theatre in Philadelphia, a post she abandoned in 1843 so that she could spend time touring with Macready. Playing opposite this renowned English actor convinced Cushman, who had not yet received star status in America despite her popularity, that her future success as a performer was contingent upon an international reputation. This discovery prompted her to journey to London in 1844, where she shortly realized her goal of becoming a star. Her English success catapulted her to fame almost overnight and facilitated an early retirement. After her British coup, Cushman resided only temporarily in the United States until the final years of her life, yet she did make regular tours to America, one that lasted from 1849 to 1852 and another from 1857 to 1858. When not on tour, she lived in Rome and in London until the 1870s, when a severe bout with breast cancer brought her back to New England, where she died in 1876.

Although she did not achieve star status until the mid 1840s, Cushman's residency at the Park endeared her to New York audiences and critics, who quickly recognized her remarkable abilities as a breeches performer. From the earliest days of her career, Cushman was regarded by critics as a masculine woman who skillfully passed in her male roles. An early review of her Romeo claimed that she could easily be mistaken for a male youth,[82] and while at the Park in 1841, her Thalaba was received with equal admiration. As Thalaba, "Miss Cushman played the part of the hero, and she was the hero indeed; she had a sword in her hand, and every chap that came upon the stage she immediately picked a quarrel with, and a fight ensued."[83] Indeed, Cushman was thought to be so masculine that one critic referred to her Romeo as a "perversion," a "monstrous anomaly" that threatened to "push [men] from [their] stools."[84]

While she met with occasional disapproval, Cushman's breeches performances were overwhelmingly popular with both critics and audiences. The remarkable press that she received in London in 1845–46, as the result of her performance of Romeo at the Haymarket Theatre, was largely responsible for assuring her prestigious standing with American critics who, eager to claim her as an eminent native star, reprinted some of these reviews so that the American public might be kept abreast of her triumphs. The *Spirit* reported that the English "press is unanimous in the expression of favor towards the sisters [Cushman's sister Susan played opposite her], and several of the leading journals are rapturous in their praise both of the young debutante and of Charlotte in her line of character. . . . Miss Cushman is far superior to any Romeo that has been seen for years."[85] Upon her return to America, Cushman was repeatedly praised by New York critics for her masculine impersonations. Her performance of Romeo at the Astor Place Opera House in 1850, for example, "received the highest encomiums," as she was said to have made the character her own.[86]

More intriguing perhaps is the criticism that surrounded Cushman's attempts at Hamlet and Cardinal Wolsey—two roles that were thought to be tests of a male actor's histrionic prowess. While New York critics puffed Cushman's Hamlet in advance and were certain that "her acute and powerful mind will doubtless present the accomplished Dane in an original point of view,"[87] few reviews exist of this performance, which took place on November 24, 1851, at Brougham's Lyceum. Unaccountably, the *Spirit* critic missed her performance despite his previous hyping and the *Albion* reviewer, while proclaiming Cushman's Hamlet "the dramatic event of the season," disagreed with her interpretation of the role, which was unabashedly and aggressively masculine. Yet, regardless of the *Albion* critic's disapproval of certain acting choices, he proceeds to analyze Cushman's performance thoroughly and justly, and praises her elocution and emotional intensity. There is no mention of any inability on Cushman's part to convincingly appear masculine; on the contrary, "the reality . . . and simplicity and earnestness of her action were inimitable."[88]

While her Hamlet received sparse coverage, Cushman's rendition of Cardinal Wolsey in Shakespeare's *Henry VIII* during her second return tour to America in 1847 was almost completely neglected by New York drama critics. Reviewers briefly mentioned that Cushman played the role (the *Albion* compared her to Macready) but did not discuss her performance thoroughly, nor did they comment on the singularity of this event; Wolsey had never been played by a woman before (or since). The *Spirit* focused instead upon Cushman's performance of Queen Katharine, in the same play, calling it "one of her most admired personations," her acting, "truly sublime."[89] This critical neglect was most likely the result of Cushman's exceptional fame. Because "Our Charlotte" was revered as America's first international star and greatest native tragedian, dramatic reviewers were perhaps unwilling to express any negative remarks. Indeed, the *Albion* critic, in writing of Cushman's Hamlet, is careful to temper his critiques with laudatory remarks that far outweigh his reservations. Considering the condemnatory criticism generally written during this period about breeches performers who attempted serious roles, Cushman's victory over the critics—or, at the very least, the paucity of harsh responses directed toward her—proves telling. Perhaps she escaped harsh criticism because she was an international star, because she had enchanted London audiences and won the crucial English seal of approval. It is also possible that her "untouchable" quality was due to her overwhelming popularity with her audiences; critics may have felt that by castigating Cushman, they would alienate treasured subscribers. As far as "Our Charlotte" was concerned, the worst critics might do was remain silent.

During the 1850s, Cushman shared the stage with another popular performer of serious male roles, Charlotte Crampton (1816–1868). Like Fisher and Lewis, Crampton performed many parts not usually undertaken by actresses, such as Richard III, Shylock, Othello, and Mazeppa—a role that was to become Menken's starring vehicle. A notice appearing in the *Spirit* on January 15, 1859, is illustrative of the type of treatment she received from the press. The *Spirit* critic writes,

> This is the second week of Miss Charlotte Crampton, and we are informed that she has improved since we saw her. A new piece, 'The Wild Rider of Santee,' was presented to display her peculiar powers and daring horsemanship, which succeeded admirably. Miss C. is well supported by the company. Our pretty favorite, Miss Sallie Bishop, executed a fancy dance in the most fascinating manner, after which a farce and a three act drama were performed.[90]

Significantly, this critic does not seem to possess firsthand evidence of Crampton's performances. While it is true that he did review her once (negatively), he does not seem to have made it for this second week of her run at the National theatre. The critic does, however, speak as though he personally witnessed the performance of "the pretty little favorite." This critical negligence regarding popular breeches actresses who attempted serious male roles perhaps suggests another form of subjugation to complement critical trends responsible for maintaining a popular image of the breeches performer as either a ludicrous anomalous woman, a societal menace, or an effeminate youth.

Many other women joined Cushman and Crampton to become relatively successful in cross-dressed performance during the 1840s and 1850s. Shaw-Hamblin, the resident queen of the Bowery, continued to impress audiences with her Ion; Celeste remained popular in her dumb-boy roles (despite negative response to her Hamlet); Fanny Wallack (and other leading stock actresses) still regularly played Hamlet for their benefits; and the craze for child stars progressed with the two Denin sisters and the Bateman twins—all four of whom won critical approbation for their rendering of adult male roles. But while many actresses, roles and/or trends within the convention of breeches continued to be popular, certain changes and shifts became noticeable during the mid-forties. As popular entertainments such as burlesque, pantomime, extravaganza, and spectacle became more prominent within the American theatre, the landscape of breeches performance changed as well. Midcentury theatrical reviews indicate that popular breeches performances were beginning to eclipse serious or traditional portrayals, as Prince Charming gained victory over the Prince of Denmark and rogues such as Jack Sheppard, that insidious yet loveable highwayman, stole the hearts of Chatham pitties. One dramatic critic, reporting on the theatricals at this establishment, gives evidence of such a phenomenon in a discussion of a certain Mr. Freer's Hamlet, which opened in March of 1845. It seems that Mr. Freer had some competition: "As a strong contrast, Miss Reynolds revived Jack Sheppard for her benefit and enacted the hero much to the admiration of the lovers of burglaries and breeches wearing heroines. The prince of Denmark knocked under to the discipline of the road and the 'lady-fair, pattering in flash' created more enthussam [sic] than the actor discoursing gifted words of melody."[91]

Jack's fame was rivaled (and equaled) by heroes in other sub-genres, equestrian melodramas being the most popular. In addition to enjoying notoriety as Mazeppa and Dick Turpin in *Rookwood*, women gained increasing approval as romantic male leads in burlesques and extravaganzas. Mary Taylor and Mrs. H. C. Timm made a memorable team in the mid-forties as they delighted audiences at the Bowery and Olympic Theatres in burlesques such as *Giovanni in Gotham* and Rossini's opera *Cinderella*. These types of roles for women continued to win approval, and by the mid-fifties critics reported that such performances meant almost certain prosperity at the box office. One critic writes of a production at the National Theatre in 1855, "Miss Hathaway as King Pretty, in 'The Fountain of Beauty,' has done more than her share in filling the house."[92]

Throughout the century, women in masculine roles had been described by critics in terms that drew attention to their underlying feminine charms, even though these actresses often played characters that boasted masculine characteristics like Norval and Ion. By midcentury, however, such strategic critical attempts to reinforce dominant gender ideology became increasingly unnecessary as certain male vehicles became progressively feminine, and playwrights began to create dashing male lovers and charming princes specifically for the breeches performer. Cross-dressed actresses were no longer simply characterized as "beautiful" and "graceful" in their portrayals of Norval and Ion, but actually *became* King Pretty. The seeming institutionalization of this critical tendency toward feminization, evident in these emerging popular breeches parts, paralleled the previously mentioned split in highbrow and lowbrow entertainment as both audiences and players began to aggregate into "legitimate" or "illegitimate" camps. Whereas breeches performers in the early century might have played Hamlet for the main feature and appeared as Little Pickle in the afterpiece, as midcentury approached these actresses began to specialize. While economic concerns and managerial influence often necessitated a varied menu for many breeches performers, a growing number of women became associated with specific types of roles. For example, Cushman and Crampton enacted an occasional Mazeppa or Jack Sheppard, but were thought of primarily as serious players, as opposed to actresses such as Fanny Herring who dominated popular stages during the 1850s and who never played a traditional role except perhaps during a benefit. A humorous letter from a rustic correspondent to the *Spirit* exemplifies this tendency toward specialization. "Wagon-Tyre" writes,

> Dear "Spirit."—When in Vicksburg, last week, I heard a horse story which I think may serve to cause a laugh, and at any rate can boast two claims to consideration from your readers—that it is *original* and *true*. You must know the celebrated tragic actress, Miss Cushman, purchased a large white horse in Louisville, and on her arrival in Vicksburg, this singular travelling companion excited the curiosity of the natives, and led them to conclude that the lady intended favoring them with some equestrian dramas. An unsophisticated Mississippian, in his anxiety not to lose a chance to see the "show," rushed to the box office to secure seats for the night's performance, but perceiving by the bill that the public were to be favored with "Romeo and Juliet" that evening, instead of the "horse opera," he judged it best to make enquiries when a style of representation more congenial to his tastes would be given. Stalking up to the treasurer, he requested to be informed on what night "Mazeppa" would be played.[93]

Mr. Tyre goes on to explain that this unfortunate patron assumed that since Cushman had a horse, she must have intended to co-star with it—a supposition so absurd that it warranted a letter to the editor. Cushman is described here as a "tragic actress" and only an "unsophisticated Mississippian" would have made the mistake in thinking that such a performer would have crossed over into equestrian melodrama.

With the exception of Cushman and a few others, the breeches performer became increasingly associated with "illegitimate" entertainment and therefore was thought to be "illegitimate" herself. Paradoxically, this relegation to illegitimacy temporarily mitigated the threat generated by many breeches performers during midcentury. The power to subvert established notions of gendered behavior—or to question and challenge the process of gender construction itself—was itself reduced by popular associations that reinforced an actress's femininity, yet the specter of the "lady-man," the woman who *did* appear masculine, who *could* pass as a man (and could therefore also appropriate male privilege through such male role playing) still haunted American critics. As middle-class bourgeois women began to articulate their concerns about domestic, social, and political inequality, a fear that women outside the theatre might also begin to "wear the breeches" became the concern of male journalists and critics—both dramatic and otherwise. Public women (actresses)—who disguised themselves as men—became especially suspect (and critics increasingly caustic) as public rights were demanded for women. "[O]n Wednesday, [Mrs. Wilkinson] undertook the part of Richard the Third. There are some fine points in her acting, but of course, as might be said of any female, she is totally unfitted for such a character. There is something repulsive in the very idea of a woman appearing in it, and though it may attract as a novelty, it cannot possibly please as a performance."[94] What had been distasteful at the beginning of the century was now "repulsive" to critics who feared that such boundary crossing was becoming far too ubiquitous. Even the exalted Cushman was, on occasion, criticized for venturing too far into masculine territory. Regarding her performances as Romeo at the Broadway Theatre in 1850, one critic allows, "If she were less masculine in her portraitures, she would be more appreciated than she is."[95] Significantly, these two notices (which both demonstrate rising critical anxiety over the breeches performer), the first from January of 1848 and the second written two years later, temporally framed what is, perhaps, the most important event in American women's history: the Seneca Falls convention in upstate New York in the summer of 1848—an event that many cite as the official beginning of the women's movement in America.

The courageous demands for equality at this convention seemed to foreshadow the collapse of binary gender prescriptions—a frightening prospect for a society invested in the maintenance of public and private spheres. At this congregation women emphatically declared their right to public citizenship. As Evans points out, "This was the essence of their radicalism: Women are citizens; their relationship to the state should be direct and unmediated by husband or children. Thus they directly challenged the doctrine of separate spheres at the heart of Victorian domesticity by asserting women's public rights as citizens."[96] Such a challenge was also voiced through the dress reform movement, spearheaded by Amelia Bloomer with the help of Stanton. This campaign, which began in 1849, was waged from the pages of Bloomer's temperance magazine, *The Lily*, and became a much debated topic in the early fifties as more and more women began to adopt this style of dress. Theatrical groups, such as the Bloomer Troupe, were created in New York where actresses performed wearing Bloomers, and satirical magazines and journals such as the English periodical *Punch* often sported satirical cartoons of women in their Bloomer "costumes," as they were called. Bloomers were thought to be highly controversial, as the following chapter explains.

Not surprisingly, Bloomers were often equated with breeches in the nineteenth century. In an article from the *Spirit* entitled "Woman, Considered as a Domestic Animal," the question of whether or not a woman has legs is satirically debated. The author magnanimously concludes that "the genus" has more than two limbs. He confesses, "The doubts we might have formerly entertained as to the precise number are dispelled entirely, by the advent of Bloomer dresses, and their inevitable concomitants breeches. Blessed then be thy name, oh, Mrs. Bloomer, who hast solved this problem for us, and made us fully aware that thy sex belonged to the class of bipeds."[97] The connections—and there are many—between the dress reform movement and the convention of breeches, add an additional political component to cross-dressed theatrics.

In the 1860s critical sentiment toward the breeches performer once more began to shift as significant changes took place within the American theatre. The craze for burlesque, equestrian spectacles, extravaganza, and pantomime occurred in tandem with increased interest in what Allen terms "feminine spectacle," and both were apparent in the theatrical sensation created by Thompson's troupe of British Blondes. In 1868 these women introduced a new type of breeches actress to the American stage—one who was politically outspoken, sexually objectified, and increasingly marginalized. The popularity of equestrian melodrama under Menken, coupled with the variety of burlesque introduced by Thompson in 1868, engendered a paradigm shift in American breeches performance that ultimately resulted in the decline of the convention in the later half of the century.

The careers of two women specifically, Menken and Thompson, significantly affected this shift. Adah Isaacs Menken (1835/36–1868), whose life dates are almost as obscure as her ethnic and spiritual heritage, was the most infamous breeches performer ever to appear on the nineteenth-century stage. Because of her adventurous spirit and her indifference to nineteenth-century standards governing proper feminine behavior, she deliberately cultivated a reputation as a dangerous woman. After growing up in various parts of the South, Menken moved to Cincinnati with her husband Alexander Menken (her first of four), where she became a scion of the Jewish community, frequently publishing her poems in the *American Israelite* and delivering public speeches. Subsequently, Menken moved to the state of New York, where she first appeared as Mazeppa in Albany in 1860. While equestrian melodramatic heroes had been popular vehicles for breeches performers throughout the century, Menken infused new life into "the horse drama" by displaying herself not only in pantaloons but also in various stages of undress. Menken was the first performer—male or female—to enact the famous scene in which the page Cassimir—who is actually the Tartar prince Mazeppa—is stripped, tied to a "fiery steed," and cast out upon the treacherous mountain terrain.

Mazeppa became popular among Bowery audiences in the 1830s due in large part to this spectacular scene. Traditionally, the brave Tartar in this scene had been "played" by a cloth dummy, since actors and actresses, not displaying the same courageous mien as the character they represented, were too timid to undertake the stunt. The critical sensation caused both by Menken's daring horsemanship and her "nudity" (she actually wore fleshlings covered with a short-sleeved white blouse, and short bloomers) cultivated a perception of the breeches performer as a sexual object and spawned a host of female imitators throughout the decade who adopted her costume and expanded upon the Menken legend. Consequently, breeches performers began to populate "lowbrow" New York theatres that showcased their talents—and their figures—through sensational equestrian vehicles.

This trend in breeches performance in the 1860s was followed by a fascination for Thompsonian burlesque. Shortly after arriving in New York from London in 1868, Lydia Thompson (1836–1908) and her company of four other women began to attract huge crowds to Wood's Broadway Theatre. Her particular brand of burlesque, which involved comic songs, skits, dances, and parodies of popular politics, and which showcased a bold display of feminine features, proved appealing to New York audiences who flocked to witness her production of *Ixion, or the Man at the Wheel*. While practically all of Thompson's productions featured the majority of her troupe in cross-dress, these actresses were not attempting to pass as men or to achieve verisimilitude. Rather, they mocked masculine behavior and manners through their gestures and words while simultaneously appearing in eroticized male garb that accentuated their feminine charms. It was this combination that ignited both critical indignation and popular appeal—both of which were apparent as Thompson and her company moved from Wood's to Niblo's Garden in 1869. At Niblo's, this troupe enjoyed the enthusiastic support of middle-class audiences (which included women as well as men) but invited such scorn from the press that the group was forced to embark prematurely on a national tour. Although Thompson's company was popular with audiences during 1869, the press continued to excoriate the Blondes for their indecent displays and vulgar subject matter. Such "hysterical anti-burlesque discourse"[98] ultimately resulted in burlesque's banishment to more pedestrian theatrical establishments during the following decade.

Yet, burlesque's deportation to minstrel halls and "illegitimate" theatres occurred at a much greater cost than its own marginalization. Indeed, the controversy that ignited over Thompson's performance engulfed the breeches performer as well, for any protofeminist subtext that might have been inferred in performances by Cushman,

Menken, and others was exposed in the candid satire of burlesque. Subtle articulations of resistance expressed by former breeches performers were now suspect as critics perceived the cross-dressed woman not as an artist, feminine youth, or "masculine lady" (if she passed), but as an anomaly, a misrepresentation, a travesty. What started in the beginning of the century as an attempt by critics to reduce the stature of the cross-dressed actress—significantly *not* through sexualization—resulted in an all-out rhetorical war against breeches performers who, in the wake of the British Blondes, were not only sexually objectified but ultimately considered to be "neither fish, flesh, or fowl of theatrical creation."[99]

Chapter 2

BREECHES, BLOOMERS, AND "BIDDY IN THE KITCHEN"

Breeches Performance as Feminist Politic

> *Dress becomes a sort of symbolic language—a kind of personal glossary—a species of body phrenology the study of which it would be madness to neglect.*
> —*Quarterly Review*, 1847

> *The Lady before us might very well pass*
> *For the gentleman viewed the wrong way in the glass.*
> —Gilbert Abbott á Beckett, 1846

> *The ultimate inversion, of course, is to transform male masterpieces into feminist statements.*
> —Carroll Smith-Rosenberg, 1985

IN THE WINTER OF 1844–1845, THE OLYMPIC THEATRE housed the celebrated team of Sarah Timm and Mary Taylor. Both women were popular with New York audiences in the early forties and won special favor with the Bowery pitties. They had a successful partnership:

Timm, described as a "showy-looking dashing, pleasing actress," played male roles while Taylor, who had a "sweet" voice and a "fine figure," acted the feminine ingenue.[1] Although reviewers had always been generous in their coverage of this pair, Timm and Taylor elicited an unusual amount of critical attention for a production of *Cinderella* that took place in December. The Olympic was crowded that night (the evening's performance was a benefit for a Mr. Howell), and the audience was reportedly extremely enthusiastic, responsive, and excited to see Mrs. Timm in her starring role as Prince Charming and Mrs. Taylor as Cinderella. During the finale, however, an obstreperous patron began to proclaim his devotion for Taylor. He stood in his seat and interrupted the performance with a rousing "Three cheers for Mary Taylor! three cheers for Mary Taylor!"[2] Although early-nineteenth-century theatre audiences had a reputation for rowdiness, their behavior became increasingly mannered as the century progressed; by 1845, audiences—at the Olympic at least—were intolerant of unsolicited outbursts. According to a *New Mirror* correspondent, Mrs. Taylor's eager fan caused a near riot, prompting motions to "put him out" from the inhabitants of the boxes and more aggressive proposals to "Kill him!" from spectators in the pit. Members of the gallery also entered the altercation; although we are told that they refrained from contributing to the noisy suggestions that were being bandied back and forth by pit and box, they silently hurled their benches over the rail. The performers apparently froze onstage, appalled and unable to remedy the situation. "Mrs. Timm alone was calm amid the storm," reported the *New Mirror* critic. She left the stage, "sprung to the box" (all the while using only one arm to "ward off the flying missiles" that rained down from the gallery), grabbed the offending man, and delivered him to the officers, telling them to "Put him out, but don't hurt him."[3] Taylor remained inert while

> Timm, from so often wearing the breeches and personating the man very likely, on this particular occasion acted the man straight out and stood her ground like a true hero.... Timm was on for the Prince at the time of the row, and was consequently arrayed in costume to do battle manfully—Taylor was doing *Cinderella*, and

as all damsels should, fainted. She, too, might have fought had she been decked in male habiliments, for it is shrewdly suspected she is not lacking in spunk.[4]

Clothes act as a sort of transforming agent in this extraordinary, and perhaps apocryphal, tale; neither Timm's physical strength (which must have been considerable if she deftly repelled flying benches with one arm), nor her negotiating skills are mentioned as contributing to her heroic deed. According to the critic, it was her breeches that seemed to give her the might, wit, and courage to execute such a feat. Indeed, Taylor, who wore petticoats, fainted—despite her alleged "spunk." Such a critical supposition—which directly links the cross-dressed actress to displays of male power—provides invaluable evidence to counter traditional views of the breeches performer as merely a sexual object. In this particular circumstance, the actress was able to do much more than simply play the man onstage; she actually became the man—the hero—in a social drama that required the skills of one who was prepared to "do battle manfully." Because of her extensive experience as a breeches performer, Timm was able to "act the man straight out," a role that critics, and perhaps audience members, saw as possible only because she had repeatedly played male characters onstage.

When stories such as this one are interpreted within the context of nineteenth-century gender ideology, the convention of breeches emerges as more than simply a leg show designed to titillate a male audience. Like dwellers in early modern Europe, who, due to strict sumptuary laws, literally wore their civic hearts upon their sleeves, nineteenth-century Americans visually communicated their social positions through their clothing as well. Cross-dressed women—regardless of their theatrical or nontheatrical status—were transgressive during this century, not simply because their attire was unorthodox, but because it transmitted a feminist message—a desire to "unsex themselves," to eschew the limitations prescribed by their sphere. While legs sold tickets and managers may have wanted to put their actresses in breeches for financial reasons, the woman who chose to play a serious or tragic male role such as Hamlet or Virginius or Claude Melnotte on her benefit night was not just exposing her legs for profit (although a desire to draw a crowd may have been one motivating factor). While some breeches actresses unwittingly participated without objection or resistance in patriarchal systems of representation that reproduced the theatrical sign "Woman," many actresses who cross-dressed *deliberately* sought to compete with their male colleagues, many considered themselves serious artists, and a few even had indirect ties to the burgeoning women's rights movement. These cross-dressed performances were not about unconditional surrender before a consuming male gaze; they were about artistry, power, subversion, and rebellion.

ANTEBELLUM GENDER IDEOLOGY AND THE ACTRESS

The gendered landscape of antebellum America is, at first glance, an easy one to survey. WOMAN was thought to be the exact opposite of man, to be, as one critic described, his "natural inferior in intellect, in energy, in strength of passions, in propelling and active powers; in ability to contend with external difficulties." Such philosophy was ubiquitous among those who shaped nineteenth-century opinion, those who tried to normalize discussions of gender asymmetry both by invoking divine prescriptions and by drawing comparisons to nature and the natural world. Man is superior to woman just as the sun is brighter than the moon, "and to argue against this because of the intellectual eminence of a few women, is like saying that night is as light as day, because the moonlight evenings of June are brighter than the foggy mornings of November."[5]

Indeed, newspapers, magazines, periodicals, and the pulpit proclaimed the prerogative of men and constructed a discourse that was authorized both by Christian and Enlightenment rhetoric and that naturalized binary gender relationships. Men were characterized as public figures, the "lords of creation," and women as their ordained subordinates. Women that lived within the boundaries drawn by a patriarchal hegemony were said to dwell within their circle of influence and thus enjoyed the "power" of domestic management, Republican Motherhood, and moral jurisdiction within the private sphere. Such women were natural women, or True Women, as they came to be known in popular discourse; they were "pure, pious, submissive and domestic."[6] Women that in any way transgressed their sphere were immediately identified as she-males or "unsexed anomalies" and were characterized or "othered" by the company they kept. "If we want masculine women," wrote the editor of an auspicious New York periodical, "we must go among savages and barbarians. We can find Amazons, and female soldiers, and female tillers of the soil, and female politicians and female generals, most easily among heathen or semi-civilized people."[7]

Fears of usurpation by so-called Amazons continually materialized as more and more women began to enter public life; however, women who sought to extend their influence beyond the hearth did so only under the mantle of altruism and argued that their moral superiority served as their passport to the public sphere. Thus women's social involvement consisted largely of mission work: women empowered to function as societal watchdogs by the revivalist proselytizing of the Second Great Awakening directed their evangelical energies towards social housekeeping through moral reform (the eradication of prostitution), temperance associations, and abolitionism.

More radical women, such as the early women's rights activist Fanny Wright and the writer Margaret Fuller, who chose to abandon legitimizing philanthropic credentials and speak openly—publicly—about female oppression, were either castigated as aberrant or dangerously sexual—either way they sacrificed their femininity. When, Ryan notes, "Fanny Wright spoke at Tammany Hall in the 1820s, she was dismissed as a 'lady man.'"[8] Similarly, Margaret Fuller's book on *Women in the Nineteenth Century*, which was published in 1845, unleashed harsh criticism that reflected deep-seated fears about social anarchism. Fuller rejected the doctrine of separate spheres and the tenants of True Womanhood outright and declared that women could do anything that men could do: "let them be sea-captains, if you will."[9] Such a clarion cry for emancipation precipitated vitriolic criticism—even from theatre journalists. Shortly after Fuller's book was released, a dramatic reviewer for the *Broadway Journal* addressed the issues exposed in her study, topics that he presently considered much more important to discuss than "things theatrical." In the first of three issues that dealt with this controversy, the critic wrote, "If there is anything clear in revealed and natural law, it is that man is the head of woman. All the beauty, all the harmony, all the happiness of life is centered in this truth."[10] One week later, this same critic continued (no doubt in response to Fuller's declaration that women could be sea-captains), "The only way in which any good can be rendered to society, is by making woman more womanly and man more manly. To make sailors of women and milliners of men, is to have imperfect sailors and imperfect milliners.... The employments of women are distinct from those of men, and the more perfect that society becomes, the more distinct they will grow."[11] To be a "public woman," operating outside the sanctioned duties of humanitarianism in nineteenth-century American society was oxymoronic, and signaled disruption or perhaps worse.[12]

Provided this context, it is not surprising that actresses—who were also "public women"—were systematically associated with prostitution in the nineteenth century. Both working class actresses and their more privileged middle-class sisters fell victim to such spurious assumptions, which, in turn, caused many women to avoid theatrical careers. In her autobiography Anna Cora Mowatt recalled that initially, "[t]he idea of becoming a professional actress was revolting"; even her closest relatives were shocked and dismayed by her "proposed *public* step."[13] "Thou leavest woman's holier sphere/For light and vain display," wrote Frances Sargent Osgood in a poem castigating Mowatt for her decision to undertake public readings.[14]

Thus antebellum gender ideology did not seem to categorically allow for working actresses, who were associated with the private sphere by virtue of the fact that they were women/wives/mothers and also had access to male dominated professions and to public spaces that they necessarily inhabited on a daily basis. For the most part, actresses were sanctioned to appear in public. As the *Arctus* critic notes in discussing Mrs. Mowatt's public readings, "The question has been discussed whether a lady should thus appear in public, but looking upon it as the exercise of one department of a reputable profession, that of the stage, we can see no more objection to the recitations of Mrs. Mowatt than to those of Mr. Vandenhoff."[15] Although professional women like Mowatt occupied both spheres simultaneously, Davis points out that they were "neither *private citizens in the public sphere nor private women in the intimate sphere.*"[16]

This liminal "semi-public" position in nineteenth-century society, however, did not exclude actresses from the controlling discourse of difference. For notwithstanding their very real achievements in a male dominated public arena, contemporary critics and journalists (both male and female) repeatedly called attention to actresses' femininity (and thus to dominant gender ideology and women's proper social place). Even the notably masculine Cushman was described by her contemporaries in terms suggestive of True Womanhood, despite her widely acknowledged manly demeanor.[17] Nineteenth-century actresses (especially breeches actresses) may have been able to blur "concepts of performance, publicity, and femininity"[18] through their work, as Davis argues, but they were still often regarded by critics as "Woman"—individuals defined initially by their opposition to men and only secondly by their accomplishments and interests. Such an emphasis on difference made the work of the female theatrical transvestite even more remarkable—and the repeated critical references to her femininity even more telling.

THE SEMIOTICS OF NINETEENTH-CENTURY CLOTHING

Despite the efforts of various critics, writers, preachers, and journalists to construct and prescribe nineteenth-century gender ideology, the average American could easily read people's "gendering" simply by looking at their clothing. Male and female fashions were emblematic of one's social power: attire indicated not only class but also marked one's place in the continuum between True Womanhood and quintessential machismo. Clothes were symbols of one's social, mental, emotional, and professional status and signified the social role performed by the wearer. Indeed, the four "cardinal virtues" of True Womanhood were all exhibited in women's apparel, the most salient one being submissiveness. Nineteenth-century female dress was designed to force women into a physically subservient position by inhibiting female movement; whalebone corsets, tight-lacing practices, bustles, heavy petticoats, and impractical shoes physically handicapped women and often invited serious illness. Moreover, cross-dressing was socially prohibited by men in order to establish gender difference and maintain patriarchal superiority.[19] As Yeats so aptly put it, "To be born woman is to know . . . [one] must labour to be beautiful."[20]

Indeed, some women went so far as to have their two lower ribs removed to facilitate tight stays and their little toes amputated so that they might fit into tiny, more delicate shoes. Feminist historian Helene Roberts suggests that nineteenth-century women were not voluntarily masochistic, but rather were seeking to reinforce a dominant/submissive relationship, to be "True" women. To experience pain through tight-laced corsets or many layers of heavy hot petticoats was simply a sign of one's willingness to be truly obediant.[21] It follows that women who rejected such conventions were not simply regarded as unfashionable but as rebels against True Womanhood, as unfeminine or masculine women.

Popular women's styles became suspect if they did not adhere to strict sartorial codes of femininity. In his 1835 conduct manual on proper feminine behavior, English aristocrat James Mackintosh laments masculine changes within women's fashion, using the "Bishop's sleeve"—popular in the 1830s—to demonstrate feminine fickleness.

> In olden times, sleeves were fashioned tight at the shoulder, descending whence, they gradually assumed width, until, nearing the wrist, they terminated in capacious ruffles. Pointblank reverse is the present mode. Bishop's sleeves, as they are called, are now in the ascendant . . . 'Tis a mode as much to be condemned for its detraction from any native beauty in the wearer, as for its intrinsic ugliness. The width of shoulder lent to the female figure by two overgrown balloons is unnatural and masculine.[22]

Mackintosh apparently did not see the attraction for women in this new style, which would allow them to raise their arms above their heads, a freedom of movement that most dresses during the thirties and forties forbade. Indeed, in the early nineteenth century, corporeal freedoms of any sort were exclusively associated with men. Women who unnaturally engaged in masculine—public—pastimes were often associated with masculine styles of dress. In a letter to the *New Mirror* (another journal that consistently reported on theatrical events), one correspondent in the early 1840s notes that a "feminist dynasty is gaining ground." Apparently a Ladies' Reading Room had opened, followed by a Club Bowling-Alley on Broadway that was set up for the recreation of women. The writer laments that "another masculine privilege has gone over to the ladies.... The luxuries remaining to our sex, up to present time are fencing and boxing—the usurpation of which are probably under consideration." Significantly this correspondent does not go on to discuss sporting activities and women's possible entrance into them, but in the very next line talks about another male prerogative that has also been "usurped": clothing. "The fashions, you would suppose, would scarcely gain by masculinifying, but the ladies are wearing *broadcloth cloaks*—for a beginning. There is another article of male attire which they have long been *said* to wear occasionally, but I am incredulous. Seeing is believing."[23] Considering the context of separate spheres and gendered social prescriptions regarding dress, cross-dressing presented the ultimate transgression.[24]

Pioneers in dress reform, such as Bloomer, disregarded such admonitions and strove to alter both the style and the meaning of women's clothing in the nineteenth century. It was in the pages of Bloomer's temperance journal *The Lily* and other midcentury women's rights periodicals that the formal women's rights movement *and* the dress reform campaign were simultaneously born.[25] Beginning in 1849, *The Lily* began to advocate the adoption of a "Turkish" outfit for women for health reasons, to counter the ill effects of long heavy skirts and tightly laced corsets. The "costume," as it was referred to, consisted of "a pair of Turkish pantaloons, wide and nearly meeting the shoe, of such material and texture as the season demanded, and of a hue adapted to the taste of the wearer; and a garment nearly fitting the person, buttoned, or permanently closed on all sides, extending just below the knee, of a material and texture that would ward off the chilly atmosphere, colored and ornamented to suit the fancy of the wearer"[26] (see figure 2.1). The Bloomer outfit also consisted of a sturdy hat, often made of straw, and a pair of sensible shoes. The pantaloons—or pantalettes as they were also called—were drawn in at the ankle with a band so that they would not drag along the floor.

While this ensemble did not closely resemble men's attire at midcentury, the pantaloons proved highly controversial during the early 1850s and engendered a caustic social debate. Entering into the public sphere to work in some capacity was worrisome enough, but to hazard such a treacherous journey without the protective and recuperative covering of one's whalebone corset and six full petticoats was unthinkable. For, as Bloomer herself recalled, "In the minds of some people, the short dress [the Bloomer outfit] and women's rights were inseparably connected."[27] *The Lily* was full of reports (both positive and negative) that linked women who tried to engage in public and civic activities with material displays of masculinity. Mrs. Swisshelm, a regular contributor to *The Lily,* observed that the "great objection urged against full citizenship for women is, that to meddle in politics is unfeminine. It would unsex her to appear at the polls. . . . Every step towards self-government is held in advance towards pantaloons and beards."[28] Another early report in *The Lily* mentions the scandal caused by actress Fanny Kemble who wore the "bloomers," was accused of cross-dressing (of parading the streets "equipped in coats, vests, and pantaloons, and all the other paraphernalia of a gentlemen's dress") and condemned for attempting to transgress beyond her sphere. Reports like this—that conflated dress reform, cross-dressing and feminism—were frequent.[29]

In an article written in 1852 for the *Ladies' Wreath,* Professor William Nevin recalls a conversation he had with a female Latin student whom he had tutored. The conversation turned to the Bloomer costume and Blanche, his student, accused him of dismissing it on the grounds of discrimination towards women. She argued, "It is not at the too lavish display of ankles in this dress that you have

Fig. 2.1: Amelia Bloomer in her pantaloons. The Schlesinger Library, Radcliffe College.

been dismayed, I fancy, but at the Turkish trowsers. You detect in these, no doubt, a disposition on the part of our sex to be overstepping their prescribed limits, to be intruding into the lordly domains of your own." The professor replied:

> To confess the truth, I have some apprehensions of this sort. To petticoat government, in a limited way, I never had any objections, but I must say that I feel seriously alarmed at this untoward display of the trowsers.... [T]hey strike me as being only one of many manifestations of that wild spirit of socialism or agrarian radicalism ... whose legitimate tendency is to drive all those possessed with it to seek after the utter demolition of all distinctive grades and orders.... Just in proportion as these levelers may succeed in destroying the natural distinctions of character and sex between us, in the same proportion also undoubtedly will they succeed in destroying all moral government and civilization.[30]

Displays of uncharacteristic female behavior—behavior that in some way undermined True Womanhood—were thought to disrupt social order, just as the material manifestation of such displays (apparent in female "drag") also appeared subversive.

Perhaps this perceived threat was due to the fact that many of the women who began to wear the "Turkish Costume" also became increasingly concerned with issues of equality. In June of 1851, Bloomer wrote an article for *The Lily* entitled "Who are the Leaders?" in which she boldly asserts, "If dress is to be a distinguishing mark between those who claim to be man's equal, and those who are willing to yield to his claim of superiority, we shall soon see a large majority of women sporting the short dress and trowsers." Bloomer argued that although there were many women who found the costume unappealing, they would "yet don it, however distasteful to themselves, rather than yield the point of equality."[31]

The Bloomer debate was not simply a popular topic among journalists but became fodder for playwrights as well. Plays that dealt with the controversy appeared in New York in the 1850s, such as a farce entitled simply *The Bloomer Costume,* which played at the Broadway Theatre in April of 1857. In addition, a group called the

Bloomer Troupe experienced brief notoriety on the New York stage in the early fifties. Unlike the plays, which satirically dealt with the subject of dress reform and women's rights, the Bloomer Troupe was not concerned with political issues. Rather, they were primarily a singing group, a collection of women who sang popular songs while dressed in the Bloomer outfit. New York critics implied that these performers, despite their "odd, unfeminine garb," attracted crowds due to the erotic appeal associated with their display of legs, regardless of the fact that the voluminous pantaloon obstructed the patron's view.[32] The Troupe's appearance in 1851 at Lea's Melodeon (also called the Palace of Beauty) along with groups of "living model statuar[ies]" corroborates such suggestions. Often referred to as "living pictures" or "tableaux vivants," the living model/performer recreated famous paintings and sculptures before a live audience.[33] While this form of entertainment enjoyed sporadic popularity between 1831 and 1870, it became especially suspect in the late 1840s as more and more managers used paintings such as Botticelli's *Venus Rising from the Sea* as a way to display partially nude bodies. That the Bloomer Troupe was performing in conjunction with the living pictures implies an attempt by the press to recuperate theatrical displays of early feminism (through bloomer-wearing) by turning the performer into a sexual object *and* by containing the threat of symbolic subversions through fetishistic description.

In addition to wearing bloomers, both onstage and off, women did actually cross-dress in public or adopt specifically male clothing. Many women put on male clothing and attempted to pass as men in order to work or to fight in wars. Women's motives in taking on male social identities stemmed either from a desire to escape patriarchal oppression (most of them sought financial independence and/or adventure) or from a romantic impulse, such as following a loved one to war.[34] Many women who posed as soldiers in order to follow their husbands also secretly wanted to escape a constrained life of domesticity. Loreta Janeta Velazquez, who fought in the Civil War for over three years as Harry T. Buford, originally enlisted in order to be with her husband but kept fighting long after he had been killed in battle. Velazquez later explained, in an autobiographical narrative of her experience, that she had always wanted to be a man: "I have no hesitation in saying that I wish I had been created a man instead of a woman."[35]

Like Velazquez, many nineteenth-century American women eagerly put on what Susan Gubar has termed "the freedom suit."[36] Female soldiers and women who cross-dressed in order to earn better wages all adopted a strategy of passing out of necessity. This strategy initially involved locating a uniform or a suit of men's clothes and tailoring it (many women padded their coats and trousers with cotton or wire netting and bound their breasts), but it also required women to *perform* masculinity, to take on the gestures, inflections, walk, and behavioral habits of men. Significantly, Velazquez consistently referred to her male masquerade as a "performance" or a play, to her male persona as Harry Buford as a "role," and to her male attire as a "disguise."[37]

Velazquez was not the only one to think of her cross-dressing as theatrical; others who tried to pass as men in public eventually went onstage to perform male roles. Hannah Gray (1723–92) and Mary Ann Talbot (1778–1808) passed as men (one as an officer in the British navy and one as a soldier in the army) and later went on to be breeches actresses,[38] and an early twentieth-century British soldier, Valerie Arkell-Smith, also tried her hand in male dramatic roles. An early American female soldier, Dorothy Sampson Gannett, provides another good example of this connection between cross-dressed cultural performance and theatrical performance. Gannett, who fought in the Revolutionary War disguised as Robert Shurtleff, sought a pension from the government after her years of service were concluded. In order to win support for her claim, she undertook a public tour in 1802 and traveled through New England speaking about her experience. She often spoke in theatres and told her story, fully cross-dressed in her uniform of a Continental Army soldier, to many incredulous but responsive audiences. After appearing at the Federal Street Theatre in Boston, she wrote in her diary, "When I entered the hall I must say I was much pleased at the appearance of the audience. It appeared from almost every countenance that they were full of unbelief—I mean in regard to my being the person that served in the Revolutionary Army."[39] Gannett, in a recuperative effort, apologized to the audience for her "uncouth" actions as the "good intentions of a bad deed," yet simultaneously acknowledged the subversive nature of her disguise. "I burst the tyrant bonds which held my sex in awe and clandestinely or by stealth, grasped an opportunity which custom and the world seemed to deny, as a natural privilege."[40] Stories like Gannett's suggest yet another example of intersecting discourses between cross-dressing, women's rights, and the theatre; such examples—which are ultimately crystallized in the breeches performer—are not uncommon throughout studies of nineteenth-century American culture.

Breeches performers shared a central and very basic need with women like Velazquez and Gannett in addition to more ideological urgings (the desire to free oneself from the limitations of the feminine "role"), and this was finding a costume. Nineteenth-century actresses were required to provide their own costumes, a task that was always difficult and more so when the clothing they were looking for was masculine. There is no indication from the visual or documented material available that the cross-dressed actress attempted to significantly alter the standard male costume for any role she played.[41] Indeed, there are at least two reports of Cushman's borrowing contemporary actor's costumes to wear herself. In 1861, Edwin Booth (1833–1893) lent Cushman his costume for Hamlet, and other reports suggest that despite their apparent rivalry (Cushman felt that Booth's interpretation of Hamlet was inferior to her own), the actress borrowed his costume on many occasions.[42] Likewise, English touring star George Vandenhoff provided Cushman with certain costume accessories when he played Mercutio to her Romeo in Philadelphia in 1843. He recollects, "Cushman was Romeo . . . I was Mercutio. I lent her a hat, cloak, and sword, for the second dress, and believe I may take credit for having given her some useful fencing hints for the killing of Tybalt and Paris, which she executes in such masculine and effective style."[43] In general, actresses consistently wore what actors wore until the late 1850s and 1860s when popular forms began to gain precedence over more serious attempts at male impersonation, and the fleshling suit became increasingly more visible onstage. Characters from antiquity wore tunics, togas, and sandals; Aladdin wore Turkish pantaloons and a short jacket; boys were usually costumed in gaily colored tunics, tights, and hats; Hamlet and Romeo wore knee-length belted tunics and tights; and Richard III could regularly be seen in a royal cloak, loose balloonlike knee breeches, tights, and high leather boots—regardless of whether Macready or Mrs. Jean Davenport played the role.

While it is inevitable that costumes varied slightly from actress to actress, most breeches performers shared certain standard clothing items and accessories. Renderings and early photographs of Cushman as Romeo, Ellen Tree as Ion, and Mrs. Henry Lewis as William Tell provide examples of the standard ensemble worn by the breeches performer during the first half of the century. As Romeo, Cushman sported a short hair cut and wore an ornamented, dark velvet, long-sleeved tunic that came to her knee, a crown, a belt with a small dagger attached, and slippers. This costume contains no unorthodox alterations from the costume worn by male Romeos; indeed, it is almost identical to the outfit worn by William Wheatley, who was popular as Romeo during the 1840s and 1850s.[44] (See figure 3.2.) Tree's costume for Ion was also a knee-length tunic, although far less ornamented and made of a seemingly lighter fabric. The garment was short-sleeved with a scooped neck line and a short toga that fell over the actress's shoulder; her shoes were sandals and her hair was shoulder length.[45] (See figure 3.1.) The artist's rendition of Mrs. Henry Lewis as William Tell is deceptive—there is almost no indication that the figure that appears in this sketch is a woman. Lewis, who was reported to have "passed" in this role[46] also donned a knee-length tunic, tights, sandals, and had a short haircut; she even appears to have worn side-whiskers (see figure 1.3). While slight differences in style, accessories and hair length must have existed, the above descriptions are in keeping with generic accounts of breeches dress throughout the antebellum period.[47]

Although actresses wore costumes that were similar to the attire of their male colleagues throughout most of the antebellum period, visual evidence exposes a common "feminine" feature among the costumes worn by Cushman, Tree, and Lewis: the accentuation of their waists. This aspect of their costume—in addition to the obvious display of their legs—would seem to draw even more attention to their femininity, yet, interestingly, their silhouette in this costume mirrors a trend within male fashion in the 1830s and 1840s. Turner Wilcox describes men's clothing during this time: "The fitted, corseted look was the fashion for *both sexes* in the 'thirties and the 'forties, and to accomplish it both sexes wore the corset.... Waist and hips were padded to accentuate the shapely silhouette. Jeweled buttons and buckles fastened waistcoats of rich colored velvet with multi-colored embroidery."[48] Although this depiction refers to men's street clothing as opposed to male theatrical costumes, it is significant that the average viewer would have been used to seeing men with the "hour-glass figure" during the exact period that these breeches performers were appearing in male dress; Cushman began playing her Romeo in 1837 and acted in it throughout the forties, Ellen Tree toured as Ion in 1837, and Mrs. Henry Lewis was popular in the mid-thirties. Wilcox also mentions that between 1830 and the late 1840s men began to wear trousers instead of tightly fitting, full-length breeches. This change was reflected onstage as well. Male characters that were popular with women in the early decades of the century, such as Goldfinch and Count Belino, often appeared in tight-fitting breeches while cross-dressed actresses photographed after 1845—significantly, about the time the dress reform movement emerges—begin to wear loose fitting trousers, long jackets and sailor suits (the sailor, William from Douglas Jerrold's nautical melodrama *Black-Eyed Susan* was a very popular role among breeches performers)[49] (See figure 2.2). As early as 1834, a note appears in the *New York Mirror* about a Miss Watson who played breeches roles and reportedly "displayed a strong *penchant* for a frockcoat and pantaloons."[50] This similarity in costumes between men and women suggests that breeches actresses tried to keep current with men's fashions both on and offstage as audiences and dramatic reviewers may have been critical of gross errors in style, and that selecting a costume was done with "authenticity" in mind rather than a deliberate desire to showcase particular body parts.

By the 1860s, breeches costumes consisted either of the Shakespearean tunic/tights combination, loose-fitting trousers, or the more titillating "disguise" worn by burlesque performers and actresses in equestrian melodrama. A craze for cross-dressed women on horseback emerged midcentury, engendered by the popularity of

Fig. 2.2: Adah Isaacs Menken as William the Sailor. Harvard Theatre Collection, The Houghton Library, Fredric Woodbridge Wilson, Curator.

Menken's portrayal of Byron's Tartar prince Mazeppa. Surprisingly, the costume worn by these actresses—actresses whose highly eroticized likeness was reproduced in newspaper sketches, photographs, and posters—is very similar to the attire that the playwright envisioned for the male actor. In Henry Milner's adaptation of Byron's poem, for example, he describes Cassimir's first costume (which is the one worn by equestrians Leo Hudson, Kate Vance, and Kate Fisher in period photographs) as a "white tunic, half full sleeve, puffed, slashed with crimson and black velvet, the tunic entirely trimmed with crimson and black velvet—white tight pantaloons—white shoes, with crimson rosettes—short mantillo worn over the left arm, of crimson cloth, trimmed with ermine—octagonal cap of crimson, with hanging pouch." Furthermore, Milner explains what the "nude" outfit is to look like, the one worn by Mazeppa when he is supposedly stripped naked and strapped to the back of a wild steed in act 2. The costume for this scene, as described by Milner, requires "flesh legs: arms and body—short tight trunks—half body of brown cloth," which suggests that all performers who played this role—male and female—were encouraged to wear fleshlings and tight short pantaloons.[51] Thus it would seem that actresses who played this role in the sixties were not deliberately trying to expose their bodies to titillate male audiences but were simply following a tradition for dress in this scene that had been established in the thirties. Certainly, this costume (and other breeches outfits) proved stimulating, and the male gaze might have successfully obscured any serious artistic intent that the actresses possessed in approaching equestrian roles. Yet, the breeches performer did not try to *deliberately* eroticize her performance by appearing in a singularly revealing costume. On the contrary, Menken—the most scandalous breeches performer in the nineteenth century—originally wore a more *modest* costume than the one described by Milner; her short white trunks were not exceptionally tight and she also added a short-sleeved white blouse to cover her fleshling top. "[T]he Menken's Mazeppa is the most modestly costumed of all we have ever witnessed," reported a critic for the *New York Clipper* in 1866 "and we believe we have seen them all."[52]

This tendency for nineteenth-century breeches actresses to ape the theatrical fashions of contemporary male actors suggests more than a simple desire to maintain verisimilitude or to respect established conventions, however. Rather, it implies that these women wanted to be taken seriously as artists and did not simply strive to play more interesting roles and to broaden their personal repertoires, but wanted instead to compete with male actors directly.

Such a desire foregrounds the dialogue that was taking place in nineteenth-century America between the cross-dressed actress and early feminism, between the private and the public, between illusion and reality, between "nature" and gender.

BREECHES PERFORMANCE AS FEMINIST SUBTEXT

Cross-dressing was the ultimate transgression—and one that actresses consistently indulged. Despite the fact that breeches performance is often thought to have been recuperative (by both nineteenth and twentieth-century critics/historians) in that it simply focused attention on an actress's leg (and thus her femininity and sexual appeal),[53] cross-dressed actresses could, on occasion, briefly escape prevailing definitions of womanhood and objectification. They could traverse beyond the limitations of domesticity and publicly present a new vision for women. By taking on male roles, certain actresses were able to critique established notions of social gender "performance" and power distribution. And as Scott argues, such a critique necessarily leads to questions about how power is institutionalized and maintained. Representative cross-dressed theatrical women implied through their performance that power was not an essentially masculine privilege, and that gender was as artificial as the painted backdrop behind them. It was in this respect that the breeches actress was political, for by appropriating male theatrical roles, she communicated a feminist subtext that critiqued hegemonic notions of feminine behavior and proclaimed the equality of women within the context of artificial gender construction.

This feminist subtext is evidenced by the fact that women who chose to undertake male dramatic characters often did so as a way to compete directly with their male colleagues in the theatre. Mrs. Sharpe's decision to play Count Belino in the *Devil's Bridge* at the Park Theatre in 1827, provides an excellent illustration of the actress's desire to challenge her male contemporary. Belino was not a standard breeches role, yet it had been played by at least one actress before Sharpe appeared in the role in December. During the previous January, the *New York Mirror* reported on Signorina Garcia's depiction of the Count at the Park and made a riveting statement about an actress's ability to compete successfully with renowned male stars. The critic declared, "This is the age of paradox and startling comparisons. They say Signorina Garcia's Count Belino is equal to Kean's Richard III!"[54] Sharpe, whose line of business had always been strictly confined to leading ladies, decided to undertake Belino for her benefit but did not receive the favorable mention enjoyed by Garcia. It seems that the reason for her harsh critical reception (the audience response was not noted) had more to do with the fact that this operetta, presently in vogue in New York, was also playing at another theatre with the celebrated Mr. Pearlman in the leading role of the Count. It was not simply Sharpe's rejection of her traditional repertoire of feminine parts that worried the critics on this occasion, but her desire to compete directly with Pearlman. The reporter from the *Albion* articulates this threat:

> On Tuesday Mrs. Sharpe's Benefit—*Devil's Bridge; Count Belino*, Mrs. Sharpe! Really, the rage for appearing in male characters is quite contagious, and if it be true that the stage is to show the "age and body of the times," it would seem that the ladies are, in real earnest, about to assume our nether garments, and we, of the ungentler sex, fast approaching to petticoat government. What in the whole range of human absurdity induced Mrs. Sharpe to play Belino, or indeed to take a benefit at all at this particular moment? Could she expect to make any impression by her voice, when she has no voice at all, (we mean for such a part,) and when an artist of Mr. Pearlman's powers is performing the same character at another house? . . . [W]e [do not] wish to speak disparagingly of Mrs. Sharpe, in parts to which her powers are equal. She is, unquestionably, a very clever woman in the line of characters generally assigned to her, and her *sphere* of acting, we are often gratified to see, gradually extends itself, and will still continue to do so as she gains experience. Her person, also does much for her, and she may be *safely* pronounced one of the most useful and improving actresses on the New York boards. Why then does she *risk* a reputation that is building up on a solid foundation, for such *visionary projects* as attempting to represent Count Belino in the Devil's Bridge?[55]

The critic marvels at Mrs. Sharpe, who appears to jeopardize her reputation as a respected woman within her "sphere" by playing a male role and by wearing garments that indicate status and privilege. Certainly, as the critic suggests, "wearing the breeches" seems to cultivate "petticoat government" as women empower themselves through the adoption of male clothing—although interestingly the adjective used to describe their reign refers to a feminine undergarment. The concept of "breeches," in this case, seems to act as a social signifier of power, a passport into public life. And the use of the word "sphere" is telling here, for it implies that the (non-breeched) actress must have paradoxically inhabited three spheres simultaneously: the domestic sphere of womanhood, the sphere of theatrical feminine caricatures that reinforced the virtues that were to be found in the first sphere, and the public sphere of work. This professional situation complicated her life by endangering her femininity for she was, by virtue of her career, presented with the opportunity or temptation to transfer her powers and influence over to the public—masculine—sphere. By creating certain lines of business or standard feminine repertories that reinforced gender ideology, the threat of an actress's becoming unsexed by her engagement in public life was abated and she safely proceeded to garner praise within the public sphere. However, once *other* markers or aspects of the public sphere became a visible part of the actress's histrionics, such as masculine dress, or roles from the male repertoire, or the desire to engage in direct competition with a male actor such as Mr. Pearlman, the primrose path to a virtuous reputation became increasingly thorny.

Sharpe's display of individual agency is significant, for she strategically requested to schedule her benefit—the actress's only opportunity to choose her own role—in December, which was unorthodox since benefits traditionally occurred in June at the end of the dramatic season. While actors occasionally took their benefits at the end of a negotiated engagement (not in June), the fact that Mrs. Sharpe continued to play for the rest of the season (through June) suggests a deliberate rearrangemet of her benefit. By deciding to have a benefit in December she would have called extra attention to her performance, thus foregrounding both her entrance into the breeches line and her seemingly deliberate competition with Pearlman (whose run as Belino would certainly not have lasted until June as plays usually ran only two or three nights in a row). Pearlman, a popular English star, had been playing Belino (in rep) in the United States ever since 1823 and had established his American reputation in this character. Sharpe's direct attempt to compete with the best Belino in America made a trenchant statement about women's equality, a statement that was further reflected in a private (and unfortunately unpublished) letter she sent to the editor of the *Albion*, complaining about the critical treatment she had received regarding her performance as the Count. The critic rebutted,

> We are sorry Mrs. Sharpe should have thought our remarks last week too severe; we assure her that we have the best feelings towards her, both as an actress and a lady. Most of our observations were general, and meant to apply to females taking in an indiscriminate manner, male parts; we confess we were sorry that she attempted Belino, and say, as we said then, that we thought it wrong on more accounts than one but she surely ought not to charge us with unfairness when she reads the concluding part of our article and which in our estimation, sufficiently atones for any severity which was exclusively applied to her male attempt.[56]

Sharpe evidently felt that the review had been unjust, probably because the critic did not evaluate her as a serious artist and did not discuss her rendition of Belino but instead engaged in a diatribe about the convention of breeches in general. It also seems as if Sharpe resented being (perhaps deliberately) "typed"; she thought of herself as an actress who could tackle any part as opposed to a limited player of ingenue roles. Following his reply to Sharpe's letter, the critic reprinted a section from his previous column in which he offered his approval of Sharpe as an actress of such feminine parts. Apparently, he thought that he could appease the indignant performer by reiterating how wonderful she was in roles that fell within her own sphere (i.e., in roles that reinforced dominant gender ideology). The critic even implied that certain male roles were acceptable, but only those that enhanced femininity such as boy parts or fairies. He spoke highly of her "generally," or when she represented her "natural" social position onstage, but found it anomalous for women to seek more serious, and therefore "indiscriminate," male roles and to attempt to compete with men directly.

Sharpe's experience provides an example of the potential power the breeches performer had to transmit a feminist message, as is evidenced by the anxiety expressed by one member of the New York theatrical hegemony in 1827. Yet, she was not alone in her ability to trouble the critics. Four years later, reviewers were still expressing apprehension over women who "acted out" of their sphere in serious male roles. A popular East Side actress, Miss Clifton, played Belino at the American (another name for the Bowery) Theatre in June of 1832; the review sounds strikingly familiar. The *Spirit* critic laments Clifton's poor choice in selecting a role that did not allow her to exhibit her womanly influence or feminine charms. He writes,

> Miss Clifton selected for her benefit the Opera of the Devil's Bridge, in which she appeared as Count Belino. We regretted this selection, as not affording an opportunity for the display of the peculiar powers belonging to this ambitious lady. She sustained herself better than was anticipated even by her friends; still she would have consulted her interest, had she chosen to appear in one of those characters in which she has so often received merited applause and universal approbation.[57]

Like Sharpe, Clifton ventures outside her line or "sphere" and therefore ultimately fails. She is not rewarded for attempting to expand her repertoire or for playing the part well, rather she is subtly reprimanded and encouraged to stick to "merited" feminine roles.

Occasionally, an actress was so talented, or so popular with audiences, that critics praised her despite the fact that she was entering into forbidden dramatic territory. The "masculine Mrs. Henry Lewis," for example, captivated Boston and New York audiences and critics in 1836–37 by playing a repertoire of male parts that included Othello, Richard III, Shylock, William Tell, and Virginius. Like Belino, none of these roles was typical fare for the breeches actress. Indeed, these characters were all serious or tragic heroes who had qualities that were not normally thought attractive in women; they were manly, powerful, wicked, and adventurous *adult* men—and all of them were presently being played by the leading male actors of the day such as Forrest, Junius Brutus Booth, and Macready. Most women did not even attempt to compete with actors like Forrest (whose school of acting was satirically described as "the muscular school; the brawny art; the biceps aesthetics; the tragic calves; the bovine drama; rant, roar and rigmarole"[58]) but by adopting his vehicles, Lewis sought to showcase both women's potential artistry as well as their ability to contend with male stars. A correspondent for the *Spirit* remarked upon her strikingly convincing impersonation of Richard III (and other leading male characters) in Boston and called her performance "commanding" and her declamation "full of power and energy." She "looked the jealous Moor excellently," was a "great *hit*" as Virginius, and closed the season as William Tell (a favorite role of Forrest's), which was reported to be her "chef d'ouvre." The *Spirit* critic concluded, "On the whole she has physical powers sufficient to give effect to any part in the Drama."[59] Interestingly, Lewis decided to take on these characters at a time when Forrest was in England, which suggests either a desire to fill his shoes, to capitalize on his repertoire while he was away, or to escape direct critical comparison to him. Perhaps it was Forrest's absence that also allowed Lewis to take center stage in New York in 1837 (once again, in his repertoire). Prior to her May performance of Richard III at the National, the reviewer writes, "To-night Mrs. Lewis is to convert symmetry into deformity—metamorphose her full and elegantly turned figure into the humped *Richard*." Rather than condemn her for her attempt, the critic continues by praising Lewis, declaring, "[S]he is a remarkable woman, and the power and truth with which she personates the most arduous tragic characters, has excited the wonder of every one who has seen her, and half inclines us to forgive her for stepping out of that sphere in which nature has qualified her so well for almost unrivaled success."[60]

In some instances, breeches actresses were thought to surpass certain male stars—even in the actor's own starring role. Cushman was said to have played Claude Melnotte in Edward Bulwer-Lytton's *The Lady of Lyons* better than Forrest, who originally made the role popular in America. On the occasion of Cushman's benefit at the end of the 1838 season (only the second year that Cushman had worked as a utility actress in New York), the *Spirit* acknowledged that "Miss C. and Mrs. Richardson" played Claude and Pauline with such "great spirit" that "we doubt if FORREST and ELLEN TREE ever elicited more general applause."[61] When Charles Kean played Richard III at the Park Theatre in 1846, the critic responded, "In our opinion, Mrs. Kean [Ellen Tree] could play the part much better than her husband."[62] Certainly, Cushman felt that she was better as Romeo than any actor during that time, and although she was not as popular as Hamlet she argued that her portrayal of the Dane was superior even to Booth's.

Judging from biographical accounts of Cushman's career,[63] it would seem that she played a mediocre Hamlet on only a few isolated occasions. Other sources (and Cushman herself) argue that this role was a far more important part of her repertoire than previously believed. Treva Rose Tumbleson in her dissertation "Three Female Hamlets: Charlotte Cushman, Sarah Bernhardt, and Eva Le Galliene," argues that while Hamlet was not a prominent component of Cushman's repertoire, the actress did play the role for 11 years and would not have continued to do so if she had been poorly received.[64] Indeed, in 1861—ten years after Cushman began to play the role—a delegation of congressmen petitioned her to play Hamlet in Washington. Their petition was published in the *Clipper* after the actress's death in 1876: "[W]e . . . respectfully solicit you to appear some evening as Hamlet, a part wherin you have lately created such a profound sensation, and one so beautifully suited to your refined and undoubted genius."[65] This request suggests that Cushman won over her audiences even if critics were ambivalent about the idea, and continued to gain notoriety for her performance long after she added it to her stock of characters.

There are many possible explanations for Cushman's original decision to attempt Hamlet, a role that was considered the ultimate test of an actor's histrionic abilities during the mid-nineteenth century. Cushman's last lover, Emma Stebbins, claimed that the actress played Hamlet for the same reason that she undertook Romeo; both characters were considered youths and it was far more sensible for a mature actress with extensive experience to act these parts—since she could still look like a boy—than it was for a young actor, who might not possess enough skill or insight into either character to undertake these roles. Therefore, an actress might not threaten verisimilitude as much as an old man.[66] Contemporary historians suggest that Cushman added Hamlet to her repertoire because she felt that the portrayals of him by major male stars at midcentury were inferior and needed to be improved—a sentiment that betrays her desire to compete directly with her male colleagues.

Throughout her career, Cushman demanded to be put on equal footing with leading men such as Forrest, Macready, and Booth. By 1849—only four years after she had solidly established her reputation—she insisted on securing contracts from her managers that mirrored those given to male stars. In a letter to William Henry Chippendale, she asserted, "My terms must be the same as those given to Mr. Macready and Mr. Forrest, in other words a clear half the house on each night, and I cannot act more than four nights in one week."[67] Cushman's ambitious and competitive nature was recognized by many. Gamaliel Bradford reflects on her ambition and her savvy as a businesswoman, "It was not her habit to entrust business affairs to others, or to let the artist's delicacy keep her out of the hot struggle of dollars and cents.... She preferred to work alone, and I am not sure she did not enjoy it. She liked to fight, she liked to drive a close bargain and get the best of it, she liked to win and dominate and control."[68] In the same year that the actress wrote her demanding letter to Chippendale, the *Spirit* aptly remarked, "I have ever looked on Miss Cushman as a woman possessing strong sense, great industry, indomitable perseverance, as well as talent; and by her *own* exertions she has climbed unaided the arduous path of her profession, and gained eminence and histrionic fame that commands the admiration of her countrymen."[69] Cushman felt most competitive with Booth (as has already been suggested by the fact that she borrowed his costume for Hamlet on numerous occasions), who returned this sentiment. She felt that his Hamlet was too effeminate and lacked backbone. It is evident that

Booth sensed Cushman's disdain, for he wrote to a friend about his suspicions in 1851: "She is down on me as an actor; says I don't know anything at all about Hamlet, so she is going to play it here in February."[70]

Cushman felt strongly about this role and approached it with reverence. Although playing the Dane exhausted her, she continually worked to improve her portrayal. In a letter to Emma Crow in 1861, she admitted that Hamlet was the most demanding part that she had ever worked on, but because he was "such a magnificent character" all her efforts might be redeemed. "I acted the part so much better than anything else I have done here," she wrote, "that I was really amazed at myself and wonder whether the spirit of the Dane was not with me and around me last night—I don't think any body here is capable of writing about it but if they do I will send it to you."[71] Cushman's last—somewhat cynical—remark implies that she was aware of the critic's anxiety about (and/or animosity towards) the serious breeches performer. She suggests that these men either would not be able to comprehend an actress's desire to be considered a genuine artist in such a weighty role and were therefore incapable of reporting on it sincerely, or that critics habitually ignored such attempts because they found them to be insignificant—or threatening. Yet, Cushman remained undaunted in her efforts to keep Hamlet in her repertoire. Stebbins recalls that performing Hamlet

> gave her intense pleasure. She alludes to it in some of her letters as the very highest effort she had ever made . . . of all her parts, this one seemed to fill out most completely the entire range of her powers . . . Miss Cushman looked the part of Hamlet as well as she did that of Romeo. Her commanding and well-made figure appeared to advantage in the dress of the princely Dane, and her long experience in the assumption of male parts took from her appearance all sense of incongruity.[72]

Cushman disagreed with previous conceptions of Hamlet. She vehemently avoided playing the role as it had traditionally been presented in the early and mid-nineteenth century, with actors interpreting Hamlet as hesitant, indecisive, and mystical. Rather she envisioned him as dynamic and manly—an interpretation that was much closer to Forrest's conception of the role. Yet she made a concerted effort to avoid the bombastic melodramatic bellowing of Forrest.[73] Cushman further abandoned the "fussy bits of business" used by Macready and the sentimental feminine tones sounded by Booth.[74] Such an interpretation of the part was unorthodox and largely unprecedented. The *Albion* commented on her "wonderfully fine" performance as Hamlet, but argued that it was based upon "a totally erroneous conception of the part—that *inasmuch* as it was Cushman's Hamlet, it was full of power and beauty—that *inasmuch* as it was not Shakespeare's, it was faulty throughout."[75] The critic claimed that his opinion was not affected by Cushman's abandonment of certain established "points," rather his views were based entirely on the text. According to the critic, the actress made her first mistake by displaying an inappropriate amount of intensity and conviction as soon as the curtain rose. She immediately appeared unequivocal and directed, which caused the reporter to wonder why she did not simply challenge and assassinate Claudius outright. The critic remarks, "The weakness, the vacillation, the turnings, the abstractions, the hesitations, the quickness to feel and the slowness to act save under momentary impulse—these are not found in the resolute consistency with which Miss Cushman invests the character.... [H]er bearing throughout ... ignores the dreamy, the mystical, the poetical, the philosophizing, the contemplative, the aimless, the endless turn of Hamlet's mind—just the very key to Hamlet's actions."[76] It is apparent from the comments of this critic that Hamlet was a role that, in the nineteenth century, was (and perhaps still is) definitively gendered. Nineteenth-century audiences read a figure onstage as either masculine or feminine—there was no intermediate category. Yet, despite the fact that Hamlet's sex was male and he was seen as a man by audiences, his mannerisms, thoughts, and emotions were perceived as somewhat feminine, as the above critic suggests. Cushman, however, did not seem to want to play a man who exhibited the same characteristics as a nineteenth-century woman, a marginal and "private" individual, especially since women were the objects rather than the subjects of antebellum discourse. Luce Irigaray argues that dominant gender ideology always locates women *outside* representation; and as Toril Moi explains, via Irigaray, "she is absence, negativity, the dark continent, or at best a lesser man."[77] Cushman, like so many breeches performers during the first half of the nineteenth century, was not content to appear as a lesser man, a boy, or an effeminate ethereal creature. Men were powerful and by appropriating their characteristics, Cushman hoped to acquire this power for herself (and to communicate its availability to other women). She wanted to claim a subject position that would allow her to transcend gender boundaries and emerge as decisive, heroic, powerful, and strong-willed, since these were all qualities that were formally forbidden to her offstage.

Cushman's desire to present a masculine interpretation of Hamlet is reflected in her approach to the role. She altered Hamlet's "business" throughout the drama so as to deemphasize his "weakness," frailty, and indecisiveness; instead, she continually reinforced his manliness. Like so many feminist critics today, Cushman seems to have read "against the text"—or at least the text established by nineteenth-century critics. It is possible that she did this for financial reasons. Perhaps the actress wanted to stimulate popular interest and create a minor sensation with her novel conception of the role, a conception that would perhaps draw crowds and generate income for her (certainly she did not play Hamlet in order to make money by showcasing her legs). Yet, Cushman's strategic decision to present a manly Hamlet seems to have arisen instead from a desire to inspire women to eschew the teachings of True Womanhood—to demonstrate that they could be strong and heroic even in situations that normally prescribed weakness and vacillation. As a revisionist, Cushman suggested that all women could rewrite their own scripts.

Apparently Cushman could "act" like a man or *perform* gender better than Booth could, but in order to do this, she first had to reconstruct Hamlet's maleness—reverse the popular gendered reading of Hamlet as effeminate. She did this by reversing standard stage practices (or, as the *Albion* critic explains, by abandoning traditional "points") and by relying heavily upon certain "suggestive" properties. When she encountered the Ghost, for example, Cushman did not appear timid, frightened, or awestruck (the standard reaction), rather she "raised her sword and stood in a menacing attitude until the Ghost's 'O, horrible!'" At this point, as she noted in one of her promptbooks, she became overwhelmed as she realized the gravity of the situation and lowered her sword, leaning on it for support.[78] Tumbleson describes her rendering of this scene:

> After the Ghost's next line, "If thou hast nature in thee, bear it not;" Cushman recovered herself and held her sword again in a very menacing manner. After the Ghost's "Let not the royal bed of Denmark be/A couch for luxery and damned incest," Cushman said Hamlet "kisses fervently *hilt* of *sword*—the Ghost should make a slight pause for this business, as [Hamlet] is solemnly devoting himself to revenge his father's death." When the Ghost mentioned the word "mother," Cushman's sword became relaxed, and her manner mournful.[79]

Cushman's use of the sword here is significant. This weapon, which might signify male power (or—in light of contemporary feminist theory—the phallus), is continually used by Cushman in a way that reinforces Hamlet's manliness. Instead of seeming frightened when he sees the Ghost, the Prince aggressively brandishes his sword; this sword/symbol of masculine power/phallus gives him support; it defines his manhood in that its use augments his strength, courage, and heroism. Cushman depicts Hamlet's pledge to take action and revenge his father's death by kissing the sword, thus acknowledging the power behind this "tool" (a recognition, perhaps, of the phallus as the ultimate signifier), the only passport to power, an object that will ensure justice and righteousness. As Jacques Lacan explains, the phallus dominates all life within society (the Symbolic Order), its presence culturally legitimizes or marginalizes. Indeed, the only time that Cushman lets her sword/phallus "relax" is at the mention of Gertrude, whose maternal body is forbidden Hamlet, and his desire for the imaginary unity he shared with her is an impulse that must be repressed. Just as it is the Oedipal crisis that precipitates the child's entrance into the Symbolic, so too does Hamlet's possible fear of Gertrude (as a woman whose betrayal indirectly emasculates both Hamlets Sr. and Jr.), cause him to remain aligned with the Law of the Father (represented by the phallus—a sword that Cushman never relinquishes) despite his painful recognition of the lack such separation with the mother engenders. Thus, through her use of the sword, Cushman could be exploring female appropriations of male/phallic power (and its unfortunate ramifications); her unorthodox performance perhaps implies that notions of privilege are deliberately gendered and that manifestos and/or markers of masculinity (such as statements of courage, weapons, clothing, even the phallus itself) are merely props to be used by anyone who chooses to play the role.[80]

By taking a singular approach to Hamlet—and by doing so at the height of the Bloomer controversy—Cushman communicated a feminist subtext about power and called attention to the myriad ways in which, as Scott maintains, "politics [or unequal distributions of power] construct gender and gender constructs politics."[81] Cushman's feminist approach to the role and to the play's production perhaps explains why her Hamlet was found "faulty throughout" by certain critics, who seemed threatened by her strong interpretation. Although they acknowledged her powerful skills as a performer, the New York press clearly outlined her "totally erroneous conception" of the role and claimed that her Hamlet lacked "princely dignity."

"WEARING THE BREECHES" BEYOND THE FOOTLIGHTS

Feminist subtexts were often communicated to audiences through a combination of actresses' male role-playing within the public arena of the theatre and their public (offstage) masculine cultural performance. Actresses who played male roles onstage, like Cushman, often embraced a variety of male social responsibilities beyond the footlights, such as managing theatres and acting as the primary breadwinners for their families. The following women, for example, played men regularly *and* managed their own theatres at some point during their career: Cushman, Louisa Lane Drew (Mrs. John), Clara

Fisher Maeder, Laura Keene, Sarah Crocker Conway, Mrs. D. P. Bowers, and Eliza Tremblin. To manage a theatre during the first half of the nineteenth century was a laborious and time consuming job;[82] these women certainly "wore the breeches" by taking on a male dominated position—a role that may have been connected in some way to their desire to wear the breeches onstage.

Some of these actresses even stimulated other women to free themselves from domestic captivity (while simultaneously threatening certain men who were equally as eager to keep them there). Certainly Cushman cultivated a score of devoted female followers, like the enthusiastic fan who wrote, "I have watched your career for many years, and being an unmarried lady have felt proud to direct other ladies who were struggling for bread, to take example from your noble career, and work out for themselves an independent and individual life.... I feel as a working woman I am under obligation to you for the footprints you leave on the sands of time."[83] Likewise, Cushman's Hamlet so electrified future artist Harriett Hosmer that the young woman immediately ushered her way backstage to meet the famous actress; shortly after their meeting, Cushman agreed to become Hosmer's patron. Hosmer eventually moved to Rome with Cushman—where they lived together in a colony of other "emancipated females"—and ultimately became one of the first American women to gain an international reputation as a sculptor.[84] Like her mentor, Hosmer also adopted a sort of masculine persona evidenced by her frenzied horse rides about town in male clothing and her tendency to conduct herself "precisely as a young man would."[85]

Italy was a place where Cushman felt that she could be of service to other women; as she stated, "[in Rome] I can help those of my own sex to work better than I can at home."[86] Even as Americans faced the outbreak of the Civil War and many American women were freed from the immediate demands of the domestic sphere in the name of progressing a worthy "cause," Cushman felt that her place was among these women artists in Rome. "I cannot be in America now," she explained to her friend, Secretary of State William Seward, "My friend Miss Stebbins who is making a ... statue of Horace Mann from Boston needs me here more than my country needs me there."[87] Cushman significantly influenced the careers of many female artists in Rome in addition to Hosmer and Stebbins, such as Sara Jane Clarke, Kate Field, Elizabeth Kinney, Margaret Foley, Anne Whitney, and Anne Brewster. Cushman's female Roman colony was a place devoid of spheres, a site where gender ideology was obscured or perhaps reversed, where women could be encouraged to foster their careers or refine their talents for employ in the male dominated public arena.[88]

Cushman dedicated her life to serving her immediate family as well as her female friends and lovers. From the age of 17, she was her mother's principle support both emotionally and financially, providing for her family (in the place of her estranged father) through her work as a singer and actress. Cushman continued to be the chief breadwinner throughout her life—a duty that weighed heavily upon her during the early years of her career, and which substantially shaped her decision making. In a letter that Cushman wrote to a Mr. Grigg of Philadelphia in the early 1840s, she discussed her burden. "I have been for a long time hoping and wishing to go to England for improvement. I am anxious to study there under some of the great masters and it [would] be putting me in the way of making much more money when I return to this country for the support of my family who have for many years been dependent upon my weekly stipend."[89] Maintaining financial security for her mother, sister and brothers was one way that Cushman proved herself head of her family, and her devoted mentorship and dogged attempts to secure work and material comforts for her siblings and nephew was another. Cushman arranged acting jobs for Susan, supported Susan's son Ned, engineered jobs for various members of her family, and augmented the income of her brother Charlie. She was, as Merrill explains, "the hero in the family and on the stage."[90]

Yet, despite her male social responsibilities and her unbounded dedication to the betterment of women, Cushman was solidly opposed to the one privilege that was the keystone of the early women's rights movement: nondiscriminatory suffrage. Perhaps the actress objected to this issue, as Merrill suggests, on elitist grounds: Cushman stated that "the vote of one good highminded woman is to be rendered completely... void by the vote of Biddy in the Kitchen."[91] Such a seemingly uncharacteristic statement is made far less shocking when one considers the context of nineteenth-century gender ideology. Cushman was the polar opposite of Biddy; she was not a True Woman, rather she already enjoyed most of the privileges of manhood. She feared that women whose experiences had been limited by a lifetime of confinement within the private sphere might naively hurt the cause of women. She was not opposed to like-minded women approaching the ballot box, but felt that "Biddy" who had been trained to "suffer and be silent," was not an adequate civic and social representative. Perhaps Cushman saw herself as forging new pathways for women, avenues that she worried would become obstructed by her domestic sisters whose goals might be limited and/or oriented specifically toward motherhood and homemaking.

Regardless of her views on suffrage, however, Cushman did articulate her feminist politics in very literal ways. In addition to supporting her family and her bevy of female artists in Rome, eschewing traditional domestic virtues (such as marriage—Cushman had a series of monogamous relationships with women but no male lovers), and working for 40 years as an independent and successful professional, Cushman's penchant for things masculine (and therefore powerful) also manifested itself in her offstage cross-dressing. Cushman's propensity to attire herself in men's clothing is evidenced, in part, by her associate John Coleman's now hackneyed "Charley de Boots" story. He reflects upon a rehearsal of *Romeo and Juliet* he witnessed in 1846:

> Towards the end of the season Miss Cushman, accompanied by her sister Susan, returned in the full flush of the Haymarket success of *Romeo and Juliet*. During her short absence, my eccentric friend had become more eccentric than ever. She had mounted a man's hat and coat, a man's collar and cravat, Wellington boots, which, so far from attempting to conceal, she displayed without reticence or restraint, as she strode about, or tucked up her petticoats, before she "polished off" Tybalt or gave the *coup de grace* to County Paris, or when she took "the measure of an unmade

grave" at rehearsal. . . . The desire evinced by *la grande* Charlotte to disport herself in masculine attire led to speculations which it would be indecorous to repeat here."[92]

Coleman goes on to theorize about Cushman's motivation to cross-dress, and suggests that her adoption of male garments was due to her desire to show off, as he calls it, her "exceptional beauty of form." In effect, he implies that Cushman looked good in male clothing and knew it; this suggests a desire on her part to showcase and perhaps eroticize a male persona. Because such a subtext was so subversive, Coleman tried to contain this potential threat by treating Cushman as an object of male desire, thus calling attention to her display of tight-encased legs. Therefore, in the spirit of almost three centuries worth of recuperative discourses that surrounded the breeches performer, Coleman reduces the cross-dressed actress to a sum of fetishized parts and attempts to render her campaigns to appropriate male dress, and therefore male power, inconsequential.

Cushman's masculine accouterments were not donned exclusively at rehearsal. In 1851, the *Spirit of the Times* noted that "*Charlotte Cushman* has been ruminating in the West, and according to reports current has adopted male attire *in toto*. Well, after the Bloomerism of Claude Melnotte, the 'tights' of Romeo and Hamlet, and sundry other 'breeches parts,' the transition is neither great nor startling."[93] This entry not only reviews the different costumes a breeches performer might wear, but, by mentioning "Bloomerism," it also directly connects Cushman's offstage cross-dressing to the dress reform campaign and women's rights. The fact that the *Spirit* correspondent was not surprised at the report, further implies that Cushman had been projecting this masculine persona for quite some time, both through her theatrical roles and her social roles. Cross-dressing outside of the theatre was only the literal manifestation of a message that she had been communicating throughout her career.[94]

Cushman was not the only breeches performer to cross-dress offstage, take on male responsibilities, or have experiences that betrayed an interest in the burgeoning women's movement and/or female emancipation. Charlotte Crampton's career also illustrates affinities between breeches performance and broader women's issues. Crampton, a popular but relatively minor actress during the 1850s, was the daughter of theatrical parents, who reportedly performed throughout Ohio and Kentucky with Alexander Drake's company. Crampton, also known as "Little Siddons,"[95] was renowned for her ability to play serious male roles. In addition to specializing in Shakespearean tragic heroes, she also was a skilled equestrian performer and was supposedly the "first female Mazeppa in America."[96] T. A. Brown remembered Crampton as "the only woman I ever saw who could satisfactorily impersonate such arduous characters as Richard III, Iago, Shylock, and Hamlet."[97] One of Cushman's biographers, William Price, described Crampton's portrayal of Richard the III as "phenomenal" and alludes to her as something of a theatrical legend in this role. He notes that she was supposedly able to pass in the character and adds, "it may well be believed, for this remarkable creature, a woman of genius, wayward, dissolute and daring, had in her the compelling fire that was akin to that which made Kean's performance so thrilling. It was of Charlotte Crampton that Macready, on his American tour, after playing with her in Macbeth said, 'There is a woman that would startle the world—if she were two inches taller.'"[98]

Crampton did, however, "startle the world" in other ways. Despite her talent, this actress never achieved star status because of her alcoholism. Her drinking bouts—like those of her Romantic colleagues—were infamous and often severely truncated her runs. Willard recalls that "one bitter cold night in Boston," after playing Mazeppa, Crampton supposedly jumped on her horse and rode it wildly through the streets in her costume, "followed by the rabble."[99] Similar to other great nineteenth-century actors who frequently "drank from the poisoned cup," such as George Frederick Cooke, Edmund Kean, and Junius Brutus Booth; Crampton's vice was said to have contributed both to her great emotion onstage and to her demise as an actress, as her productions would often close abruptly despite her brilliant, albeit inebrious, performances.[100]

Crampton's questionable reputation was further enhanced by the fact that she had four husbands: Charles Wilkinson, Charles B. Mulholland, Harry Clifton, and James Delmor Grace. Significantly, none of these men's last names were Crampton, which suggests that this actress retained her maiden name throughout her career and thus independently established her reputation and her identity as a performer—keeping this persona separate from her identity as a wife and mother. Regardless of Crampton's equivocal reputation, she was able to achieve a great deal more than most women within a relatively brief life span. In addition to her success in tragic breeches parts in Boston, New York, Providence, and Cincinnati, Crampton also acted as a vivandiere (a cross-dressed camp follower) during the Civil War and, ironically, as a temperance lecturer—two positions that would have proven worrisome to male advocates of True Womanhood. As indicated by Bloomer's temperance magazine *The Lily*, devotion to this topic immediately signaled an individual's sympathy with the "Woman Question."

Crampton further demonstrated her independence as a politically minded woman after her son was drafted into the Union army during the early years of the Civil War. Knowing that she did not have the political influence to release him or the money to get around the Conscription Laws, she used the only tool that was then available to her: supplication. Appealing to government officials personally or through petitions (women's one political right in the early nineteenth century) was the only option for women who sought recognition in the public sphere. While Crampton did not engage in a large scale petition campaign, such as the Women's National Loyal League's petition to Congress in 1865, she was reported to have made a personal appeal to Lincoln after learning of her son's conscription. The extraordinary thing about her request is the manner in which she went about making it. She did not simply write a letter, as so many women did, but rather traveled on foot from Wheeling, West Virginia to Washington to personally solicit favor for her son from the president.[101] It is difficult to know how her pilgrimage was conducted or financed. Did she perform her repertoire of tragic heroes along the way? If so, what kind of statement would this have made considering the fact that she was on a trek to exercise her sole political privilege as a woman. Although most of the details of her life remain obscure, Crampton's social and theatrical role-playing emerge as central features of her biography. Crampton was a renowned player of strong male heroes (already a risky undertaking) and a woman who openly participated in activities that would have been associated with feminism at midcentury. Her offstage cross-dressing as a vivandiere, her public speaking engagements about temperance, and her personal attempts to intervene in government decision making, suggest a connection between performing masculinity and attempting to claim its privileges in the public sphere.

Although many actresses who played within their proper sphere, such as Fanny Kemble, still demonstrated a desire to appropriate some degree of male social power throughout the century, breeches performers stand out as some of the boldest adventuresses in this respect. Cross-dressed actresses continued to scandalize audiences and critics throughout the century by their audacious forays into public life. In the 1860s, for example, Menken and Thompson (perhaps the most notorious breeches performers of the nineteenth century) communicated feminist messages offstage that were perhaps a bit incongruous with their sexualized bodies that were being displayed onstage. Menken, who was also married (and divorced) four times, conveyed her feminist convictions through her appearance ("her hair was outrageously short-cropped"[102]), her social habits (smoking, drinking, gambling and, on occasion, offstage cross-dressing), her radical thoughts concerning love and marriage, her attempt to control her own career and fashion her public image, her constant struggle to advance herself as a poet, and her continual expressions of sympathy concerning women and women's issues. Indeed, while performing in California, "The Menken" went so far as to cultivate a masculine persona and engage in gender play both on and offstage—a social and theatrical performance of masculinity and femininity recognized by her audiences.[103] Even as a teenager growing up in the relatively small (and aptly named) city of Liberty, Texas, Menken expressed herself as an independent thinker and avidly endorsed the idea of women's equality. As early as 1855 (approximately ten years before she became an international star), Menken wrote an article for the *Liberty Gazette* about the "double standard," which was becoming an increasingly salient topic among early feminist thinkers. She charged,

There are many young men, alas! too many! who imagine it adds to their dignity to play off mean jests, to bandy unclean doubts of woman's honor; and this even passes as a wretched substitute for wit. Let those remember, who dare to whisper vulgar suspicions of any woman's purity (even though it is darkened) if compared to their own would appear as the immaculate white of angels! And they should also remember, that for her blasted character *they alone* are answerable.[104]

In another article for the *Gazette* entitled "Fugitive Pencilings," this young "female liberationist," as she was described by the editor, declared, "Oh! mothers! believe me, there are other missions in the world for women, other than that of wife and mother."[105] One such mission was writing and, as Sentilles points out, Menken's essays and poems in support of Judaism, published in Cincinnati in the late 1850s, might also have communicated a feminist subtext by indirectly alluding to abolitionism, a galvanizing issue for early female reformers, as readers might have gleaned similarities between two (or three) oppressed peoples. Moreover, in her poetry she deliberately summoned images of Deborah, an Old Testament woman and powerful judge with "warlike spirit," who became a sort of poetic raisonneur for Menken.[106]

Despite Menken's sexual iconographization during the 1860s, she continued to cultivate an image of herself as a serious artist, actress, and poet and, according to Sentilles, probably identified herself with the Jewish community in Cincinnati (and claimed—falsely—a Jewish heritage) in order to further her career as a poet. Menken, who had written poems since her childhood, initially earned respect for this art in 1857–8 after many of her poems appeared in the *Israelite,* a Jewish periodical published in Cincinnati. While it is true that she derived her income from performing in the theatre (even in Cincinnati), poetry acted as her controlling Muse, and she ultimately succeeded in publishing a collection of her poetry, *Infelicia,* in 1865.

Menken consciously used the theatre as a way to promote (not only her body but) her poetry and her politics. For example, fearing that knowledge of her Louisiana birth would spawn rumors that she was a secessionist, she had pamphlets printed up for her Broadway debut that outlined her patriotism and distributed them to the audience before the curtain rose. It is unlikely that this plan could have been conceived of as a publicity tactic or box-office contrivance, since the pamphlets were not passed out until after the audience members had already bought their tickets and were seated in the house. It is more likely that Menken was using the negative press that she had received to her advantage. Most women did not have the opportunity to broadcast their politics (sincere or concocted) to audiences—or their poetry. The flyer that Menken had her crew circulate read:

> The Management of the Broadway Theatre wishes to announce that attacks on the patriotism of Miss Adah Isaacs Menken are without warrant. Miss Menken makes no secret of her birth in Louisiana, but proclaims no fealty to that misguided state. She is a loyal and trustworthy Citizen of the United States of North America, and she joins with other patriots in the devout wish that those states which have seceded will return to the fold of the Union.[107]

On the opposite side of this notice appeared Menken's poem *Pro Patria—America, 1861*. While it is possible that Menken was in fact a Southern sympathizer—she was arrested in Baltimore one year later on charges of being a Confederate spy—and simply deceived her Broadway audience on this occasion to advance her reputation as a poet and ensure good houses for the rest of her run, she did manipulate the medium to express her "political" views and to cultivate an alternative artistic image. Inherent in such an attempt at self-promotion was a desire on Menken's part to compete, to construct a public persona for herself as an artist or celebrity (something Sentilles discusses at length), and to perhaps imply that women's political and artistic expressions—and not her simply legs—were worthy of exposure.

Lydia Thompson was another breeches performer who publicly asserted her independence during the late 1860s/early 1870s. One episode from her career conveys this independence particularly well. While Thompson—who received mixed reviews as a burlesque performer throughout her career in the United States—was performing in Chicago in February of 1870, some unflattering criticism caused a scandal and near riot. She and her troupe of British Blondes had been playing successfully at Crosby's Opera House in two of their starring vehicles: *The Forty Thieves* and *Ixion*. Wilber F. Storey, editor of the *Chicago Times,* saw Thompson's performances and harshly reviewed the company, comparing the English burlesquers to prostitutes. He claimed that Thompson and the Blondes "made an unnecessary and lewd exhibition of their persons, such as would not be tolerated by the police in any bawdy house; they have made use of broad, low and degrading language, such as men of any self respect would repudiate, even in the absence of ladies; that their entertainments have been mere vehicles for the exhibition of coarse women and the use of disreputable language unrelieved by any wit or humor."[108] Thompson responded to this charge in turn. On the evening immediately following Storey's excoriating critique (February 24, 1870), Thompson, her husband and manager Alexander Henderson, their publicist Archie Gordon, and another member of the company, Pauline Markham, waited for Storey outside his Chicago home. When he emerged, the men accosted him and restrained him while Thompson and Markham horsewhipped him (in front of his wife). The assailants continued to the theatre, were arrested after the performance that evening, made an appeal to the judge, were asked to pay a small fine, and went onstage in *The Forty Thieves* the next night. After a successful performance (in a male role), Thompson came out onstage to address the audience and convey her version of the event that had recently taken place—and which was, by this time, well-publicized. She explained to the audience that "The persistent and personally vindictive assault in the *Times* upon my reputation left me only one mode of redress.... They were women whom he attacked. It was by women he was castigated.... We did what the law would not do for us."[109] While it is true that Thompson specialized in burlesque (a form that quickly became associated with feminine spectacle), she also specialized in cross-dressing and played male roles in costumes that were often no more revealing than those that had been worn by breeches performers for decades. Indeed, perhaps it was not simply the genre in which she played (and the sexual titillation and gender parody associated with it) that caused Thompson to appear transgressive in the 1860s, but the combination of her cross-dressing and her offstage demonstrations of power—as the Storey incident details.

Because she was an actress, the breeches performer was a "semipublic" woman. Yet, unlike the Juliets, Paulines, Ophelias, and Black-Eyed Susans who populated American stages, women like Sharpe, Cushman, Crampton, and Menken (who occasionally played men who did not undress) attired themselves in a costume that symbolized authority, agency, and emancipation. By putting on this "freedom suit," the cross-dressed actress, on occasion, extended the prerogative of the male character she played to include a broader public arena. She simultaneously took on male social roles in a larger civic theatre, where she also performed masculinity and played at being an aggressor, a competitor, a serious artist, a manager, a breadwinner, and a decision maker. Actresses who sought to free themselves from the confines of domestic ideology simply "put on the breeches" and transcended the gendered landscape of nineteenth-century America. However, the feminist subtexts communicated by such performances of masculinity—whether in a theatre or on the street—signaled social anarchy, and those who sought to unsex themselves and journey towards a more independent identity were rigorously castigated or insidiously controlled through deliberate discourses of containment.

BREECHES PERFORMANCE AND CRITICAL ANXIETY

Regardless of the popularity enjoyed by breeches performers, critical anxiety increased as more and more women attempted serious male roles. Just as True Women were anathematized for failing to live up to any of the "four cardinal virtues," and just as male journalists expressed concern about the possible chaotic outcome of the dress reform campaign, so also did many dramatic critics fear the female transvestite, whose performance of gender threatened to transcend its theatrical context. While certain cross-dressed performances were generally found to be acceptable (the boyish youth, the idealized fairy, or the effeminate romantic hero) since they reinforced dominant gender ideology and were, therefore, innocuous, leading male vehicles such as Hamlet, Belino, Iago and Romeo were strictly forbidden to actresses. Although arguments could be made (and were) that questioned both Hamlet and Romeo's masculinity, these roles, by virtue of the fact that they were Shakespearean tragic heros, were exclusively out of a woman's line of business or "sphere." An excerpt from *The Lily* illustrates how clearly these "lines" were drawn. Aunt Fanny, a regular correspondent for the paper, explains, "Women may toil and strive; perform the most unwomanly labor—mix with men anywhere, through the market, the street, the lecture room, the church, the theatre—the steamboat, the rail-road-car, the stage and she is in our 'Sphere,' so say our masters. But let her not dare to come in competition with *man* in those things that make him her master."[110]

Critical uneasiness over the breeches performer may have stemmed, in part, from the profound influence that the theatre held over its patrons. In 1811, the editor of *The Cynick* proclaimed, "Next to the sacred institutions of religion and the almost as sacred establishments of a free press, the theatre possesses the greatest influence over the minds and the manner of men."[111] Similarly, the very first issue of the *Spirit* featured an article about the awesome power and influence of the stage. Theatre could save people from tyranny and exhort others to uphold democracy. The writer of this article humbled himself before this mightly persuasive institution, because, as he allowed, "we have *reason* to respect its influence and reverence its power."[112] Perhaps this influential capacity can, in part, account for the copious theatre stories that abound about nineteenth-century audiences who suspended their disbelief to such an extreme that illusion actually became reality. The *Theatrical Censor*, for example, carried an early story about a spectator who watched a performance of *As You Like It* and jumped onstage to help Rosalind after Oliver's bloody handkerchief caused her to faint in act 4. Constance Rourke recounts another example,

On a small stage in a Kentucky village a gambler's family was pictured as starving and a countryman rose from one of the boxes. "I propose we make up something for this woman," he said. Someone whispered that it was all a sham, but he delivered a brief discourse on the worthlessness of the gambler, flung a bill on to the stage with his pocketbook, advised the woman not to let her husband know about it or he would spend it all on faro, and then with a divided mind sat down, saying, "Now go on with the play."[113]

David Grimstead similarly tells tales that illustrate extraordinary audience engagement; "a sailor's jumping up onstage to give aid to a dying Jane Shore," and "a Worcester woman's pleading with the gamester to stop his criminal behavior" are coupled with anecdotes of audience members who actually stopped productions of *Coriolanus* ("because 'three on one' was not a fair fight") and *Othello*. As Grimstead explains, a New Orleans boatman was irritated by Othello's grieving over the loss of the handkerchief and exclaimed, "'Why don't you blow your nose with your fingers and let the play go on.'"[114]

Audiences—while fully aware that they were watching a play—often believed what they saw. And judging from the intense alarm that often emanated from the pages of theatrical journals concerning the breeches performer, it is safe to assume that certain critics believed as well. Certainly, these spectators usually knew that the performer was a woman (from reading newspaper notices and/or play bills) and did not, of course, fancy that she had miraculously been transmogrified, but rather they witnessed a woman's momentary ability to appear convincingly masculine, to pass briefly as a man onstage and therefore blur gender boundaries. Even though such trespasses were—like Iago's villainy—ephemeral, critics felt threatened by the fiction's seeming truthfulness; they perceived a woman's desire to adopt the dress, the role, and the privilege of manhood and believed that this desire was potentially disruptive even *after* the curtain had dropped. Furthermore, critics regarded the usurping cross-dressed actress not only as potentially dangerous to men, but also as presenting a very real threat to other actresses in general and herself in particular. Indeed, breeches were not simply linked to women's rights, for in the minds of the male theatrical hegemony this costume was also capable of disqualifying women from any "natural" entitlement they might have otherwise had to wear instead the sacred mantle of True Womanhood. In its first mention of a woman in a breeches role (1806), for example, the *Theatrical Censor* remarked upon the success of Mrs. Jones as Patrick in *The Poor Soldier*. The critic notes, "The novelty of the undertaking excited great interest, and doubtless attracted a better house than any other cast; but still we must say, whatever precedent there may exist for it, it is a part in which we never again wish to see this favorite actress. It is *unworthy* of her."[115]

Because of the ideology of separate spheres, performing masculinity and performing femininity were mutually exclusive in nineteenth-century America. And since the performative nature of gender was not always consciously acknowledged or readily articulated, to act masculine was to simultaneously dislodge one's femininity. True Womanhood was sacrificed when actresses played characters who were unchaste, aggressive, and irreverent. These qualities, while usually found in a male villain (or hero—many had flaws that were acceptable to nineteenth-century audiences),[116] were not completely restricted to masculine characters. Lady Macbeth, Mrs. Haller *(The Stranger)*, Millwood *(The London Merchant)*, and many others also possessed "unwomanly" attributes. A double standard becomes apparent here when one considers the disparity between the way breeches performers were perceived as opposed to actresses in leading female lines. Critics did not worry that Siddons was dangerously ambitious or possessed a hidden nefarious nature just because she played Lady Macbeth, or that Anne Brunton Merry was perhaps unfaithful to her husband[s] after playing Mrs. Haller too many times. Yet when actresses such as Clara Fisher undertook roles like Goldfinch in *The Road to Ruin* in 1827, critics worried that these portrayals might threaten to pollute their womanhood. A critic for the *Albion* exemplifies this tendency as he discusses Fisher's enthusiasm for breeches roles:

> They may afford room for the display of her talent, but that display must be made at the expense of a great deal of good taste and delicate feeling. Other media can be found, equally calculated to

exhibit her versatility, without being equally certain to compromise her feminine charms. Goldfinch is a profligate debauchee, and his language is in unison with his character. Now we cannot endure to see a young lady whom we know to be lovely, innocent, amiable, and pure, struggling to put on the swagger and impudence of a debauchee, talking his language and imitating so far as she can his vulgarity and vice.[117]

Despite the popularity of female dramatic characters that were far more wicked than Goldfinch, Fisher endangered her femininity because she played a man who possessed these qualities. Fisher was revered by New York critics as an icon of feminine virtue, perhaps because of her age (she starred in New York as a teenager) and her small stature. Although she was considered a brilliant actress, critics found it difficult to reconcile her angelic image with the stage pictures she so masterfully painted. After she played Norval, for example, one critic wrote, "A strong appeal is made to the imagination when we are asked to believe that so frail and delicate a creature has put to flight 'a band of fierce barbarians,' and is capable of worsting in single combat the ferocious Glenalvon. . . . [O]n the whole we prefer to see her in such parts as Albina, Helen Morret, and Leticia Hardy."[118]

Even Cushman, who was widely acclaimed to be the best breeches performer in America, was occasionally admonished not to go too far for fear of risking her status as a True Woman. In December of 1849, the *Spirit* critic confessed that if Cushman "were less masculine in her portraitures, she would be more appreciated than she is. But whatever physical advantages may limit her theatrical success, she is undoubtedly an intellectual gem of the purest character."[119] Although Cushman was condemned for seeming too manly, her tendency towards masculinity was still, paradoxically, considered a physical "advantage" by critics. Masculinity was perhaps always considered essentially "good," yet inappropriate for a woman to exhibit; a woman's "goodness" came from her physical *dis*advantages: weakness, submissiveness, and sexual inhibition. A few months after this comment, the *Spirit* critic again advised, "We perceive a suggestion that, having distinguished herself as Romeo, she ought to undertake other male characters, but we hope she will not adopt any such style of personation. Nothing which is calculated to destroy the effeminacy of her action, should be entertained by an actress."[120] This comment is significant, for it traces the proliferation of the threat throughout the century. By 1850, Cushman was advised not to play other male roles, while in 1830 she performed them constantly at the Park. Either the reviewer was not familiar with her career history—which would have been unusual considering Cushman's fame by this time—or was choosing to ignore the fact that wearing breeches was an extremely popular convention in the 1830s. Regardless, it seems that a critical effort was being made both to contain the further adoption of this practice by actresses as well as to discourage stars from expanding their breeches repertoire.

One year later (the year she added Hamlet to her stock of characters), a similar review was published regarding Cushman's Romeo in *Tallis's Dramatic Magazine and General Theatrical and Musical Review*. In this article, the critic introduces, and subsequently tries to answer, a question that he had heard many people ask lately: Should Cushman stop playing male roles, or was she "justified [in] continuing this experiment?" He confesses that he thinks she should indeed refrain from playing men, and goes on to say that he found even her phenomenally successful London performance of Romeo in 1845 questionable because it was "an impeachment of her powers as an actress."[121] Even Romeo was beginning to be seen as a role that would challenge the credibility of an actress's power to act her feminine parts—both onstage and at home.

Playing men removed women from their pedestals and placed them on equal footing with their supposed masters. This thought was distasteful to some male critics and audience members, who preferred the old arrangement, but inviting to women who strained against the confines of the hearth. A good illustration of this principle comes from the pages of Benjamin Brown French's journal. While in Philadelphia in 1835, French, who was a theatre aficionado, decided to take in a matinee (probably at either the Walnut Street or Chestnut Street Theatre). Celeste, the famed Parisian dancer and breeches actress, was the star attraction that afternoon. Because this actress spoke very little English, she earned her American reputation in "dumb boy" roles that did not require her to speak, in plays such as *The Broken Sword, The Dumb Brigand,* and *Deaf and Dumb.* Although these dumb boy roles were usually regarded by most critics as innocuous, some viewers—French included—found any breeches role demeaning to women. His diary entry for November 6, 1835, details his displeasure with actresses like Celeste:

> Celeste has a *penchant* for performing male characters. I dislike it, I would never see a female upon the stage in male attire, could I avoid it, and it is only pardonable under circumstances where in actual life such disguise would seem to be necessary [he is talking about disguise roles here]—but a female in breeches, through play after play, and character after character, though it shocks not *my delicacy,* for I never carry any with me to a Theatre—still it lowers the female character in my estimation, especially when I see the most respectable female audiences gazing on with much apparent satisfaction. It ought not to be tolerated by the respectable of the female sex.[122]

Even though such transgressions were contained within the imaginary world depicted onstage, French suggests that the breeches performer still "lowered" herself or marred her reputation in general. By becoming a man—even for a few hours—she was somehow less of a woman, less virtuous, less submissive, less angelic. The danger, therefore, did not simply lie with the male viewer's exposure to the woman in breeches, since French admits that he felt immune to any subversions he might encounter at the theatre. Rather, he claims, it was the women—on both sides of the proscenium arch—who were threatened by this convention: the actress risked compromising her femininity and the "respectable" female spectator (a term that draws attention to the *other* women in the theatre—prostitutes and lower-class women) chanced being corrupted by disruptive ideas. Indeed, French implies that his distaste towards the convention was exacerbated by watching women watch the cross-dressed actress. The female attendees at the theatre that afternoon were part of the performance for French, whose anxiety mounted as he pondered the spell that actresses like Celeste might cast over other women. For as French gazed upon the women in the audience, they in turn "gaz[ed] on [Celeste] with much apparent satisfaction"; this suggests that the anxiety that the breeches performer engendered in the male critic or audience member was not individualized. In other words, male critics and viewers like French were not just worried about a small percentage of theatrical women whose performances betrayed signs of rebellion. Instead, they perceived the breeches performer as one who possessed the power to sway other women, to initiate a petticoat government, to obliterate crucial gendered demarcations concerning social behavior, relationships, and work, and to therefore unravel the very fabric of American society.

This underlying—perhaps largely unconscious—anxiety over women's theatrical cross-dressing explains both the constant critical lamentations over actresses who jeopardized their sacred femininity and the frequently vitriolic dramatic reviews. As we have seen, many critics simply denounced the convention altogether and found undeserved fault with talented actresses simply because they chose to play men's roles. Mary Barnes's Norval in 1817 "pained" the critics, for example, in spite of the fact that she executed the role with undeniable skill. She was acknowledged to be accomplished, animated, and correct in her interpretation, yet because she was a woman she nearly ruined the critic's enjoyment of the play. As the *American Monthly Magazine* critic lamented, Barnes

> came so short, in her stature and the might of her arm, of what the whole probability of the incidents required, as almost entirely to mar our enjoyment of the scene. There should be verisimilitude in the *looks of an actor,* in his figure and muscular strength, as well as propriety in his costume, correctness in his readings or adaptation in his voice and gesture.... And where is the propriety of a delicate female, small even for her sex, totally deficient in size and vigour of limb, and in fullness, energy and masculine melody of voice, attempting to personate a young man of heroic stature, and majesty of mien, as well as of unconquerable valour? If the story had brought Young Norval before us at the age of 15, when his imagination began to kindle at the recitals of the hermit, and his soul pant to break from obscurity, and prove his parentage by

deeds, we think we should have been completely satisfied with Mrs. B. for her representation. Instead of the strength that could enable her "to play her weapon like a tongue of flame," and an aim to shelter the Grampian vales, and of "four armed assailants" strike to earth, "from which they never rose again the fiercest two" ... She could scarcely unsheathe her sword, and we regretted that Mrs. B. should undertake the part at all.[123]

Barnes was talented but unacceptable because her womanly frame threatened verisimilitude. Indeed, the critic questions the "propriety" of Barnes' playing Norval, an interesting choice of words considering that the term "propriety" was also a neoclassical precept, and certainly an elemental part of the standards being used to judge this performance. According to neoclassicists, the concept of verisimilitude also extended in a more specific way to characterization. Each character was required to follow proper decorum, a behavioral prescription for all humanity; categorized according to gender, race, class, age, profession, and global/state/civic community, individuals in particular classifications were attributed particular qualities. Thus, governed by neoclassical principles of decorum, playwrights constructed, actors played, and critics looked for stereotypes: those who behaved according to type were successful while those who deviated from established rules of conduct were thought aberrant. Thus by abandoning her proper sphere and playing Norval, a masculine character, Barnes rejected feminine propriety and therefore appeared "preposterous."[124]

Not all critical sentiment, however, was the innocent by-product of neoclassical logic, as is evidenced by the following review of adolescent star John Howard Payne's performance of Norval. The young American Roscius, as he was called, earned a great deal of popularity for his rendition of the role in 1809. He was billed as an "infant prodigy," despite the fact that he was in his late teens when he first acted the character. The *Thespian Monitor* reported on his performance in strikingly contradictory terms:

> Upon his appearance [Payne] was greeted with as loud applause as ever has been heard—His figure is very small, and not profuse in

beauty; his utterance is not quite clear, his tones wanting a degree of roundness which time may yet supply them with. His voice is weak, and his words though tolerably well heard by those who are near, are not sufficiently distinct to those who are at a distance from the stage. His gesture is clothed with "manly readiness," and his movement with it over the boards, is as graceful, easy, and dignified, as that of the oldest veteran of the stage; but we think he overloads his speeches with too much emphasis and action.[125]

Payne, unlike Barnes who played the role eight years later, was applauded loudly despite the fact that his performance seemed inferior to her rendition in almost every regard. Described as small and unattractive with a weak inarticulate voice, Payne is nevertheless said to possess "manly readiness"—a quality that Barnes could never attain. In 1817, the *American Monthly* journalist marvels at Barnes's ability even to draw her sword and scoffs at her desire to embody a character who must "play his weapon like a tongue of flame" and "worst" the savage Glendower in single combat. Judging from the earlier review of Payne, however, it seems the critic should have been equally as dubious about the young Roscius, who, notwithstanding his lack of skill, small frame, and billing as an "infant," was perceived as "manly."

When Barnes played female roles, Juliet for example, she was exalted as "the first female performer of her day,"[126] but in breeches she was considered a sort of gender pirate—dashing and compelling, even triumphant, but fundamentally deviant. Indeed, no one could deny her virtuosity in male roles, not even the critic who covered her performance of Hamlet in 1820 for the *Ladies' Port Folio*. Yet while her skill as a performer was acknowledged, she was simultaneously admonished for her trespass:

> We do not hesitate to declare that in our opinion the part was as ably represented by this lady, as we have ever known it by any of her sex; this being the first, and we earnestly hope the last attempt of the kind within our observation. In truth, we protest against such an invasion of man's prerogative. We do not think a female ought in this instance to have worn the breeches and have at-

tempted to counterfeit "man's fair proportion," either for her own, or her husband's *benefit*.[127]

The *Port Folio* critic then goes on to compare Barnes's undertaking to an episode in Thomas Cooper's career. Cooper was acting in Philadelphia, and because he was having a difficult time procuring a full house, he rented an elephant and featured the animal in his next performance. This lark proved successful as audiences flocked to see Cooper's novel addition, an undertaking not unlike Barnes's "jumping into breeches." Cooper's elephant and Barnes's Hamlet were similar oddities, the critic implies, embraced only because desperate times called for extreme measures.

Critics, through their negative reviews, repeatedly hinted at the threat posed by representative cross-dressed actresses. Barnes was denounced for playing men in the early century and Fisher in the twenties. In 1839, the *Spirit* critic discusses Mrs. Shaw's inclination towards male parts and suggests that appearing in breeches was "esteemed fatal to the fairest of names."[128] In 1848, a journalist found a Mrs. Wilkinson "repulsive" in the role of Richard III,[129] and in the fifties and sixties breeches actresses like Fanny Wallack and Sarah Crocker Conway (both popular New York actresses) were either ignored by the press or marginalized.[130] Even Cushman, who garnered far more fame than an actress like Barnes, was castigated for her transvestism. Yet, if negative dramatic notices of cross-dressed women were emblematic of critical anxiety over the specter of petticoat government, the fact that Cushman—the most powerful actress in the nineteenth century—was also targeted as dangerous proves unsurprising. More incredible was the degree to which Cushman was found transgressive in one of her most celebrated roles—Romeo.

Romeo was largely responsible for catapulting Cushman to stardom. Because of her unprecedented success as the young lover at the Haymarket Theatre in London during the 1845–46 season, Cushman went from being a respectable American actress to an international star. She was lionized by the British elite, lauded by the majority of London critics, and glowingly remembered at home—by most. One English critic, residing in America, would certainly not have raised his voice to match the fever pitch sounded in London. George Vandenhoff obviously did not foresee Cushman's 1845 sensation when he bitterly reproved her Romeo in America three years before. Vandenhoff, an itinerant English star, was traveling through Philadelphia in 1843 and was engaged for a short time at the Walnut Street Theatre, then under the management of Cushman. While under Cushman's direct employ,[131] Vandenhoff played Mercutio to her Romeo, an experience that inspired the following invective:

> Romeo requires a *man* to feel his passion, and to express his despair. A woman, in attempting it, "unsexes" herself to no purpose, except to destroy all interest in the play, and all sympathy for the ill-fated pair: she *denaturalizes* the situations; and sets up a monstrous anomaly, in place of a consistent picture of ill-starred passion and martyr-love, faithful to death. There should be a law against such perversions; they are high crimes and misdemeanours [sic] against truth, taste, and aesthetic principles of art, as well as offenses against propriety, and desecrations of Shakspere [sic]. In his time women did not appear on the stage at all; now they usurp men's parts, and "push us from our stools."[132]

Cushman usurped Vandenhoff's part in more ways than one. In addition to being his employer, she also borrowed his costume, and, because of her popularity in the role, restored Romeo's position as the principle male character in the play—an honor that Mercutio had previously held after Charles Kemble gave up Romeo to play this part a few years before. This review does not merely betray an annoyance or irritable distaste for the convention as articulated by French and certain members of the New York press. Rather, Vandenhoff is clearly threatened by Cushman, who as a man (and as his boss) is not merely unwomanly but perverse, not simply preposterous but monstrous, an unnatural emasculating creature.

Both Vandenhoff and the *Port Folio* critic, who likened Barnes's Hamlet to an animal act, voice a direct concern about such "invasion[s] of man's prerogative" and hope to discourage all future attempts by openly expressing their disgust and by conjuring up images evocative of a side show. Women like Barnes and Cushman who played serious male roles—while beloved by their audiences—were critically rendered as freaks, as ominous curiosities; like Cooper's hired elephant, they metaphorically loomed over their male colleagues, monstrous in appearance and immensely powerful in their capacity to disrupt prevailing order—to revolutionize. They alarmingly commanded center stage (as opposed to balconies),[133] captivated audiences, and freely roamed through public spaces—unruly and in desperate need of supervision. Such beasts found their keepers as marked discourses of containment materialized within dramatic criticism, which were effective in undermining the image of the manly or unsexed breeches performer. Rather than luxuriate in their misgivings about cross-dressing, many critics constructed alternative representations of the breeches actress to counter feminist subtexts communicated by actresses like Barnes, Cushman, and Crampton. So as to erase visions of the manly usurper, reviews instead re-membered the cross-dressed actress in hegemonic terms: she was no longer a man but a boy, no more a masculine force but a feminine icon. Through such discourse, rhetorical "keepers" contained subversive "acts," caging the elephant after the exhibition.

CHAPTER 3

MAPPING THE BO[D]Y FEMALE

Immaturity, Femininity, and the Antebellum Actress-as-Boy

> [The actress-as-boy] is charming in a little piece called Nature and Philosophy, *and has a class of characters in which she invariably awakens the warmest admiration. Without the energy to sustain the heavier parts of the drama, she has a naivete, and, if we may be allowed to speak, an infantine grace, which makes her a valuable as well as beautiful ornament of the stage.*
>
> —New York Mirror, 1825

> [W]hat there was of the woman just served to indicate juvenility, and no more.
>
> —Athenaeum, 1846

THE RICHMOND HILL THEATRE'S BENEFIT SEASON OF 1832 enjoyed a particularly successful performance by a relatively minor—but popular—player known only as Mrs. Russell. A favored breeches performer that spring, Russell delighted New York critics and audiences by presenting a series of boy roles. Regardless of her appeal in these parts, it is surprising that she chose to play a boy for her benefit at the Richmond Hill, since these occasions were (for the breeches performer) traditionally reserved for more challenging tragic or serious adult roles. While most actresses who specialized in breeches roles chose Hamlet, Norval, or Count Belino as their benefit pieces, Russell selected Julian, the "Peasant Boy"—an unorthodox choice for an actress who was routinely compelled by managers to play these types of roles throughout the regular season. Perhaps Russell anticipated the warm encomiums bestowed upon her efforts by select members of the New York press. The *Spirit* critic was exceptionally effusive, calling Russell's personation of Julian "nature realized" and declaring that the role had never before been played with such truth:

> Her fine person, sweet tenor voice and graceful language was everything externally the part required; and her truly lover-like attentions towards Rosalie were so strictly natural they gratified without disgusting the most fastidious female present. But when in the boyish, off-hand manner she slightly spoke of her encounter with the wolf, she even exceeded all our expectations. The *bonne bouche* was in her last scenes. Her resignation to the will of heaven, the noble assertion of her innocence, her air, voice, and manner, was—we cannot express it. The eye gazed, the mind exulted, and the heart sympathized with the suffering boy. It was true excellence.[1]

Both Russell's decision to play Julian on her benefit and her triumph in this role can be explained in part by New York's fascination with the actress-as-boy. Notices of plays featuring dumb and blind boy roles and melodramatic characters such as Julian filled the theatrical columns of New York newspapers during the early decades of the nineteenth century. Indeed, during the first three years of the *Albion's* circulation (1823–1825), the only breeches roles ever listed in the theatrical record were boy parts. Theatrical boys such as Little Pickle in *The Spoil'd Child,* Colin in *Nature and Philosophy; or the Youth Who Never Saw A Woman,* Paul in *The Pet of the Petticoats,* and Paul and his brother Justin in *The Wandering Boys* were far more popular vehicles for women than the

Shakespearean tragic hero and the adult melodramatic male lead. While critics were suspicious of Barnes's Hamlet and Sharpe's Count Belino, they were enchanted by women who portrayed boys.

Theatre historians suggest that women played boys during the nineteenth-century for utilitarian reasons (as there were simply more women in the company than young men) or to enhance nineteenth-century conceptions of verisimilitude, since even mature actresses were thought to resemble boys more closely than adult male actors.[2] Such explanations are far too simplistic, and ignore gender as a category for historical analysis despite breeches performance's female subject (sometimes object). Rather than simply accept critical (and historical) associations between the cross-dressed actress and the boy as "natural" expressions or as pragmatic managerial maneuvers, discourses of containment must be identified and deconstructed. By casting women as boys and by critically reinforcing the actress's boyishness, male playwrights and critics maintained prescriptive codes for women—codes that were being jeopardized by the burgeoning women's rights movement, the dress reform campaign, and the increased popularity of breeches performance. By creating a wider public awareness of the connections between femininity and immaturity through strategic dramatic reviews, play selections, and casting choices, theatrical patriarchs attempted to launch a coup on petticoat government and to script gender upon the female body through boyish metaphor.

An examination of the ways in which women were associated with boys (and children in general) during the first half of the century will expose such patriarchal strategies and will thus challenge and/or expand upon traditional explanations. Furthermore, by venturing down more gendered avenues of historical inquiry, dramatic reviews like Russell's can be deciphered to expose the specious innocence of terms such as "fine," "sweet," "graceful," "slightly," "resign[ed]," "noble," and "suffering." For although the stories that the actress-as-boy played out on stage were often about courage, valor, and masculine rites of passage, critics interpreted these tales differently. Peasant boys, young warriors, and fairy tale heroes were presented by playwrights, cast by managers, and read by critics not as young men but as adult women. Actresses who played boys were not perceived as subverting stereotypes; rather, they reinforced dominant gender ideology. Such representations rendered the performance of the cross-dressed actress innocuous and, as Marjorie Garber might argue, literally and figuratively took the "Peter" out of Peter Pan.[3]

THE ACTRESS-AS-BOY

The tradition for breeches performance in America always relied heavily upon the image of the actress-as-boy. From the eighteenth century onward, this convention was largely based on the perception that a woman could convincingly appear youthful or "boyish." If women wore the breeches at all during the eighteenth and early nineteenth centuries, it was almost always to enact a boy. Only on rare occasions, such as a benefit night, would a woman undertake an adult male role. Indeed, between 1759 (the year that marked the first breeches performance in America) and 1800, nearly all the male roles played by women on the New York stage (on nonbenefit nights) were boy parts. Of the approximately 34 breeches performances that took place during this time, only four featured women in adult male roles (see Appendix 1). This pattern was also discernable in the early nineteenth century; however, instead of playing pages and young princes, cross-dressed actresses began to star as boys in weightier melodramatic characters. Leading boy roles became institutionalized during the first half of the nineteenth century as an increasing number of plays were written with juvenile male leads; such plays gave rise to a succession of boyish types.[4]

While the increase in plays with boy roles is noted by historians, no attempt has been made to question either the institutionalization of boy characters within the American dramatic canon or the practice of systematically casting women in these parts. A precedent for casting women as boys out of necessity was established during the eighteenth century, and scholars have been content to accept this explanation for the nineteenth century as well. Certainly there is some merit in this suggestion, for women often were asked to play the juvenile lead by managers who did not want to go to the expense of hiring another actor. Even as late in the century as 1865, such arrangements were being made. Clara Morris recalls having to play boy roles for the Cleveland Academy of Music during her tenure there as a ballet girl in the mid-sixties. While she was rapidly singled out as a talented young performer and therefore given more bit parts than the others (an opportunity that helped her advance in the ranks), the page roles were divided up among all of the girls in the ballet company. Morris explains, "It must not be thought that I had in the first place a monopoly of the small parts; far from it, but the company being rather short of utility people, if the ballet girls could play speaking servants, it not only saved a salary or two to the manager, but it was of immense advantage to the girls themselves."[5]

Actresses were also thought to play boys because they physically resembled them; they could convincingly pass as youths because of their small frames and high voices. In 1809, for example, the *Thespian Monitor* reported that, "Mrs. Wilmot's figure is admirably calculated for the male apparel, and in the character of Little Pickle in its *tout ensemble,* she never can be exceeded."[6] This sentiment was echoed by the *Spirit's* assessment of Mrs. Russell's Julian, who had "everything externally the part required."[7] In addition, many boy roles were artistically demanding and required a skilled player, and adult women were thought to possess the necessary experience as well as the desired appearance. In her nineteenth-century biography of Cushman, Stebbins attributes the actress's success as Romeo both to her histrionic ability (as an older and more experienced actress) and to the public's desire for verisimilitude. "It is well known that there is no character in the whole range of drama so difficult to find an adequate representative for as Romeo. When a man has achieved the experience requisite to *act* Romeo, he has ceased to be young enough to *look* it; and this discrepancy is felt to be unendurable in the young, passionate Romeo, and detracts from the interest of the play. Who could endure to see a man with the muscles of Macready, in the part of the gallant and loving boy?"[8]

Stebbins—like many critics and historians who have written about Cushman's achievements—tries to explain away the actress's extraordinary career as a breeches performer by placing her in the context of a utility actress. Cushman did not want to play boy/men's

Fig. 3.1: Charlotte Cushman as Romeo. Harvard Theatre Collection, The Houghton Library, Fredric Woodbridge Wilson, Curator.

parts, argues Stebbins, but was "obliged" to do so during her residency at the Park Theatre because the plays contained more male roles than there were male actors to fill them. While subsequent research on Cushman has found this explanation to be incorrect,[9] the desire on the part of biographers and historians to attribute the phenomenon of breeches performance (specifically women as boys) to utility playing and verisimilitude seems deliberately recuperative and/or evasive—especially considering the fact that many actresses who played boys continued to do so long after they could claim recognition as a utility player or capitalize on their slender boyish figures. Both Barnes and Cushman played boy roles even *after* they achieved star status. And at this point in their careers, they would have had more control over their own repertoire than a utility player would have possessed. Additionally, both of these women acted the boy well into their fifties (Barnes did not begin playing boys until she was in her mid-thirties), which suggests that verisimilitude was not always the central casting requirement. This is not to say that the actress-as-boy failed in the role if her appearance seemed at odds with nineteenth-century standard conceptions of a male youth. Cushman continued to thrill her audiences despite the fact that by 1855, her matronly figure was more suited for Lady Montague or for the Capulet Nurse than it was for Verona's young male lover (see figure 3.1). Similarly, the *Spirit* critic continued to praise the popular breeches actress, Elizabeth Trewar Shaw-Hamblin, for her portrayal of Ion even though there seemed to be little or no physical resemblance between the two. In November of 1847, the critic wrote,

> Mrs. Shaw continues to draw crowds at this house nightly. Mrs. Shaw, as our readers either know from the pleasure of having seen her, or from good report, is a very fine looking lady, with very superior attainments and was, when her figure was more fragile than it is now, a most captivating actress. Even now when she is much heavier, her reading having lost nothing by the change, she fails not to interest her audiences and to impress them with the ability which she possesses. The personations of Ion, and Julia in The Hunchback, and Mrs. Haller in The Stranger during the week have been equal to her reputation. The press have kept her before the people by very eulogistic notices, and the people have crowded together to see and hear her.[10]

Cushman and Shaw may have appeared too old for the boy roles they played, but other actresses were criticized for looking too youthful. While the *Spirit* praised Russell's performance of Julian, they found her presentation of Colin—a lad of seventeen—to be unsatisfactory. Although they commended her on her acting, they noted that Russell "looked some years younger than she should have."[11] Reviews such as these imply that traditional explanations surrounding the actress-as-boy are inconclusive. This type of breeches performer did not always look the part, nor was she only playing such roles to convenience handicapped theatrical companies. We must, therefore, look beyond the traditional school for explanations regarding the popularity of the actress-as-boy and investigate broader cultural connections between femininity and immaturity.

WOMEN AND CHILDREN

Like Romeo, Cushman supposedly began to court the fair Juliet (and Albany audiences) when she was still a teenager. Her first recorded performance of the young Montague took place in April of 1837 at the Pearl Street Theatre in Albany, and was repeated a few weeks later at the Old National Theatre in New York City. The critic from the *New York Mirror*, who at this time was still unfamiliar with the popular new actress, reproduced a review of Cushman's Romeo that had previously appeared in the *Morning Courier*, written by a "contemporary in her favour." In their critique, Cushman's anonymous champion draws a remarkably clear connection between the actress and the boy. They write, "Her personal appearance, voice and manner are singularly adapted to the performance of juvenile male characters; and a casual observer would have found some difficulty on Saturday evening, in realizing the fact that Romeo was played by a girl not yet out of her teens."[12] This comment is somewhat misleading, however, since Cushman would have been 21 in 1837. While the critic simply may have been misinformed, it is also possible that he deliberately sought to cultivate this affiliation between womanhood and adolescence. If Cushman and Romeo were reported to be contemporaries, New York audiences would not have to exert too much energy in suspending their disbelief. With her strong slender frame, her bold features, square jaw, and moderate height, Cushman may easily have passed for Montague. Likewise, since it is evident that this reviewer perceived Romeo as a youth, the actress's vocal quality—which was usually reported to be deeper than most women's—might be thought to match that of the teenage lover. Yet the *Mirror* critic also points to a third quality possessed by Cushman that has little to do with her ability to appear or sound boyish. Her "manner" was also "singularly adapted" to young or "juvenile" roles—an observation that betrays a less superficial association between the woman and the boy.[13]

Indeed, within nineteenth-century American society and culture, a woman's domestic life, limitations, and privileges mirrored that of a boy's (or of a child's in general) in multiple ways. Like children, women were thought to be weak, delicate, irrational creatures who could not thrive outside their private domestic environment. A woman's moral superiority and angelic nature helped to stoke the home fires yet simultaneously extinguished her civic spark. Mary Wollstonecraft argues that because of their limited sphere of influence and their restricted access to education, women were kept in an "infantile" state. In her controversial yet influential book of 1792, *A Vindication of the Rights of Women,* Wollstonecraft draws on this common parallel between women and children. She begins her study by asking her female readers to forgive her for perceiving them differently than men viewed them. Wollstonecraft proclaims that, contrary to most men, she fails to think of women as being "in a state of perpetual childhood, unable to stand alone."[14] Such a puerile condition is the result of a poor education, argues the author. A woman's early instruction focuses on the acquisition of a variety of inconsequential ornamental skills; "meanwhile strength of body and mind are sacrificed to libertine notions of beauty, to the desire of establishing themselves—the only way women can rise in the world—by marriage. And this desire making mere animals of them, when they marry they act as such children may be expected to act,—they dress, they paint, and nickname God's creatures."[15] Wollstonecraft likens women to children and also to childish objects; women are the playthings of men, "created to be the toy of man," and must "rattle" or "jingle" according to his whim.[16]

As Wollstonecraft (qua Shakespeare) implies, marriage—the ritual that, for most, heralded the entrance into womanhood—was responsible for legally reducing women to the status of children, and thus strengthened the ideological connection between the two. While certain privileges like the right to vote were denied women regardless of their matrimonial standing, many others were revoked as soon as the marriage license was signed. In terms of legal matters, an unmarried woman or "femme sole" enjoyed many of the same privileges as nineteenth-century men; she could own property, accrue debt, draft a will or contract, sue or be sued. Yet under coverture (the legal status of married women), wives had neither rights nor responsibilities. They could not be held accountable for most civil offenses, were excused of all debts, and were exonerated for any crimes they committed within their husband's presence. The husband bore all the responsibilities and experienced all the privileges. Indeed, until the second half of the nineteenth century, a married woman or "femme covert" had few rights under the law and could no longer civilly operate as she had prior to matrimony. Her husband controlled all financial decisions and property, took full legal responsibility for his wife, and had complete custody over the children. Furthermore, women who suffered abuse at the hands of their spouses had a difficult time obtaining a separation or a divorce. Even abandoned women could not escape patriarchal control, for their property would still remain within their husbands' jurisdiction.[17] Marriage united two individuals, but once wed, the law recognized only one partner.

Early feminists—both male and female—acknowledged this state of "perpetual childhood" and took formal steps to remedy the situation in 1848 at the first women's rights convention in Seneca Falls, New York. Selected items from their "Declaration of Sentiments" (a protofeminist rearticulation of the Declaration of Independence) convey both the frustration and anger felt by the convention's participants and the extent to which women in American society publicly acknowledged their "infantile" condition. The Declaration stated, "The history of mankind is a history of repeated injuries and usurpations on the part of man toward woman, having in direct object the establishment of an absolute tyranny over her. To prove this, let facts be submitted to a candid world." A list of women's infantilizing restrictions and limitations ensues, outlining her inability to vote, earn decent wages, or own property (if married); her necessary submission to laws that were written without her consent or consideration; and her moral irresponsibility within society. The writers of this document aptly summarize a woman's legal powerlessness, arguing that because man has "deprived [woman] of her first right as a citizen, the elective franchise, thereby leaving her without representation in the halls of legislation, he has oppressed her on all sides," and "has made her, if married, in the eye of the law, civilly dead"[18] or civilly childlike.

As the Declaration of Sentiments suggests, women were infantilized during the first half of the nineteenth century because their legal status left them, like children, dependent upon an adult male provider. Additionally, women were thought to share certain biological traits with children. As Elizabeth K. Helsinger, Robin Lauterbach Sheets, and William Veeder point out, women's "relegation to the lower evolutionary level of children" was justified by scientists, as well as lawmakers, who ventured all the way back to antiquity to validate their claims of dominance. "Drawing upon authorities from Aristotle (women never transcend the childlike state) to Darwin (children of both sexes resemble women more than boys do men), scientists defined women's traditional traits—intuition, fidelity, charity—as "infantile." Resembling children in cranial structures and dimensions, women are supposedly more susceptible to infant diseases."[19] Such legal and scientific/physiological parallels between women and children may have been reinforced socially as well, since both parties inhabited the same sphere (a better explanation for women's susceptibility to childhood illnesses) and were forbidden access to public life. Although childhood supposedly prepared boys for manhood, male children were far more influenced by domesticity and femininity. As the industrial revolution displaced many middle-class men from the home, boys had much more contact with their mothers; women raised them, dressed them, and impressed their moral codes upon them. A boy's world was domestic like his mother's, and his appearance—at least for the first few years of his life—was feminine. Indeed, the clearest manifestation of women's influence upon boyhood was sartorial. "All children began life clothed in the image of femininity," and boys did not shed their gowns and petticoats until the age of six.[20]

Philip Greven, whose scholarship focuses upon different approaches to child rearing in early American society, provides further evidence of this practice through his discussion of portraits painted of children during the first half of the nineteenth century. Regardless of whether or not artists rendered boys or girls, the feminine appearance of most paintings' subjects made it so difficult to establish their sex, Greven explains, that later art experts were forced to simply label portraits as "Child." He describes, for example, a painting from 1833 of young Edward Salisbury Rich, who wears a long gown with puffed sleeves, a necklace, and carries a flower. Similarly, another portrait, this time of twin children, reveals a boy and a girl who are dressed identically in feminine outfits. Moreover, the hair of both children is cut short, as was the practice throughout the 1840s. According to Greven, "the feminization of boys in terms of clothing and physical appearance . . . continued unabated until at least the middle of the nineteenth century."[21] Interestingly, the most significant rite of passage in the life of the boy came with "breeching," the term used to describe his abandonment of feminine attire for male clothing. Being "breeched" meant liberation for the boy on some level, just as it did for the cross-dressed actress. Although boys could not yet escape the influence of the private arena, their clothes acted as visible emblems of difference between themselves and the females who shared their sphere; "[w]ith great clarity a boy saw that 'female' meant fettered and 'male' meant free."[22]

In addition to appearing feminine, boys were also expected to display certain behavioral characteristics that closely resembled the cardinal virtues of True Womanhood. Excerpts from nineteenth-century women's magazines and journals depict the model boy as innocent, obedient/submissive, pure, self-sacrificing, and morally superior—all qualities that were expected of women as well.[23] Even Bloomer's temperance paper *The Lily,* whose writers sounded a rallying cry for early feminism, reinforced this association between the woman and the boy. The early issues of this paper carried a section called "The Youth Department" that featured story after story on the thoughtful and generous boy. One anecdote relates a visit to the dentist made by two brothers. The younger brother expresses anxiety over the procedure that awaits him after witnessing the older brother's pain. The littlest is comforted by his elder sibling, however, who belays the younger's fears and boosts his courage despite the fact that he himself is suffering. Such "real benevolence" and selflessness—which were both thought to be "natural" feminine qualities—should be exhibited by all boys, expresses the author.[24] In the following issue, the editor reprints a "Word to Boys," a piece that originally appeared in the *New York District School Journal*. This article, which lectures boys under a series of rubrics such as "Be polite," "Be kind to everybody," "Never strike back," and "Avoid vulgar common-place slang phrases," might just as well have been written for women, since its tone and message so closely resemble the exhortations directed towards ladies of all ages. To be polite, for example, boys must act "benevolent[ly]" and commit themselves to "the graces of the heart; whatever things are true, honest, just, pure, and of good report. The true secret of politeness is to please, to make happy—flowing from goodness of heart—a fountain of love."[25]

Boys, like their mothers, were conceptualized in popular literature as yielding, innocent, and pure. Submission for women translated into obedience for boys. In an 1831 issue of the *American Baptist Magazine,* an evangelical minister, Francis Wayland, declared that children had a duty to obey their parents' command: "Authority belongs to one, submission to the other."[26] Likewise, a child rearing manual, published in 1833, mandated that obedience was the most worthy virtue a mother could instill in her children, and without it, "all other efforts will be in vain."[27] Certainly, women were the ideal teachers of this lesson since the principles they passed on to their children guided their own lives as well. Ideally, children mirrored their mother's spotless characters and were described in the same terms. Boys as well as girls were perceived as "holy," "beautiful," and "sanctified." Cloistered from the polluting daily transactions of public life, women and children remained untouched by the world. A poem published in 1839 portrays the child as a sort of moral tabula rasa or an immaculate "bright mirror." Entitled "Child at Prayer," the first two stanzas describe the purity of children:

> Pour forth each holy, white-rob'd thought,
> —Yes, bend in prayer, my child!
> Lift up thy heart to God, for thou
> Art pure and undefil'd.
> In the green beauty of thy youth,
> With an unsullied heart,
> In thy rejoicing and thy truth,
> Choose thou the "better part."[28]

Because girls were expected to be *essentially* pure, the majority of advice that emanated from the pages of domestic journals and women's periodicals concerned boys. Rhetorical questions concerning boys such as, "Is there in that face ought that speaks of sin and shame?"[29] (asked by a contributor to *Godey's Ladies Book*), were countered with antimasturbation material that assumed that as boys neared adolescence, the answer to this question would increasingly be yes. Just as young women were taught to prize their chastity above all other feminine virtues, pubescent males were commanded to remain pure and to refrain from participating in supposedly tainted rituals. So important was the need to abstain from "knowing thyself," that antimasturbation reformers (whose moralizing climaxed between 1830 and 1850) threatened pubescent young men with promises of death and disease.[30] While notions of "purity, piety, submissiveness and domesticity" take on slightly different meanings when applied to boyhood as opposed to womanhood, affinities between these behavioral codes are significant. Both women and boys were marginalized from the world of men. They were seen as private/domestic individuals without any legal rights or responsibilities; they were powerless, financially dependent, morally superior, and somewhat ornamental. Despite myriad allusions to their significant qualities (beauty, purity, charm), these societal Others were relegated to the wings of nineteenth-century American life, to play out their private theatricals in isolation.

THE ACTRESS-AS-BOY: FEMININITY AND IMMATURITY ON STAGE

When framed by such undeniable ideological connections between femininity and boyishness/immaturity, traditional views of the actress-as-boy as simply a utility player seem incomplete, and arguments about verisimilitude become significantly more complex. It is especially interesting that the number of boy roles for women grew in tandem with the threat generated by the cross-dressed actress. Perhaps the male theatrical hegemony hoped that by casting women as boys and by critically praising their exemplary ability to perform boyishness on stage, they would be able to mitigate mounting anxiety about female usurpation. Critics feared and were repulsed by Barnes's Hamlet, yet they eulogized her Myrtillo—responses that make perfect sense in light of the fact that the former role conjured up images of petticoat government and the latter only of petticoats.

Artistic connections made between femininity and immaturity, or between the actress and the boy, reinforced legal, scientific, and social parallels between the two. Boy roles in melodrama were especially emblematic of this relationship, as young heroes repeatedly betrayed feminine qualities. A good example of this principle can be found in William Diamond's play *The Broken Sword*. As hinted above, this play's boy role, Myrtillo, was always played by an adult actress and was introduced to American audiences by Barnes on April 28, 1817. The play saw its first production in London, however, on October 17, 1816; a Miss Luppino is listed in the playbill as the original Myrtillo, which suggests that the role was indeed written for a woman.[31] The main action of *The Broken Sword* takes place at Baron Zavior's mansion, which is nestled among the Spanish Pyrenees. As the play opens, the residents of the mansion are preparing for two events: a festival to celebrate the return of Claudio, the Baron's son, from the wars, and a remembrance mass for the dear Count Luneda, who was brutally murdered six years before. Myrtillo, Luneda's son (and described in the playbill's dramatis personae as "A Dumb Orphan"), has lived happily with the Baron and his family since his father's death, which he witnessed and which rendered him mute. The boy was discovered by the

Baron's brother, Captain Zavior, who brought him home and adopted him into the family. Before the return of Claudio, Rosara—the daughter of the Baron (all the other women in the play are dead)—and the Captain show Myrtillo a bust of his father that they secured from the Count's estate and that they erected in the garden as a tribute to Luneda. Myrtillo is moved by this likeness of his father and rushes to embrace the statue.

Shortly after this scene, Claudio returns with his friend Colonel Rigolio, whose seemingly honorable nature becomes suspect when he reacts strangely to the mention of Myrtillo's name. Furthermore, upon entering the garden, Rigolio sees the bust of Luneda, drops to his knees, and is overcome by violent emotions. After learning that Myrtillo swears that he can identify the murderer of his father, Rigolio flees the mansion and journeys to a shepherdess's cottage. Here he meets Estevan, the old valet of Luneda, who has just escaped from a galley slave ship, where he was unjustly sentenced to a life of hard labor for the murder of his master, the Count. Rigolio, who, unbeknownst to Estevan, was the one who framed him for the murder six years before, sends the valet back to the Baron's home with a message. Estevan arrives with Rigolio's note (which states that Estevan is Luneda's murderer), is apprehended, identified by his long lost friend Myrtillo, and exonerated.

Realizing that Rigolio is still at large, the Baron puts together a search party—consisting of all but Rosara—to look for the villain. Myrtillo spies him on an old bridge that is suspended above a torrent, which has been swelled by the ominous storm that simultaneously rages. Despite the evils that Rigolio has committed, the self-sacrificing boy runs to help him; Myrtillo confronts the villain, who strikes the torch out of the boy's hand with his sword and in doing so loses the tip of his blade. After he strikes, he throws Myrtillo off the bridge into the torrent. Myrtillo is saved with the help of Estevan and a servant Pablo. Believing that the boy is dead, Rigolio returns to the mansion where his sword identifies him as Myrtillo's attempted murderer. He is arrested and identified by the boy as Luneda's killer. The play ends as Myrtillo rushes onstage and exclaims—in the first words he has spoken in six years—"My father's murderer! . . . Justice! Justice! Justice!"[32]

This melodrama reinforces dominant gender ideology and thus foregrounds the association between immaturity and femininity in various ways. For example, Myrtillo—who the audience knows is an adult woman—is constantly being rescued by men. Like legions of melodramatic heroines, his is a story of virtue in peril. Captain Zavior (whose name unsurprisingly sounds like "savior" spoken with a Spanish accent) brings him back from the woodland scene of his father's murder and adopts him, and, in doing so, provides him with a luxurious life among the Baron (another "zavior") and his family. Similarly, Myrtillo is saved by two men from the torrent: Estevan, who jumps in after him, and Pablo, who throws him a rope. Myrtillo was even delivered by Estevan before the play's action began, as Estevan relates a story of rescuing the boy from a wolf many years before; when the two are finally reunited during the play, Myrtillo identifies Estevan by a scar on his neck produced by the wolf bite. In a sense, the boy is also saved at the end of the play by Estevan, who tricks Rigolio into bearing his sword, therefore exposing himself, and by the male police force who arrive to formally apprehend the villain.

In addition to his constant need to be protected by a male hero, Myrtillo resembles the nineteenth-century woman in many ways. Both have a difficulty expressing themselves—symbolic of the fact that women had no public voice during the first half of the nineteenth century. Myrtillo is also constantly described as "little," an "infant," and an orphan—conditions that further emphasize his dependence upon male champions and his marginality within the dramatic text. He is a sweet, loving child who brings quiet joy to the Baron's family but who cannot engage in public discourse. As the costume note in the play's text makes clear, Myrtillo is an ornamental character. Arrayed in a "light blue tunic, with black satin bindings and rows of white bell-buttons," "gray tights," a "hat to match" his outfit, and a pair of "yellow morroco lace-up boots," Myrtillo appears almost jesterlike. This boy/woman's outfit, which both amuses and tinkles musically (as its bell-buttons shake with movement), also sounds faint echoes of Wollstonecraft's likening of women to men's toys, that "jingle" and "rattle" to produce male pleasure.

Myrtillo's inferior or submissive position is established in the second scene of act 1 as Captain Zavior tells his story of rescuing the boy from the woods. The Captain recalls,

> From the thick bows of the chestnut, suddenly slipped down a little boy, who cast himself upon his knees in the path before me. His features were convulsed and pale, and his poor piteous eyes, that were raised beseechingly to mine, ran over with salt water as fast as the scupper of my own brig, when she had shipped a sea.— "What cheer, young messmate?" cried I. His lips opened, as if to return my hail, but no utterance followed.[33]

In this scene, the boy figure seems almost like a wood sprite or a fairy (another delicate Other) as he suddenly emerges from the tree. The inferior position of the boy/woman is enhanced by the image of Myrtillo falling on his knees before Zavior in supplication. This might also bear an erotic interpretation, for not only does Myrtillo kneel before Zavior, but he opens his mouth. Because the role of the boy was written for, and always presented by, a woman, Zavior's tale may have titilated audiences members in a way that might have caused the actress to be objectified, thus further reducing her in stature. Whatever the interpretation, the image produced by Zavior and Myrtillo functions as an almost Brechtian *Gestus* representing dominance and subservience: the man towers over the boy/woman, who has no power, no voice, and no alternative but to become dependent upon the male hero.

Given this objectification or dependence, it is not surprising that the breeches actress both thrived in this role and was described by critics in feminine terms. From its first production onward, the play—which was usually presented as an afterpiece (therefore maintaining a marginal position within the evening's entertainment bill)—was well received by New York audiences. *American Monthly Magazine* gave a full plot summary of the play shortly after it premiered and announced that "the piece ... was received by the audience with decided approbation." The critic continued to review the acting, giving Mr. Simpson, the actor who played Estevan, a long paragraph and Mrs. Barnes only two sentences. Of Barnes, the critic wrote, "Mrs. Barnes in Myrtillo, was irresistibly charming. Her appearance was lovely, her action easy, appropriate and eloquent."[34] The *New York Evening Post* also recommended the production and stated that the "managers have judiciously cast it to nearly the whole strength of the company, and it is uncommonly well got up and supported throughout."[35] Barnes continued to be popular in this role through the early years of the 1830s; in 1832, the *Mirror* announced that she was "emphatically excellent" as Myrtillo.[36]

Barnes was not the only actress who was praised as the "Dumb Orphan." In 1823 a newcomer to the New York theatre, Mrs. Clarke, played Myrtillo for her debut. The *Mirror* critic noted, "She supported Myrtillo (a dumb boy) in the afterpiece of the Broken Sword with . . . success; and we predict that she will be thought a valuable acquisition to our dramatic corps."[37] Likewise, at the Chatham Garden Theatre two years later, a Mrs. Waring was reportedly well received in the role by both critics and audiences.[38] As the virtuous "heroine" Myrtillo, the actress-as-boy could confidently take the stage and win audiences without fear of being thought anomalous.

Another popular dumb boy role—which was also consistently played by a woman—was Theodore (also known as Count Julio) in Thomas Holcroft's "historical drama" *Deaf and Dumb; or, The Orphan Protected*.[39] Set in Southern France, the play opens in a room in the palace of Harancour. In this room hangs a "whole-length portrait of a Boy," the young Count Julio (also described in the dramatis personae as "deaf and dumb"), who once had possession of Harancour despite his youth but has been supposed dead for several years. Because of the Count's death, the estate was given over to the boy's uncle Darlemont, a former merchant. Eight years prior to his acquisition of the palace, Darlemont allegedly took his nephew to Paris to cure his affliction. Rather than seek help for the boy, however, Darlemont dressed him in rags and left him on the street to die as a beggar so that he could gain control of the Count's wealth and possessions. Upon returning to Harancour, he reported that the boy had been administered a nostrum and died. Meanwhile, Julio is found by the police and taken to De L'Eppe, the famous Parisian teacher of the deaf and dumb. De L'Eppe temporarily adopts Julio, whom he calls Theodore and whom he suspects to be of noble birth. Eventually the teacher learns of the boy's past and pledges to help him find his home and restore justice. In act 2, scene 1, he declares, "If, as I fear, you are the victim of unnatural foul play, grant me, Providence, to unmask and confound it."[40] De L'Eppe and Theodore travel throughout France looking for the boy's home and finally discover Harancour. Theodore is recognized by St. Alme, Darlemont's honest son, and by other servants to be Count Julio, and is restored to his rightful position after Darlemont is denounced as the villain.

Like *The Broken Sword*, this play also reinforces dominant gender ideology. Julio and Myrtillo are cut from the same dramatic cloth, for both boys are unable to speak; display characteristics such as virtue, selflessness, and a loving heart; are victimized by male villains; and require—like the traditional melodramatic heroine—the aid of a male deliverer. Julio's character, like Myrtillo's, is repeatedly described in feminine terms: he gestures with "eloquence," his "every look" is "affectionate," and his "heart [runs] over with benevolence." Even though his communication skills are limited to signs and symbols, Julio still demonstrates these womanly qualities. De L'Eppe, the only one who can understand him, gives evidence of this when he tells St. Alme, "[Theodore] calls you friend; he speaks to you in smiles and tears, the language of the heart; his only language."[41] Julio is also indirectly compared to the play's female ingenue, Marianne, the beloved of St. Alme. After Darlemont takes the young Count to Paris and strips him of his social status (the woman is once again brought to a lowly position), he then reduces him to the position of a pauper. Indeed, Holcroft refers to Julio as a "beggar" (or one who has become completely dependent), which is the same word Darlemont uses to describe Marianne. Furious with St. Alme for refusing to marry the wealthy girl who has been selected for him by his father, Darlemont exclaims, "[Y]ou dare to make a mockery of my solicitudes, and audaciously reject power, rank, and fortune, for the interested transactions of a beggar."[42] Once again, the male is conceived as powerful and the female as base. While it is true that Julio is restored to power at the end of the play, justice is made possible only because of the help of Julio's male savior, De L'Eppe.

Deaf and Dumb, also known as *Abbe De L'Eppe or The Dumb Made Eloquent,* was a popular mainstage piece during the very early years of the nineteenth century. Theodore may even have been the very first role played by a breeches actress in New York in the nineteenth century. The *New York Evening Post* lists a Mrs. Hodgekinson as playing Theodore in December of 1801 at the Park Theatre; prior to this date, a young male actor, Master Stockwell, played many of the boy roles at the Park, such as Tom Thumb and Fleance. Mrs. Hodgekinson was favorably reviewed by the *Post,* who acknowledged that, "On the whole, the Abbe de l'Eppe may be pronounced a well-constructed and highly interesting play, and when well appointed in its principal characters, must be eminently successful." The critic continues to praise Hodgekinson, whose exhibition of "the *joyful* emotions of *Theodore"* allowed her to distinguish herself.[43]

A revival of interest in Theodore occurred when Celeste adopted the part in the 1820s and played it along with other dumb boy characters such as Myrtillo, Manuel in *The Dumb Brigand,* and Florio in *The Forest of Bondy.*[44] Although critics decried many of these plays as dramatic literature, the boy characters continued to charm audiences. On November 17, 1827, for example, the *Albion* featured a review of *Deaf and Dumb* and found Celeste's characterization of Theodore—which was described in feminine terms—to be the only redeeming thing about the piece. The somewhat disgruntled critic writes, "That very trumpery piece of business, *Deaf and Dumb,* has been twice performed. We call it *trumpery,* for trumpery it is, in spite of the excellent acting which was thrown away upon it. . . . *Celeste* plays the dumb boy very prettily. . . . The play is manifestly attractive and will continue to be so—inspite of our censure."[45] One year later, another actress was similarly commended by the press for her portrayal of the boy (the title role) in *The Dumb Savoyard.* This play's scenic effects—particularly its diaroma— made it a bit more palatable to the *Albion* critic:

> The most fascinating piece that has been produced for a long period is the *Dumb Savoyard,* and is one of those that will have a long and profitable run if duly fostered by the manager and not

prematurely withdrawn to make room for other novelties. The point of the *Dumb Savoyard* consists in a magnificent moving scene of about 7000 feet of canvas. The Dumb S. was played with uncommon feeling and effect by Mrs. Hilson.[46]

The popular enthusiasm cultivated by these types of breeches parts is significant. While female Hamlets and Norvals drew crowds on isolated annual benefit nights, the boy—especially the dumb boy—was a regular feature on the New York stage. Indeed, feminized youths who had no voice (literally or figuratively) comprised the majority of the breeches boy characters during the first half of the nineteenth century. Perhaps this was because the condition of being dumb seemed to be concomitant with femininity, since women were supposed to be weak, passive, quiet, and serene. Cross-dressed actresses who played these parts simply reemphasized qualities that they were already thought to possess; they simply showcased their own femininity. Just as nineteenth-century leading ladies could not avoid playing roles that perpetuated the Madonna/Whore image of women, neither could the breeches actress escape playing "herself"—inspite of her cross-gendered portrayals.

Another more frequently enacted boy role, Paul in *The Pet of the Petticoats* by J. B. Buckstone, provides a final example of this association between boyish characters and femininity. This play is described as an "opera" because it also contains several songs, yet it much more closely resembles today's musical comedy. The "Pet" was played by many actresses throughout the 1830s and 1840s, and provided an early vehicle for Cushman while she was still working as a "walking lady" at the Park. This play, like *Deaf and Dumb,* is set in France. The curtain opens on a convent, however, instead of an opulent estate, and reveals Job the gardener, investigating the ground around the convent wall for footprints (he suspects that someone has been trying to trespass). As he continues his search, the owner of the prints—Chevalier St. Pierre—makes another attempt to scale the wall and is apprehended by Job. St. Pierre explains that he is simply trying to see his wife, who has been separated from him by friends who felt she was too young to marry, and convinces Job to give her a note. Job delivers the message to Julia St. Pierre, who learns that her husband plans to storm the convent (along with his fellow Dragoon officer, Belair, who also wants to retrieve his wife Emma) in order to rescue her. While Job is talking to Julia, the rest of the girls are engaged in dancing lessons and conversation about their "pet" Paul. All the girls adore this boy who lives among them at the convent. Nicknamed Poll after their beloved but deceased parrot, Paul is constantly showered with gifts and attention by the boarders. He is the nephew of the Mother Superior and has been sent to this institution by his mother to get a "feminine education," because life outside this cloistered community seemed too rough for him.

Much to the girls' dismay, Paul is informed that he must leave the convent immediately for a vacation with his mother. After a tearful goodbye, Paul is escorted by Job to a Parisian tavern, the Golden Lion, where he is to meet his old nurse Jenny who will take him to his mother. Upon reaching the Inn, the boy meets a beautiful opera star, Madame Bravura, who is to debut at the theatre that evening. Paul is smitten by her, as are St. Pierre and Belair who temporarily forget about their wives and compete with one another for the affection of the prima donna. Paul overhears them make a wager about who will win the Madame first and vows to revenge his friends Julia and Emma. He reads two solicitous notes written by the officers (which he has been asked to deliver to Bravura) and answers them back himself, arranging false assignations with both men in remote parts of the city. Paul proceeds to make love to the singer himself in "true military style," a technique he has picked up from the Dragoons, but is discovered by Job and the officers. In order to make amends for his trick, Paul promises to reunite Belair and St. Pierre with their wives that evening. The first he dresses up as Job, who has subsequently become drunk and passed out, and the second he disguises as his nurse Jenny, who arrived at the inn to fetch Paul but was so tired that she immediately retired. The three arrive at the convent, the men are returned to their wives after a series of complications, and Paul, who now feels that he has become a man, renounces his feminine education and joins the Dragoons.[47]

This play is different from the others, in that Buckstone concentrates on the education of Paul and on his transition from feminine boyhood to manhood instead of focusing only on the boy's femininity. Because rites of passage are emphasized over the simple narration of a boy's life, performed gender characteristics emerge more clearly in this play, and nineteenth-century polarities between woman/boy vs. man are fortified. During the first half of the play, Paul's feminine persona is established. To the residents at the convent, Paul is an ornament: he is pampered, idealized, and constantly referred to as the girl's "pet" Poll. It is significant that the pet that Paul replaces is a parrot—a bird who imitates the actions and behavior of its owners (in this case, the young women at the convent). Paul, too, acts like a girl and is so feminine that Job questions his true gender identity. When asked by St. Pierre who Paul is, Job replies, "I don't know what he is—he's not a man, and not exactly a boy; but we call him Poll."[48] Job's description is especially provocative considering the layering of gendered attributes that were present in performance: a woman played a boy, who was not exactly a boy and certainly not a man. Indeed, Paul is instead a pet, an actress/woman-as-boy whose performance of gender is innocuous because it is barely a performance. Job continues to remark upon Paul's femininity, explaining, "His mother sent him here to have him educated in innocence, and brought up as pure and as virtuous as a girl, because his father was a sad rake, and the poor mamma feared that the son might, when he grew up, follow in his papa's footsteps.... And the young fellow has, indeed, been educated in innocence; for I really think he don't know whether he is a boy or a girl."[49] While Job may have been confused about Paul's gender identity, it is likely that the audience was not, since Paul's most salient characteristics were in supposed harmony with the actress's "essential" feminine nature.

Paul's association with the girls at the convent is strengthened both by his preoccupation with his appearance and his desire to parrot the boarder's lifestyle. For example, Paul does not respond positively to the literal petting he receives from the young ladies. His frustration stems both from a lack of sexual attraction to any of the girls (perhaps because he is still a "boy" or because he is really a woman—both variables would produce the same end),[50] and from a "feminine" desire to remain unmussed. "I never know a moment's peace, for they are continually wanting to kiss me, and I'm sick of it; besides, it spoils my hair, and makes me so untidy."[51] Paul goes on to explain that the reason he is so irritable and does not want to be bothered has to do with his lack of sleep. The Mother Superior has forced him to sleep in the old pavilion by himself (since he is male) and, as a result, he is "always frightened." He details the story of his aunt's rage when he confronts her with his request to be allowed to sleep in the girls dormitory, and laments her refusal to comply. Once again, Poll, like his namesake, seeks to imitate the girls' lifestyle. He has none of the qualities respected in a young man (principally courage), and instead is timid, frightened, and seeks the protection of women. When Paul is compelled to leave the convent, he refers to the girls as his sisters and promises he will cry often as a sign of his loneliness. Finally, Paul resembles the feminine boy in his expression of the cardinal virtues of True Womanhood. He is called a "young priest," which suggests that he is pure, pious, and innocent. That Paul's image is representative of these virtues is evidenced by a song he sings to Madame Bravura:

> The pious child who loves to walk
> In Virtue's pleasant ways,
> Will live respected all his life,
> And happy all his days.
>
> But he who noisy is, and bold,
> And heeds not what is said,
> Will ne'er be noticed—ne'er be lov'd—
> Nor pitied when he's dead.

The innocent life that Paul has heretofore led lies in stark contrast to the world of the Golden Lion. Indeed, his life within the feminine sphere of the convent (men are not allowed to enter except to garden and teach dancing) has ill-prepared him for this indecorous world of men. The male environment of the tavern is clearly established as soon as the curtain opens in act 2, for the Dragoons are discovered "drinking, smoking, dicing, and card playing." The lyrics of their song narrate the visual image they present as they sing, "Women, gaming, drinking/Are the soldier's due;/And, to our thinking,/Pleasant wages too."[52] Job, however, is not worried that Paul will become corrupted by the officers who frequent the Golden Lion; rather he is concerned that the youth will be ruined by the opera singer, whom Job refers to as a "devil in Petticoats." Paul is too consumed by his new educational experience to share Job's fear; instead, he reflects on all the things he has learned since he left the convent. He remarks, "The Soldiers . . . say nothing but 'Cannons and fireballs!' 'bombs and mortars!' and 'damn it.'"[53] By the end of the play, Paul has adopted this speech and uses it to confound and scandalize the Mother Superior and the girls who once knew him as their feminine peer. In a defiant act of rebellion against all the convent stands for, Paul ends the play by directly disobeying his aunt. He barks, "Silence; fireballs and furies, will nobody hear me? . . . [F]rom this day, I renounce my feminine education. I am enamored of the army—and if Mimi [his favorite and most loyal friend at the convent] will wait patiently, she shall be the wife of a Captain of the Dragoons; this is, if our Commanders-in-Chief before us [the audience] think that a Pet of the Petticoats has sufficient skill, courage and talent, to head a Company."[54] Paul has matured by the end of the play and directly asks the audience to approve his passage from feminine boyhood into manhood. Of course, this transition could never truly be sanctioned for the actress-as-boy who may have sought transcendence from the shackles of prescriptive womanhood, yet within the liminal space of the theatre, where boys could be girls and vice versa, fictional crossings were sustained.

Women who played boys were often described as "pettish."[55] Even Cushman, who was widely believed to have masculine tendencies, played the ornamental Paul on at least seven occasions during her tenure at the Park Theatre.[56] Regrettably, Cushman was not a major star at this point in her career and was not given a great deal of press, so it is difficult to assess her performance of the Pet. Another Charlotte, Mary Barnes's daughter, Charlotte Barnes, was popular during the mid 1830s, however, and was recognized as a breeches performer by the *Spirit of the Times*. "Miss Charlotte has a line of her own of the most popular characters. . . . We allude of course to her *Little Pickle,* and *Poll the Pet,* and *Pages* without number. The Washington bucks insist upon seeing her in the *Pet of the Petticoats.*" [57] It is interesting that of the roles listed here (Little Pickle, Paul, and the ubiquitous page), it was Paul who was the most popular with a male audience. Perhaps this had to do with the fact that Little Pickle was such a mischievous boy, a prankster, and far less feminine than other boy roles that were standard vehicles for breeches performers. The "Washington bucks" may have wanted to see the actress-as-boy in a role that would showcase her femininity—and her legs. By hinting at the sexual allure of Barnes as the Pet (an observation that rarely surfaced in reviews of cross-dressed boys), the *Spirit* writer reduces the threat imposed by Paul's renunciation of his womanly associations for a manly lifestyle. Critically interpreted as titillating, the actress in breeches only amuses as she absurdly ventures to reject a femininity that she clearly cannot escape; unlike Peter Pan, she *cannot* lose her shadow, for reflections of her womanly figure and exposed leg follow her everywhere, even into the newspapers—which is why boy roles such as Paul were, as the *Spirit* suggested, "the most popular characters" for cross-dressed actresses to undertake, both with critics and with audiences.

Breeches actresses played many other boy roles in addition to Myrtillo, Theodore, and Paul, and were repeatedly described by critics in feminine terms throughout the first half of the nineteenth century. For example, as Zamora in a 1805 production of *The Honey-Moon,* Mrs. Whitlock was called a "pretty smooth faced boy"; as Little Pickle in 1806, the "beauties of [Mrs. Jones's] performance ... were indescribably charming"; and as Aladdin in 1817, Barnes's reportedly expressed great "naivete."[58] In the mid 1820s, the *Mirror* reviewed a series of actresses whose boy roles also reinforced dominant gender ideology. In the afterpiece entitled *The Blind Boy,* Barnes "imparted additional beauty to the beautiful drama"; the critic was so moved by the piece that he declared, "Praise is almost superfluous in speaking of her."[59] Similarly, an actress at the Park, Miss Johnson, was applauded for her ability to portray "beautiful boys," and was especially recognized for her rendition of Colin in *Nature and Philosophy.* The associations between femininity and immaturity in this review are striking: "She is charming in a little piece called *Nature and Philosophy,* and has a class of characters in which she invariably awakens the warmest admiration. Without the energy to sustain the heavier parts of the drama, she has a naivete and if we may be allowed to speak, an infantine grace, which makes her a valuable as well as beautiful ornament of the stage. In the afterpiece her appearance was uncommonly splendid, and she was frequently greeted with well-deserved applause."[60]

Notably, the character of Colin was closer to manhood than he was to boyhood, being almost 18 years of age when the play begins. Although he is old enough to marry (which he does at the end of the play) and proves himself a man before the play begins by conquering wolves and lions in the forest where he lived for 15 years, Colin is perceived by this critic as a boy. Other viewers recognized Colin's manly qualities, however, which calls into question the sincerity of the review of Miss Johnson's performance. In 1832, the *Spirit* correspondent applauded a Miss Vincent for most "valorously" playing the part of Colin. He continued, professing that "ultimately [Colin] did ample honor to the manhood of his assumed sex by the fervency of his assumed kisses and the voluptuous earnestness of his amorous dalliances with the modest 'Eliza.'"[61] Rather than conceptualize the breeches actresses as similarly passionate or courageous like other young men such as Norval, Ion, or even Romeo, the *Mirror* critic chooses instead to emphasize the actress-as-boy's "infantine grace" and beauty; Miss Johnson's Colin was re-membered as ornamental—an image, crafted by the *Mirror* critic, to counter other, possibly threatening, representations by women who wore the breeches.

Critics often coupled remarks about feminine qualities with allusions to childhood, and, in many cases, the actresses who played male roles were actually children. Charles and Fanny Kemble's celebrated production of *King John* at the Park Theatre, for example, featured a "very promising little girl" as Prince Arthur: "[W]e intend a just and high compliment when we say, that in Miss Wheatley's spirited personation of the 'beauteous boy,' our conception of the character was fully realized. She is an exceedingly smart child and with suitable attention to her education may hope to reach an enviable distinction in theatrical fame."[62] However, because adult actresses were often described as "girls," it is sometimes difficult to discern their ages. An article about a benefit performance in Boston, for example, mentions an actress playing both Julian, the "Peasant Boy," and the adult character Bob Nettles from *Parents and Guardians* at Kimball's Museum in 1855. Miss Fanny Brown is described as a "pretty girl," a "pretty young lady," and a "promising little actress," yet there is no indication that she is an "infant prodigy," nor does it seem likely that a child belonging to the troupe would receive a benefit unless she had achieved star status, which she had not.[63] Therefore, is it difficult to tell whether the critic is literally referring to a child actress or whether he is talking about an adult actress in childish terms. Regardless, reductive critical strategies seem to be at work, considering the frequency with which the actress—of any age—was associated with juvenility.

Indeed, if a traditional argument regarding adult actresses playing boys is based upon the fact that there were not very many juvenile male players in the companies, why were boy characters also said to be "fully realized" when played by girl actresses? Girl actresses were equally as scarce in nineteenth-century American acting troupes, which suggests that girls could "fully realize" juvenile male roles not because they were children but because they were female. Furthermore, why were all the child stars in nineteenth-century America—with the exception of two—female? The answer, again, seems to lie in this ubiquitous association between childishness and femininity—a concept perhaps rooted in the theory that connections to immaturity would undermine the subversion of female cross-dressing. Both the actress-as-boy and the girl actress-as-man were popular conventions during the first half of the nineteenth century, and although the variables differed, the end products were similar. Cross-dressed actresses who played boys ultimately could not transcend their sex; their characters—like all fictional boys—lived in a theatrical Never Never Land; they would never grow up, both because the actress could not change her sex (or "evolve" into a man), and because the dramatic boy was trapped within discourse. Likewise, the "pretty little girl" who played Shylock or Richard III was less threatening than the adult woman, for children's actions were seen as unconditionally innocent: as men, they were perceived to be at play rather than at work.[64] Girls did not fight for women's rights, nor did they try to work outside the home, vote, or war against the status quo. Regardless, neither the juvenile or adult actress could ever be a man; they were constricted by their femininity and the childlike powerlessness that confined them to their roles as ornaments or novelties, as "beauteous smooth-faced boys" possessing "infantine grace."

Clara Fisher's career as child star exemplifies this perceived symbiotic association between femininity and immaturity. Fisher was born in England in 1811 to a father who was a theatre aficionado. From an early age, she was acquainted with theatrical personalities and the business of the stage. At the age of five, Fisher debuted at the Drury Lane in David Garrick's *Lilliput,* that was played in conjunction with the fifth act of *Richard III,* which featured her in the title role. Interestingly, the actress recalls that all of the characters in Garrick's piece, with the exception of Gulliver, were young girls.[65] Until Fisher's theatrical star rose, girls played the "Little People," while male infant phenomena, like Master Betty, played more sophisticated characters.[66] Yet, as Laurence Hutton implies, male child stars never seemed to achieve the sustained popularity that female child stars enjoyed. While boys like Betty quickly escaped Londoners' remembrance, actresses like Fisher proved to have more enduring success.[67] Fisher quickly eclipsed the memory of Betty when she won the hearts of English and American audiences in the late teens and early twenties. She reflects, "Since Master Betty's time, which I think, lasted only two or three years (from 1804 to 1806 or 1807), there had been no precocious children upon the stage, the time seemed to be ripe for my appearance, and I had the whole field to myself"[68]—a field that she controlled for many years.

Fisher took American audiences by storm when she arrived in New York in 1827. Still billed as a child star although she was 16, Fisher played a series of roles (most of them adult men) that included Norval, Dr. Pangloss, Dr. Ollapod, Scrub, Sir Peter Teazle, Goldfinch, Crack, the Mock Doctor, Myrtillo, and Moggie McGilpin.[69] While it is true that Fisher was occasionally reprimanded for undertaking specific male roles (especially the profligate Goldfinch), she was generally well received by New York critics, who focused on three primary "attributes" in their reviews: her talent, her youth, and her femininity. While the majority of reports recount Fisher's performances as exhibiting amazing histrionic abilities, some, significantly, found certain vehicles "very puerile."[70] If the piece, itself, was not thought to be childish, often the performance was described in terms that suggested juvenility. Fisher's Norval, for example, was perceived by the critics as a boy. Although Norval had almost always been regarded by critics as too manly for a woman to play (as was the case with Barnes), Fisher's rendition of the young Douglas was praised for its childish tones. "The delivery of Miss Fisher was very felicitous. There is something in the musical flow of the verse of Douglas which suits the lisping modulations of youthful innocence."[71] The *New York Mirror* also fixated upon Fisher's age and called her a "highly gifted girl . . . now bursting into womanhood." While such a description suggests that Fisher was at least thought to have reached adolescence, the critic goes on to reinforce her childish status. After comparing her to a "wonderful dog" and a "learned pig," the *Mirror* critic states, "[U]nlike most precocious prodigies, Miss Fisher's talents grew with her growth . . . and she is now one of the most pleasing versatile, and accomplished little actresses, that it is our good fortune to witness."[72] Although she had matured since her former days as a Lilliputian, she was still regarded as a pleasing "little actress."

Fisher, herself, attributed a great deal of her popularity to her young age. In her autobiography she remarks,

> I have intimated that I attributed much of the extraordinary success I achieved in New York and all the principal cities, when I first appeared, to my extreme youth. I believe I was the first very young person to appear in these light, acceptable plays. Soon afterwards dozens came over, or were brought out on the American stage, but when I, a mere child, played women's parts, or even "breeches parts," as they are termed, every lady in the profession was seemingly old enough to be my mother.[73]

Fisher's reference to her "extreme youth" is curious considering that there were certainly other actresses playing in New York who were not much older than 16 and who were not regarded as infant prodigies.[74] One explanation for this seemingly mistaken conception of Fisher's might have to do with her socialization. It is possible that the actress's perception of herself as a "mere child" was reflective of parental opinions. Fisher describes her father's protective nature and his desire to keep her secluded in a private world when she was not acting. She writes, "He had a great aversion to my being seen or talked to, and would frequently say, 'My child, now that you are on the stage, and so young, keep yourself from public view, except professionally, and let nobody come near you. The less you are seen and known as Miss Clara Fisher, outside of your immediate duties in your respective characters, the better for you.'"[75]

Fisher's earliest lesson concerned learning this distinction between public and private; the aim of this lesson was to make sure she knew which sphere should be her primary home. It is possible that such instruction and imposed confinement within the private arena enhanced a youthful self-image. She acknowledged, for example, that because she was "regarded as a mere child by [her] parents," she was forbidden from acquainting herself with her fellow actors in New York. This insistence on maintaining a private existence is, of course, evocative of femininity as well as immaturity. The press viewed Fisher as a sort of feminine icon, an image that, no doubt, was furthered by her "youthful innocence." As one critic remarked, "Miss F's person is well-formed—her face pretty and very expressive—and, when we add to her other numerous recommendations, that she is a spirited and pleasing singer, we think we may safely say . . . she is one of the most piquant and delightful intellectual treats, that has for some time been set before [us.]"[76]

Within this framework, the girl actress in serious male roles could escape critical vitriol—as Fisher's successful early forays into Shakespearean tragedy prove. Inspired by Fisher, many female child stars literally graced the nineteenth-century American stage, such as Jean Davenport, Louisa Lane (later Mrs. John Drew), Ellen and Kate Bateman, and Susan and Kate Denin.[77] Aside from Payne, who enjoyed a brief period of success before Fisher's arrival, and Master Burke, who was popular in the 1830s, all of the celebrated infant prodigies in America were female. Of the young actresses listed above, almost all of them specialized in tragic adult breeches roles. In 1838, for example, "Little Miss Davenport" won over New York audiences with her Richard III, yet commentaries on her performances were still riddled with references to her youth and her femininity. The critic for the *Spirit* noted that Davenport was favored in adult roles as opposed to children's roles such as Prince Arthur and "Young Norval"[78] because in the guise of the tragic hero she could present an exhibition that would "astonish us by its extraordinary perfection in the person of a child." Davenport's sense of perfection did not spring from her precocious acting abilities alone; the *Spirit* critic exposes her other selling points as he continues, "One thing at least is certain, did we not feel an interest in this blond and florid little English beauty, we should not have noticed her, and least of all given her one word of advice. She can make her fortune before she is eighteen, if managed judiciously, and that she may do so, she has our best wishes—and who knows—unless we get too far 'into the lean and slippered pantaloon'—what an old bachelor may be left to commit, in 'mere oblivion.'"[79] Davenport proved to be both the perfect child and a potentially stimulating woman—two qualities that distanced her considerably from Gloucester and made her/his triumphant reign on the New York boards considerably more palatable.

Legal, physiological, social, and cultural discourse propagated this image of the woman-as-boy or woman-as-child. Whether upon the stage or in the drawing room, a woman's powerlessness was reinforced by this association with immaturity, just as a boy's marginality was foregrounded through his ties with the feminine. This popular conception of the woman as inhabiting a "perpetual state of childhood" helped to defuse another popular nineteenth-century image: the woman who wore the breeches. As Anne Russell suggests, nineteenth-century male "myth-makers"[80] had a vested interest in the construction of the feminine boy image, for by reducing the woman to the status of a child, they could perpetuate not only her infantile state but social gender asymmetry in general. The actress-as-boy and the girl-actress-as-male-adult were sanctioned by the male theatrical hegemony because their performances were seemingly harmless, yet these benign representations did not emerge "naturally." Like Pinochio, the nineteenth-century theatrical "boy" was manufactured and manipulated; the image he projected was the exclusive creation of his puppeteer. Pinochio could speak, dance, sing, and partake in myriad adventures: the "boy" could be at once a male youth and a woman, an impotent man or a fairy. His charm captivated and his diversity was impressive, as long as the puppet master controlled the presentation and no strings were cut.

DISCOURSES OF CONTAINMENT

In his study of cross-dressing, written during the late 1970s, Peter Ackroyd makes it clear that an ideological investment in the innocence (read femininity) of the actress-as-boy transcends nineteenth-century dramatic criticism. All "male impersonators," according to Ackroyd, are engaged in "sentimental" and "harmless" reversals, and are limited by their femininity since their cross-dressing could never fool an audience. Indeed, the breeches actress's disguise was always transparent, he argues; it always revealed "a feminine, noble mind in a boy's body."[81] Ackroyd's conception of the cross-dressed actress is strangely reminiscent of the New York press's summation of actresses such as Barnes, Russell, and Celeste; his assessment of the cross-dressed actress suggests that conceptions constructed in the nineteenth century remain influential. Yet, why was (and is) the actress-as-boy thought to be so unobjectionable (so completely untransgressive in her transvestism), and how were (and are) such images crafted and sustained? Theories of language as symbolic can help to answer these questions and can decode the seemingly harmless sentimental message generated by the juvenile breeches performer.

In the first chapter of her book, *Disorderly Conduct,* Smith-Rosenberg discusses the symbolic and political casts that language takes on; she theorizes about the ways in which discourses are created by powerful male authority figures to oppress, marginalize, or re-encode images of women. It is the feminist historian's job, argues Smith-Rosenberg, to analyze such discourses and to outline the ways in which language is used as a social agent as opposed to a social mirror. S/he must explore "the complex ways language, transposed into myth, distorts reality, so that what is too conflicted to be spoken directly can nevertheless be said."[82] In her own research, Smith-Rosenberg uses the medical community as an example of the way hegemonic institutions try to control marginal groups—specifically women—through language. Smith-Rosenberg argues that language indirectly betrays the speaker's social positioning and his/her relative power. However, those who employ or construct such symbolic languages—the "opinion setters" as she terms them ("male physicians, publishers, educators, and religious leaders")—speak in many different tongues. It is for this reason that Smith-Rosenberg keeps her definitions of language deliberately broad. For her, language can include "grammar and dialect, unconscious symbols and self-conscious metaphors, conceptual systems, folk narratives, and political or sexual discourses." Not limited to words, language can also be found in a host of "nonverbal forms," such as dress codes, consumption habits, religious practices, and expressions of sexuality. According to Smith-Rosenberg, these things "constitute shared systems of signs or symbolic languages rooted in, and expressive of, social relationships and social experiences."[83]

Smith-Rosenberg's model may be appropriated and applied to early- and mid-nineteenth-century dramatic criticism as well. Women who cross-dressed and acted out of their sphere also needed to be contained so as not to disrupt social order. The medical profession contained threatening women (who demanded education, the right to work outside the home, and fertility control) through propaganda about nonreproductive/"unnatural" females, while dramatic critics contained the subversive activity of theatrical woman by constructing images for them—like the boy—that reinforced dominant gender ideology. By expanding one's analysis in this manner (and not simply detailing the events that took place in the theatre on one particular evening), theatre historians may explore the ways in which critical words, categories, and ideologies (e.g., the actress-as-boy) mirror the organization of society as a whole. If questions surrounding the "distribution of power and the nature of social organizations" are placed at the center of one's inquiry, then the historian will have entered into "an analysis of language as political discourse."[84]

"Boyishness" acted as a discourse of containment during the first half of the nineteenth century. This can be seen in the many ways the New York press used this image in relation to the breeches performer. Critics may have distorted the symbolic "language" of the cross-dressed actress by seeing one representation and reading another: the boy appeared before them but the reviews and performance reports re-membered a woman. Peggy Phelan's distinction between "seeing" and "reading" theatrical performances proves helpful here. Phelan argues that seeing is the act of viewing and reacting to visual and conceptual information onstage—a relatively one-dimensional nondiscursive analysis, yet nevertheless, one that is made by many audience members. Reading, on the other hand, involves translating the image into language or constructing a meaning for the nondiscursive (translating into symbols what Phelan refers to [via Lacan] as the pre-Oedipal—or pre-Symbolic—impulse).[85] Feminist theatre historian Elizabeth Drorbaugh, for example, uses Phelan's theory to explain the consistent reading of the contemporary cross-dressed performer as homosexual. There is nothing about the image that says that the performer is gay, yet the viewer perhaps expects or anticipates this association and produces an opinion based not on what s/he *sees* but on a societally influenced *reading*.[86] Likewise, the actions of the nineteenth-century dramatic critic may be similarly assessed. The woman in male attire, even within the theatre, evoked for the "seer" social taboos that were cloaked by the "reading." By reading the actress-as-boy as a woman, critics could draw upon a common nineteenth-century association, reinforce femininity, and move the performer away from threatening alternatives. If the actress-as-boy was perceived as a woman, s/he was no longer seen as a young *man*, a male child who would undoubtedly grow into privilege and power. Moreover, ubiquitous associations between the breeches performer and feminine youthfulness might counter or perhaps dispel anxiety generated by the players of serious/tragic male roles, and in some way redeem the convention as a whole. Yet, while it is true that cross-dressed boys presented less of a cultural menace than their tragic fathers, they still posed some danger. Indeed, some nineteenth-century dramatic boys, such as Colin, Romeo, and Ion, were interpreted by certain critics (and by certain actresses) as young men, which potentially cultivated fears about female usurpation. When read as a woman, however, the actress-as-boy would, like Peter Pan, never grow up nor ever leave the marginal and "private" space s/he inhabited.

Perhaps the most persistent attempt to "read" the actress-as-boy as a woman can be seen in the critical tributes bestowed upon Ellen Tree during her first tour of America in 1836–1838. Tree arrived in New York in December of 1836 and immediately began a long engagement at the Park Theatre. During her residency at the Park, she played a number of popular leading women's parts before she starred in the title role of T. N. Talfourd's play, *Ion: or The Foundling of Argos* on February 2, 1837.[87] This role was a standard component of Tree's personal repertoire and one she had often performed in London before crossing the Atlantic. Eagerly anticipating Tree's New York debut, the *New York Mirror* reprinted an article that had previously been published in the *London Times*, and which foreshadowed future American criticism. Before ever witnessing Tree's histrionic powers, New York audiences knew of the "beauty and excellency of her acting" as well as her "charming" mien. The *Mirror* critic touted Tree as an icon of womanhood: she was beautiful, affectionate, delicate, and "eminently feminine." He writes:

> She has a woman's energy, and woman's passion, and woman's tenderness, and woman's weakness. She cannot unsex herself. In Ion, for instance, she is not a whit masculine. She becomes not Ion, but Ion becomes Ellen Tree—most beautifully and eloquently delivering Sergeant Talford's [sic] beautiful and eloquent reveries. Yet she has nothing cold or methodical, or, least of all, lack-a-daisical about her. Energy—nay, fierceness, if need be—she can develop most decidedly. Passion can flash and lighten from her deep dark eye, and scorn distend her exquisitely-chiselled nostrils, and contempt curl her very beautiful lip; but still all is emphatically feminine. She is evidently of the stuff of which the maids, wives, and mothers who daily surround us, are fashioned.[88]

Notably, this article reappears in the *Mirror* for no other reason than to celebrate Tree's femininity. The London writer discusses no other roles by Tree, nor does he give a detailed history of her career; rather he simply outlines her womanly features and makes it very clear that despite her reputation as a breeches performer, she "cannot unsex herself." Even her ability to enact masculine traits is continually countered by references to her femininity. Tree's performance as Ion is not void of energy, passion, or scorn, yet these "manly" expressions obviously light across the face of a beautiful woman. While her motivation might have been to play the righteous indignation of a heroic prince, her "masculine" efforts could not upstage the captivating feminine presence that held center, complete with "deep dark eye," "well-chiselled nostrils," and a "very beautiful lip."

Unlike Tree's supposed rendition, however, Talfourd's Ion was a brave and masculine young man. Although he is described in the text as both boy and man, he is always presented as strong and heroic. Ion is similar to many boy heroes in nineteenth-century drama in that he is a foundling. Early passages in the play reveal characteristics typical of the orphan: he is described as innocent and gentle, "our sometimes darling," mild in nature, and a "rare infant."[89] Yet while he might have possessed feminine qualities in his early boyhood, Ion has gone through a change *before* the action of the play begins. Agenor and Cleon—two Argonian sages—note his metamorphosis:

> His form appears dilated; in these eyes,
> Where pleasure danced, a thoughtful sadness dwells;
> Stern purpose knits the forehead, which till now
> Knew not the passing wrinkle of a care:
> Those limbs which in their heedless motion own'd
> A stripling's playful happiness, are strung
> As if the iron hardships of the camp
> Had given them sturdy nurture; and his step,
> Its airiness of yesterday forgotten,
> Awakes the echoes of these desolate courts,
> As if a warrior of heroic mould
> Paced them in armour.[90]

The report of this change is timely, for shortly after the sages' conversation, Ion reveals his newly awakened manliness in volunteering for a dangerous mission—a rite of passage—that betrays courage, leadership, and a sturdy nature.

Argos suffers from a plague that threatens to destroy the entire city. The local priests/sages of Apollo blame the king, Adrastus, for the pestilence because he ignores their advice, occupies his time with wild debacles, and refuses to make necessary sacrifices to the gods. Although the king shuns the sages' admonitions, he does send a messenger, Phocion, to the Oracle at Delphi to learn Apollo's prophesy concerning the plague. After weeks of waiting for Phocion to return, the sages under the command of Medon, the High Priest of the Temple of Apollo at Argos and Phocion's father, decide that more immediate measures must be taken. Medon asks for a volunteer to go to the king, beg the monarch to renounce his life of revelry, and persuade him to meet with Apollo's priests. Such a job is dangerous, however, and such ambassadors scarce because the king thinks that there is a plot against him and that everyone who tries to council him is a traitor. Even though the last man who was sent to the king was instantly killed, Ion bravely requests this post. Rather than fear the king, Ion boldly addresses him and charges him to repent and to listen to the gods. As they converse, the youth quickly endears himself to the king (who admires Ion's courage) by appealing to his emotions; Ion asks Adrastus to remember his childhood and his first love—memories that serve to soften his "marble" heart. During the course of their conversation, in which the king speaks of his deceased beloved wife, Adrastus realizes that Ion (who strongly resembles this woman) is his long lost son; the king relays this news to Ion and dies shortly afterward. After a series of events, Ion becomes king himself, yet before being crowned, the young warrior learns from the returned Phocion that according to Apollo, *all* of the King's line must die in order to rid the city of the plague. Rather than flee, Ion quickly proceeds with his coronation and as soon as he is instituted as king and is publicly acknowledged to be the son of Adrastus and rightful heir to the thrown, he takes his own life.

Under Talfourd's pen, Ion appears to be a fearless tragic hero and an honorable strong man—qualities that were thought unnatural in a woman. Considering the possible subversion involved in similarly—critically—crowning the breeches actress, the New York press devised a way to praise Tree's inspired performance while simultaneously undermining Ion's masculine nature. It is possible that Tree, who was very popular in this role, might have been seen by some as representing Talfourd's true Ion (the honorable man and noble king), yet critics read her portrayal differently. For them, all textual references to Ion as a "man" and a "brave monarch" were forgotten;[91] Tree emerged as a feminine boy, a fairy, a "stripling youth." The *Albion* reporter, who admittedly gave Tree's performance more critical attention than other current theatricals, called Tree a "new and brilliant star." She is an actress, he asserts, "whose fame having for some time reached this western world from a distance, is now to establish itself through the direct judgement of an American audience." This comment suggests that the *Albion* reporter read articles about Tree that were printed prior to her arrival in New York (such as the one reprinted by the *Mirror*) and may have been familiar with previous critical celebrations of her femininity and reports of her inability to unsex herself. Certainly his first description of her echoes the *London Times's* sketch: "In Miss Tree . . . we see more of the woman than of the actress; and while her quiet propriety imparts its charms, that charm is sweetly but greatly heightened by the music of her tones and the exquisite purity of her pronunciation."[92]

Tree was indeed regarded as a feminine icon, as opposed to an actress who could transform herself into other—especially manly—characters. Like Ackroyd's description of the female theatrical transvestite, Tree was exactly "what she seemed to be"—a woman. According to the critics, many of the qualities of True Womanhood were apparent in Tree's performance. The *Albion* writer noted her "warmth of feeling" and "her earnestness of purpose" as the Prince. All masculine tendencies are explained away by this critic, who is quick to counter manly displays with feminine feeling. He allows, "Never but once is Ion supposed to lose temper, and that is when a succession of messengers enter, to interrupt his desire of soothing the heart of Clemanthe [Medon's daughter and Ion's beloved], and the beautiful manner of atoning for that solitary hastiness is touching to the highest degree. . . . We feel fully warranted in saying that the acting of Miss Tree was [as] perfect as human powers could make it; it was a treat of the very highest order."[93] In addition to the review, the *Albion* commissioned an engraving of Tree as Ion that showcased her femininity with an illustration of small feet, luxuriant black curls, long graceful neck, and ornamental tunic (see figure 3.2).

The *Albion* reviewer was not the only critic to place Tree on a pedestal. The *Mirror* reviewer also reinforced this image of Tree as feminine, yet curiously refrained from reporting on her performance of Ion. Because Tree's tour had been so heavily publicized before her arrival in America and because her Ion was so popular on both sides of the Atlantic, the *Mirror's* decision to ignore her debut as the Argonian foundling is telling. Perhaps the critic could not reconcile a woman in this tragic male role and refrained from trying to make allowances for Tree's undertaking, or perhaps the critic did not want to risk popular disdain by criticizing an actress who had become such a public favorite. Regardless of the reasons why, the *Mirror* critic's failure to mention Tree's Ion did not stop him from contributing to Tree's feminization. He recommended the versatility of her acting power in general and marveled at her attractiveness. "Her peculiarly ladylike appearance, and the excellence of disposition that seems to beam from her countenance, make Miss Tree [one] of the most attractive persons we remember upon the stage, and it is surprising what effects the last of these gifts has upon the favour of the publick."[94] By ignoring Tree's performances of Ion (she had played the role at least twice since February and would repeat it two more times that spring), the *Mirror* critic possibly tried to erase the public's memory of a woman in such a manly role, or at least tried to restructure that memory by fortifying the image of Tree as an uncommonly feminine woman. Indeed, the *Mirror's* only other mention of the actress occurred in July of 1838, when the paper published a poem that had been penned for Tree in Washington by John Quincy Adams. Reported to be "one of her most distinguished admirers," Adams wrote,

> 'Tis Nature's witchery attracts the smile;
> 'Tis her *soft sorrows* that our tears beguile;

Fig. 3.2: Ellen Tree as Ion. University of Illinois, Theatrical Print Collection.

> Nature to thee her fairest gift imparts:
> She bids thee fascinate, to win all hearts—
> The wife, the queen, the wayward child we see,
> And fair perfection, all abide with thee.[95]

Adams's poem reflects several essential notions about womanhood. Tree, the woman, is Nature personified (which reifies the man/mind vs. woman/nature polarity); she is emotional, soft, beguiling, fascinating, and can embody all images of virtuous femininity. As wife, queen, and child, Tree's ornamental status within the male American mind is confirmed and her feminine perfection established by one of patriarchy's highest representatives.

While the *Mirror* ultimately made its point concerning Tree's femininity, the *Spirit of the Times* critic was more direct in confronting her rendition of Ion. Rather than avoiding mention of her performance, this paper gave a lengthy account of the actress's efforts as Talfourd's hero. Interestingly, however, the *Spirit's* review of Tree's Ion was preceded by another dramatic review, describing her performance in a disguise role. On February 4, 1837, a brief notice appears in the *Spirit* concerning Tree's Rosalind and her Viola. The critic writes, "Would that Miss Tree selected still oftener Rosalind and Viola—the most delightful characters in her line, and to our stage the most novel. In these we believe her to be perfectly unsurpassed."[96] Significantly, this notice predates the *Spirit's* discussion of her Ion (which appeared on February 11) by one week, regardless of the fact that Tree played Ion on February 2 (which would have given the reviewer plenty of time to submit an article for the February 4 issue). Although other New York papers featured articles about Tree's Ion in the February 4 issue, the *Spirit* chose to postpone their notice regarding her breeches work and to write instead about Tree's disguise roles. It is not surprising that a critical assessment of Tree as a tragic male hero is prefaced by a favorable report of the actress as Rosalind and Viola. While it is true that both characters don male apparel for a portion of the dramas in which they appear, they eventually abandon their masculine disguises and return to their "original" feminine identities (and duties). The critic's remark that Tree is unsurpassed in these roles implies that the actress's area of theatrical expertise lies ultimately with characters who privilege the feminine over the masculine—a suggestion that both undermines the threat of her decision to play Ion and anticipates the critique of her Ion as a feminine boy.

Rather than confront the incongruous coupling produced by this extraordinarily feminine actress attempting a character who was—according to the text—both a young masculine warrior and a noble prince and king, the *Spirit* reporter, like the critics from the *Albion* and the *Mirror,* proved equally evasive. This critic could not address Tree as a tragic male hero and therefore created another character for her to play instead, a character that poorly resembled Talfourd's aggressive foundling. Talfourd's Ion was transformed, in the imagination of the *Spirit* correspondent, from a young courageous man into an ethereal fairy, a morally superior, dainty sprite. Ion no longer appeared as the stoic youth that Agenor and Cleon described, the courageous prince who was not afraid to face death at the Palace of Argos or to sacrifice himself in order to save his city from devastation. Rather he becomes a character who "is purely the creation of the imagination, having no prototype in humanity, yet the natural product of a superstition, refined and ennobling, that seeks for the ideal of moral perfections in a sphere elevated above the walk of the perfect of mortals." The reviewer concludes that only a woman could play such an untainted goddess: "Who of earthly mould may venture to impersonate a being wrapt in the consciousness of his inspiration by the 'elder gods'? ELLEN TREE."[97]

Continuing in the same vein, the critic tries to read against the literal text by insisting that Ion is not a brave young man but a "fanciful creation," an "ethereal essence as subtle as thought and as evanescent." Tree could never be a man, implies the critic, but she might make a wonderful fairy. Additionally, this capricious and somewhat inconsequential (certainly erroneous) image of Ion is critically enhanced by the repeated references to his youth. The *Spirit* reporter suggests,

> We should look on Miss Tree's enactment with a free fancy—giving loose to all that is creative in our imagination, feeling, as did the poet who engendered the creation we are listening to, that the fair being whose melodious tones are thrilling us with an agony of delight, is not of this nether world, earthly, but some disconsolate Peri, who for the nonce palpably reveals to our baser senses that "stripling boy" whose frame and soul is suddenly instinct with a

high conviction that the gods are about to make him at once of the avenger of his country and the victim of their offended majesty.... With some feeling did we listen to Miss Tree's Ion and to us the impersonation was complete—perfect. To us it was no objection that she was acting the part of a male—like a worshipper of the Grand Lama, who recognizes his God in a child, we could see the visible divinity though emanating from the lineaments of a woman.... Ion was but a stripling—a youth not suddenly *corporeally* magnified into the proportions of herculean strength, but mentally and miraculously endowed with all the feelings and attributes of a hero, made vivid to his own mind by his education and ready faith in the superstitions of this country.... A thousand times easier is it for us to realize the tender, pure, but souled youth in the faultless gracefulness and feminine figure of Miss Tree, than it would be in the gigantic proportions of Forrest or yet in the wiry outline of the elder Kean.[98]

Tree's threat in undertaking a tragic male hero was contained by the New York press, who constructed a discourse of femininity and boyishness around the actress's performance and "read" her Ion as a woman. By arguing that Ion was a morally superior "Peri" who could only be played by a female, the *Spirit* critic reinforces the nineteenth-century association between women and immaturity, and creates a familiar image of feminine weakness and beauty to counter threatening images of female strength, independence, and courage.

In addition to using the image of the actress-as-boy to enhance connections between femininity and juvenility, New York critics also employed this "symbolic language" to contain or control breeches performers in other ways. The male theatrical hegemony also reinforced dominant gender ideology and reduced women to nonoffensive positions by expanding their "readings" of the actress-as-boy to include passionlessness, impotence, and marginality in addition to continuing to interpret her as youthful and feminine. Critics drew once again on broader social associations between women and boys in their attempts to recast young dramatic heroes as Victorian women.

A good example of this critical tactic can be seen in midcentury responses to cross-dressed Romeos—specifically Cushman's. Regardless of Romeo's talent with a sword, his fierce expressions of anger, his aggressive desire to avenge Mercutio's death, and his substantial displays of courage, some nineteenth-century critics interpreted his character as more feminine than masculine and more youthful than manly. In the preface to Cushman's 1850s promptbook of *Romeo and Juliet*, the editor delights in Romeo's effete and boyish qualities; he remarks, "How admirably is the boyishly-passionate and impatient character of Romeo, with his 'womanish tears' and his 'unreasonable fury,' preserved in his dying exclamations!"[99] A discussion follows in which Romeo is compared to Hamlet (another character that was sometimes interpreted as being both feminine and youthful).[100] The editor, however, vehemently disagrees with past critics who try to draw parallels between the two. He especially objects to William Hazlett's theory that "Romeo is Hamlet in love." According to the editor, Romeo is instead "a froward, unreflecting boy. His whole demeanor conveys the idea of one who has been the curled darling of his parents, and a spoiled child. Hamlet is a meditative, philosophizing man of thirty. The two characters have few traits in common. Hamlet himself declares, that he is 'not splenetic or rash'; but these are, of all epithets, the most applicable to the impetuous son of Montague."[101]

Romeo was not only seen by some critics as an impulsive and "spoiled child" (an interesting description considering the popularity of the breeches role Little Pickle—another famous "spoiled child"), but also as a hysterical womanly man. Reporting on Charles Kean's Romeo in New York in 1830, the *Mirror* critic notes the difference between the young Montague and other Shakespearean heroes such as Othello, Richard III, and Shylock. Romeo—even when played by Kean—is significantly less masculine; his feelings, while serious and immediate, are not "manly and spirited." Neither are his emotions "of the philosophic description which runs through Hamlet," rather they are "of a morbid cast, which, without becoming sentimental, gnaws and corrodes the mind, and initially drives it to despair."[102] The *Mirror* commentator implies here that Romeo's mental instability incapacitates him and ultimately leads to his death. Such a conjecture possibly suggests another reason why women were successful as Romeo during the nineteenth century. Given popular notions surrounding women and hysteria, it is not surprising that Romeo's character was believed by some critics to be closer to a woman's than a man's in this respect. As is demonstrated in the Friar's cell in act 3, scene 3, Romeo is driven to the brink of madness by emotional stress or by a passion that has gone out of control. Because women were thought to experience similar symptoms in the nineteenth century, it follows that a woman might have been viewed by certain critics and managers as being better equipped to interpret and express Romeo's emotional range. Moreover, as Smith-Rosenberg points out, hysteria was closely associated with failed femininity, with "[e]motional indulgence, moral weakness, and lack of willpower."[103] Romeo's failed masculinity—his inability to, as the Nurse says, "stand up and be a man" [3.3.96]—corresponds to similar feminine gender crimes; interestingly both end in hysteria, a medical umbrella term that signified sex role transgression and social inversion.

In addition to being regarded as possessing feminine characteristics, Romeo was also read as a boy by certain nineteenth-century critics. As Romeo (a role she played most frequently during the 1840s), Cushman appeared to certain Victorian spectators not as a man but as an "impetuous youth." Noah Ludlow remarked that Romeo "requires a boy" for "no man that was not born an idiot would feel or whine his love out in such a lackadaisical way."[104] Laurence Hutton supports this sentiment, as his memory of Cushman's performance demonstrates: he states, "The constitutional susceptibility of Romeo's character was depicted by her in its boldest relief—a particular phase of the nature of the young Montague, which no male actor, unless he were a mere youth, could efficiently and satisfactorily portray."[105] Similarly, after witnessing Cushman's triumphant run as Romeo at the Haymarket Theatre in London, the *Athenaeum* critic added that "what there was of the woman just served to indicate juvenility, and no more."[106]

As a "boy," Cushman was considerably less threatening to male audiences. Women as men were "perverse," "monstrous anomalies," but as boys they remained marginal and therefore innocuous; as an adolescent, Romeo/Cushman occupied a position that reflected his/her inferiority to men both socially and sexually. While nineteenth-century boys may not have been physically impotent, they were perceived as socially impotent because of their peripheral status within the domestic sphere. Boys were not regarded as sexual creatures but as moral icons, as feminine. Indeed, once a boy did reach adolescence he was urged by preachers and parents to refrain from premarital sexual relations, early marriage, and/or masturbation—admonitions that served to fortify a sense of impotence. The actress-as-boy contributed to such images of adolescent impotence. In her study of the cross-dressed actress, Straub argues that cross-dressed "[w]omen assuming masculine sexual prerogative are 'insipid,' and their love-making 'conveys no ideas at all'; they are in short, failed men, and, as such, would seem to offer no threat whatsoever to masculine sexuality."[107] By coupling Cushman with this marginalized image of the boy or the "failed man," certain nineteenth-century critics constructed a discourse that contained the breeches actress by implying that as a woman she could never be a real man, only an ineffective substitute.

The concept of impotence furthered the success of Cushman's cross-dressed Romeo, however, by abating fears of sexual transgression. Because Romeo was such a passionate lover, Victorian moral codes may easily have been upset. Yet, women, like boys (or like women-as-boys), were represented as sexless, "impotent," or as Nancy Cott argues, passionless. This prevalent belief that middle-class white women were devoid of sexual desire was also absorbed by the press to contain anxieties concerning gender transgression and the cross-dressed actress (as boy). Regarding Cushman's 1845–46 London performance of Romeo, for example, the *Britannia* critic writes that "it seems that females may together give us an image of the desire of the lovers of Verona, without suggesting a thought to vice.... [T]o give an adequate embodiment of the true feelings of this play, would certainly outrage the sense of a modern audience, were the performers of opposite sex."[108] Furthermore, Coleman declared that Cushman's "amorous endearments were of so erotic a character that no man would have dared to indulge in them *coram publico.*" [109] As Merrill aptly points out, "in many ways, being a female Romeo was an asset.... Since nineteenth-century 'respectable' women were generally believed to be sexually chaste, the love performed by two women, however ardent, was seen by most as innocent."[110] In addition, it is important to note that this theory of Victorian passionlessness (whether it operated in England or America) explains an ideology that was both self-conscious and political, a doctrine that should be placed "in the vanguard of feminist thought." Cott remarks that the "serviceability of passionlessness to women in gaining social and familial power should be acknowledged as a primary reason that the ideology was quickly and widely accepted."[111] Therefore, in addition to passionlessness being a recuperative measure administered to contain the threat of women assuming male roles, it should also be regarded as an ideology that afforded women certain displays of power and freedom that normally would have been forbidden to her.

While members of the male theatrical hegemony attempted to mitigate anxieties engendered by the breeches performer through manipulating the image of the young male hero (by presenting him as boyish, feminine, impotent, socially nonessential, and passionless), others used the image of the boy to control women (and social patterns in general) in other ways. In his book *Melodramatic Formations,* Bruce McConachie argues that paternalistic elite males exercised social influence by controlling the theatre between 1820 and 1835. By patronizing and producing melodramatic productions that contained malleable (feminine) boy characters, these men encouraged a hierarchical system that ensured their own dominant position. According to McConachie, patricians frequented, owned, and managed the theatres, and used the theatre buildings for their own social performances to display their benevolence and wealth; they sat in the boxes, indirectly controlled benefits and repertoire selection, and used the corridors and private rooms to negotiate business deals. Plays presented at patrician-controlled theatres were designed to hold a particular mirror up to nature, and, as McConachie explains, the fairy-tale melodrama of the 1820s and early 1830s offered such a tailored reflection through stories that assuaged paternalistic fears concerning loss of power "over their children, their cities, their nation."[112]

An analysis of *The Wandering Boys,* the fairy-tale melodrama that McConachie uses to prove his theory, reveals further patrician anxieties. McConachie does not focus on gender in his interpretation of the text and context surrounding Mordecai Noah's play; thus, it is important to add that patrician men also worried about losing control over their wives, mothers, and daughters. Since, as Smith-Rosenberg argues, hegemonic prescriptions tend to intensify during times of social upheaval, the paradigmatic shift from paternalism to mercantile capitalism is informative in that it exposes female oppression as well as patrician anxieties, and both are evident in the fairy-tale melodrama. McConachie argues that patrician males felt threatened by the rise of mercantile capitalism. These men were committed "ideologically to hierarchical social and political relations," and worried that the mobilization resulting from emerging capitalist operations would disrupt their authority. They found solace in plays such as *The Wandering Boys* that were structured by a "hierarchy of affection and control," plays that favorably represented a strong male figure presiding generously over powerless dependents. McConachie neglects to mention, however, that the individuals being controlled, in this case the two boys Paul and Justin, were always played by women. Moreover, the part of Justin was specifically written for a woman, as a letter from Noah to William Dunlap reveals.[113] Paul and Justin resemble other melodramatic boys—Myrtillo, Paul, and Julian—in that they betray feminine qualities and are dependent on the protection and benevolence of a male hero.

The dramatic formula apparent in *The Wandering Boys* is familiar. The play is set in a remote town in France and although there is no date given, it is evident that a feudal system governs the inhabitants of the hamlet Olival. A king, who is discussed but never seen, rules over France; under his direct control is a villainous Baroness who, along with her nefarious assistant Roland, reigns over Olival and the surrounding area. Through a series of depraved events, this pair usurped the former beloved ruler, the Count de Croissy—who is believed to be dead at the onset of the play's action. As the curtain rises, the peasants gather for a wedding, but before the ceremony begins the senior villager, Hubert, customarily reads an order, made years before by the Count, which states that any orphans who appear in Olival during a festival (such as a wedding day) must be provided for by the community. The Baroness also has an interest in abandoned children, for under her decree, any strange boy that enters the village must be taken to the castle to be scrutinized by her and by Roland. Unbeknownst to the villagers, this process is undertaken so that the Baroness can ensure that the two, supposedly deceased, sons of the Count do not come to Olival and try to regain their rightful place. Although they were reportedly killed along with their mother years ago in a castle fire (set by the Baroness), she continues to worry about their unlikely return. The boys, Paul and Justin (who are unaware of their true identity as the Count's heirs), do indeed return and are adopted by the residents of the village. Shortly after they are embraced by the peasants, the boys are called to the Castle where the Baroness and Roland identify them (through the discovery of a box containing letters that establish their royal claim) and subsequently try to poison them. Meanwhile, the Count, who escaped from a pirate den after being accosted while voyaging to Sicily, returns to the Castle in the disguise of a deaf porter in hopes of eventually regaining his power. After overhearing Roland and the Baroness (his niece) discuss the true lineage of the wandering boys, the Count vows to rescue his sons. He succeeds first by saving them from the poisonous wine that is offered to them and then by ushering them safely back to the village. Roland hears of their escape but is thwarted in his attempt to apprehend them, for on his arrival he meets the king's army who have come to intervene on behalf of the Count. Roland and the Baroness are placed in the dungeon and the Count and his sons enjoy a blissful reunion.[114]

Patrician audiences favored melodramas such as *The Wandering Boys* because, as McConachie points out, such plays were "imbued with the ideology of traditional paternalism."[115] Because the king never appears, the Count enjoys the supreme position in a hierarchical system—despite his displacement by the Baroness—by ultimately controlling and resolving the situation. Even when he is not present, the Count's influence is apparent through old customs that still remain a central part of village celebrations. The Count rescues the boys, triumphs over the usurpers (with the help of the ultimate patriarch, the king), and maneuvers his way back into power. The tableau in act 5 functions as a *Gestus*, reinforcing this patrician privilege. As McConachie explains, "By the play's end, the reunited family poses with happy peasants and villagers for the final tableau, an organic hierarchy of loving relationships centered on paternal affection."[116]

Yet while fairy tales have potentially emancipatory themes, McConachie points out that the victims who escape oppression ultimately champion patrician ideology, as liberating messages from the folktale tradition become apologies for "patriarchal conservatism."[117] Although they dominate the action of the play, Paul and Justin are not the heroes; rather the victor is the Count—the all-powerful father. This father/child relationship, which, McConachie argues, was so important to antebellum elite males, was perhaps best represented theatrically by breeches actresses like Fisher and Barnes—who were both popular as Paul in the 1820s. McConachie discusses Fisher's contribution to paternalism, stating:

> Clara Fisher helped her male admirers to fantasize a father-child relationship that was pleasing and necessary for them. It was as a child, after all, that Clara Fisher first won applause, and she continued in childlike roles long after reaching maturity. Significantly, her popularity plummeted after she married in 1834. . . . Above all, commentators on her acting singled out her vulnerability on the stage, a characteristic that elite fathers in need of bestowing paternal protection and affection must have cherished. In short, the accepted definition of Clara Fisher as virtuous, vulnerable, and obedient allowed the fathers in her audience to define themselves as moral, benevolent, and commanding.[118]

What McConachie does not make clear, however, is that Fisher could facilitate this aggrandizement of patrician privilege only because she was a woman. Male elite security was not simply cultivated by watching melodramatic fathers dominate boys. The image of the boy was indeed manipulated by an upper-class male hegemony to reinforce paternal ideals, but significantly the boy was always a woman—a reality that exposes the construction of such discourses of containment. Like Myrtillo, Paul, and Julian, the orphan pair in Noah's drama continually display feminine characteristics; indeed, even McConachie refers to them as "heroines."[119] The boys, described as "pretty lads," are honest, charming, and powerless to effect their own fate; the only difference between the brothers is that Justin tends to be more anxious and tearful than Paul, who is comparatively blithe. Here again, however, two images of women emerge to offset the evil Baroness: the insecure and weak dependent and the charming engaging companion.

As these stereotypes suggest, gender demarcations in this melodrama are clearly outlined. There are only three women in this play (not including Paul and Justin): one is a simple country virgin, the second is an evil Baroness, and the third is a foolish old maid (a female grotesque) who is ridiculed by fellow villagers. While no truly noble women dwell in Olival—except for the marginalized and cross-dressed Paul and Justin—valiant men dot the rural French countryside. Roland is the only unsympathetic male character in the play, which is interesting considering that he is also the only servant of a powerful—but usurping—woman. In contrast to Roland is the kind, loyal, and hardworking Hubert; the dependable servant Gregoire (who remains faithful to the Count regardless of the Baroness's takeover); and the benevolent and mighty Count himself. Men are described as the "Lords of Creation," and misogynistic comments about women (made most often by Hubert) appear comic rather than pejorative. Significantly, the two cross-dressed characters in the play acknowledge the artifice of such rigidly prescribed gender stereotypes. In act 2, the boys talk of Roland as a "great lady's man" (meaning that he is the Baroness's steward, not that he is an adventurer) and Paul remarks, "Lord, 'tis mighty easy to be a great man—'tis only to stamp your foot, be pompous, and pretend to more consequence than you have a right to.'"[120] Such a statement, which foregrounds the performative nature of gender itself, demonstrates that anyone can be a "great man."

Subversive messages like this one—delivered by the woman in breeches to the patrician patron—suggest the need for the above varieties of containing discourse. Even though melodramatic male heroes were often boys, they still had the power to transgress beyond proper gender boundaries: regardless of the character's age, when a woman "put on the breeches" the potential for offense existed. This is why critics and playwrights needed to remind patrons repeatedly of the boyish/feminine status of the images that played before them. By constantly reiterating the ubiquitous nineteenth-century association between femininity and immaturity (and all that came with both: passionlessness, social impotence, and marginality), male critics secured a sure pathway for the male patron, free from the specter of the Baroness of Olival. Rooted in the knowledge that men were men and boys were "girls," the theatrical male hegemony could enthusiastically applaud the efforts of Barnes and Fisher, while Paul, Justin, and Myrtillo could confidently continue to control the hearts—if nothing else—of antebellum audience members.

BEYOND DISCOURSES OF CONTAINMENT

Yet, other possibilities may have existed for the actress-as-boy. Cross-dressed actresses in boy's breeches were not necessarily always marginalized figures, nor were they exclusively read as constructed recuperative images. Rather the actress-as-boy could also have been interpreted as "a transvestite," as an emancipatory changeling boy. Not simply the physical manifestation of an artificial discourse of containment, the boy breeches performer may have participated in a symbolic language of his/her own by signifying either a "category crisis," as Garber argues, or a space of possibility, an alternative sphere where unorthodox gender configurations expanded prescriptive nineteenth-century sex role definitions.

In *Vested Interests,* Garber grapples with the complexities of the Peter Pan Syndrome in her attempt to discover why Peter Pan is (almost) always a woman. A brief history of J. M. Barrie's play, originally composed in 1904, reveals a long line of female Peters. Garber points out that Peter had been female from the first, and it was not until 1982 that a major professional English company, the Royal Shakespeare Company, introduced a male Peter (not counting the Disney movie). This "drag" rendition of *Peter Pan* was interestingly perceived as a tragedy. By showcasing a male lead, the play was elevated "'from the ghetto of children's theatre into a national masterpiece,' as well as restoring the author's putative intention. In other words, the presence of a female lead in the title role relegated the play to the marginal backwaters of kid's stuff, and, at the same time, to the carefree playing fields of comedy."[121] This assessment of *Peter Pan* recalls the critical feminization that Talfourd's *Ion* experienced once Tree appeared in the role; the presence of a woman reverses the tragic tone and literally renders all activities onstage child's play. Like his nineteenth-century melodramatic comrades, Peter Pan never grew up because he was a boy *and* because he was a woman. What might have appeared as an incongruous inversion (the woman who becomes male) is embraced, suggests Garber, as the masculine character is read as a feminine boy. She argues, "Rather than detecting 'masculinity' behind the woman, the audience of *Peter Pan* detects 'femininity' behind the boy. This discontinuity, oddly, produces not consternation but reassurance. Love for—or cathexis onto—a 'boy' turns out to be love for or cathexis onto a woman, after all."[122] Once again this association between femininity and immaturity contributes to the popularity of the female Peter.

Yet Garber also offers a more complex answer to her question of why Peter is a woman. She concludes that the role must be played by an actress because the character is ultimately a "transvestite." As Garber explains, the appearance of the transvestite in cultural representation indicates a "category crisis" (or cloaked tensions between two conflicting polarities) and such category crises are evident throughout *Peter Pan*.[123] Garber's theory proves illuminating if appropriated for nineteenth-century cross-dressing studies as well, for the transvestite in the form of the actress-as-boy also reveals specific examples of category crises. As McConachie's discussion of *The Wandering Boys* suggests, Paul and Justin are also good candidates for the transvestite role. Their appearance in the text-as-performed seems to have exposed tensions between the patrician elite (represented by the Count) and the mercantile capitalist (represented by forces that try to break or pollute the benevolent feudal system—the Baroness and Roland).

Moreover, the actress-as-boy (or the breeches performer in general) as transvestite certainly uncovered broader tensions between men and women. The anxieties expressed by male critics over the cross-dressed actress in tragic or serious (sometimes melodramatic) adult male roles may have inspired and fueled the appearance of the actress-as-boy on the American stage. Because women played both types of breeches parts throughout the century (men and boys), the constantly reinforced image of the woman as a feminine boy may have sprung from a repeated reaction to the category crisis signified by female Hamlets throughout the century. Indeed, it was not simply the tragic breeches performer that produced such worries about gender transgression; the actress-as-boy also conjured up images of petticoat government, as the recuperative remarks (the discourses of containment) surrounding Tree's Ion and Cushman's Romeo demonstrate. The convention of breeches perhaps became more palatable as the image of the performer/character became more childish and feminine because gender categories were unambiguous.

Additionally, the nineteenth-century transvestite may have signaled a further category crisis between boys and the women with whom they were constantly identified. For while the association between the two was widespread and culturally reinforced, Anthony Rotundo argues that nineteenth-century boys created an alternative "culture" in order to distance themselves from the feminine domestic world that enveloped them. Boy culture, argues Rotundo, provided its members with a way to escape the private sphere and allowed boys to create a separate sphere in between the public and private.[124] The neighborhood and its surrounding areas provided boys with a chance to break away from their mothers' environment and explore qualities that were in contrast to the cardinal virtues that they were learning at home. Rotundo explains that their games were often violent and competitive and their rituals frequently cruel. Most importantly, boyhood activities "provided special opportunities to enter and imagine the roles of adult males."[125] In this respect, boys were similar to breeches actresses who used their acting vehicles for similar purposes. Boys, like actresses, also had to do a great deal of negotiating between public and private, repeatedly adjusting to the alternative (and often discrepant) values presented in each world. As Rotundo explains, boys shifted back and forth from "an atmosphere of cooperation and nurture to one of competition and conflict; from a sphere where intimacy was encouraged to one where human relationships were treated as means to various ends;

from an environment that supported expressive impulses to one that sanctioned aggressive impulses; and from a social space that was seen as female to one that was considered male."[126]

While all actresses had to deal with this constant exchange between spheres, certain performers were more skilled at making the crossing. Some even seemed to act between the spheres, to inhabit a third space of possibility beyond gender prescriptions. While most breeches performers were perceived as threatening, ridiculous, feminine, or juvenile, other exceptional cross-dressers—specifically Cushman—managed largely to escape vitriolic criticism or recuperative discourses of containment. As transvestite, Cushman exposed category crises, and as Androgyne she transcended such categories altogether. While it is true that she was, on occasion, read as both a boy and a "monstrous anomaly," she also singularly deconstructed such readings through her ability to present a double image. Associations between boys and femininity and between the cardinal virtues of True Womanhood and immaturity were forgotten in the wake of Cushman's captivating cross-gendered performances. And deliberate hegemonic strategies to manipulate the boy image on the nineteenth-century stage in order to control and/or contain women were rendered useless as Cushman turned her histrionic/feminist vision toward Verona.

CHAPTER 4

ACTING BETWEEN THE SPHERES
Charlotte Cushman as Androgyne

Art Thou a Man? Thy form cries out thou art;
Thy tears are womanish, thy wild acts denote
The unreasonable fury of a beast.
Unseemly woman in a seeming man!
Or ill-beseeming beast in seeming both!

—*Romeo and Juliet* [3.3.119–123]

How little do they see what is, *who frame*
Their hasty judgement upon that which seems.

—Charlotte Cushman, 1837

ON DECEMBER 29, 1845, CHARLOTTE CUSHMAN did an extraordinary thing at the Haymarket Theatre: she convincingly transformed herself into a young man. Audience members who witnessed this performance were captivated by "the transmuting power" of Cushman's "genius" as she became Romeo. This production (and Cushman's Romeo in general) continues to fascinate both contemporary theatre historians and lesbian and feminist scholars, who are equally impressed with Cushman's seeming ability to create an unsettling paradox.[1] Anne Russell, for example, discusses the positive reception that Cushman's Romeo received, and questions how the cross-dressed actress could have been so successful "in a period when dominant gender ideologies assumed clearly delineated separate spheres for men and women, when stage reviewers as a manner of routine assessed the 'womanliness' or 'manliness' of characters and performers."[2] As Russell explains, the nineteenth-century audience member, critic, and/or commentator read the human figure on stage as either male or female; indeed, such antithetic thinking was pervasive throughout nineteenth-century culture. Cushman was unique, however, in that she repeatedly defied such categorization, both in her theatrical performances and in her "private" life.

As a breeches performer—and as a nineteenth-century woman—Cushman was exceptional. Although other breeches actresses such as Lewis and Crampton were reported to have convincingly "passed" as men onstage on specific occasions, the transmogrifying powers recognized in Cushman were *continually* marveled at by critics and audience members. As one of her nineteenth-century biographers pointed out, Cushman was no "ordinary trespasser" into male territory. "[T]he power of her Romeo... is too strongly attested to admit of doubt; and it presents angles of view that are helpful in considering her extraordinary genius. In her near or actual approach to the achievement of the illusion of manhood on stage Charlotte Cushman stands alone."[3] Her ability to completely lose her female identity in Romeo was not an isolated incident noted by a single critic, but was a phenomenon that was repeatedly remarked upon by spectators on both sides of the Atlantic. Moreover, Cushman largely evaded harsh critical representations and limiting discourses of containment (sexual objectification, infantilization, and feminization) constructed to mitigate the threat of female usurpation. While other actresses were condemned for their unauthorized gender trekkings into forbidden masculine terrain, Cushman was celebrated as an intrepid explorer. Such singular Victorian histrionics are easily explained by scholars interested in Cushman's career, who claim that her prowess as an experienced breeches actress and her magnetism as a notably manly woman (and "butch" lesbian) account for her success as the youthful effeminate Romeo. To understand Cushman's success as a breeches performer only in these terms, however, is to simplify (and obscure) an extremely complex historical moment: Cushman, an international star, "passed" as men on the nineteenth-century stage and was lionized for her cross-gender portrayals by a public trained to read performance texts within a binary framework.

An alternative focus on Cushman is required in order to fully understand and appreciate her power as a cross-dressed performer: she was an androgyne, one who could construct and present a *double image* that was concomitantly subversive and ameliorating. Perceived by her public as simultaneously womanly and masculine, Cushman was compared to her male contemporaries such as Macready rather than to other actresses, and was often described by the press as "manly."[4] Such reports might lead to assumptions that Cushman embodied an ambiguous sexuality for her audiences, that her masculine qualities negated her femininity and vice versa, resulting in a nonspecific amalgam of indefinite characteristics. But a neutral role was an ideological impossibility in the nineteenth century where all aspects of existence (including entertainment) were conspicuously gendered. Rather than being seen as sexually equivocal, Cushman was perceived by nineteenth-century viewers as doubly sexed, or as the twentieth-century historian Charles Shattuck reflectively labeled her: "half-woman, half-man."[5]

The *OED* defines androgyny as the "union of sexes in one individual," thus an androgynous person is one who is "at once male and female."[6] In referring to an androgynous state or person, nineteenth-century critics also used the term "hermaphrodite" or "hermaphroditical," which, according to the *OED,* bears a similar meaning: "Consisting of, or combining the characteristics of, both sexes; more generally, combining two opposite qualities or attributes."[7] Cushman figuratively and theoretically conceptualized such a union. She was rarely noted as seeming *intersexual* or as generating a sexless nongendered image; rather, this actress was described as one who could represent both sexes through one body. In roles such as Romeo, for example, her physical appearance was regarded as both masculine (as opposed to boyish)[8] and womanly—feminine is not a word that ever seemed to describe Cushman. In reports like those of John Coleman, who couples a description of the actress's "ample and majestic bust" and "waist of a woman" with an account of her convincing manliness, she seems to corporealize both. Coleman allowed that,

> As a rule, actresses of refinement and sensibility, when they assume male attire, betray their female origin by quaint little movements, the lower limbs are apt to cling helplessly together, the knees are instinctively bowed inward, while a numerous other quaint and pretty *minauderies* suggest the existence, and, indeed, the very essence of feminine charm. Not a shadow of these dubieties were observable in our new Romeo. . . . [H]er figure, except in the central region before indicated, might have been that of a robust man.[9]

Androgyny was a narrative that was frequently employed to interpret and explain Cushman's performances, yet this narrative was not limited to her theatrical endeavors. Hermaphrodism shaped the actress's offstage image as well. In a tribute delivered upon her death in 1876, the Reverend W. H. H. Murray of Boston remarked, "In her the strength of the masculine and the tenderness of the feminine nature were blended. She seemed to stand complete in nature, with the finest qualities of either sex. Her strength was that of a man, her tenderness was that of a woman. She was Samson and Ruth in one."[10]

In order to explain how such an identity was constructed by—and for—Cushman, this double image must be elucidated, and the messages produced and possibilities suggested by it must be decoded. Cushman's status as a "masculine lady" allowed her to create an alternative category, a space between separate spheres, where androgyny held sway, and gender's artificial nature was foregrounded as popular notions of manliness and True Womanhood were transcended. In order to illustrate this theory, Cushman's exceptional forays into masculinity are explored through a juxtaposition of her theatrical roles—specifically Rosalind and Romeo—and her nontheatrical experiences. Such an analysis expands historical conceptions of Cushman as a gifted tragedian, skilled breeches performer, and international star. Certainly, she was all of these things. But she was also a boundary crosser, a breaker of conventions, a thespian capable of performing masculinity and femininity just as she performed Romeo, an actress who—despite meticulously placed signposts designating male from female—traversed beyond the gendered landscape of Victorian theatre and culture in her ability to "seem both."

"PASSING"

From the beginning of her career in 1836, Cushman was recognized as an accomplished breeches performer in addition to being regarded as a skilled leading lady. Her particular reknown as a player of male roles was ubiquitous; critics in New Orleans, New York, Albany, and Philadelphia joined in chorus, lauding her as "undoubtedly the best breeches figure in America."[11] Despite ten years of domestic success playing both men and women, Cushman had yet to be recognized as a star; her career lacked the British stamp of approval so necessary for the antebellum performer. She achieved this distinction in 1845 with her performance of Romeo at the Haymarket.

Although Romeo became the most celebrated role in Cushman's English repertoire and established her reputation, two preceding characterizations helped to secure her international fame. Cushman initially introduced herself to London audiences as Bianca in Milman's *Fazio* at the Princess Theatre. As Bianca, the deceived wife, Cushman's energy inspired spectators, who remarked upon her "real, impetuous, irresistible passion" and marveled at her protean ability to deftly proceed through a gamut of different emotions. Yet, perhaps the most provocative—certainly the most unusual—comment made concerning her London opening appeared in the *Herald*, whose critic began his review by discussing Cushman's extraordinary resemblance to Macready. Described as "tall and commanding," the actress was compared to her English dramatic peer in several ways. Her face was said to be "curious" and reminded the critic of the actor; in addition, the "tones of her voice" and her "mode of speech" evoked a similar recollection.[12] What initially struck this reporter was not her broad emotional range or her passionate intensity, rather it was her masculinity, her semblance to Macready physically and vocally. Similarly, another London reviewer contrasted Cushman's style with popular British actresses who, unlike their American sister, were "very ladylike."[13] Even in female roles like Bianca, Cushman was described by the London press in masculine terms—a critical insight that perhaps foreshadowed Cushman's unprecedented triumph as Romeo a few months later. Unlike Lady Macbeth, however, Bianca had no "masculine" tendencies and proved an unworthy vehicle for displaying Cushman's androgynous characteristics. This role was directly followed by two specific performances in London that deviated from standard nineteenth-century fare, two roles that more clearly exhibited her androgyny and established Cushman, already touted as London's "first actress," as a "very dangerous young man."[14]

Cushman played Rosalind for the first time at the Princess Theatre on February 27, 1845. While critics were impressed with her performance in *As You Like It,* not all aspects of her Rosalind were successful. According to the *Observer* critic, Cushman's portrayal of the heroine in the early scenes of the play was flawed; the depiction of Rosalind sans Ganymed seemed forced and uninspired. "It was not . . . until she re-appeared in male disguise, in the forest of Arden, that her powers had fair play. This transformation from woman to man had the same effect on her as on the famed Tiresias, of Argive fable. Her mind became masculine as well as her outward semblance; and on the assumption of the manly garb she would seem to have doffed all the constraint of her sex and her country."[15] Cushman's success was directly linked to her assumption of male dress for as long "as she retained these outward and visible symbols of the stronger sex" her gestures, "voice and manner," seemed natural and her performance persuasive.[16] Male dress, therefore, engendered delight and power and proved to be crucial to both actress and character; in order for Rosalind to test and ultimately win Orlando, she must transform herself into a boy, just as Cushman did not completely woo her London audience until, as Rosalind, she too became Ganymed. Despite her initial shortcomings as Rosalind, her portrayal of Ganymed was so effective that the *Observer* critic declared Rosalind to be the best thing Cushman had yet done before an English audience. As another London critic testified, Cushman and Rosalind were "one and the same thing. If ever we looked upon, heard, conceived Rosalind, it was upon that occasion.... Miss Cushman *was* Rosalind."[17]

American critics reacted similarly to Cushman's Rosalind. After returning from England in 1849, Cushman starred in *As You Like It* at New York's Astor Place Opera House during the third week of May, 1850.[18] She was heralded as "the best living Rosalind" in a review by the *Spirit of the Times* critic Gemotice, who also focused on her particular strength as Ganymed. According to this critic, Cushman took a unique approach to the role. Throughout the nineteenth century, the role had been played by actresses who emphasized Rosalind's femininity and downplayed—or simply ignored—her masculinity as Ganymed. As Gemotice explains, Ellen Tree's approach was typical: Tree was completely convincing as Rosalind in the early scenes of the play, appearing as "the most delicate and refined, the most lady-like and chaste" actress that he had ever seen in the role. But upon entering Arden, where she was called to "suit her at all points like a man," Tree's gentle feminine Rosalind was sorely unconvincing. Her portrayal of Ganymed was so "soft" and "fair" that the critic wonders how Orlando ever believed the disguise (although it is possible that critics feminized her portrayal of Ganymed like they had done with Ion in order to contain the threat of her masculine performance). Cushman, on the other hand, was reported to be a manly, saucy Ganymed. Gemotice explains that while some spectators found her innovative interpretation of Rosalind "too boisterous, rough and turbulent," he felt that she conceived and executed her part in "the true way." He argues that Rosalind puts on a "'swashing and a martial outside,'" when she makes up her mind to "'outface' the cowardice of her sex 'with semblance.' And this Charlotte Cushman does; this Miss Kean affects to do, but stops short of the mark."[19] Rosalind's "mannish dash" is evident from the very beginning of the play, Gemotice urges, and is meticulously expressed by Cushman throughout. Before she even assumes her masquerade, Rosalind appears somewhat masculine in her unabashed attempt to resume her conversation with Orlando after the wrestling match and in the candid recounting of her feelings for Orlando to Celia. As Gemotice explains, Rosalind confesses her love "in somewhat franker terms than those of womanly diffidence. The suggestion of the male disguise occurs to her mind, as if 'the wish were father to the thought.' ... Now this, under favor, we think is the Rosalind of Shakespeare, and, still under favor, that it is the Rosalind of Charlotte Cushman."[20] The *New York Herald* lent support to Gemotice's encomium in its cursory yet favorable account of the actress's efforts in *As You Like It;* while this paper did not detail specific aspects of the production, it declared that Cushman's acting "approached near perfection.... [S]he was greeted with the most enthusiastic and rapturous applause."[21]

English and American critics were impressed with Cushman's skill at performing masculinity in the role of Rosalind, yet they were astounded by her interpretation of Romeo. Popular though she had been as Bianca and Rosalind, Cushman's London debut as Romeo (which she played to her sister Susan's Juliet on December 29, 1845, at the Haymarket Theatre) absolutely captivated British audiences (see figure 4.1). Reviewers marveled at her virtuosity as the Italian lover, for she seemed to pass as a man rather than to simply create a convincing illusion of masculinity as Rosalind. The majority of London papers acknowledged her ability to *become* Romeo, to change her shape, to transform herself into someone else. Sheridan Knowles, perhaps Cushman's most fervent admirer, described act 3, scene 3, in which Romeo is made aware of his banishment, as "a scene of topmost passion; not simulated passion—no such thing; real, palpably real.... I particularize this scene," he added, "because it is the most powerful, but every scene exhibited the same truthfulness.... There is no trick in Miss Cushman's performance: no thought, no interest, no feeling seems to actuate her except what might be looked for in Romeo himself were Romeo reality."[22] The *Athenaeum* reviewer agreed that the role of Romeo was well suited for Cushman, "whose style of acting is so masculine (we say this to her credit) ... [s]he is eminently fitted to do justice to the poet's idea."[23] Additionally, Lloyd's *Weekly Messenger* discussed the "glowing reality and completeness" of Cushman's performance, the *London Times* declared

Fig. 4.1: Charlotte Cushman as Romeo with Susan Cushman as Juliet. University of Illinois, Theatrical Print Collection.

that "the illusion was forcible and perfect," and the *Britannia* critic remarked, "Miss Cushman, as Romeo, gave an illustration of the character startingly [*sic*] real. Singularly masculine in her energy and her decisive action, this lady might pass for a youthful actor with little chance of her sex being detected. She was, therefore, the creation of the poet. . . . Romeo has never been so truly interpreted before."[24]

The almost unanimously positive response to Cushman's Romeo in London caused American critics to sit up and take notice. Cushman had always been popular in this role, yet it was not until she had achieved approbation from the London press that American reporters directed serious critical attention to her portrayal of Romeo.[25] The occasional paragraph in the New York newspaper that sketchily outlined the actress's achievements during the late 1830s and early 1840s gave way to full-length articles by 1846 about the wonders engendered by "Our Charlotte." Readers in New York could track her theatrical career much more precisely after her London debut as Romeo, and trade papers such as the *Spirit* kept audiences at home abreast of her accomplishments at the Haymarket by reprinting London reviews.[26] When she returned home to tour in 1849, she was welcomed by wildly enthusiastic audiences and approving critics. American reporters churned out eulogies that were equally as fervid as, and largely identical to, those penned by their English colleagues—a phenomenon that suggests that Yankee reporters were eager to remind Old World admirers that this newly "international" luminary still shone brighter at home. Yet, while Cushman's Romeo was almost always treated favorably by critics, her acting in general was received ambivalently, a pattern that suggests that the praise surrounding her Romeo was rendered justly. Periodic harsh assessments of her mechanical style and her supposedly limited comic skills seems to indicate a lack of puffing on the part of the New York press, international fame or no. Notices from the *Spirit of the Times* that pronounced Cushman's Romeo worthy of the "highest praise" appeared in tandem with candid statements concerning her flaws. One critic allowed that "many have been, and will be, most agreeably disappointed in the performances of Miss Cushman."[27] Cushman was occasionally condemned for her tendency to "attitudinize," a practice undoubtedly learned from Macready and other members of the "Statuesque" school of acting. Such critiques seem strangely at odds with descriptions of her performance as Romeo, however, which was regularly singled out for its extreme "realism." For example, one of the *Albion's* critics mentions this bombastic school in a review of Cushman's Romeo (and rants against it with equal vehemence), stating that although the actress has a proclivity toward this type of presentation, her performance as the young Montague is eminently truthful. Even this dubious spectator confesses to "being carried captive at her will, by the earnestness, the intensity, and the thorough *naturalness* of her embodiment of the passions and emotions which she has to depict. . . . [T]here is a freshness and truthfulness in her conception, that we confess never to have seen equalled."[28] Similarly, the *New York Herald* professed that her "style presented a total abandonment of the performer, in the varied action of the scenes; and after the death of Mercutio, all that power, energy, feeling, and passion, evolved by the circumstances, were depicted with a fervency and truthfulness which swept over the audience with tremendous effect." Her triumph, upon returning to New York after her London engagement, was so great and the applause so tumultuous that, according to the *Herald* critic, her performance at the Astor Place Theatre in 1850 had to be stopped for several minutes in the middle of act 2. Throughout her initial run in 1850, the crowds she drew were unprecedented: "We have never before seen such a large assemblage within the walls of the Broadway Theatre."[29]

New York reviewers, like their London contemporaries, were almost in awe of Cushman's power as Romeo. Many of them crowned her the greatest Romeo—even the greatest performer in general (despite her somewhat antiquated style)—that they had ever witnessed. Describing act 3, scene 3 in the Friar's cell, one critic wrote, "the tortures of mind and agony of soul [were] exhibited so truthfully by this distinguished actress, [they] surpassed anything we have ever seen."[30] Like select London critics, certain American reporters doubted that this Romeo could have been played by a woman. Even as late as 1857, when Cushman (now 41) was making her second American tour as Romeo, the *Albion* critic described her as remarkably convincing. He wrote,

> No mortal can believe that the stately and impassioned figure before him is that of a woman—that those earnest and thrilling tones were designed by Nature to utter "blest rejoinders" rather than "desolate entreaties;" that the *Romeo* before him ought, in strict veracity, to answer *Juliet's* question from the balcony, "wherefore

art thou Romeo?" with a frank denial of the soft impeachment, and protest himself no "him" at all.... Her transformation is complete.[31]

Apparently Cushman still looked the part, regardless of her matronly figure and sagging jowls. Indeed, in 1858, *Porter's Spirit of the Times* claimed that she was "in face, form, and general makeup, a most perfect specimen of the impetuous and yet loving Romeo."[32] (See figure 4.2.)

Yet, it seems curious that critics were so impressed with Cushman's particular transformation, since they as professionals were well versed in the notion of disguise as a central tenant of performance art. Did not all theatre spectators expect such displays, and were not all actors expected to change their appearance and character, to pass from one thing to another? Cushman's Romeo startled audiences because it disrupted both their expectations as participants in a theatrical event (as perhaps any gifted performer might do) *and* their gendering. For brief moments during her performance of *Romeo and Juliet*, "Our Charlotte" actually *seemed* to be a man and crossed a boundary that was unthinkable, unexpected, and largely unprecedented. English critic J. M. W. describes this bizarre phenomenon in his review for the *People's Journal*. Reflecting upon her Haymarket performance, he writes:

> Her voice is deep-toned, and with that *timbre sonore* which a high authority tells us is not the "most excellent thing in a woman." Her figure, her gait, her gestures, are manly; at least, they are so in *Romeo*. Had I not known that the part was played by a woman, I do not think I should have suspected her sex. Whether all this be the effect of *the transmuting power of genius*, I know not, but am inclined to believe it is. I should not be at all surprised to see her play Juliet as well as she plays Romeo—to see her womanised into the impassioned girl.[33]

It is interesting that in addition to the previous critical sentiments concerning Cushman's ability to persuasively act both masculine and natural, J. M. W. also speculates on the efficacy with which

Cushman might move from Romeo to Juliet, from man to woman, just as Ganymed does—to deftly undergo *transmutation* or change momentarily from one nature, form, or substance into another. This reading of her talents might suggest gender's social construction, for, as J. M. W. points out, Cushman can *play* at man just as she can *play* at woman—she can assume a male role and in like turn be "womanised." Her manly appearance, walk, and movements were not products of any essential qualities the actress might have had—although this was a common explanation—but rather were due to her "transmuting power of genius."

Yet, it is more likely that J. M. W. mentions Cushman playing Juliet for another reason. If Cushman did indeed pass as Romeo, as the above critics imply, she successfully crossed certain borders between masculinity and femininity. In order to contain the threat implied by such illicit traveling, J. M. W. tries to remind his readers that while Cushman effected a magnificent Romeo, she could also easily play his feminine counterpart; she is still a woman, he implies, despite her manly figure, gait, and gestures—and not only a woman but potentially "Juliet," an ideal woman, a "bright angel" and "dear saint" [2.2.26, 55]. This implication also problematizes the idea of "passing." Cushman might have been convincing as Romeo, yet the audience always knew that she was an actress *playing* a male role: spectators and critics read the advertisements, went to the theatre, watched the performance, and read the reviews knowing that Romeo, like Ganymed, was a woman.

Issues of passing were further complicated by the nineteenth century's emphasis on the dissimilarity between men and women. This cultural focus on difference made Cushman's performance as Romeo even more remarkable—and the continual critical references to her "true" sex even more telling. Critics, like J. M. W., cited their foreknowledge of Cushman's sex (a crucial detail in their reviews) as the only factor that inhibited an otherwise flawless masquerade as Romeo. Theatrical illusions, however, as critics well knew, could be dispelled almost as easily as they could be conceived. No matter how engaged a spectator was in the performance, they were eventually distanced from the fantasy as the curtain dropped, gas jets were turned up or down, and the orchestra began to play. Knowles described his experience in witnessing Cushman as Romeo in the Friar's cell: "I listened and gazed and held my breath, while my blood ran hot and cold. I am sure it must have been the case with every one in the house, but I was all absorbed in Romeo, till a thunder of applause called me to myself."[34] The *Albion* critic, who shared Knowles's awe for Cushman's acting in this scene, commented upon the passion that she instilled into every moment of her performance. Both the early "gentler passages" of the play and the "climax of passionate emotion which presages the catastrophe of this 'true love'" were inspired. He continued, "But it is this climax, naturally enough, which most affects the public mind, and the silent shudder of anticipation which runs through the house as the despairing *Romeo*, convinced that all is over, prepares to shuffle off the mortal coil, could not be more genuine if that scene of suicide were a dread reality."[35] Two points are made by this critic: he emphasizes Cushman's intensely natural dramatic conception, yet he also makes it clear that what his audience watches is an illusion. The scene "could not be more genuine" if it were reality, claims the *Albion* journalist, yet by making this distinction he foregrounds the artifice and once again reminds his readers that Cushman is an actress playing a role. Regardless of her unusual talents and genuine performance, this critic implies that Cushman is a female weaver of illusions but not Romeo.

Although critics may have had an easier time maintaining their perspective, audience members would have been distanced from the reality of the performance as well. Even if standard frequent disturbances during the performance were minimized due to Cushman's mesmerizing acting (one witness declared that "from the beginning to end, except where a fitting opportunity offered for a delighted audience to give expression to their feelings of pleasure, all was still as the grave"[36]), viewers would be aware of Cushman, and not Romeo, when the play ended. The curtain call initiated a shift out of illusion as did periodic responses—pleasant or unpleasant—from the audience, limited as they might have been. For example, the *London Times* reported that, "at the conclusion of the performance the sisters were called before the curtain with honest, unfeigned enthusiasm by a crowded audience."[37] Before the grand drape at the Haymarket Theatre (or the Astor Place Theatre), the audience confronted the sisters Cushman, not Montague and Capulet. Cushman, who had so effortlessly *become* Romeo, now appeared once more as Cushman, just as Rosalind ultimately abandoned the role of Ganymed.

THEORIZING THE ANDROGYNE

As J. M. W.'s comment and the above discussion of "passing" indicate, Cushman presented a double image to her audiences. By figuratively housing two gender identities within one frame, she possessed the capacity to display both intermittently through the same body. This potential capability of hers to "seem both" man and woman allowed Cushman to play a third part, that of the androgyne. Four distinct functions of androgyny—as I conceive it—contribute to an understanding of Cushman in this role. As androgyne, Cushman had the power to transcend gender boundaries, to break established conventions, to critique existing gender polarities, and to introduce a third sphere or alternative space of possibility for women to rival traditional conceptions of True Womanhood.

Phyllis Rackin, in an article concerning the Boy Heroine on the English Renaissance stage, draws upon mythological conceptions of the androgyne and uses this image to negotiate exchanges between Elizabethan theatrical performance and cultural representations of gender. While she specifically discusses the androgyne as s/he appears in plays by Shakespeare and his contemporaries, I feel comfortable applying her formula to Cushman, as I believe this metaphor holds equal promise for revealing insights about nineteenth-century performance and gender. Rackin writes, "The androgyne could be an image of transcendence—of surpassing the bounds that limit the human condition in a fallen world, of breaking through the constraints that material existence imposes on spiritual aspiration or the personal restrictions that define our roles in society. But the androgyne could also be an object of ridicule or an image of monstrous deformity, of social and physical abnormality."[38] As Rackin points out, the androgyne was a figure who could move beyond borders: gender boundaries, social precepts, and standard expectations (within the family, society, and the theatre) were transcended as the androgyne escaped such limitations. This (anthropological) position of liminality—that state of being between established categories—engendered both power and disdain; liminal individuals, like Cushman, simultaneously inspired spectators and disrupted existing norms. Liminal figures paradoxically empower themselves through their marginal positioning (by escaping the limits of gender prescriptions); they also absorb "all the chaotic power of formlessness and disorder."[39]

By appearing to be "half-woman, half-man" and transcending established codes of gendered behavior, Cushman made a statement about the constructed nature of gender, about one's ability to *perform* their masculinity and femininity. In *Gender Trouble*, Judith Butler theorizes (male-to-female) drag as a self-consciously subversive act that foregrounds the performative nature of gender and exposes what seems natural as artificial. *"In imitating gender, drag implicitly reveals the imitative structure of gender itself—as well as its contingency."* Butler goes on to argue that audience members delight in drag performances. The spectator's pleasure mounts as they begin to recognize "a radical contingency in the relation between sex and gender"—a contingency that, according to Butler, appears radical only because it is performed within a cultural context that has traditionally conceived of gender as "natural" or "normal."[40] Cushman could enchant audiences with her transfiguration because the audiences recognized her performance as drag: she was an actress—immutably sexed—putting on the clothes, adopting the gestures, and assuming the behavior of a man. Yet, by performing gender on stage, Cushman may also have generated a more subversive statement about the potency of ideological female-to-male drag on and offstage—a message that if recognized would produce anxiety rather than amusement. Butler argues that we perform our gender everywhere: on the street, in the classroom, in the bedroom, and in the workplace—a theory that may have been even more true in the nineteenth century. She explains that gender does not allow for or give genesis to a stable identity, nor does it prescribe natural actions. Rather we create ourselves and establish our identity through a repeated series of stylized acts that script our bodies for precise public consumption. More importantly, Butler asserts, "If the ground of gender identity is the stylized repetition of acts through time, and not a seemingly seamless identity, then the possibilities of gender transformation are to be found in the arbitrary relation between such acts, in the possibility of a different sort of repeating, in the breaking or subversive repetition of that style."[41] By exposing through her theatrical and nontheatrical performances both the "radical contingency between sex and gender" and the tenuous nature of masculine and feminine identity, Cushman-as-androgyne critiqued hegemonic institutions (of which gender is one) and threatened certain nineteenth-century men with her cross-dressed theatrics and her "male" public image. Indeed, select contemporaries of Cushman's gleaned her subtextual message and regarded her as a "monstrous anomaly."[42]

This capacity to appear menacing, in addition to her constant efforts to break theatrical and social conventions, demonstrates a third aspect of her androgyny: tricksterism. Carroll Smith-Rosenberg's conception of the trickster figure, as it appears in nineteenth-century popular literature, adds an additional layer to the theory of the androgyne. Tricksters break existing taboos, "violate categories, and defy structure." Tricksters are both empowering and dangerous because of their determination to shatter traditions. According to Smith-Rosenberg, they represent not only the contingency of gender but of order or social tradition, and illustrate "disorder" by living outside institutionalized community. The trickster personifies Butler's theory as s/he continually constructs her/himself and thus battles convention. As Smith-Rosenberg argues, "the Trickster personifies unfettered human potential. She/he constitutes the ideal feminist hero."[43] Trickster-like, Cushman was indeed regarded as a sort of shape shifter, as a woman capable of "passing," at least momentarily; it was for this reason that her performances of Romeo were regarded as extraordinary. "Her rare, wondrous, and most surpassing talent," was noted for its marked difference from other renditions of Romeo—even female Romeos. The *Athenaeum* reviewer termed Cushman's effort "an eminently unusual performance," and the *Herald* critic testified, "It is very unusual to see a female represent the character of Romeo, and in such a manner as Charlotte Cushman fills it."[44]

Because she broke conventions and defied antithesis, Cushman was able to inhabit an alternative sphere between patriarchal categories, between "male and female," public and private. As Garber points out, such a "third" space calls into question the validity of the binary; it "questions binary thinking." To challenge antithetic cognitive patterns is to create a category crisis that is symptomatized either by a preoccupation with or a disregard for the act of cross-dressing (both symptoms were exhibited in reviews of Cushman's Romeo). As is demonstrated below, Cushman's social and theatrical androgyny created a site where gender contingencies were exposed, existing categories of male and female were expanded, and future opportunities for women were imagined.

CUSHMAN AS THE ANDROGYNE

As we have seen, Cushman's power to transform herself into a man was initially recognized in her performance of Rosalind. The actress's androgynous image allowed her to move fluently between the sexes—a quality that proved particularly useful in the Forest of Arden, a place where "gender reversal and outright gender denial escalate to the point where gender and dress cease to constitute significant categories."[45] As the *Observer* remarked, "Cushman *was* Rosalind," a character who also moves easily and deliberately between male and female identities. Just as the boy actor on the English Renaissance stage added to the multiple layers of gender identity in playing Rosalind-Ganymed-"Rosalind" and highlighted such gender boundary-crossing in the Epilogue, Cushman-as-Rosalind-as-Ganymed-as-"Rosalind" also drew attention to the contingent nature of gender.[46]

Catherine Belsey discusses this phenomenon in the Shakespearean comedies. In referring to disguise roles such as Rosalind, Belsey remarks, "Even while it reaffirms patriarchy, the tradition of female transvestism [boys playing women] challenges precisely by unsettling the categories which legitimate it."[47] Because Shakespeare's character is continually alternating between a male persona in Ganymed and a female persona in Rosalind, the notion of a stable identity is disrupted regardless of the fact that the audience knows that Rosalind is affecting Ganymed. Taking pleasure in the knowledge of the disguise, Belsey argues, produces delight for the audience, but such delight can also be undermined. The notion of identity in *As You Like It* is momentarily called into question "by indicating that it is possible, at least in fiction, to speak from a position which is not that of a full, unified, gendered subject. In other words, [*As You Like It*] can be read as posing at certain critical moments the simple, but in comedy unexpected, question, 'Who is speaking?'"[48]

As gender identity is destabilized in this comedy, the image of the androgyne is fortified, since a double image (which contains the potential for "seeming both") replaces shattered singular conceptions of male and female.[49] Rosalind reaffirms this position in the Epilogue as she declares, "It is not the fashion to see the lady the epilogue" [5.4.198] and then proceeds to state, "If I were a woman, I would kiss as many of you as had beards that pleased me" [5.4.214, 216]. As Belsey observes, "The lady is not a woman."[50] Paradoxically, Rosalind declares that she is both a lady *and* not a woman. The riddle is solved, Belsey suggests, through conventions of Renaissance casting, yet how does one resolve this riddle in cases of nineteenth-century performance where the "not woman" (formerly the Elizabethan boy actor) is indeed a lady?

Belsey finds the post-Renaissance portrayal of this character (women playing the part instead of boys) to be ineffective in this respect. She suggests that when women play Rosalind the disguise becomes transparent and only with the boy actor does the "extratextual sex of the actor ... seem significant. Visually and aurally the actor does not insist on the femininity of Rosalind-as-Ganymed, but holds the issue unresolved, releasing for the audience the possibility of glimpsing a disruption of sexual difference."[51] Belsey dismisses too easily the actresses' potential to create a similar schism. Because she has difficulty resolving the issue of Ganymed's occasional harsh sentiment toward women (his "conventional invective" in 4.1.150–155), Belsey argues that the disguise in post-Renaissance productions must be transparent since a female performer in the role of the protagonist could not convincingly mock women. Yet, what Belsey fails to acknowledge is that, as a woman, Cushman might be mocking (even more appropriately) the popular image of women briefly illustrated by Rosalind-as-Ganymed (who speaks as "Rosalind"). Just as she spoke out against "Biddy in the Kitchen" offstage, Cushman might have been speaking out against the image of Biddy onstage. A woman who was "more jealous . . . than a Barbary cock, . . . more clamorous than a parrot against rain, more new-fangled than an ape, more giddy in [her] desires than a monkey," [4.1. 150–153] lacrymose, changeable for the sake of being antagonistic, and hysterical perhaps deserved such censure in Cushman's opinion. By claiming the autonomy of Ganymed's voice and by, following Butler's suggestion, engaging in a "different sort of repeating, . . . in the subversive repetition" of stylized acts (different because Ganymed plays Rosalind to show Orlando a stereotypical and unappealing side of femininity), Cushman could draw attention to unattractive aspects of female gendering and possibly introduce a new kind of woman in Ganymed.

Furthermore, the transparency of the assumed disguise might be negated in an actress who, like Cushman, "doffed all the constraints of her sex" in becoming Ganymed, therefore once again rendering the issue unresolved. If boy-as-woman-as-boy-as-woman can disrupt gender prescriptions so can woman-as-boy-as-woman; the potential for calling the constructed nature of gender into question is equally compelling for the female transvestite or male impersonator who momentarily passed on stage as Cushman was reported to have done. Yet this issue is further complicated by the double image: the girl is really a girl-boy. Cushman is Rosalind is Ganymed is "Rosalind" is *both* in the Epilogue just as the audience can simultaneously believe the actress's masculine masquerade and acknowledge that a woman controls the disguise.

Belsey hints at the importance of the double image in her closing discussion of the play's gender issues by invoking the feminist theorist, Julia Kristeva. Belsey makes reference to Kristeva's influential article, "Women's Time," in which the theorist briefly outlines her own version of a third generation or space, an alternative sphere. Kristeva writes, "In this third attitude, which I strongly advocate—which I imagine?—the very dichotomy man/woman as an opposition between two rival entities may be understood as belonging to *metaphysics*. What can 'identity,' even 'sexual identity,' mean in a new theoretical scientific space where the very notion of identity is challenged?"[52] In lieu of trying to live out a gendered "identity," which Kristeva suggests is impossible in this post-structuralist age, an individual must internalize difference or, as she says, "interiorize the founding separation of the sociosymbolic contract."[53] Belsey argues that Kristeva's concept of the third attitude aids a post-structuralist reevaluation of Shakespearean comedy—specifically *As You Like It*—because it reveals "a plurality of places, of possible beings, for each person in the margins of sexual difference, those margins which a metaphysical sexual polarity obliterates." Yet Belsey misses the true significance of the double image by embracing the concept of a third space or a "gap" through which we might "glimpse a possible meaning, an image of a mode of being" that does not depend upon the existing system of difference. She makes it clear that this third state is "not a-sexual, nor bisexual but [that] which disrupts the system of differences on which sexual stereotyping depends."[54] Such a statement suggests that Belsey has missed Kristeva's point about the significance of what I have been describing as the double image—an image that *is* bi-sexual in that it is ideologically hermaphroditical. While it is true that the interiorization of difference creates new possibilities beyond "male" and "female," older categories must exist prior to the establishment of the third attitude. A new "possible meaning" that disrupts the old *necessitates and is dependent upon* the old. The double image therefore requires/insists upon the patriarchal gender polarities that preceded it. In order for Cushman-as-Rosalind to critique established categories and point to new possibilities, she must be able to define and explore the existing polarities. Male and female *create* the double image, which, I believe, is the third attitude, the Kristevian internalization of difference.

Despite her ability to break theatrical and social conventions by performing Rosalind in a nontraditional way (that hinted at gender's constructed nature and transformed Rosalind from Tree's feminine icon to the trickster), Cushman/Rosalind/Ganymed's prerogative as a boundary crosser proves ultimately ephemeral. For while Rosalind hints at new possibilities and critiques existing categories, she ultimately remains powerless to change them. She might challenge the legitimacy of patriarchal categories, as Belsey suggests, but her final capacity to affect definitive change is limited. For Ganymed—regardless of his influential power, his magical associations, and his ability to "do strange things" [5.1.59]—remains invisible at the end of the play as Rosalind discards the signifiers of manhood and surrenders her power to Hymen. As Gayle Whittier argues, the comic disguise-role heroine in Shakespeare's plays always reinforces conventional notions of femininity; her motives spring from essential feminine qualities: "purity, piety, submissiveness and domesticity." "Dialogic wit," she explains, "often depends on their consciousness of the disguise as no more than a disguise. And the costume itself is temporary, a symbol of the plasticity of androgyny, but not androgyny itself.... Tragedy, then, is the only stage on which to explore the dramatic portrayal of the ... androgyne."[55]

Whittier's point appears especially apt in relation to Cushman's Romeo, for while her portrayal of Rosalind was successful, it in no way compared to the overwhelming and widely celebrated victory that she experienced as Romeo both at the Haymarket and in American theatres during her subsequent tours to the United States. Regardless of Rosalind's remarkable qualities, she was not an entirely effective vehicle for Cushman—all issues of passing aside. Despite her androgyny, Rosalind's potential ability to create a true "category crisis" (which was, according to Garber, the transvestite's most influential function in culture) was severely limited since her motives, as Whittier points out, were essentially hegemonic. The transvestite, Garber argues, creates a cultural category crisis by fracturing definitive gender role prescriptions or by "calling attention to cultural, social, or aesthetic dissonances." She explains this crisis as "a failure of definitional distinction, a borderline that becomes permeable, that permits of border crossings from one (apparently distinct) category to another."[56] As Whittier implies, Rosalind must live out the fate of all Shakespearean comic heroines and marry—an event that reestablishes distinct categories. Her appropriation of a male role is not ultimately threatening to audiences, nor are her indirect attempts to proselytize about gender convincing, for she neither remains in the mystic woods of Arden where girls can be boys, nor does she (as a nineteenth-century actress rather than a boy) hint at the possibility of homosexual love like the crossed-dressed Romeo. As the tragic hero, Cushman could explore androgyny (its implications and its benefits) more extensively. With Romeo, the pretexts for Cushman's cross-dressing change as her gender-bending becomes more accomplished, her border-crossings more advanced, and her androgyny more dangerous.

As Romeo, Cushman proved to be so accomplished in her impersonation that many critics expressed subtle fears that she would completely loose her own female identity in the young Montague. The *Athenaeum* critic, for example, praised her repeatedly—despite his general dislike of the convention of breeches, which he referred to as a "mistake"—calling her performance superior to any he had seen in years, her acting extraordinary, and her male masquerade impeccable. Yet, while he enthusiastically declared, "In all, Miss Cushman is [Romeo's] adequate representative," this critic also expressed a concern over her ability to so completely transform herself. Cushman's repeated forays into masculinity, he feared, would eventually prove destructive both for her and for the art of the theatre in general. "Assuming possession of a masculine mind and a corresponding style" may achieve "mischievous" results, the critic worried, and eventually cause Cushman's feminine traits to disappear altogether.[57] Such a critical reaction is a testimony to the actress's capacity to momentarily pass as Romeo, to briefly become a man and in doing so move beyond gender limitations, to initiate a category crisis and test the permeability of borders.

Regardless of the press's apprehension about her transgressions, English writers were actively engaged in the process of cultivating the masculine persona that Cushman had revealed in her performances as Rosalind and Romeo. After her London debut as Romeo, she was repeatedly compared to Macready both physically and in terms of her theatrical style. This constant association between her and the most prominent male actor in England at the time perhaps reinforced her masculine image (for it proved that she was, on one level, perceived by the public as masculine) and helped to explain to audiences her "transmuting power of genius." The *People's Journal* correspondent recalled, "At first I was struck by her likeness to Macready, both in person and in manner; afterwards I became convinced that this likeness was entirely the work of nature; and that Miss Cushman does not *imitate* Macready."[58] Gilbert Abbott á Beckett made perhaps the most famous comparison between the two in a poem he composed for the *Almanack of the Month*. After witnessing *Romeo and Juliet* he wrote:

> What figure is that which appears on the scene?
> 'Tis Madam Macready—Miss Cushman, I mean.
> What wondrous resemblance! the walk on the toes,
> The eloquent, short intellectual nose—
> The bend of the knee, the slight sneer on the lip,
> The frown on the forehead, the hand on the hip;
> In the chin, in the voice, 'tis the same to a tittle,
> Miss Cushman is Mister Macready in little.
> The lady before us might very well pass
> For the gentleman, viewed the wrong way in the glass.
> No fault with the striking resemblance we find,
> 'Tis not in the person alone, but the mind.[59]

Although this poem was undoubtedly satirical, it did attest to the frequent associations that were being made between Cushman and Macready. It is also significant in that Beckett implies that Cushman did not simply resemble the great actor in terms of her physical appearance but also adopted a masculine mind. In his recollections of the stage, the former English actor Dutton Cook also remembers certain similarities between Cushman and Macready, and suggests that in addition to looking and thinking like a man, the actress also behaved like one. "The likeness to Macready—a likeness which applied not merely to features and 'trick of face,' but also to gait and gestures, tone of voice and method of elocution—has been from the first observed; and no doubt gained force when the actress personated a male character."[60] Cushman's masculine image was further enhanced in private circles by her fellow actors who, because of her "enterprise and straightforwardness," referred to the actress not as Charlotte but as "Captain Charlotte."[61] Similarly, Coleman, who referred to Cushman as "Charley de Boots" because of her tendency to cross-dress at rehearsals, recalled, "Airy young gentlemen of these days [the 1840s] would have said that she was a 'deuced good fellow,' and so she was!"[62]

Because she embraced this male persona, Cushman-as-androgyne was reportedly able to lose her "identity" (temporarily) as the *Athenaeum* critic feared, and in doing so perhaps challenged the validity of such a definitive state. As one American critic remarked, she "abdicate[s] her identity, and loses herself in the heir of Montague. And this so completely, that she makes herself not only an adequate *Romeo*—but the actual *Romeo* of the actual English stage."[63] Cushman was much more celebrated in this role than in her numerous other male parts, and was praised for her Romeo while other actresses were being castigated or (occasionally) objectified. With efficacy she played the changeling, transformed her identity, and *became* Romeo.

One explanation for her unprecedented success in this particular role seems to lie in the character of Romeo, her kindred spirit, who emerges from the text not as the fair Montague but rather, as the Friar describes him, "an ill-beseeming beast in seeming both" male and female. As Russell suggests, Romeo was "a site of contradiction," a liminal character whose "unsettled" qualities made him particularly attractive and accessible to actresses.[64] Indeed, Romeo's liminality is continually reiterated by the text; from the very first scene in the play in which Romeo exclaims, "Tut! I have lost myself; I am not here: This is not Romeo, he's some other where,"[1.1. 196] to his ultimate death in the Capulet's tomb, Romeo—like Cushman—embodies the androgyne. He is always changing, often transgressive, and constantly in the process of crossing boundaries, both social and sexual.

Romeo's sudden transferal of love from Rosaline to Juliet at the beginning of the play initially betrays his mutability. This shift of affection is significant not only because it gives evidence of his variable nature, but also because Cushman was the first to reincorporate any mention of Rosaline back into the play. In the spirit of Macready and other nineteenth-century theatre artists who tried to rescue Shakespeare's texts from the "improved" sentimentalized versions of Cibber, Garrick, and Tate, Cushman's production of the play at the Haymarket in 1845–46 gained interest from British critics because of her attempt to restore the original text.[65] The *London Times* established that Cushman and company "played the characters of Romeo and Juliet, not in the ordinary acting tragedy with which David Garrick favored the world, but in the tragedy as written by Shakespere. . . . [T]he chief difference between Shakespere's play and Garrick's adaptation, is that, in the former work, Romeo is represented as in love with Rosaline before he sees Juliet. . . ."[66] Cushman's 1852 promptbook also provides evidence of this change. In the introduction to this copy of *Romeo and Juliet*, which the editor states was "arranged and remodeled by Garrick about the year 1748, and which has been, from that time to our own, the preferred acting edition," Cushman's notoriety as a textual reformer is observed: "Garrick's omission of the allusions to Romeo's first love, Rosaline, has been often condemned; and Miss Cushman, the American actress, who has lately won so much fame on the London boards by her impersonation of Romeo, has been commended by many English critics of high literary repute for the restoration in her performance of those passages in the first act of the tragedy, wherein these allusions appear."[67] Because, as many critics have suggested, Garrick's extraction of Rosaline from the original text was probably done in order to make Romeo's love for Juliet singular and thus more sublime, Cushman's representation of Romeo as capricious rather than steadfast further exemplifies her possible attempt to use this character as a vehicle through which she might explore changeability and explode simple conventions. Indeed, Cushman efforts to reestablish the original text and to play "the actual Romeo of the English stage," demonstrate her desire to break with long-held theatrical conventions.

Cushman broke other dramatic conventions in her interpretation of the role. Romeo had long been regarded by the English stage as a two-dimensional character, a young man who simply recited a string of passionate speeches and made certain expected "points." It was the wilder darker role of Mercutio, and not that of Romeo, that was the coveted part among actors during the first half of the nineteenth century. Yet, something about the young lover appealed to Cushman and allowed her to breath life into the role. One London critic pointed out that,

> The glowing reality and completeness of Miss Cushman's performance perhaps produces the strength of the impression with which she sends us away. The character, instead of being shown us in a head of disjecta membra, is exhibited by her in a powerful light which at once displays the proportions and the beauty of the poet's conceptions.... All Miss Cushman's stage business is founded upon intellectual ideas, and not upon conventionalisms.[68]

Similarly, the London *Times* described Cushman's Romeo as a "creative, a living, breathing, animated, ardent human being. The memory of the play-goer will call up Romeo as a collection of speeches delivered with more or less eloquence, not as an individual."[69] Like the trickster, Cushman broke with established traditions both by restoring the original text and by approaching the character in a unique way. She did not regard Romeo as a "head of disjecta membra" or "a collection of speeches" but rather could see the logic behind his seemingly liminal and fractured—or double—persona. Androgyny provided the link between Cushman and Romeo and made the paradoxical familiar, the contradictory rational.

Romeo's character seems unsettled from the very beginning of the play. His abrupt shift in affection from Rosaline to Juliet further reinforces both his changeable image and his transgressive nature, since his forbidden desire causes him to find himself beyond the compass of social and political ordinance. As he seeks midnight asylum in the Capulet's orchard, Romeo, cloaked by the night, appears precarious, chameleonic, and "with love's light wings" scales the orchard wall for, as he tells Juliet, "stony limits cannot hold love out" [2.2.66–67]. Love further conditions Romeo's mercurial and paradoxical nature after it indirectly prompts him to slay Tybalt in act 3, scene 2. Juliet reflects upon this, asking:

> Did ever dragon keep so fair a cave?
> Beautiful tyrant! fiend angelical!

> Dove-feathered raven! wolvish-ravening lamb!
> Despised substance of divinest show!
> Just opposite to what thou justly seemst—
> A damned saint, an honorable villain! [74–79]

As this passage demonstrates, Romeo also tests gender boundaries in addition to social and physical boundaries. Although it causes Juliet pain, Romeo's slaying of Tybalt is an act that re-asserts his masculinity and that transforms him into the opposite of what he previously seemed to be. No longer the gentle lover, he engages in an aggressive maneuver, yet he does this immediately after he declares that love has emasculated him. After Mercutio's death Romeo declares, "O sweet Juliet, [t]hy beauty hath made me effeminate [a]nd in my temper softened valor's steel" [3.1.114–115] and then proceeds a few lines later to revenge his friend's murder. This ability of Romeo's to rapidly shift between gendered attributes and/or behavior is first illustrated in act 1, scene 5. Romeo illicitly gains passage to the Capulet's festivity (perhaps his first trespass), where he encounters Juliet. Throughout their first scene together, Romeo seems to be the aggressor. However, as Marianne Novy points out, his dialogue with Juliet "puts aggression at a distance. He speaks humbly about his 'unworthiest hand' [1.5.93]; if his touch is sin, it is 'gentle' [1.5.94]; if it is too rough, he would prefer 'a tender kiss' [1.5.96]. Thus his initiative is that of a pilgrim to a saint and claims to imply the dominance of the woman, not the man."[70] After the party, Romeo dismisses his male comrades and scales his rival's wall (another bold and aggressive action) to gaze up at Juliet's balcony; but once inside Juliet's garden, he again forfeits his masculine control. Act 2, scene 2 finds Juliet "both literally and figuratively above" Romeo, as Whittier points out, a position of dominance further emphasized by Romeo's comparison of Juliet to the sun or "the solar (male) principle which will extinguish the female one, 'kill the envious moon.'"[71] Romeo's progressive intimacy with Juliet parallels his movement towards an androgynous state—or double image—as he layers feminine gender traits upon his male gender identity and proves that he can move deftly between them. During the street fight he is "made effeminate" by Juliet's beauty, quickly resurrects (or erects) his "valor's steel" to kill Tybalt, and then shifts back to the feminine as he apes his lover's expressions of despair and adopts certain characteristics that are thought to resemble Juliet's. This is evidenced by the Nurse's remark to the Friar in act 3, scene 3, "O, he is even in my mistress' case,/Just in her case!" [3.3.84–85]. The Friar notices Romeo's protean nature even earlier in the play. Upon first meeting the enamored Montague in act 2, scene 3, he inquires about Romeo's new passion, asking: "[A]rt thou changed? Pronounce this sentence then: women may fall when there's no strength in men" [79–80]. If Romeo belies social decorum in courting Juliet, he also crosses gender lines, suggests the Friar, since it is unmanly for one to be so drunk with love and so inconsistent. If men can be so affected, the Friar hints, women may fall as well; both sexes are threatened if men do not maintain the roles, duties, and expectations that their gender prescribes. As Butler might say (and as the Friar implies), Romeo fails to "do" his gender right.[72]

Romeo's seeming liminality (his ability to move between categories) is furthered by his banishment. Verona's Prince, in rushing "aside the law," [3.3.26] forces Romeo outside the boundaries of his city, thus rendering him physically, socially, and spiritually marginal. "Romeo is banished," Juliet laments, "There is no end, no limit, measure, bound,/ In that word's death; no words can that woe sound" [3.2.125–126]; Romeo continues this sentiment, exclaiming, "There is no world without Verona walls . . . /Hence banished is banished from the world, . . . Thou cuttest my head off with a golden axe/And smilest upon the stroke that murders me"[3.3.17, 22–23]. This act of cutting off his "head with a golden axe" implies castration as Romeo becomes emasculated by being thrust outside the community that contains Juliet, or that which defines—and threatens—his manhood. By metaphorically losing the definitive sign of his gender, he, like the trickster, moves "beyond gender."

The display of emotion that results from the news of his proposed banishment further exemplifies Romeo's lack of a singular and/or stable gender identity. Romeo, whose display of violence toward Tybalt reaffirms his manhood in Verona's eyes (as Novy argues "Verona's definition of masculinity by violence is partly

Romeo's definition as well"[73]), also expresses a "womanish" passionate despair in act 3, scene 3; like Cushman, Romeo's androgyny allows him to experience various gender characteristics through one body. As noted above, the Nurse remarks upon Romeo's similarity to Juliet during his outburst in the Friar's cell and then immediately commands him to "stand up" and "be a man" [3.3.88]. When he fails, he becomes, as the Friar bemoans, "an ill-beseeming beast in seeming both" man and woman, a creature who "shamest thy shape, thy love, thy wit," whose "noble shape is but a form of wax, /Digressing from the valor of a man" [3.3.12,122, 126–127]. In discussing Romeo's predicament in Shakespeare's Verona—a world, like Victorian America, signified by rigid social restrictions—Whittier notes that Romeo's displays of feminine traits might be seen as "perverse" or abnormal; "[a] man, more than a woman, is likely to undergo such censure since, by conventional stereotype he 'loses' (male) power in the role exchange, while a woman 'usurps' it (gains it however, falsely)."[74]

This perception of Romeo as anomalous, "an ill-beseeming beast," recalls Rackin's discussion of the androgyne as a figure who connotes images of monstrosity as well as liminal power. Significantly this view of Romeo was also expressed by some of Cushman's critics who viewed her androgyny as threatening. After playing Mercutio to her Romeo in 1843 at the Walnut Street Theatre, Vandenhoff, as noted in chapter 2, issued the first serious barb against Cushman's Romeo. Vandenhoff described her performance as "hybrid," and charged, "She looks neither man nor woman in the character—or both; and her passion is equally epicene in form." Rather than being praised for her genius, she was branded for her "perversions" as her performance "denaturaliz[ed] the situations" of the play.[75]

Vandenhoff, who performed under the management of Cushman at the Walnut Street Theatre, was not the only one to feel threatened by her Romeo. Despite the fact that the actress was his friend, Coleman also expressed anxiety over her impersonation and tried to undermine the fervor with which London critics praised Cushman's Haymarket performance. He reductively expressed that "it was by no means the abnormal performance described by Mr.

Sheridan Knowles and other indiscreet adulators; it was simply the effort of a monstrously clever woman—but it was not Romeo."[76] While Coleman's word choice may be indicative of sentiments regarding transvestism (and lesbianism) in 1904, when he wrote his memoirs, it is still significant that Cushman is not simply described by him as a clever woman but as a "monstrously clever woman," for this labeling is reflective of earlier Victorian criticism as well. Vandenhoff's comment coupled with Rackin's discussion of the androgyne as "an image of monstrous deformity" and "social and physical abnormality," further illuminate Coleman's phrasing. Such terms work to invalidate Cushman's potential influence as a serious artist, for the woman who is too clever, too much like her polar opposite, is unnatural, an anomaly, a monster, or "a very dangerous young man."[77]

Moreover, George Fletcher, in a chapter from his *Studies of Shakespeare* entitled "New Perversion of This Play *[Romeo and Juliet]*, In Its Late Revival at the Haymarket Theatre," advocated the restoration of the original text in 1845 by Cushman (to whom he never refers by name), but declared that in regards to a woman assuming the part, he would "waste no words upon demonstrating the disgustingly monstrous grossness of such a perversion.... To pursue this consideration in all the detail into which it would naturally lead us, would be so overpoweringly repugnant to our own taste and feeling, that we must at once decline the task."[78] Fletcher refuses further comment concerning this transgression and characterizes the London critics who claimed that Cushman passed as Romeo as "men with so little manhood as to have almost lost all sense of the essentially different manner in which this passion, especially, manifests itself in the two sexes respectively."[79] This antithesis that Fletcher creates between "the monstrous *epicene expression* of the part" and "the *essential* conception of it" is especially interesting when perceived in light of gender theory.

Fletcher's essentialist position—quite literally articulated in his essay—is as opposed to the notion of an artificial construction of gender expressed in Cushman's Romeo as, Fletcher believes, man is to woman. Since, according to Fletcher, an actress, regardless of her virtuosity, can in no way represent the essential nature of masculinity, it would seem that the only other option would be for her to create a simulated representation of it. Yet if this manufactured portrayal is convincing—as many critics claimed it was in Cushman's case—then gender and not the actress proves to be unnatural.

Fletcher's vitriol demonstrates the profound effect that Cushman's performance must have had on him, and in this way provides further proof of the inherent threat that she represented to certain critics. Fletcher goes so far as to declare a state of theatrical emergency that he seeks to remedy by calling for an immediate remounting of the play with a male Romeo. Cushman's threat as androgyne is made palpable in Fletcher's remark: "It is no longer a question of rendering this drama adequately on the whole,—but of expelling the intensely gross misconception of it lately impressed on the minds of so large a portion of the London public. . . . [T]here is little cause to fear that so unnatural an outrage on the great master genius of our country as that recently perpetrated at the Haymarket Theatre, will ever more be tolerated on the London stage."[80] The anxiety voiced by critics like Vandenhoff, Coleman, and Fletcher regarding the actress's literal assumption of a male role seems indicative of an underlying fear that her transvestism was (or would become) figurative as well. Erroll Sherson perhaps best articulates the reason behind these fears in a remark he made concerning Cushman as a breeches performer. He writes, "Personally I have an idea that what made her go on the stage was a great desire to 'wear the breeches.'"[81]

Yet, Cushman was perceived as dangerous by these male critics for reasons that extended beyond the typical alarms sounded by other actresses who attempted breeches roles. Certainly, as Vandenhoff declared, Cushman threatened to "usurp men's parts" and "push" them from their "stools," yet her performance indicated that she was not simply a mouthpiece for the advancement of petticoat government like former cross-dressed actresses. Rather, Cushman-as-Romeo seemed to make a much more revolutionary statement about the legitimacy and stability of gender identity. Through her performance as androgyne, she demonstrated that gender was, as Butler argues, "an identity tenuously constituted in time—an identity instituted through a *stylized repetition of acts.*"[82] And it was for this reason that she appeared so menacing to critics like Vandenhoff.

These critics responded to the potential social disruption signaled by Cushman's androgyny. Her double image was especially ominous because it suggested that women could embody masculine power and authority; they were not destined to express only the prescribed gender traits found in True Womanhood but could be anything they wanted to be; they could push beyond the limits of the "feminine" and seek new definitions for themselves. Only a double image implied the potential for such freedoms, however, since an ambiguously sexed image would negate the power of the masculine and therefore limit female potential. Viewed within this context, the negative criticism rendered by Vandenhoff, Coleman, and Fletcher becomes even more debilitating. Vandenhoff argued that Cushman "looks neither man nor woman in the character—or both." By seeming "neither" or "both," Vandenhoff undermines the power of the double image by suggesting that Cushman is "epicene" or intersexual, that her gender identity seems blurred or undecipherable rather than seeming double—intermittently both masculine and feminine. Likewise, Fletcher rails against the "epicene expression of the part," and while he clearly states his disgust at such amorphous representations, he perhaps subtly implies that Cushman is perverse and monstrous but at least not powerful; she muddies her gendering but does not momentarily deny it all together by alternately claiming a masculine identity. Coleman communicates a similar subtext by declaring that Cushman "is not Romeo." If Romeo is the androgyne, if his persona is paradoxical, his identity protean and his gender phenomenological and not natural—as the original text suggests—then Cushman is not the true "creation of the poet," as the *Britannia* claimed she was. By arguing that her performance was "by no means the abnormal performance described by Mr. Sheridan Knowles and other indiscreet adulators," he suggests that, contrary to popular opinion, she did not really achieve a true impersonation of the character; her performance was not exceptional nor was it "transmuting." In denying that Cushman truly embodied Romeo, Coleman forbids her access to the powers of androgyny.

Interestingly, this subtle campaign to discredit Cushman (or potential future androgynes) by undermining the double image was recognized (and/or anticipated) by Cushman's friend, the early

English feminist, Geraldine Jewsbury.[83] Jewsbury, like many other nineteenth-century women (such as Kate Field, Mary Howitt, and Louisa May Alcott), regarded Cushman as a sort of early feminist icon. Her androgyny was idealized by these women who recognized in the actress an ability to display qualities that had, in the past, been thought desirable only in men. Jewsbury admired Cushman as a woman of genius and used her as a model for the principal character in her novel *The Half Sisters,* written in 1848. Independent women, such as Jewsbury, who also desired to transcend domesticity, recognized the alternative sphere that Cushman-as-androgyne had created for herself and sought to join her there. This is reflected in Jewsbury's novel, in which the protagonist Bianca Pazzi (the character inspired by Cushman), an actress, also embraces a double image through her unusually public (and therefore masculine) life. The novel tells the story of two half sisters, Bianca and Alice, who, though quite different in temperament and opinion, both fall in love with the reprehensible Conrad Percy. Conrad, Bianca's benefactor, eventually transfers his affections and loyalty from Bianca to Alice (who is a married woman) after becoming disgusted with Bianca's acting career. For Conrad, Alice represents the irresistible True Woman while Bianca's status as a professional, despite her extreme success, defeminizes her and renders her undesirable. Significantly, Conrad's castigation of Bianca bears a striking resemblance to the negative remarks made about Cushman by Vandenhoff, Coleman, and Fletcher. Jewsbury's astute perception of the male critical tendency to defuse the power of the androgyne is evident as Conrad asks:

> [W]hat is it that professional life does for women? Take Bianca, if you will, as a specimen, she is one of the best, and what has been its effect? It has unsexed her, made her neither a man nor a woman. A public life must deteriorate women; they are thrown on the naked world, to have to deal, like us men, with all its bad realities; they lose all the beautiful ideal of their nature, all that is gentle, helpless, and confiding... All that a professional woman achieves, then at such a grievous cost of all that is charming in her nature, is only to do what a man would have done much better.

> The intrinsic value of a woman's work out of her own sphere is nothing ... she strides and stalks through life, neither one thing nor another; she has neither the softness of a woman, nor the firm, well-proportioned principle of a man; from her contact with actual things she is slightly masculine in her views, but the woman spoils the completeness; she cannot attain, at least she does not attain, to manly prudence and grasp of intellect. She is a bat in the human species; when she loves like a man, and yet expects to be adored as a woman—the good gods deliver us from all such.[84]

Whether played out onstage by Cushman or written about in the pages of a novel by Jewsbury, the trenchant satire of hegemonic investments in the doctrine of separate spheres is evident. Conrad's monologue, like Vandenhoff's memoirs, is constructed to undermine the influence of androgyny. Women who tried to accomplish masculine goals in the public sphere, who tried to expand their horizons beyond the hearth, were excoriated. The appropriation of male goals and "contact with actual things" is not empowering, suggests Conrad, but deteriorating. Bianca "unsexed" herself by becoming a professional woman and by living between spheres; she appeared "neither male nor female . . . neither one thing nor another." No female attempt to assume a masculine persona could ever be complete, suggests Conrad and Cushman's critics; rather it renders the woman monstrous as she "strides and stalks through life."

Despite the fact that this monologue of Conrad's was obviously written by Jewsbury in order to parody male critiques of female ambition, the analogy of the "unsexed" actress to the bat is apt. Although undesirable to men such as Conrad, women such as Bianca—like Romeo—also possess wings that can scale "stony limits." Yet rather than appearing monstrous, Bianca, as androgyne, emerges from the novel as a heroine who has retained the best of both worlds. Ultimately she succeeds at acting between the spheres and enjoys both a professional life and love—though happily not with Conrad—leaving the shackles of True Womanhood for Alice to wear. Jewsbury's poignant statement about the benefits of androgyny appears increasingly cogent in the second volume of her novel, for while Bianca finds wealth, love, *and* professional satisfaction, Alice finds only an early grave.

As androgyne, defined by both disorder and power, Cushman appeared threatening to Vandenhoff and others who possibly understood the full implications of the image and message that she broadcast from both sides of the footlights concerning the social construction of gender. If Romeo-as-androgyne could move beyond traditional conceptions of gender, so could Cushman-as-Romeo and possibly all women. Yet if Cushman did indeed exhibit trickster-like characteristics through her androgyny, if she represented a disruptive figure who "exist[ed] to break taboos, violate categories, and defy structure," it is curious that her transgressions—so vehemently noted by critics like Vandenhoff—went largely unrecognized. Rather, such comments remained within a critical minority, greatly overshadowed by the multitude of admirers who delighted in her transformation.

Various discourses functioned to contain the perception of Cushman as transgressive. Several of the actress's contemporaries argued that Cushman undertook the role in order to bolster her sister Susan's career. While this theory has since been discredited, the exonerating concept of "sisterly love" provides a compelling explanation. As Merrill (via Nancy Cott) argues, the Victorian doctrine of "passionlessness robbed Cushman, as a woman, of sexual desire and made her lovemaking platonic thereby legitimizing it."[85] In addition, cultural associations between boyishness and femininity may have contributed to the actress's success as Romeo because his status as a youth—a lesser man or socially impotent boy—worked to contain the perception of Cushman as transgressive.

Cushman's androgyny also contributed to this containment process. While Cushman was perceived as masculine, she was also always acknowledged as an actress, a woman "in drag." The double image seemed to delight audience members who could indulge in her gender trespasses, safely supposing that they were temporary. In her article, "Mrs. Siddons Looks Back in Anger: Feminist Historiography for Eighteenth-Century British Theater," Ellen Donkin discusses the London audiences' tacit endorsement of subversive activity onstage and relates this phenomenon to the concept of female subjectivity and the male gaze. She employs the theory of the male gaze, originally articulated by feminist film theorist Laura Mulvey, to discuss the supposedly "closed system" of audience spectatorship in eighteenth-century England. The actress performed the role of "Woman," a culturally constructed and male-fashioned image of what women were expected to be like, rather than representing actual female experiences on stage. Because she was not in control of the discourse or the subject of the narrative in which she appeared, she maintained an object position. Events and characters were rendered, as Donkin points out, "to reward the eye of the heterosexual male subject"; the actress did not do the looking, rather she was the object of this subject gaze. Donkin argues, however, that women could disrupt this seemingly closed system by claiming subjectivity through the actual *performance* of the text. While the text that they were engaged in representing may have been one that reinforced cultural ideas of femininity, their performance—their actions on stage—allowed them to undermine this narrative. Such displays of female autonomy were not repulsed by eighteenth-century British audiences, for as Donkin explains, "although audiences demanded from the text the comfort and familiarity of the norms of Womanhood, *what in fact they responded to in performance was something that potentially ruptured that comfort and familiarity.*"[86] While certain critics—perhaps even a majority of them—might have expressed anxiety about the usurping powers of the emasculating female artist (her subjectivity onstage is the "something" to which Donkin refers), audiences may have been captivated by the "potential for danger" and perhaps relished disruptions that they could regard as innocuous as long as all such rebellions remained safely behind the footlights.

Donkin's study has provocative implications for nineteenth-century performance as well, for her theory of the audience's delight in the actress's subversion may well help to partially explain Cushman's popularity as Romeo with both critics and audience members. Cushman was almost excessively emotional as Romeo, yet rather than interpreting this as feminine (reading Cushman as an object), most viewers simply believed—and took momentary pleasure in this belief—that they were witnessing the reality of the despairing Montague—the male subject of the narrative. As one critic described,

So high ran her frenzy of grief, so real was the air of a "mind distraught" with which she repelled the Friar's counsel and reasoning that when, with unexplained desperation, she dashed herself upon the earth, "[t]aking the measure of an unmade grave," all that is extravagant and unreasonable in Romeo's behavior was forgotten in the ardour of his love, and the house was roused to the wildest excitement, as if by some tragic event in actual life. There was a pause before the recollection that Romeo's misery was but feigned, enabled it to thank the impassioned performer in volley after volley of applause.[87]

The critics who responded positively to her Romeo, calling it "truthful" and "natural," rewarded her for her ability to assume the subject position (the male persona) so convincingly, yet despite their wonderment over Cushman's transformation, they were ultimately reminded that she could never be the subject, that her masculine impersonation was "feigned"; while she was regarded as "half-man" or a masculine lady, she was also always a lady, a True Woman. As a nineteenth-century woman, Cushman was limited to an object position in the eyes of her male viewers—a position that would ultimately always be reinforced through theatrical convention. This recuperative situation worked in Cushman's favor, however, for it allowed her some freedom in her determined efforts to adopt, if only momentarily, the voice of the subject.

In Cushman's case, the audience would have been familiar with a traditional style of representation for Romeo, a style that she challenged both through her innovative interpretation and through her sexed female body. Regardless of the fact that Cushman was playing a male role, spectators might have expected her to act like a woman, to, as Coleman remarked, "betray [her] female origin by quaint little movements." Breeches performers were generally not expected to pass, and if they did their success proved to be, for many viewers, "a kind of failure correspondingly great."[88] This was not the case with Cushman. Her androgyny, her double image, allowed her to paradoxically assume the subject position even though she remained an object, to pass as a man onstage and to be thought of as masculine offstage, without incurring public scorn. The power she communicated onstage and in her "private" life was so enchanting that she was celebrated for it rather than castigated. Moreover, the spell that Cushman wove over her audiences with her impersonation of Romeo *enhanced* her reputation as a great actress and woman; she was a more amazing lady in the public eye because she could become a man. As William Price points out, Cushman's masculinity (expressed both through her professional work and through her nontheatrical achievements) positively affected her reception as a nineteenth-century woman. She was publicly respected for her willingness to take on the headship of her family and play "the part of a man in these serious relations of life." She transacted her public business over private affairs fairly and honestly without sacrificing her femininity, he explains, and this forceful manner translated to her performance of masculinity onstage. Forgoing all the "disturbing concerns of feminine emotion," yet still remaining "pure" and "true," Cushman reaped the fruits of her androgyny and was recognized, according to Price, as "a woman of rare genius."[89] Because men held a much more esteemed position in Victorian society, Cushman may have been regarded as simply striving to reach a higher status, to improve herself, and this was a pursuit that she could follow without surrendering her "truest intents." As the androgyne, Cushman could transcend gender, break conventions, disrupt expectations, move beyond restrictive sex role prescriptions, *and* be rewarded for her efforts.

OFFSTAGE ANDROGYNY

Cushman played the androgyne off stage as well. As Price mentioned above, she could enact male social roles successfully without threatening her status as a respectable Victorian woman. She directly competed with her male colleagues, demanded the same wages as men, supported her family (which included various female lovers), and controlled her own business affairs and real estate ventures after 1858.[90] By traveling outside her sphere and taking on traditional male responsibilities, Cushman furthered her image as a masculine woman and triumphantly played the androgyne as she broke accepted conventions and deftly crossed social gender boundaries through her public male role-playing, her lesbianism, and her offstage cross-dressing. Cushman was successful in acting between social categories and suggested new possibilities for her Victorian sisters by creating a new sphere with expanded roles for women. Like her Romeo, Cushman's embodiment of the social androgyne was largely accepted by the public. Her masculinity, while being recognized by some as eccentric, reinforced a perception of her as a strong woman and added to her meritorious public persona. This double image allowed her, once again, to claim a liminal position that facilitated an escape from, and critique of, domesticity and traditional femininity.

Years before critics made associations between the actress and Macready, Cushman adopted a male persona that colored her personal life as well as her professional career. As Cushman's biographers relate, Cushman's youth was spent climbing trees, assuming male parts (Bluebeard) in childhood games, and smashing doll's heads open so that she could investigate their brains. All such activity was aptly summarized in the statement that opens an early diary of Cushman's: "I was born a tomboy."[91] Cushman celebrated this self-imposed label despite the fact that the word tomboy was used pejoratively in the nineteenth century as a derogatory term for a girl who eschewed her femininity. As Stebbins explained in her biography of Cushman, the word "tomboy" was applied to all little girls who betrayed a will of their own. "It was the advance-guard of that army of opprobrious epithets which has since been lavished so freely upon the pioneers of women's advancement and for a long time the ugly little phrase had the power to keep the dangerous feminine element within what was considered to be the due bounds of propriety and decorum."[92] Games and activities that were, according to Stebbins, "considered exclusively and strictly masculine" were off limits to girls in the 1820s when Cushman was growing up. It is significant, therefore, that upon reflection, Cushman selected this term to describe herself, thus recognizing her own transgression and attempting to escape discourses of containment by appropriating and celebrating such aspersions.

The actress's early masculine self-image was also noted by those who grew up with her. In writing about Cushman, one childhood friend juxtaposes Cushman's extraordinary accomplishments in the public sphere and her success in expanding the private sphere with her "masculine masquerade." She recalled the actress as an individual of "grand force" who,

> conquering her work, had freed herself from the conventions and traditional judgements of the stage; and I think that, in her private and individual relations, her friends took that same impression of her as of a grand soul having conquered life and itself, so that she might fairly exercise the right to do as she pleased—to be her own gracious, individual self. It was that spontaneity in a woman of the world that held its unfailing charm over men of the world and over multitudes of young women, which made them kneel to her.... I shall never forget our first meeting after many years of absence.... She seated herself in front of me, holding both my hands in the sincere grasp of hers, while she went back over the times when, as she said, we were boys together, albeit I had not such a penchant for a masculine masquerade as she, with the glory of her Romeo behind her, might reasonably entertain.[93]

As her "boyhood" friend suggests, Cushman succeeded in living outside social prescriptions. Unlike most Victorian women, Cushman lived an alternative lifestyle within nineteenth-century society, a lifestyle that contemporary historians, particularly Merrill, explain provides evidence of her lesbianism. She never experienced any fulfilling romantic relationships with men nor did she ever marry. Indeed, she violently rejected entry into traditional matrimony, for as she once told Coleman, "No *actor* should ever marry at all, or, if *she* does, she should quit the stage!"[94] Rather, Cushman was a partner in at least two "female marriages," as Elizabeth Barrett Browning remarked,[95] one with English actress Matilda Hayes and one with the sculptor Emma Stebbins, her most enduring and beloved companion. Before her longer more serious relationships with Hayes and Stebbins, however, Cushman engaged in numerous other relationships and flirtations with women.[96]

Although Cushman's own family members betrayed some concern over her unorthodox relationships, romantic friendships between women were not generally perceived as threatening during the nineteenth century. Women, whose strong bonds were cultivated through female kinship networks, boarding schools, and church groups, could unabashedly express both verbal and physical affection for each other without exciting any marked Victorian speculation because, as Lillian Faderman points out, "sound women were asexual." Until late nineteenth-century sexologists categorized love between two women as "inverted," women could cultivate romantic friendships, write passionately of their female lovers, and live monogamously with other women for indefinite periods of time. For as Faderman explains, "It was doubtful enough that [women] would concern themselves with any form of sexual satisfaction, but that they would seek sexual expression without a male initiator was as credible as claiming to hear the thunder play 'God Save the King.'"[97]

Even Cushman's dissenters did not express concern over her relationships with women. For Coleman and others, her crimes lay in attempting to usurp male privilege and in trying to "wear the breeches," not in homosexuality, which was not even an acknowledged practice for women during the mid-nineteenth century. Such critical insouciance regarding Cushman's personal life is illustrated by an anecdote told by Coleman about an early conversation he had with the actress. Though the contemporary critic would undoubtedly find in this conversation evidence of Cushman's lesbianism, Coleman did not indicate that her sentiments were at all "unnatural." He recalls that while still a theatrical novice, Coleman received some coaching from Cushman, who also gave him advice about his future career as an actor. She urged him to study all the great tragic roles and reminded him how fortunate he was to have all the "divine girls" from Shakespeare's canon to woo:

> Bless your lucky stars that you've pull of the Bard himself, who was condemned to see all those lovely creatures murdered by beastly, scrubby, chubby, louts of boys, while you, you villain, you've the pick of creation to make love to! And the beauty of it is, they never worry, never fool you; when you're tired of one, you can declare on to the other without making either of 'em jealous. My God! were I a man, instead of a wretched, miserable woman with a face like an owl.[98]

Cushman does not simply speak like an older and wiser theatrical legend giving advice to a fledgling actor. Rather she speaks with authority as a fellow female admirer and as one who lives vicariously through Coleman. She envies his position as one who can love many different women without having to remain monogamous to one; she longs, it seems, to enjoy his sanctioned privilege as a theatrical (and perhaps social) playboy.

It is important to acknowledge Cushman's lesbianism in light of her success as a breeches performer, her penchant for male roles in general, and her overall fondness for Romeo in particular.[99] Indeed, the knowledge of Cushman's lesbianism suggests another possible layer in her performance of Romeo and explains, as Merrill argues, the reported sense of "truth" that seemed to accompany her exhibitions of passion. The majority of English and American critics remarked on Cushman's exceptionally fervid lovemaking. Coleman reported that her "amorous endearments were of so erotic a character that no man would have dared to indulge in them *coram publico*," and Weston Marston claimed that, "[a]s a lover, the ardour of her devotion exceeded that of any male actor I have ever seen in the part."[100] Likewise, Knowles described act 3, scene 3 as a "scene of topmost passion" and the *London Times* commended Cushman for her acting in the banishment scene and remarked that her passion broke forth with "irresistible violence."[101] In America, the *Herald* critic was amazed by the "fervency and truthfulness" of her passion and added that in the banishment scene "the torture of mind and agony of soul exhibited so truthfully by this distinguished actress, surpassed anything we have ever seen."[102] Ten years later (despite her age and her portly silhouette), Cushman's skill as a lover was still recognized by New York papers; the *New York Daily News* stated in 1860 that she played the role with "immense vigor and a touching tenderness that is seldom to be noticed in her feminine assumptions . . . Her love making is inimitable, and may be studied with advantage by young men with crinoline fascinations that they don't know how to attack."[103] The *Herald* parroted the sentiments of the *Daily News* critic in a review that came out the same day, allowing that, "There is perhaps not one of her impersonations in which she is more happy, or a *role* in her *repertoire* more suited to her peculiar power, voice and energy."[104]

Through Romeo, Cushman could express her passion for women without condemnation. Indeed, Romeo is passionate, lively, ambitious in furthering his suit, and yet also expresses deep pain in the course of the play as his early melancholic disquisitions over Rosaline and his outpourings to the Friar in act 3, scene 3 signify. Perhaps Romeo's lamentations over Rosaline, the Petrarchan idealized woman, and his unrequited love, struck a cord with Cushman; such expressions may have echoed her own sentiments in a century where women were forbidden even heterosexual desire. Moreover, as Merrill's study makes clear, Cushman's sapphic Romeo provided a lesbian subtext to which women in the audience responded. This would explain the actress's extreme popularity with her female fans, as evidenced by her childhood friend who marveled over the "multitudes of young women" who came to "kneel" to her. Such a patron might have experienced profound empathy with Cushman/Romeo when in act 3, scene 3 the Friar related the verdict that would define her/his relationship to both society and love: "banishment."

Cushman's tendency to break conventions and "defy structure" was emotionally and theatrically manifested through her lesbianism and physically manifested through her offstage cross-dressing. The *Spirit of the Times* reported that during her midwestern tour in 1851 Cushman publicly adopted "male attire *in toto,*" and added that because of her repeated portrayals of male characters ("the Bloomerism of Claude Melnotte, the 'tights' of Romeo and Hamlet, and sundry other 'breeches parts'"), her "transition" into a "man" offstage was "neither great nor starling."[105] Both Coleman and Herman Melville also attest to Cushman's offstage practice of cross-dressing; they recall her tendency to appear at rehearsals wearing Wellington boots and a man's coat, hat, cravat, and collar over her feminine apparel.[106] Both the *Spirit* account and the reports by Coleman and Melville strikingly reinforce Cushman's androgynous image. While it is true that she did perhaps attempt to pass by appearing in male drag "in toto," her famous face betrayed her to the *Spirit* reporter (or his informant), and further cultivated her double image. Her silhouette would have been read as exclusively male since women never wore men's clothes ordinarily, yet upon closer scrutiny, the woman would have been recognizable beneath her male habiliments. Furthermore, Cushman's rehearsal clothing, as described by both Coleman and Melville, included elements of male dress in addition to female petticoats, which she did not abandon. The Harvard Theatre Collection contains at least three photographs of Cushman wearing a bow tie or male cravat, and the same outfit is also featured in an oil painting by William Page, rendered in 1853.[107] Her selection of outfits that were comprised of elements from male and female wardrobes allowed Cushman to "seem both," to play the androgyne offstage by foregrounding the artificial nature of gender construction. The androgyny implied in Cushman's sartorial markers suggests that women like herself could *perform* male social roles as well as female ones—a reality symbolized by her penchant for boots and bow ties.

By appropriating male dress in addition to male behavior offstage, Cushman lent additional puissance to her male representations onstage and implied that women could compete with men in reality just as they could in illusion. Cushman gives evidence of a direct link between the two in an interview with LaSalle Corbell Pickett in which she describes a performance of *Romeo and Juliet* at the National Theatre in Boston during the 1851–52 season. Cushman recalled, "I was playing Romeo to Miss Anderson's Juliet when, just as I was revealing the rapture of my love, a man in the audience gave vent to a sneeze so loud and so grotesque that I knew he had manufactured it for that occasion." Cushman immediately stopped the play, escorted Miss Anderson off the stage, returned to the footlights, and "announced that if some man did not put that person out I would have to do it. It was done and I got more cheers for that irregular interpolation than for any of the scenes written for the original Romeo."[108] This event juxtaposes Cushman's masculine roles—both theatrical and social—and therefore accentuates not only her facile ability to move between Romeo and her offstage role as female star but also the affinity between these two roles. Indeed, Cushman seems to discuss three figures in this story: herself as star; Shakespeare's Romeo, or as she says "the original Romeo"; and Cushman/Romeo, the androgyne who can move between the other two roles with ease and simultaneously embody both. Cushman, the actress, broke the fourth wall and appeared as woman, but at the same time took on a masculine role in violating accepted norms of female behavior (taking charge of the situation, escorting Juliet offstage, and commanding members of the audience to expel the obnoxious patron) and "breaking taboos" in the process.

In conclusion, Cushman's androgyny can be interpreted in multiple ways. It acted as a metaphor for critics who were impressed by her great powers of transformation yet could not ultimately categorize her as male. Yet, by appearing as "half-man, half-woman," Cushman became both a symbol of transcendence in an age of antitheses and a "monstrous anomaly"; in addition to being perceived as concomitantly male and female, she was acknowledged as both a genius and a threat. Her extraordinary abilities allowed her not only to convincingly perform masculinity as Rosalind/Ganymed and move beyond gender in her portrayal of Romeo, but also allowed her to act between social spheres, thereby calling the legitimacy of this ideology into question. Like Smith-Rosenberg's trickster, Cushman demonstrated the "contingency of order" and of gender as she warred with convention and personified, in her social and theatrical roles, "unfettered human potential." Indeed, Cushman expanded possibilities for the nineteenth-century middle-class woman, whose life was defined by antithesis. By appearing both masculine and feminine she undermined binary prescriptions and proved that women could select from a varied menu of gendered attributes. Cushman's androgyny suggested to her nineteenth-century followers that identity need not be polarized or essentialized; rather it might be envisioned as a rich tapestry: complex, textured, handmade or *individually* crafted, varied, and essentially (neither "male" nor "female" but) unique.

Chapter 5

THE DECLINE OF BREECHES PERFORMANCE

The leg business is a business which requires legs.

—Olive Logan

IN 1860, LAURA KEENE MOUNTED A PRODUCTION of John Gay's *The Beggar's Opera* at her theatre in New York. Once considered a staple within the American repertoire, Gay's play was now referred to by critics as "a curiosity only," yet it managed to attract a crowd for the benefit of "two pretty debutantes," Miss Willoughby and Miss Melvin. While the former went unmentioned by the *Albion* critic who reviewed the production, Melvin was recognized for her portrayal of Captain Macheath, a role that had been a popular breeches vehicle since the Restoration. Unlike Peg Woffington, who supposedly impressed London audiences with her convincing impersonation of the dashing male hero, Melvin did not appear manly at all but rather "looked as much like a woman as it is possible for a woman to look." The *Albion* critic continued, "Miss Melvin may easily do better than to evoke dim ghosts of musical highwaymen, in chestnut curls, and pink satin tights."[1] Nineteenth-century spectators may have grown tired of the cross-dressed Macheath's criminal crusades, yet they were becoming increasingly enthusiastic about "chestnut curls" and "pink satin tights." As the description of Melvin suggests, breeches performance in the 1860s privileged alluring costumes over serious dramatic endeavors, as legs rapidly became a much safer guarantee of sizable benefit houses than displays of manly sword play or skilled histrionic expression. Such a trend in breeches performance was influenced by the rise of variety entertainment in the 1860s. Indeed, as burlesque spectacles like Keene's *The Seven Sisters* (which featured "large numbers of pretty women" or "short-petticoated ladies"[2]), "leg shows" in the manner of the 1866 hit *The Black Crook,* and "horse operas" like *Mazeppa* became standard New York fare, critics began to lament "the extinction of the Drama in New York."[3]

The Drama was not the only endangered species on the New York stage during the 1860s. In their brief mention of the convention of breeches in America, theatre historians note that the breeches performer was equally in danger of cultural erasure and/or marginalization during this decade, as the cross-dressed player of Hamlet, Romeo, and Claude Melnotte largely vanished from the theatrical scene and popular performers of burlesque and equestrian melodrama were relegated to lowbrow theatres. Two principle explanations have been posited regarding this phenomenon in the 1860s: the proliferation of realism within the American theatre, and the overwhelming interest in popular entertainment forms. Both of these theories lack analysis and evidential support.

Other possible reasons for this decline must be explored, such as the marked shift in critical response to the breeches performer during the 1860s—a shift that reflected the neglect of traditional players, the sexual objectification of the equestrian breeches performer, and the vilification of the burlesque actress in 1869. Two actresses in particular—Menken and Thompson—significantly contributed to altered critical perceptions of the cross-dressed actress during this decade; the influence that their careers had on the critics and on the decline of the convention (which was significantly influenced, I think, by critical response) must be investigated as well. The "Naked Lady" and the British Blonde irrevocably transformed cross-dressed representation at the end of the 1860s; their combined forces inspired a change in the convention of breeches both with regard to the performance of gender onstage and to the critical consumption of female transvestism. Breeches actresses were no longer regarded as boys, "ladies," or even androgynes with the power to appear both male and female. The female cross-dressed performer became instead a highly specialized, dangerously sexual actress with certain transgressive powers—powers that were ultimately contained through her physical marginalization within lowbrow theatrical establishments—haunts that were only frequented by "dim ghosts."

DECLINE OF BREECHES

As early as 1855, breeches performances in certain cities were recognized as subversive and were thus eliminated from the repertoire. William Wood provides evidence of this in his *Personal Recollections of the Stage* as he reflects upon the unfair treatment previously given to a female dancer in Philadelphia and the double standard displayed by local audiences. He recalls, "An unaccountable severity on the score of dress *in dancing* prevailed, while an exact as well as ungraceful imitation of men in the performance of male characters by women was tolerated to an extent which it would be dangerous *now* [1855] to follow, even in a minor theatre."[4] While this view might have been extreme (New York audiences could still see breeches performers regularly throughout the 1850s and 1860s), it does suggest that female expeditions into masculine territory were becoming increasingly suspect.

While breeches performers were often harshly criticized and viewed as threatening during the first half of the nineteenth century, late-nineteenth-century responses to the cross-dressed actress became much more acrimonious, which perhaps explains the marked decrease in the number of male roles being played by women as the century progressed. Very rarely did examples of positive criticism and/or innocuous reports pepper the columns of "Things Theatrical" as they had during the first half of the century; rather, breeches performance repeatedly met with harsh criticism or no criticism at all, which was perhaps more damning. Actresses who played men's roles were taken less seriously in their dramatic pursuits, and were instead often considered eccentric and immoral: they were "mongrels"[5] who "mocked masculinity" and "belittled the drama."[6] Critical responses during the later half of the nineteenth century made it quite evident that the breeches actresses had permanently fallen from grace because of her association with the burgeoning leg show. And although certain types of breeches performances remained popular with some audiences until the turn of the century, the practice of cross-gender casting was largely eliminated from the American theatre by 1900.

The most frequently offered explanation for the decline or transmogrification of this convention involves the ascendancy of realism in the American theatre. Although certain actresses such as Eva Le Gallienne and Judith Anderson continued to play roles like Hamlet in the twentieth century, these performances were regarded as novel and secondary to the realistic vehicles that established their stardom. Indeed, there was seemingly no place for the transvestite, the octogenaric Dane or Little Eva in the so-called legitimate (albeit still in many ways alternative) theatre of Ibsen and Hauptman.[7] Ferris notes this theory of the decline, allowing that the "advent of dramatic realism at the end of the nineteenth century . . . stopped the majority of actresses playing men's roles," yet explains that those who did achieve notoriety were not necessarily regarded as "oddities" but as female stereotypes in male clothing. She continues, "[T]he male roles retained in an actress's repertoire displayed a lack of traditional male virtues, such as strength and willpower, and in some cases were almost deemed unsuitable for actors."[8] As Ferris notes, roles like Hamlet (whom Erica Munk calls "a waffling neurotic prone to violent fits"[9]) that continued to be played by actresses such as Bernhardt and Le Gallienne simply reinforced dominant gender ideology. Because threatening messages concerning women usurping male power were defused when the agents involved in this coup on masculinity were themselves regarded as effeminate, such parts could be retained within an actress's repertoire even after the convention had become unpopular. Yet, while it may have been easier for critics to argue that roles like Hamlet and Romeo were perhaps less masculine than their Shakespearean big brothers, Othello and Richard III, most late-century commentators condemned *any* foray into manhood within the traditional repertoire.

As was the case during the first half of the nineteenth century, the critical response to the breeches performer after 1860 was still somewhat contingent on genre as well as character. Burlesque, equestrian melodrama, and extravaganza provided acceptable material for the breeches actress, but serious drama remained outside the limits of appropriate subject matter. One late century New York critic remarked, "The time seems to have passed when the feminine element essay masculine roles in tragedy,"[10] and another claimed that performances of Shakespearean heroes by women "are novel if not interesting though they 'make the judicious grieve' that estimable ladies who have many personal charms and acknowledged domestic virtues should attempt what Heaven never intended they should do and no one but themselves and a few misguided friends seem to be specially interested in."[11] When the genre was thought to be fatuous, "lowbrow," or insignificant, the performers were similarly regarded as less threatening, yet when the genre was to be taken seriously, then those acting as conduits for such profound dramatic expression must be thought sincere. Such was the case with tragedy and/or serious drama and perhaps even more so with realism. As William Price explains in his biography of Cushman written in 1894, "burlettas and the romantic opera seem to demand this paradox" (women as men) and in such cases art "takes no offense." He continues:

> It would seem easy to establish the limits of feminine intrusion. A point is reached at which the question of taste arises. We may say that it is impossible for a woman to act with sincerity, by reason of temperament and mental characteristics, and elemental nature, in certain roles essentially masculine—the illusion is impossible. The highest degree of success, we may say, is a kind of failure correspondingly great; and finally we may urge that only eccentricity and a desire for notoriety can be at the bottom of such performances.[12]

In reflecting upon the tradition of female Hamlets, the New York critic, William Winter, concurs with Price's views regarding the inability of the actress to convincingly portray masculinity. He writes in 1911, "Women sometimes succeed in creating an actual, if fleeting, illusion of masculinity in presentments of dashing young cavaliers, or of roguish girls masquerading as such ... but the great, serious male incarnations of dramatic poetry have never been, and they never can be, adequately impersonated by females."[13] Century-old arguments against women playing serious male roles, therefore, applied to fin-de-siècle breeches performance as well. For while it may have been foreseeable that Shaw's Marchbanks could be played by a woman, certainly Morrell, Ibsen's Torvald, or Strindberg's Captain were off limits. According to later nineteenth-century critics, the "illusion [was] impossible" despite the degree of talent an actress might possess. For as the age of realism dawned within the American theatre, the ability to create a convincing "illusion"—a term that was becoming more and more narrowly defined—became paramount.

Provided this context, the traditional breeches performer was asked to perform an impossible feat. Although actors throughout theatrical history continually endeavored to hold their "mirror[s] up to nature," late nineteenth-century reflectors revealed images that were startlingly different from previous "natural" conceptions. Events and ideologies such as the industrial revolution, August Comte's theories and the ascendancy of Naturalism in literature and drama, and Darwinism and the growing emphasis on science, transformed the cultural looking glass as well, necessitating a much more precise and "scientific" interpretation of "nature." While outside the boundaries of realism, actresses such as Fisher, Cushman, Lewis, and Crampton may have momentarily "passed" as men (or boys) onstage (especially given that they were perhaps being evaluated according to more neoclassical conceptions of "truth"—masculinity was an "ideal" that could be played as actresses were scrutinized for showing life as it "should be," rather than as it existed beyond the footlights), modern audiences were not quite as willing to suspend their disbelief. Perhaps a Johnsonian argument pointing out the absurdity of such strict adherence to seemingly natural "rules" may have better served a late nineteenth-century American audience, who could neither imagine nor tolerate displays of incongruous gender play amidst actual tables, chairs, and tea services.[14] As scripts, lighting, sets, and costumes became increasingly realistic, the cross-dressed actress of more traditional or classical roles became increasingly displaced.

In addition to the advance of realism within the American theatre, the rise of variety entertainment, specifically burlesque, is also indirectly cited by Edwards as being partially responsible for the convention's decline. (Other historians do not mention this phenomenon as a contributing factor.) Breeches performers who could not convincingly pass as men in the new realistic dramas were increasingly unwelcome within the ranks of the mainstream theatres, while in burlesque halls, this very handicap became their signature. As breeches and trousers were exchanged for pink tights and fleshlings, the convention of female theatrical transvestism literally lost its legitimacy as it was largely transformed into what Olive Logan so aptly termed "the leg business"—a "business" that was gradually deemed unacceptable for mainstream audiences and ultimately marginalized within the American theatre. Yet how did this process of marginalization take place, and how did variety entertainment alter the way in which breeches performance was perceived by the public? Neither of these questions are answered by Edwards, who implies that the leg business had something to do with the transformation and/or decline of breeches performance, but does not explain or define the "significant changes" that precipitated such a shift in female theatrical transvestism during the 1860s.

Previous theories concerning the decrease in breeches performance (both traditional and popular), therefore, are informative yet incomplete. Other explanations must be examined in order to achieve a more complete understanding of how breeches performance began to decline after midcentury. The elimination of the benefit system, for example, also significantly affected the serious breeches actress. For with the eradication of benefits during the second half of the nineteenth century, cross-dressed performers who aspired to play Shakespearean tragic heroes and melodramatic adult male leads lost their principle performance opportunity (since benefit nights were the only occasion on which actresses—who had not achieved star status—could choose their own roles). Benefits, as

Russell points out, were "special performances at which boundaries were transgressed and risks were taken. Announcements of benefits frequently include the phrase 'for the first time,' indicating that many nineteenth-century performers used benefits to try out new roles or new lines of business."[15] Indeed, the benefit was a sort of liminal space where the breeches actress could explore gender identities without worrying that such experimentation might cost her a job. When benefits were denied actresses, experimental performance projects ceased as well.

As theatre became increasingly "industrialized" in the 1860s, actors and actresses lost many of their privileges. Dudden reports that in the sixties, there was a general reduction in salaries for utility performers (the walking ladies and gentlemen, ballet girls, and supernumeraries) and an increase in "job acting," which meant that managers could hire performers for individual productions and forego the seasonal contract. In addition, the "traditional benefit performance, in which a performer had some influence over her own compensation, was eliminated."[16] While benefits did not entirely disappear in the 1860s, as Dudden implies, managers began to think them unprofitable and made efforts to curtail them. Actors and actresses were known to withhold their best performances until their benefit nights, which hurt business and irritated their employers. Such conduct caused managers to limit benefits to leading players and ultimately convinced them to revoke the privilege altogether.[17] One critic for the *Albion* explains the behavior that precipitated these managerial decisions regarding the elimination of the benefit. He writes,

> The present fashion converts the established season of theatrical benefits into a season of individual drummings up and exasperating rivalries. The comic man counts the house of the leading juvenile with knitted brows and anxious eye, if he discovers a dozen more dollars taking their ease in their orchestral chairs than smiled upon him with their candid faces on his own night, he forthwith ceases to be comic, sets to gnawing his heart in comfortless [despair] and very probably dives into the nearest 'saloon,' to wash the horrible reality out of his thoughts.[18]

In addition to remarking upon the destructive competition between the players, critics also complained about the "dreadful old plays" that were remounted on benefit nights. In an age when spectacular vehicles (that often privileged transformation scenes and dioramas over great acting) were occupying most Broadway houses, many actors looked to the classics to provide weighty material that might showcase their talents.

Yet other performers were more interested in drawing a crowd. Because more traditional fare was threatened by popular interest in extravaganza and spectacle, breeches performers—like their managers—often realized that they might make more money by choosing a popular vehicle for their benefit rather than a more artistically satisfying role like Norval or Richard III. For example, Menken repeatedly played Mazeppa on benefit nights throughout the early 1860s, even though she favored other parts. Similarly, the Bowery celebrity Kate Fisher also played Mazeppa on her benefit night, resulting in a theatre "crowded in every part," a standing ovation, and "a magnificent floral tribute . . . composed of almost every variety and hue of natural flowers."[19] While such benefit choices certainly enhanced actresses' pocketbooks, repeating popular roles like Mazeppa on benefit nights further narrowed current perceptions of breeches performance and fortified associations between the actress and "illegitimate"—seemingly less serious—types of theatrical entertainment.

Another contributing factor to the decrease in breeches performance during the second half of the nineteenth century was the press's disregard for the tragic and/or serious player of men's roles. Even Cushman's male performances were critically neglected despite her midcentury reputation as America's most highly acclaimed actress. The *Albion* critic's response to her month-long engagement at the Winter Garden in October of 1860 is indicative of critical approaches to serious roles during the 1860s. Hamilton, the critic, reports on Cushman's performances of Bianca and Mrs. Haller throughout the month, yet neglects to even mention that she played Cardinal Wolsey in Shakespeare's *Henry the Eighth*. For example, on October 6, he reports that his column will cover theatrical events that occurred over the last six days. Cushman performed Wolsey on October 1, 2, and 3, but there is no review nor any indication from this critic that these singular performances ever took place. Considering the novelty of this event—an actress had never played this role before on the English-speaking stage— Cushman's extreme fame as Romeo in the 1840s and 1850s, and the publicity that her tour of America had received prior to her arrival, it is almost unbelievable that Hamilton could overlook this portrayal, even if to condemn it. This critical silence can perhaps be explained by the actress's unorthodox choice in selecting Wolsey and by her unprecedented popularity among American audiences. The role of the Cardinal was thought to be out of the breeches performer's line: the character was not a youth or a romantic hero but a man—authoritative and cunning—and was currently being played by many of Cushman's male contemporaries. Such an undertaking could not be sanctioned by critics like Hamilton, who possessed no discourse with which to contain the celebrated actress since this character was neither a boy nor an effeminate male (although other critics who reviewed her Wolsey tempered their praise by remarking upon Cushman's femininity and her singular talents as a breeches performer).[20] The only option left to this critic would have been to criticize her performance, but because Cushman was such a recognized breeches performer and was so loved by her audiences, it might have been difficult for the *Albion* to criticize her without stirring up too much public ire—especially if such negative criticism threatened to test the loyalty of their readership. Because condemnation would have proven too costly, the paper had no alternative but to ignore her.

Actresses who played men's roles in Broadway hits were also strangely absent from the columns of the theatrical reports. Mercutio's review of *Rosedale, or the Rifle Ball* exemplifies this tendency to marginalize the more serious breeches actresses. In his first review of the play, this critic, otherwise known as William Winter, discusses the text, the characters, and the cast at length, but makes no mention of Emma LeBrun who played Sir Arthur May, the only breeches role featured in the production. In the following issue, Mercutio writes about the performance again, this time giving a detailed analysis of the individual performances; yet, once more, the breeches role is not mentioned.[21] The only breeches role in a new drama to attract critical attention in the early 1860s was Sam Willoughby in Tom Taylor's *Ticket-of-Leave-Man;* on both occasions that this play was reviewed by the critics, the actress playing Sam was given a brief but favorable mention. Not surprisingly, Sam was a boy role, and the *Albion* critic noted that because an actress played the part "the impulsiveness of boyhood" was added to the performance.[22]

The critical practice of ignoring "legitimate" breeches performance continued to be operative throughout the rest of the century, as is evidenced by the press's treatment of Charles Hoyt's enormously successful play, *A Trip to Chinatown,* which was produced in 1891. Although Hoyt's farce contained two breeches roles— Willie Grow and Tony Gay—the actresses who played these parts throughout the long run were forgotten by New York critics. The *New York Dramatic Mirror* refused to review the play at all, and bemoaned the farce as a detriment to the American drama. "The *Mirror* does not admire the class.... It has arrested the serious dramatic development of this country, coarsening public taste and discouraging effort in higher and better directions."[23] In addition, the *Spirit of the Times* and the *Spirit of the Times and the New York Sportsman* both reviewed the play with no allusion to any breeches performers, and the *New York Times* wrote about the play but neglected to comment on either actress.[24]

This critical silence seems to have stemmed from a desire to avoid expressing negative sentiments (as may have been the case with Cushman's performance of Wolsey), or it was perhaps an indication that the breeches performer no longer rated as a significant part of the New York theatrical scene, that the convention was employed less and less frequently in regular drama. Breeches actresses may also have been neglected on purpose by dramatic journalists who hoped that by rendering the breeches-wearing actress critically nonexistent, audiences might loose their interest and stop patronizing this usurper of male privilege. Another explanation for such critical disregard lies in the so-called extinction of the Drama. For as more traditional performances were eclipsed by novelty acts, circus shows, and spectacular equestrian melodramas, the rare actress who donned the tights and tunic of Hamlet became increasingly eclipsed by the woman in the fleshling suit. Legs not only sold seats in the Bowery during the 1860s, but also facilitated a critic's feast in the Cold Cut Room.

EQUESTRIAN MELODRAMA AND THE SEXUALIZATION OF THE BREECHES PERFORMER

While it would be safe to assume that women who played men's roles during the first half of the nineteenth century were frequently admired for the novelty of their attire (as well as for their dramatic character choice), the widespread adoption of fleshlings by breeches performers who played Mazeppa in the 1860s marks a significant change in the way cross-dressed actresses were perceived by the critics. Breeches allowed women to display their legs, yet, unlike the silk bodystocking favored after midcentury, the term "breeches" did not always signify tight-fitting or exceptionally revealing costumes. The breeches actress wore spacious trousers and turkish pantaloons (Bloomer-like garments) in addition to snug knee breeches. Even the infamous Menken wore loose-legged pants when she portrayed the sailor William in Jerrold's *Black-Eyed Susan* or the French Spy (see figure 5.1).

In the 1860s, a craze for equestrian melodrama erupted in New York. The most popular of these melodramas was *Mazeppa,* which featured a scene in which the principal male character would appear partially or entirely nude. Such a display facilitated the need for the fleshing suit—a costume that ultimately became representative of breeches performance in general during this decade. The *Clipper* critic describes a typical fleshling outfit, worn by a popular "Mazeppa," Kate Vance. The costume "consists of a complete suit of closely-fitting, flesh-colored tights, encasing the entire form, from neck to feet, unencumbered or disfigured with drapery or anything else excepting brief trunks around the loins."[25] Although some actresses did "disfigure" their silk suit by wearing a (usually white cotton) blouse in addition to their trunks, the general idea surrounding the adoption of fleshlings was to give the audience the impression

Fig. 5.1: Adah Isaacs Menken as the French Spy. Harvard Theatre Collection, The Houghton Library, Fredric Woodbridge Wilson, Curator

that the actress was nude (perhaps by Victorian definitions she actually was) (see figure 5.2). Because theatres were often poorly lit and because houses like the Bowery and Niblo's Garden were so large, spectators might have suspected that the actress was indeed naked.

While breeches performers wore silk tights before the 1860s, the traditional tunic/tights combination was indeed modest when compared with Vance's undress uniform. Yet, any view of a woman's leg must have been both novel and perhaps erotic during a period when such views were strictly reserved for private showings. Prior to mid-century, however, drawings, photographs, daguerreotypes, and etchings do not suggest any overt or deliberate attempts by the breeches performer to display her body in ways significantly different from

Fig. 5.2: Adah Isaacs Menken in fleshlings. Harvard Theatre Collection, The Houghton Library, Fredric Woodbridge Wilson, Curator.

the male performer of her day. Actresses, prior to the 1860s, were not attempting to objectify themselves as some contemporary scholars imply, nor were they critically objectified by the male press. Critics may have felt privately stimulated by such displays but did not collectively *focus* on the erotic aspect of breeches actresses' apparel until the 1860s.[26]

Prior to this time, social anxieties (expressed through critical aspersions) engendered by "masculine" women who strove to appropriate male power by "wearing the breeches" were controlled through discourses of boyishness and femininity. During the 1860s, however, a shift in the nature of critical discourses transpired as New York critics began to systematically focus upon the body of the actress as opposed to her talent, her voice, her age, her masculine disguise, or her dramatic interpretations; not surprisingly, such discourses arose with the adoption of fleshlings by the equestrian breeches performer and with innovations in photography that, through the *cartes de visite,* allowed spectators to inspect more closely and to consume more frequently the female form.[27] The sexualization of the breeches performer by the American press, however, must not only be regarded as a publicity campaign designed to attract audiences in an age of increasing industrialization (although this certainly influenced critical rhetoric). Nor were such discourses simply direct responses to changing costume trends or uncontrollable expressions of desire exhibited by select members of a male dominated press. Rather, the discourse spun alongside the silk fleshling suit was, on specific occasions, deliberate and marginalizing, a specious narrative created to tell a frightening story about a "horrible prettiness" that threatened the American family and society at large.

According to Dudden, American theatre historians often cite Henry Jarrett, Harry Palmer, and William Wheatley's 1866 production of *The Black Crook* as the original "leg show" (although this extravaganza featured no female cross-dressing). Allen argues, however, that the theatre became gradually "feminized" (or preoccupied with displaying the female form) prior to (or during the early years of) the 1860s with the growing public clamor for ballet, the emergence of "living pictures" or tableaux vivants, and the proliferation of equestrian spectacular melodrama. All three of these entertainment forms featured women's bodies, and thus privileged the exposure of legs over artistic expression.

Ballet was introduced to New York audiences in 1827 as Madame Hutin made her American premiere. While her performance—and her costume—proved somewhat controversial (Hewitt recounts that upon seeing Hutin, all the female occupants of the boxes rushed from the theatre "after an exclamation of horror"[28]), the dance's subsequent associations with "romantic ballet" proved redemptive. Celebrated dancers such as Celeste and Fanny Elssler made ballet more palatable for American audiences as they introduced a style of ballet that transported audiences to fairy kingdoms and witches' covens; female dancers transcended their scantily clad corporeal shells and became "swans or butterflies or celestial bodies." This emphasis on a supernatural world de-emphasized the body of the romantic ballerina, argues Allen, and thus contained fears regarding immodesty posed by translucent skirts and pink tights.[29]

Living pictures, tableaux vivants, or "model artist" shows, which became popular in the 1830s in New York museums and theatres, featured actors and actresses in performed versions of famous paintings and sculptures. The performers, dressed (or undressed) appropriately, would assemble themselves, along with backdrops and properties, to create a sort of living still life that would be shown before an audience. After a few minutes, the curtain would fall and another representation would be prepared. Women's bodies often became a salient component of such displays, as art works such as *Venus de Medici* and Hiram Powers's *Greek Slave* offered ample opportunity for exposing nude women. As this practice became increasingly feminized (meaning that women's bodies were featured above other subject matter) and therefore increasingly popular, press reactions became, in many cases, increasingly vitriolic. Class associations, however, often influenced the outcome of such criticism. As Dudden points out, "The organizers sought to cloak themselves in the aura of high art by claiming connection to the royal academies of London and Paris, and by representing scenes from the Bible as well as from classical painting and sculpture."[30] While exhibitions that were housed in upper-class establishments could succeed in disguising themselves as "art" and thus escape critical aspersions, most living picture galleries were located in the Bowery, in store fronts, or concert saloons. The living pictures "hanging" in such halls were judged to be so transgressive that city officials attempted to eradicate these shows in 1848.[31]

While ballet and living pictures were popular vehicles for the exhibition of female bodies, actresses who participated in these enactments, like melodramatic boys Julian and Myrtillo, were mute. Such was not the case with equestrian melodrama however, for Menken—as Mazeppa—was bound but not gagged as her fiery steed galloped across the stage of the New Bowery Theatre in 1862. Equestrian melodrama, the last example of feminine spectacle in Allen's trilogy of feminization,[32] had featured breeches performers in the leading male roles for years, and some actresses, such as Fanny Herring, established their reputations in equestrian parts like Dick Turpin and Eagle Eye. The infamous, free-spirited Menken, however, proved unprecedentedly subversive, for regardless of the fact that many women had previously donned breeches in "horse operas," Menken became notorious for taking hers off.

Prior to her move to New York to seriously pursue her acting career in 1859, Menken had spent most of her life performing in the South and the Midwest. Breeches roles had never been a standard feature in her personal repertoire during her early career, rather her regular offerings included leading lady roles such as Widow Cheerly in *The Soldier's Daughter*, Bianca in *Fazio,* and Parthenia in *Ingomar, or the Barbarian* (although she did occasionally play a variety of different roles—some male—in protean comedies). One of Menken's first appearances in a leading masculine part occurred in Dayton, Ohio in 1858. Regardless of her esteem as an actress and poet among members of the Jewish community in Cincinnati, Menken journeyed to Dayton to play Jack Sheppard in *Sixteen-String Jack* in an effort to expand her repertoire and further her reputation as an actress. The *Israelite* reported on the positive reception she received both from her Dayton audiences and from the local press:

> We are glad to notice the favorable impression that our ingenious poetess makes on the people of Dayton. She played a short engagement there. The press is entirely in her favor. The *Empire* spoke thus of her the other day: "MRS. ADAH ISAACS MENKEN—This charming actress and beautiful woman took a benefit on Saturday evening and played her unrivaled character of 'Jack Sheppard,' to a crowded and enthusiastic audience. Her success in Dayton has been decided, and she justly merits it, for she is, undoubtedly, the most versatile actress in the Union.... So much talent combined with youth and beauty can not fail to gain for their possessor a high and brilliant position in the dramatic world of art."[33]

This celebratory review, however, neglected to mention an episode that proved far more destructive to Menken's career than the above puff proved helpful. The Dayton audience who attended the actress's benefit included 75 members of the Dayton Light Guards, a local militia corps, who responded to Menken's performance with wild enthusiasm. After throwing a dinner celebration in her honor, the men awarded her with the commission of Captain of the Light Guards. Though the ceremony was supposedly innocent, rumors of indecent conduct traveled back to Cincinnati, soiled her reputation with Menken's family, and contributed to marital problems between her and Alexander (although such rumors obviously did not influence the *Israelite* editor). After a series of increasingly bitter quarrels over the actress's refusal to renounce her career, the Menkens obtained a rabbinical divorce in July of 1859; shortly afterward, the "Captain" fled to New York to further her theatrical career.[34]

Although a capricious marriage to, and subsequent bitter divorce from, pugilist John C. Heenan inhibited her early New York career and further wounded her reputation, Menken did enjoy tremendous popular acclaim for her Mazeppa in Albany in 1861.[35] Her costume, or lack of one, caused a grand critical sensation in this city, for the actress supposedly appeared naked in the climactic scene of the play in which Mazeppa is sent to his death by an evil Count. The Count, in trying to eliminate this competitor for the hand of the lovely Olinska, orders Mazeppa to be stripped, strapped to a wild horse, and turned loose in the desolate Asian desert to be chased by wolves and tormented by vultures. It was for this scene that Menken traded her breeches for fleshlings; such an outfit certainly provided valuable publicity in both Albany and New York City. Yet while it is true that Menken often used "humbug" to promote her own career (therefore empowering herself to some degree), evidence exists to suggest that the actress was exploited by her New York managers. Louis Adler writes, "According to [Menken's] account, she was 'ordered' never to answer questions from the press or anyone else as to whether she wore tights or was really nude. The wardrobe mistress, Emma Hazeltine, was also sworn to secrecy."[36]

Publicity ploys regarding Menken's supposed nudity communicated certain messages to audiences all over the East coast, as Menken toured numerous cities in 1861 and 1862. Poster images of a nude woman in a vulnerable position, strapped to the back of a large black rearing horse, were coupled with scandalous gossip regarding the actress's character. Many of the sensational rumors circulated about Menken dealt with her precarious relationship with Heenan. Certain New York newspapers denied that their marriage had even taken place, a stance echoed by Heenan himself after the story began to attract widespread attention. The situation was additionally aggravated by Alexander Menken, who wrote a letter to George Wilkes, the editor of *Wilkes' Spirit of the Times,* shortly after the boxer married the actress, denying that he and Adah were legally divorced. He referred to his former wife as an aberrant and indecent woman, an "adventuress," an "incubus and [a] disgrace," and condemned her "superlative impudence and brazenness."[37] Menken promptly responded to Wilkes in an attempt to clear her name, yet she received no support from Heenan who was in London at the time training for an important match with the English prize fighter, Tom Sayers. Heenan's reluctance to respond to Menken's constant stream of letters was followed by his rejection of her altogether—an event that prompted the actress to contemplate suicide in December of 1860.[38]

In addition to advertising campaigns that championed her as "the Naked Lady" and the damning press coverage that resulted from the Heenan affair, the *New York Illustrated News* printed a four-part story of her life that enhanced the public's understanding of Menken as a subversive figure. The article, which appeared in March and April of 1860, cited Heenan as Menken's fourth husband, as opposed to her second, and presented a detailed narrative of her experiences as an "adventuress." Although much of the report is probably apocryphal, nineteenth-century New York readers supplemented their knowledge of Menken (who was already regarded as a marked woman due to her first divorce and subsequent rejection by Heenan—events that were fodder for the penny press for months) with this report. This biography portrayed Menken as a slave owner, a three-time divorcee, an offstage cross-dresser, an infidel, a prima donna, a "wild" poetess with a "crude intellect," and a creature associated at every turn with scandal. It is not surprising, therefore, that she was perceived by some as a threatening figure throughout the 1860s, a woman who could usurp male power and battle against Victorian prescriptions. The *Illustrated* explains, "Mrs. Menken was christened Captain Menken by her friends and acquaintances. Nor was the title an inapt one, for she is one of those beings not content to travel quietly in the beaten path, nor fall into the ranks of her countrymen in an orderly manner. She was born to command—to take the lead. She issues orders like a General—demands obedience—and is determined to be prominent in whatever sphere of life, society or circumstances place her."[39]

Menken's writing career contributed to this image of her as a strong independent (and perhaps more respectable) woman, a Deborah, as discussed in chapter 2. Her submissions to the *Israelite* demonstrated her desire to engage in public discourse, to voice an opinion on topical political concerns facing the Jewish community. For example, Menken wrote an emotional defense of Shylock (which received national publication), an essay protesting the papal abduction of an Italian Jewish boy, Edgar Mortara, and a defense of a Jewish member of Parliament, Baron Lionel de Rothchild.[40] Menken's reputation as an aggressive "public" woman also may have been enhanced by the national press coverage given to her commission as captain in the Dayton Light Guards (although stories about this event circulated months after the incident had occurred). Allen Lesser reports that upon hearing about her honorary militia title, Stuart Robson, a successful Shakespearean actor, declared, "By the living jingo, what next? In the case of female suffrage, Adah Isaacs Menken will be nominated for the Presidency—yes, and be elected too!"[41]

Like Cushman, Menken violated nineteenth-century conceptions of True Womanhood and passive domestic femininity. As Sentilles argues, she was a "self-made man" in antebellum society, and constructed for herself an identity that allowed her both to rebel and to gain access to patriarchal privileges. In a sense, Menken created her own containing discourse by using "the tropes of Victorian femininity to express her rebellion" against True Womanhood. Her poems, published weekly in the *Sunday Mercury*, characterized her as a woman wronged by male spoilers[42]; indeed she became the victim of the double standard, the subject of her early "fugitive pencilings," whose "blasted character" was solely the fault of men. Thus, Menken manipulated public sentiment and cloaked her subversions by simultaneously presenting herself as the helpless woman and as the feminist who touted a popular cause in the double standard. In doing so, Menken capitalized on early feminist rhetoric about prostitution since female reformers, like those involved in New York's

Female Moral Reform Society, blamed men for sexual transgressions and regarded the fallen woman as the unfortunate victim.

Menken's public image was shaped by many hands, however, and while the New York penny press turned her into a celebrity, as Sentilles explains, it also eroticized her and in so doing changed public conceptions about breeches performance. Early in her New York career, reporters repeatedly sexualized Menken in their reviews, perhaps as a way to contain her threat. Menken was a divorced professional woman with a "reputation" who persisted in furthering her career despite the web of sensationalism that surrounded her, *and* she was popular with audiences. Such a combination of beauty, talent, box-office appeal, and ambition coupled with an emerging masculine persona and penchant for breeches roles could certainly provoke anxiety among "opinion setters." Like boyishness and femininity, sexual objectification seemed to operate as another discourse of containment, for by reducing Menken to a sum of fetishized parts, male critics could control the danger implied by her societal transgressions as an outspoken forceful woman; they could undermine her symbolic power as a transvestite by portraying her as a sexual—and therefore uncontrollable—female while simultaneously reinforcing her femininity, and thus her weakness, through their constant foregrounding of her sexed body. She was not to be regarded either as a serious artist capable of communicating important moral (or political) lessons, or as a strong innovative woman—a nineteenth-century Madonna—who took commercial control of her own commodified body; she was, instead, a fleshling suit, a woman who prostituted herself and would expose body parts to satiate male desires for a price.[43]

New York reviews of Menken's breeches roles during the 1860s demonstrate this process of sexualization. Even before her success as Mazeppa in Albany, Menken was noted by critics for her physical attractiveness; her acting skills were always considered secondary. On March 24, 1860, the actress performed William in *Black-Eyed Susan* at the Bowery, and although this role was never played in fleshlings or tights but in the loose-fitting trousers necessitated by a nautical uniform, Menken's beauty was still privileged over her histrionic prowess. The *Clipper* critic states, "First and foremost, therefore come we to Adah Isaacs Menken, whose name has been so prominently before the public of late. Not being satisfied with seeing her name only, she has been solicited to gratify the 'Metropolitans' with a sight of her lovely features, and a specimen of her abilities on the dramatic boards."[44] By 1862, after she had achieved local fame as Mazeppa, Menken had become sufficiently recognized as a breeches performer and was popular enough that the *Clipper* critic juxtaposed her name with the most successful breeches and equestrian actress presently in New York, Fanny Herring.[45] Reporting on activity at both the Old and New Bowery theatres, the critic writes:

> Jack Sheppard will . . . be repeated with Miss Fanny Herring as Jack. . . . Adah Isaacs Menken commences her engagement at the New Bowery this evening, opening in the "Three Fast Women." Thus, we are to have two dashing actresses on the east side this week, Fanny Herring at the old theatre, and Adah at the New. Both wear their hair in that tantalizing style which helped to make the Western girls so popular, and we suppose the "young fellers," and the old ones too, will go one eye on each of the ladies, and descant upon the fair proportions of "ye seductive beauties." "We'll be there, you'll be there," and a lively time there will be in the Bowery this week.[46]

The critic's reaction to the hairstyles of Herring and Menken is especially telling, for both of these women had their hair cut short like men in the style of actresses Lucille and Helen Western. Rather than react negatively to these unfeminine boyish haircuts, the critic turns this feature (that may have once been perceived as a threatening or inappropriate fashion for a woman) into a sexual asset; indeed, the reviewer calls the actresses "tantalizing" and suggests that such a style makes "girls popular." He then immediately proceeds to describe a seemingly split male gaze, as one man will watch two different women enact different roles (in Menken's case she played three separate characters in *Three Fast Women*). Although the spectator— who is clearly male—"sees" four different characters on two separate stages, he "reads" them similarly. Herring is not read as Jack

Sheppard (or even as Herring-as-Sheppard), and Adah is not read as one of the three characters found in the protean comedy; rather, both are consumed as "seductive beauties" whose "fair proportions" prove much more compelling than a daring equestrian stunt or a quick change.

Although both actresses clearly had a great deal of talent in addition to their fine figures, it was always their legs that drew the crowds to the theatre. The *Clipper* critic even remarked upon Menken's masterful work in *Lola Montez* and the *French Spy* and noted that in both "she evinces a degree of talent and originality that is quite charming." He confessed, however, that he was "rather surprised that she should favor such trash as 'Sixteen String Jack,' and dramas of like character."[47] Unfortunately, this critic did not go on to ponder the degree to which Menken, still a relatively minor actress at this point (despite her success in Albany), had the power to select her own repertoire. Indeed, given a choice, she would have preferred the Widow Cheerly, Bianca, Beatrice, or Rosalind, roles that she liked to play but that were not nearly as profitable as equestrian melodramas, protean comedies, and spectacle.[48] As Dudden points out in her discussion of Menken's Albany engagement, the actress did not initially have the power to choose her own roles. Dudden explains, "Playing the naked hero in *Mazeppa* was not her idea if we can believe the boast of a theatre manager." Apparently John B. Smith, the manager of the theatre that rivaled the house in which Menken was playing, advertised that he would be giving away free beer on the night of Menken's benefit. After deliberately stealing her audience and leaving her destitute, Smith offered to hire her to play Mazeppa. Menken, whose options were extremely limited, agreed to play for Smith and "[a]fter a flurry of suggestive publicity, including the parading of a set of horses billed as 'the Menken stud,' she opened to enthusiastic male audiences and played three record-breaking weeks."[49] Dudden goes on to explain that while women, like Menken, had been treated as sexual objects by male managers throughout the nineteenth century, as the theatre became more industrialized women became increasingly commodified.

Despite the minor disruption in theatrical activity caused by the war,[50] legs continued to sell tickets and managers intended to capitalize on this current trend as much as possible. For example, in the same issue of the *Clipper* that commented on Menken's selection of "trash," a description of Charles Gayler's rendition of Shakespeare's *The Tempest* is given. The popularity of the production did not seem to hinge on the manager's innovative dramatic choice *(The Tempest* was not a popular play in America during this time) as might be expected, but rather on the large congregation of female supernumeraries (whom Gayler added to the production), who were "about as good looking a lot of 'pretty waiter girls' as have [been] seen for a long while or since the music halls closed." The critic's reference to "pretty waiter girls" suggests that he is making a link between the supers and the group of women employed by concert saloons in the Bowery; the waiter girls, who wore relatively short dresses (ankle-length) and low-cut blouses that exposed their bosoms, were permitted to drink and socialize with their customers as well as serve them. The saloons, which featured variety acts as well as these attentive waitresses, were regarded as dens of iniquity by bourgeois members of society who eventually succeeded in putting enough pressure on city officials to have the saloons closed in April of 1862. Allen argues that the focus of the bourgeois objections to these theatres were centered upon "the waiter girl and her actual or possible connection to prostitution."[51] By referring to the company of female supernumeraries in *The Tempest* as "pretty waiter girls," the critic tacitly implies that they are selling more than simply dramatic entertainment. This is further evidenced by the *Clipper* critic who goes on to describe what he saw as the real "beauty" of the performance. The supernumeraries, he explains, "don't confine themselves to affording the audience ocular demonstrations of well-formed nether limbs that a view from the stage yields, but they march around the parquet on a platform erected under the boards thereby affording the occupants of the parquet seats a splendid chance for a closer scrutiny of the aforesaid nether limbs." He goes on to discuss the "choice exhibition" of the evening, the appearance of Miss Emily Thorne, an English *"blonde,"* who proudly displayed a "splendid pair of legs." She was not ashamed of her most salient feature, reported the critic, but displayed her legs "much to the edification of the amorously disposed of the audience, to whom a beautiful form and face of the feminine gender is *the* attraction of attractions at our public places of amusement."[52]

Thorne and Gayler's corps of female supernumeraries were joined by a number of cross-dressed members of the "feminine gender," for Menken's brief appearance as Mazeppa in 1862 at the New Bowery Theatre inspired many imitators. A plethora of breeches actresses aped Menken's performance style and her costume and thus further cultivated and intensified the critical focus on actresses as sexual objects. As one critic noted, "Male actors have no business to play Mazeppa any more. It is decidedly out of their line, since Adah Menken donned the tights, and showed what an actress could do with the part. It gives a splendid chance to display the fine points of the female figure, and if there were no other merit about it, that of itself would be sufficient to attract the fast young men about town."[53] By 1866, the New York *Clipper* would boast that "many a fresh and fiery Mazeppa, many a luscious and sculpturesque French Spy [a disguise role in Menken's repertoire] will make their debut on the dramatic course, attired in those undress costumes which never fail to make such characters attractive to 'venerable roues' and aged young men."[54]

Leo Hudson was the first disciple of Menken's to gain extreme notoriety as she played to packed houses at the New Bowery in the fall of 1863 (see figure 5.3).The *Clipper* critic introduced her, stating, "[W]e are to have a fresh Mazeppa this week at the New Bowery, and Leo Hudson is her name. She is to appear in *puris naturalibus,* or rather in flesh colored tights, and is to run in *porpria persona*—do the riding herself. Miss Leo, if 'she is all my fancy painted her,' will create a sensation, and allure many of us 'young fellers' to the New Bowery."[55] Hudson became even more popular with audiences (though certainly less infamous) than Menken herself. She played throughout the fall and winter at the New Bowery and upon one occasion "drew together one of the largest—if not *the* largest—crowds ever seen within the walls of that establishment."[56] The review in the *Clipper* claimed that hundreds of people were turned away at the door for this performance, hours before the curtain even rose.

Fig. 5.3: Leo Hudson as Mazeppa. Harvard Theatre Collection, The Houghton Library, Fredric Woodbridge Wilson, Curator.

It is likely that such fervent interest in Hudson's Mazeppa was inspired by reviews similar to those found in the *Clipper*, that mention the actress's "flesh colored tights" immediately after introducing her to his readers. Critics did not seem to be interested in the fact that Mazeppa wore several different costumes throughout the course of the play or that he engaged in heroic battles and parried with evil Counts. Similarly, Hudson's acting background and biography were initially unimportant to the *Clipper* critic, who seemed to regard Hudson as the fulfillment of his personal erotic fantasy (since he hopes that he will discover that "she is all [his] fancy painted her") rather than a potentially gifted actress with enormous drawing power.

The *Clipper* did provide a biography of Hudson in a later issue; however, it was confined to one brief paragraph in a weekly column about the lives of popular stars and was placed on a different page from the theatrical reviews. The columnist reported that Hudson was originally born in England in 1839 and had played all over the world prior to her engagement at the New Bowery. She was one of the original members of the New York Hippodrome's company and was featured as the principal equestrian. Indeed, Hudson was the first woman in that company to perform the "terrific leap" over a canal that had been specifically excavated in that theatre for daring animal stunts.[57] However, despite her previous experience and her daring, critics still attributed Hudson's popularity to scanty attire: "Shape does it, and pretty girls who travel on their shape never play to empty benches."[58]

Kate Fisher succeeded Hudson as Mazeppa in 1864. She was innovative in introducing additional ramps to her act (a trick introduced in Gayler's production of *The Tempest*) that extended her climactic ride into the parquet and around the first circle of boxes, which allowed audiences to get a better look at her "nude" body. Sketches of Fisher as Mazeppa, featured on the front page of the *Clipper* in January of 1864, give some indication of what her costume looked like. In one large picture she appears dressed as a king or royal figure, and in two smaller pictures she is seen wearing only a pair of "brief trunks" and a short strapless blouse that covered only her breasts. Such a juxtaposition of images suggests a sort of crude striptease, as it implies that potential viewers will see Fisher in an elaborate male costume that she will eventually shed throughout the performance. As one reviewer put it, "She performs the business well, dresses magnificently, and undresses deliciously."[59] Kate Vance, another popular Mazeppa in 1864, perhaps undressed even more deliciously than Fisher, for a picture of her in the March 26 edition of the *Clipper* shows a woman who appears to be completely naked except for a pair of short white pantaloons that came to mid-thigh. There was no attempt to make Vance look masculine in this rendering, since her hair appears to have been worn long and her breasts were accentuated in the picture. In addition, Vance was positioned on the horse with her legs straddling the back of the animal, which implies that the actress was both vulnerable and perhaps willing to comply with consumer fantasies.

Like Hudson and Fisher, Vance had considerable experience as an actress and was reportedly a rather serious artist. Vance's performance was even described by the *Clipper* critic in aesthetic terms, as he likened her Mazeppa to a moving sculpture or a piece of living art. He reveals that in her "undress, or summer costume, the beauties of the female form are displayed in all their loveliness, and to make the living picture more complete, the actress puts herself in various artistic positions, bringing still more prominently into view the handsome points and muscular developments of the human form."[60] Although puffing was increasingly deplored by respectable New York critics, alliances made in the Cold Cut Room may have still prevailed into the 1860s, which explains the critical impulse to "legitimate" feminine spectacle by associating it with fine art. Yet, regardless of the motive behind the aesthetic analogy, Vance was still unmistakably objectified by the press. Significantly, the critic uses the term "living picture," which suggests that he is doing more than simply trying to remind his readers of another entertainment form that sanctioned the display of women's bodies using aesthetic arguments. By conceptualizing Vance's Mazeppa as a living picture, the critic implies that the breeches performer is no longer an actress or an actively creative artist, but an *object* of (sexualized) beauty. Audiences were no longer encouraged to attend performances in which women played men in order to judge their artistic merit or their convincing ability to affect masculinity (or even their equestrian skills). Rather, the more an actress appeared to be a woman—silent, naked, restrained by ropes, and lashed astride a wild horse—the more popular, the critic implies, she would presumably be with contemporary male spectators.

The *Clipper* critic's attempt to turn Vance's erotic display into high art may also be explained by the highbrow/lowbrow ideology that governed entertainment and criticism during midcentury. By conceptualizing Mazeppa as a living picture (albeit still an eroticized living picture), this critic may have been trying to attract a larger, more diverse clientele to the Bowery—a gesture that would have aided local managers, for as the decade progressed, entertainment became increasingly homogeneous. The popularity of equestrian melodrama in New York reinforced public conceptions of the breeches performer as a lowbrow or marginalized entertainer, since she was rarely mentioned by critics like the *Albion's* Hamilton and Mercutio, who only reviewed activity at "highbrow" theatres such as Wallack's, Wood's Broadway, Laura Keene's, Niblo's, and Burton's (where traditional breeches performances were rare). As audiences became more uniformly "classed" after the Astor Place riot, the evening entertainment bill lost its heterogeneity as well. Working-class Bowery "b'hoys" and "g'hals" revelled in witnessing Hudson, Fisher, and Vance's daring jaunts around the parquet, while more "sophisticated" audiences were supposedly interested in entertainments of a different kind. As one critic explained:

> Managers and actors, like newspaper writers, and publishers, work to make their money. They understand the tastes of their patrons, and they endeavor to gratify those tastes. "Rosedale" would not run more than a week or two at either of the Bowery theatres; neither would Jack Sheppard be likely to meet with a very favorable reception at Wallack's. . . . Kate Fisher might attempt the loving Juliet at the New Bowery, but it would be "for one night only," for the habitues would boo it a bear; while her Mazeppa would hold them night after night as tight as she is held on the bare back of the "fiery untamed steed."[61]

Because papers such as the *Albion* almost never discussed sexualized equestrian breeches performers and rarely discussed women who played men at all, conspicuous displays of female sexuality *seemed* to be absent from highbrow theatres. Spectacles such as Keene's *Seven Sons* prove that this was not the case, however. Highbrow theatres profited from the leg business as much as lowbrow theatres, but disguised this fact by critically side-stepping (or completely ignoring) this business. Newspaper coverage of spectacles like Keene's *Seven Sons*, which was sparse, served to perpetuate the spurious notion that such presentations were fancied by "the prurient alone."[62] Indeed, critics seemed to define the highbrow theatres according to what the lowbrow theatres were not, and equestrian breeches performers (because of their Bowery associations) were regarded as the theatrical "low other" of the 1860s. Allen borrows this term from Peter Stallybrass and Allon White and interprets their low other to be "something . . . reviled by and excluded from the dominant social order as debased, dirty and unworthy, but that is simultaneously the object of desire and/or fascination."[63] This middle-class fascination with the low other may, in part, explain both the phenomenal sensation caused by Menken's return to New York in the spring of 1866, where she played at a "highbrow" theatre, and the criticism that surrounded this sensation.

After a highly lucrative tour of the West Coast and London, Menken, now an international star, returned to New York. As soon as she arrived in the city, managers descended upon her and aggressively vied for her business. Yet after she named her price—$500 a performance—only George Wood remained to negotiate with Menken and agreed to hire the actress for a 24-night engagement despite her comparatively outrageous fee. Menken's performances of *Mazeppa* were sold out a week in advance as spectators braved even an ominous cholera epidemic to flood the house of the Broadway Theatre. While audiences responded favorably to Menken's breeches performance, certain critics were less than enthusiastic. Once again, class seemed crucial in informing critical response; writers like Winter of the *Tribune* seemed disturbed or threatened that Menken, a lowbrow breeches performer, would have the audacity to display herself at Wood's, which had traditionally catered to a middle-class audience. Furthermore, before her arrival in New York, rumors had spread throughout the city that Menken would do the thrilling bareback scene absolutely naked. And although, as Lesser points out, only a small group of civil reformers "cared very much about the naked women who danced at stag parties or behind the red curtains of certain houses on East Fourteenth Street, it was an entirely different matter when a woman threatened to appear in the same state on a public stage," on Broadway, before a middle-class audience.[64]

Beyond the Bowery, this actress, regardless of her international star status and her powerful friends, was considered social anathema by critics like Winter. As long as breeches performers in the

Mazeppa line played in Lower East Side theatres, the danger that they might corrupt more refined patrons and disrupt strict middle-class moral and gender codes was contained.[65] Menken's fame, however, allowed her to cross class lines when she arrived in New York in 1866. In addition, this honorary Captain of the Dayton Light Guards not only secured a relatively prestigious engagement at Wood's theatre but defiantly named her price and chose her role, thus asserting control over New York managers. Winter's extremely vitriolic review in the *Tribune* betrays both his anxiety about Menken's supposed assault on middle-class sensibilities and his deliberate attempt to sexualize and marginalize (or perhaps remarginalize) an increasingly powerful public woman. He writes,

> To announce that Miss Adah Isaacs Menken would appear at the Broadway Theatre in the character of Mazeppa was to announce that a woman would exhibit herself, in public, in a condition closely bordering upon nudity; and such an announcement, of course, was calculated to draw together an immense concourse of spectators. Such a concourse greeted Miss Menken's first appearance last evening. The Broadway Theatre was densely crowded. The audience, composed chiefly of males, was the coarsest and most brutal assembly that we have ever chanced to see at a theatre on Broadway. Every variety of dissolute life was represented in it. The purple nose, the scorbutic countenance, the glassy eye, the bull head, the heavy lower jaw, the aspect of mingled lewdness and ferocity—all was there. Youths, whose attire exhibited an eruptive tendency toward cheap jewelry, loll upon their seats, champing tobacco, and audibly uttering their filthy minds. The atmosphere fairly reeked with vulgarity.... Such was the audience to whom the stalwart proportions of Miss Menken were duly exhibited. It is unnecessary to say that the spectacle was cordially applauded. To speak of Miss Menken as an actress would be to waste words. She has not the faintest idea of what acting is. She moves about the stage with no motive, and therefore, in a kind of accidental manner; assumes attitudes that are sometimes fine, and sometimes ridiculous; speaks in a thin, weak voice, and very much as a mild and hungry female might order tea and toast; and, in short, invites critical attention not to her emotional capabilities, her intellectual fits, or her culture as an artist, but solely to her physical proportions. These, we may as

well say, at once—to have done with a trifling topic—are, in many respects beautiful. That any purpose connected with dramatic art is served by their public exhibition is offensive to good taste, we are distinctly certain. Miss Menken's praises as an actress have been loudly sounded; but if artistic greatness is to be acquired by such means as Miss Menken has chosen for its pursuit, there would seem to be no good reason why the majority of females should not acquire it, if so disposed.... The appearance of Miss Menken's Mazeppa at a theatre on Broadway is nothing less than a grievous discredit to the acted drama in this metropolis.[66]

Winter was correct in saying that Menken had been widely trumpeted, for many papers merited her achievements. However, critics were collectively hesitant to praise her acting, commenting instead on her "exhibition of physical beauty."[67] The *Clipper* carefully selected the most laudatory remarks from all of the New York papers and edited them in such a way that the assembly of comments resembled a full-blown puff (not surprising considering the editor, Frank Queen, was a good friend of Menken's), despite the *Clipper's* claim that all notices, including their own, were "unbought and therefore unbiased." The most blatant example of this dubious editing appears in the *Clipper's* rendering of Winter's review from the *Tribune*. The first line of the review as the *Clipper* quotes it (as they claimed "word for word") reads, "To announce that Miss Adah Isaacs Menken would appear at the Broadway Theatre in the character of Mazeppa was calculated to draw together an immense concourse of spectators."[68] Winter's primary point about Menken's performance being simply a vehicle for nude display was entirely lost as the *Clipper* cloaked his excoriations through skillful editing. His caustic reflections were contained just as Menken's transgressions might have been. Although the *Clipper* critic dismisses the issue of her "nudity" by stating that her Mazeppa is "the most modestly costumed of all we have ever witnessed," he does objectify the actress. In comments reminiscent of Hudson's review (in which she was likened to a "living picture"), the *Clipper* compares Menken's body to the "Greek Slave," a sculpture exhibited in New York in 1864. Women as well as men delighted in spending hours contemplating this "nude work of art," the critic explained, just as the

Broadway Theatre was packed night after night with elaborately dressed ladies as well as gentlemen who came to witness Menken as an "art" object. In short, the *Clipper's* elaborate puff functioned as a sexualizing narrative as well as a lionizing tribute; though Menken's "praises" may have been "loudly sounded" as Winter suggests, her triumph was not as sure as the *Clipper* implied. For underneath this glorious puff ran a much more ominous subtext that robbed the breeches actress of artistic legitimacy and implied that the real power behind her performance lay in her fleshling suit. Certainly Menken did achieve international success, made it to Broadway, and controlled New York managers in the process; yet while she may have entered the theatre on April 30 as an artist, she was re-membered by the press as an object—a mere collection of "admired anatomical developments."[69]

Winter's review is equally marginalizing but considerably more direct. He does not try to recuperate Menken's performance by rendering it a piece of high art. Rather, he lists in one (lengthy) paragraph many of the various critiques that were leveled at the breeches performer in the 1860s. Menken was not an actress, despite her impressive credentials and elaborate theatrical accoutrements. Her performance was instead "a grievous discredit to the acted drama." She did not appear manly, masculine, or powerful despite the fact that she played a male role; her body was womanly, sensuous, her gestures undirected, and her voice "thin" and "weak." She was a salacious character, displaying her body onstage before an audience whose appearance and behavior were far from middle-class. Indeed, Winter described those attending the Broadway that evening as alcohol-sodden male barbarians or flashy youths sporting cheap jewelry and scatological mindsets—a portrayal that was designed to explode any associations that might have been made between Menken and more bourgeois consumers. Yet, such an account is at odds with the *Clipper's* description of the decent gentlemen and ladies who attended the theatre "in all their brilliant and variegated plummage."[70] Perhaps Winter distorted the image of the audience in an attempt to undermine Menken's potential power as a star. If the patrons were vulgar then the performer may be as well, since by 1866 theatre managers were strategic about targeting their products to what they considered to be a very specific and clearly defined market.

Other critics shared Winter's disdain for Menken's *Mazeppa*. For example, Bayard Taylor, the *Spirit of the Times* critic, ignored the actress completely and reviewed only Menken's horse, Black Bess. As Lesser relates, Taylor "studiously avoided even a single mention of the Menken's name. In the only sentence of his blast that referred to her, he said: 'So far as the person called in the bills 'Mazeppa' is concerned, he (I use the gender of the character) is best *on* the mare, and the worst *off* that I have ever seen or expect to see.'"[71] In addition, Winter wrote another review under his pseudonym Mercutio for the *Albion*, in which he declared the performance "one of the most disgraceful exhibitions of immodesty and intellectual poverty that have ever been made in New York." He goes on to declare that "Miss Menken is not an actress in any sense of the word. She presents herself merely as a specimen of physical beauty."[72]

Because of Menken's influence (which was significant), the image of the breeches actress shifted from an innocuous boy, a feminine hero, or even a directly transgressive masculine woman to a silent sexualized object, a "low other"—no more talented than a horse and no more professionally empowered than a "pretty waiter girl." Moreover, the few serious performers, such as Cushman, who did attempt to play a male character during the 1860s, were generally ignored (or contained) by critics as their efforts were eclipsed by the legion of fleshling-clad equestrians that dominated the Bowery stages. Any potential for gender transcendence or consideration as a talented artist—even as an actress in the broadest definition of the word—disappeared as more and more cross-dressed women figuratively mounted Menken's fiery steed.

THOMPSONIAN BURLESQUE AND THE VILLIFICATION OF THE BREECHES PERFORMER

Despite the anxiety that Menken's "nude work[s] of art" caused critics like Winter, her performances of *Mazeppa* ultimately seemed less worrisome to the American press when compared with those of her blonde sisters from across the sea. Even though Menken represented a "new model of theatrical femininity: independent, ostentatious, outspoken, free-spirited," as Allen argues, her press-constructed image (which she perhaps contributed to) as a sexual object contained any threats that her ambitious nature and unconventional womanhood may have engendered by reinforcing her essential femininity and reducing her to an object position. In addition, her position as a melodramatic actress may have limited her transgressive powers since audiences could identify her performance within the context of a familiar and comforting melodramatic narative.[73] Burlesque, on the other hand, with its blatant mockeries of masculinity and indiscreet condemnations of the American gender system, could not cloak its subversions within a formulaic moralistic genre; unlike equestrian melodrama, unmitigated satire was burlesque's raison d'etre. Because the trespasses of burlesque breeches stars such as Thompson could not be sanctified within the framework of recuperative melodramatic ideologies, these performers were eventually removed from mainstream theatres—an event that further marginalized the breeches performer and contributed to the emerging image of her as a dangerously sexual "low other."

While Thompson's influence on the leg business has been well documented, an investigation of how Thompsonian burlesque specifically affected the convention of breeches requires further attention.[74] The burlesque of the British Blondes parodied classical and cultural texts; a loose story provided a skeleton to be fleshed out with songs, comic bits, and political commentary. And while Thompson and her colleagues' cross-dressed performances were eroticized by critics in the 1860s and 1870s, their performances never resembled the striptease of the early twentieth century. Like Menken, Thompson and her troupe (composed of Ada Harland, Lisa Weber, Grace Logan, Pauline Markham, and Aggie Wood) also played at Wood's Broadway Theatre in New York, where they debuted on September 28, 1868 in *Ixion, or the Man at the Wheel*. All of the women in the company, with the exception of Markham, were cross-dressed, and Thompson assumed the title role. The critic for the *New York Times* reviewed the production favorably and even suggested that Thompson was convincingly masculine as Ixion. The critic states,

> It is hard to judge her as an actress, in a disguise that robs her sex of all its charms, for Miss Thompson has to swear, swagger, and be otherwise masculine as *Ixion,* but as to the manner in which she plays this part this must be said, that she is lively, vivacious, and spirited, and although some exceptions may be taken to her costume, and that of her companions, no one can do so from artistic reasons; the statuesque is certainly not violated in this respect; nature has her own.[75]

The critic implies that Thompson's masculine apparel necessitated a masculine interpretation of the role. Because she put on a male "disguise" that undermined her personal femininity, the actress was compelled to affect manly behavior. Yet, he immediately points out that "some exceptions may be taken" to Thompson's costume, which suggests that the tunic and tights she wore as Ixion (although it bore no significant difference from other tunic/tight ensembles worn by breeches performers throughout the century) was too exiguous and did not in fact "rob her sex of all its charms." This curious juxtaposition of a masculine performance style and an eroticized costume continued as a critical theme throughout Thompson's career in New York. And while this incongruous combination did not seem to confound the *Times* critic, it soon proved extremely disconcerting to select members of the New York press.

In February, Thompson's troupe moved to Niblo's Garden for a second engagement. Though the company had received favorable notices during their run at the Broadway, critical sentiments regarding the Blondes changed markedly after they began to play at Niblo's. Despite their popularity with audiences, who often enjoyed the breeches actress even when critics did not, Thompson's brand of burlesque was not regarded by the press as harmless satire, as innocuous Broughamian lampoons, but as gross distortions of Victorian propriety. In fact, New York critics were so disdainful of Thompson's theatrics that they mounted a seeming rhetorical war on the Blondes and constructed what Allen calls a "hysterical antiburlesque discourse."[76] This discourse was largely inspired by an altercation between certain New York critics and theatre managers, and Alexander Henderson, Thompson's manager. Henderson offended members of the American theatrical hegemony through a supercilious speech in which he trumpeted his own accomplishments and condemned New York critics for their naive treatments of burlesque, not understanding that the ensuing controversy would add to the profit he already enjoyed. Moreover, Allen argues that the main reason behind the press's attack on burlesque had to do with the specific threat generated by the Blondes, for the troupe's coupling of sexual display with subversive gender parodies proved too controversial for New York critics.

Plays like *Ixion* provided only a basic plot augmented with topical illusions, popular songs, and imitations of famous—often notorious—male figures. Indeed, Thompson and her Blondes would parody honorable and dishonorable male contemporaries, adopt their language and their gestures, and sing songs and dance in imitation of well-known artists—all of which was standard fare for the burlesque performer. Because their routines did not require them try to *pass* as men, even thought they played men or performed masculinity, they were in a sense similar to their equestrian melodramatic sisters, who because of their "undress" did not seem convincingly masculine.[77] Yet there was a crucial difference between these two varieties of breeches actress that Allen neglects to point out: one was telling a story *as* a man, and the other was telling a story *about* men. One assumed a male voice and carried out daring actions within a definitively patriarchal world, and the other turned this world upside down and boldly exposed the prerogative of the storyteller and the constructed nature of the tale.

Unlike performers of THE DRAMA (Olive Logan's term for "legitimate" theatre) or performers of equestrian melodrama, burlesque actresses' representation of male characters focused not upon conveying the illusion of masculinity or telling a man's story, but instead foregrounded the construction of masculinity or of the masculine fable—a dangerous act to perform. Similarly, breeches performance was often read as subversive by the press throughout the century because critics sensed a disturbing subtext underneath the cross-dressed performance, a subtext that implied that women could "wear the breeches" in every regard. Thompsonian burlesque turned the breeches performer's subtext into text. Rather than subtly imply, as the breeches performer did, that women could play at masculinity just as well as men could, the British Blonde privileged an uncloaked, parodic *performance* of gender that was unprecedentedly bold and unmistakably clear.

Significantly, the "hysterical antiburlesque discourse" that bombarded the American public regarding Thompson and her Blondes repeatedly discussed the female burlesque player as a cross-dressed actress and, in some instances, actually conflated the burlesquer with the breeches performer. Writers and journalists found burlesque's transparent quoting of masculinity worrisome. William Dean Howells was perhaps the most perplexed by the burlesque actress, whose performance he regarded as paradoxical; she was a sexualized woman—in costumes that accentuated her bust, waist, and thighs—who appropriated the gestures, postures, and attitudes of manhood. Reflecting on a burlesque review he witnessed in Boston, Howells recalls, "[T]hough they were not like men, [they] were in most things as unlike women, and seemed creatures of a kind of alien sex, parodying both. It was certainly a shocking thing to look at them with their horrible prettiness, their archness in which there was no charm, their grace which put to shame."[78] Allen explains that Howells was scandalized by the burlesque's parodic representation of manhood. Indeed, what Howells witnessed was not traditional breeches acting (women sincerely attempting to play a male role just as they would play a female one) but unabashed *impersonation*.

In an article written in 1869 for *The Galaxy*, Richard Grant White stated that burlesque was "monstrously incongruous and unnatural."[79] White does not stop here however, as Allen implies, but goes on to discuss burlesque and cross-dressing at length. Burlesque appeared unseemly to White for several reasons, but the chief element that perplexed him was the actresses' adoption of male clothing. White felt that American audiences no longer appreciated real feeling or emotional depth. The only thing that would move spectators in 1869, he declared, was spectacle. Cross-dressed actresses were popular with audiences, he claims, because they added spectacle/beauty to ordinary performances; they contributed an illusion of masculinity, yet it was manhood "in a monstrous form... dressed for incongruity's sake, as well as for a display of their beauty, in the costume of men centuries ago."[80] Because White's discussion/critique of the breeches convention (which he refers to generically) is used to contextualize his examination of Thompson's performance, it is clear that he conflates the two, that he regards Thompson as a breeches performer—an association that is not explicitly articulated by Allen. Yet, despite White's contempt for breeches performance in general, he admired Thompson but made sure to contain the threat of her "monstrous form" (which might inspire and empower as well as invite anxiety) by championing her femininity. Thus, like many critics before him who reviewed the breeches actress, White employed a discourse of femininity to reduce the burlesquer and transform her from a "creature of alien sex" into a "lady." White remarked that Thompson played with a "daintiness" that other actresses lacked, and her charm was so intoxicating that "[i]t was as if Venus... had come upon the stage." Furthermore, he disagreed with dissenters who castigated Thompson's leg display, arguing that audiences should familiarize themselves with the fine points of a woman's body: "They seem to me quite as important, and I think they are quite as interesting, as those of a fine horse."[81] While hybrid transformations seemed menacingly prophetic of some absurd new world order or system of defiance, White tried to lend some comfort to his readers by unlocking the secrets of Thompson's stage charm. She was not a usurper of patriarchal rule but a benign goddess, or, if this was not completely ameliorating, a fine animal like Menken.

Such pejorative recuperative critiques echo discourses of containment that were used to mitigate threats generated by the breeches performer throughout the century. Even the specific language used by the most notorious disseminators of the antiburlesque hysteria was reminiscent of phrases that had been used for decades to describe the breeches performer. In 1807, for example, the actress Eliza Poe's performance of Little Pickle was referred to as belonging to an alien sex, to a "class of beings termed *hermaphroditical,* as the uncouthness of his costume seemed to indicate."[82] Likewise, Barnes's was called "preposterous" in 1817,[83] and Cushman a "monstrous anomaly." Such a parallel between the terms used to describe the burlesque actress and previous criticisms of the breeches performer are telling, for they suggest that on some level both types of male impersonation were communicating similar messages.

These messages, however, fell on deaf ears. Even Logan, the one critic who might have been sensitive to subtle protofeminist articulations, was oblivious to all such whisperings. Indeed, this former actress turned lecturer, journalist, and women's rights activist fervently disapproved of burlesque and proved to be the breeches performer's most destructive adversary.[84] For while other critics employed rhetoric that was reminiscent of negative descriptions of breeches actresses, attributed the transgressive nature of Thompson's performance to her cross-gender portrayals, or *suggested* that there was a connection between Thompsonian burlesque and the convention of breeches, Logan directly associated the burlesque performer and the breeches actress (of both traditional and popular roles) through her writings. She charged that *all* participants in the "nude drama" were enemies to "THE DRAMA." Logan's opinions about the theatre, like Winter's and those of other New York critics, were largely shaped by class prejudice: industrious ballet girls (despite their lower-middle-class status) and respectable actresses like Fanny Janauschek and Rachel were welcome within the theatre, but breeches performers like Menken (who were "neither fish, flesh, nor fowl" of the theatrical creation) and "yellow-haired nudities" like Thompson must remain contained within lowbrow variety halls and concert saloons.[85] Like Winter, Logan betrayed her fear that "the practices of the haunts of the degenerate working-classes had taken over the same stages where Shakespeare's creations once walked."[86]

In a chapter from her book *Apropos of Women and Theatre* (1869) entitled "About the Leg Business," Logan writes, "In this chapter, whose main facts were set down before the fever for 'blonde burlesque' raged in our theatres, I treat principally of a style of performance which the above-named women illustrate, and which is already fluttering in the last agonies of death."[87] In this statement of intent, Logan makes it clear that although the leg business thrived before Thompson sailed to America, she and her company could be seen as representative of this previously established "style of performance." The style of performance that Logan refers to is clearly nonburlesque breeches performance, specifically equestrian melodrama. Significantly, Logan prefaces her statement of intent with an acrimonious castigation of "Mazeppas," whom she distinguishes from the plebeian (yet "hardworking" and therefore redeemable) ballet girl. These women, a few of whom Logan identifies by name (even though she says that this is an ungracious thing to do), "are neither actresses, pantomimists, nor ballet-girls."[88] Menken, Felicja Vestvali, and Leo Hudson are all explicitly noted by Logan as belonging to this class of nonartists; all of them were breeches performers. Yet none of them confined themselves to equestrian melodrama, which is the style of breeches performance that falls under Logan's umbrella term, "the leg business." Regardless of the fact that Menken regularly played Jack Sheppard, the French Spy, and Black-Eyed Susan's lover, William the sailor (in trousers), and Vestvali had leading male roles in opera and also played Romeo, Logan felt justified, because of their public display of body parts, to denounce them as "shameless and unworthy."

Logan's vilification of Menken is understandable given the context of the actress's scandalous reputation and the bad press she received at the hand of reputed critics in 1866, but why does she also single out minor actresses like Hudson and Vestvali? The answer seems to lie in the fact that neither of these women perfectly fit Logan's model of the witless, blonde, clog-dancing "creature." They obscured Logan's image of the Other—a figure who, once defined, facilitated indisputable definitions of good and bad (the virtuous actress was defined by what the "nudity" was not) and substantiated Logan's cause. Breeches actresses like Hudson and Vestvali blurred the lines between the shameless and the respectable, creating lax boundaries that Logan felt compelled to reestablish and reinforce.

Hudson—whom Logan describes as "a person whose name is thoroughly associated with the Mazeppa, Dick Turpin, Jack Sheppard school"[89]—made a particular impression on Logan in the 1860s. After witnessing a play that Logan had written and produced on Broadway, Hudson sought out the former actress-turned-playwright for a copy of the script because the role of the heroine, "a woman of tender feelings" and "holy passions," appealed to Hudson. Logan was astonished that an actress in Hudson's line could be interested in such a part. "What sympathy had the 'French Spy' with a heroine, tearful, suffering, and self-denying? What was the chastening influence of anguish and repentance to Jack Sheppard and his jolly pals who 'fake away' so obstreperously in the burden of the chorus, and the pockets of the unwary?" Confounded by this "seeming inconsistency," Logan asked an acquaintance of Hudson's to explain the equestrienne's actions and was told that "Leo hates the leg business as much as anybody; but, bless you, nothing else pays nowadays,—so what can she do?"[90] Such a bald statement about the actresses' position within a profession that allowed her little freedom to express herself artistically, failed—ironically—to illicit any sympathy from Logan. Rather than being regarded as a seeming poster girl for the exploitive practices of the leg business, a victim of a systemic problem that Logan was committed to redress, Hudson was cast by Logan as an anomaly, a nonactress whose combination of exposed legs and masculine roleplaying made her unfit for other "feminine" roles and, significantly, for Logan's feminist cause; instead, Hudson was not categorical and therefore dangerous.

Yet, for Logan, Hudson's transgressions may have extended beyond her lowbrow theatrics. On June 1, 1867, the *Albion* critic reported that Hudson had left the Bowery and taken her Mazeppa to Barnum's, where "Mr. Barnum is making rapid strides in the work of rendering his lecture-room a place of 'intellectual amusement,' where ladies and children may repair without danger to either their morals or their manners." Because Barnum could not secure Menken for an engagement at his theatre, he hired Hudson, who supposedly played in "the most approved style" and made "a decided sensation."[91] While it is true that Barnum worked strategically to solicit a solid middle-class audience, who would not normally have patronized East Side theatres featuring equestrian melodrama, he was also a savvy businessman who understood the drawing power of women in fleshlings. Despite the questionable fare, Barnum successfully encouraged respectable patrons to visit his establishment by calling his theatre the American Museum and his performance space a lecture-room. What, in some respects, resembled a sensational collection of side show attractions began as a proclaimed educational laboratory, a place where the entire family could come to be edified as well as entertained. Icons of angelic femininity were associated with his name, and while Hudson was no Jenny Lind, her affiliation with Barnum would have signaled a marked rise in status for the equestrian breeches actress (*and* a marked rise in box-office receipts for the manager). Thus sanctioned, Hudson appeared before an eager and responsive audience of women and children to prove that the leg business was perhaps not so "shameless and unworthy." Logan's anxiety that actresses like Hudson were usurping the interest in the "legitimate" player may have been fueled by such instances, and may have ultimately provoked her to speak out about the need to eradicate this business.

Vestvali, a Polish actress whose real name was Felicja Westfalewicz, also fell victim to Logan's poison pen. Significantly, Vestvali was primarily a singer and a Shakespearean actress and never played Mazeppa or any role within the equestrian line.[92] Logan acknowledges that this actress—whom she describes as "a failure on every lyric stage, both in Europe and America"—was not a complete stranger to art, but states that if Vestvali was an artist, she was a poor one. Actresses such as Vestvali, Logan argues, "do not either act, dance, sing, or mime; but they habit themselves in a way which is attractive to an indelicate taste, and their inefficiency in other regards is overlooked."[93] By condemning Vestvali, whom Logan rightfully admits was not a typical "Mazeppa," the writer not only conflates traditional repertory offerings (Vestvali as Romeo) with burlesque, but also confuses the popular equestrian with the Shakespearean player, simply because they all shared similar costumes. This suggestion that Logan denounced all wearers of breeches, despite their seemingly hierarchical status within the profession, points to an inconsistency in her argument—a position that was strictly governed by her highbrow/lowbrow philosophy—and provides a possible explanation for the ultimate marginalization of the breeches actress and decline of the convention in the latter half of the nineteenth century. Logan cleverly avoids all mention of actresses like Cushman who regularly wore breeches while engaged in enacting "THE DRAMA." If taken to its farthest logical conclusion, however, her argument might also implicate even the scions of the theatrical world. Logan read the breeches performer monolithically and regarded her as a nonactress who was willing, without exception, to reveal herself on a daily basis "before the gaze of thousands of men... in satin breeches, ten inches long, without a vestige of drapery upon [her] person."[94] The costume and not the entertainment vehicle implicated the breeches performer. It did not matter to Logan if the actress in question played Romeo or Ixion; if she displayed her legs she was suspect. *Any* actress associated with the leg business must be scorned, marginalized, and must forgo work in the "Theatre," as Logan narrowly defined it, and must instead pursue a career in lowbrow entertainments. Those who continued to play within middle-class theatrical environs were found to be threatening to Logan because such performers limited opportunities for the respectable young actress who sought work in the Theatre (since it was one of the few careers open to women in the 1860s, and one that supposedly ensured equal pay for equal work).

Not all respectable young actresses agreed with Logan, nor did they find honest work in the theatre and breeches performance to be mutually exclusive. In a letter to the *New York Times,* written shortly after Logan's diatribe on the breeches actress appeared in print, an anonymous actress (yet clearly one who had played breeches roles) exposed certain inconsistencies in Logan's argument. This actress wrote to amend a gross injustice that she felt Logan had bestowed upon all theatrical women, for Logan was a widely recognized writer—she had published one book and her numerous articles appeared in a variety of big city dallies and periodicals—and proved extremely influential. The author of the letter confirms this and laments Logan's power, which was ironically wielded at the expense of the respectable minor actress/ballet girl. She writes, "Unable to obtain more than fictitious hold upon the stage, Olive Logan glided from the boards to the lecture field, and having there an advantage denied other actresses—that of speaking directly to the public—and by dint of forcing her views upon them, her statements have come to be listened to and accepted as facts, by those already prejudiced against the stage."[95] One of these "facts" involved the illegitimacy of the nonactress/breeches performer, the entertainer in tights or satin breeches. As the actress writing the letter points out, this was a particularly bold statement for a *former* breeches performer to make publicly. According to the writer, Logan played a number of male roles throughout her career as a performer. Like most actresses, she began as a "walking lady," which necessitated playing the occasional page or boy and, as the author of the letter makes clear, wearing the breeches. Logan's costume was probably "somewhat longer than the 'ten inches' pattern she now so mercilessly condemns," remarked the actress/author, but the fact that Logan donned such clothing at all demonstrates her "willingness to appear thus attired before the gaze of thousands of men." Not only did Logan appear as boys and pages, but she also played Sebastian in *Twelfth Night* at the Broadway Theatre, claimed the letter writer, which again caused Logan to resort "to the artifice which she now decries in 'padded-limbed creatures.'" Logan's assumption of Sebastian is especially interesting considering the play already contained one cross-dressed disguise role in Viola. The fact that Logan played a breeches role in a play that already featured a disguise role suggests either a particularly strong desire on the part of the management to showcase feminine sexuality (in adding another part that would have necessitated a display of female legs) or an equally strong desire on the part of Logan to perform a male character (or an error on the part of the letter writer, who might have meant to say Cesario).

However, considering both the power the manager had over the actress and his thirst for a profit (which he knew he could make by featuring legs), and the walking lady's utter lack of bargaining power or artistic freedom, Logan's early repertoire of breeches roles need not make her a hypocrite. Yet, as the writer of the letter is quick to note, Logan would have had control over her character selection once she achieved star status, which she did during the Civil War. The author continues, "As a star she could select her own roles, wear what costumes she liked; and yet with all these advantages she voluntarily appeared in the drama of 'Don Caesar de Bazan' choosing the part of the drunken hero, and wearing the breeches that did not reach the knees, with her form unconcealed and unrevealed save by a cape or diminutive cloak that fell a little below the waist behind."[96] The actress decries Logan's hypocrisy in castigating breeches performers who had no control over what roles they could play and might not have volunteered to wear breeches "ten inches long." Furthermore, the writer added that by condemning all breeches performers as "indecent women," Logan slandered the "virtue of every woman that has ever trod the boards," from Sarah Siddons, who played Rosalind and Hamlet, to Ellen Tree, who won success as Ion. Logan, and not the cross-dressed ballet girl (who dressed scantily upon compulsion), proved reprehensible, concluded the anonymous actress; such a "large class of inoffensive players," she added, should be defended from further prejudice.

This letter is not only significant because it exposes Logan's duplicity. By setting out to prove that Logan herself was a breeches actress, the author of the letter to the *Times* also proves that the breeches actress was under attack as well the burlesque performer, that the two forms had become associated in the public mind. Indeed, when drawing on examples of actresses that Logan maligns (Sarah Siddons and Ellen Tree), the author mentions only breeches performers and actresses who played disguise roles, as opposed to burlesque players like Thompson. Logan's repertoire is not discussed to show how many burlesque roles she played, but to establish her as a former breeches performer. While the author's primary motive in writing this epistle was to defend the minor player against slander (for enacting roles over which she had no control), this letter also suggests that prejudice against the breeches performer was as ubiquitous as Logan's published critiques.

Given the sexualization of the equestrian breeches performer, the hysterical antiburlesque discourse circulated in 1869, and Logan's castigation of all breeches actresses (burlesque or otherwise), it is no surprise that breeches performance almost completely disappeared after 1869, except for popular forms that were contained within lowbrow theatres. The critical destruction (and simultaneous construction) of sexualized Mazeppas and burlesque blondes in the 1860s proved fatal for the breeches performer who, according to critics like Howells, White, and Logan, polluted both THE DRAMA and society. Moreover, the objectifying rhetoric that surrounded the New York Mazeppa craze and the critical war waged against the post-Thompsonian burlesque performer irrevocably stigmatized the convention of breeches on the American stage. Any subtextual messages that were generated by female Hamlets, Romeos, and even Jack Sheppards about women's ability to appropriate male power were erased as the breeches performer became associated in the popular mind with the "leg business." Her male impersonation could no longer be viewed as an innocent attempt at representation. Rather, because of her costume, the breeches performer was associated with the burlesque actress, who was thought to be ominously sexual, untalented, incongruous, and unnatural.

TRENDS IN BREECHES AFTER 1869

Although the entire nature of the convention was altered in the wake of Thompsonian burlesque, breeches performance never entirely vanished from the American theatre. Yet after burlesque became institutionalized in 1869, most breeches roles were within burlesque pieces.[97] Equestrian melodrama was still performed in the Bowery, but was less popular than burlesque; as this newer entertainment form became the rage, breeches actresses who had previously starred in melodrama began to act in burlesque. Although breeches performers still appeared in theatres offering burlesque entertainment, the number of male roles played by women markedly decreased in the last three decades of the century. Edward's dissertation, for example, lists only four major breeches actresses who performed in the 1870s, and none in the 1880s or 1890s. Furthermore, according to Edwards, the minor actresses who played during these years almost exclusively appeared in burlesques and spectacles. The four major actresses who did play breeches roles in the 1870s—Minnie Maddern Fiske, Rose Coghlan, Clara Morris, and Fanny Buckingham—never became famous for their breeches performances (which they performed only during their childhood); their success came from female roles that they played later in their careers. Minor actresses who continued to play breeches roles probably did so under the authority of the management that employed them, as the actress who wrote to the *Times* regarding Logan suggests. Although specific women continued to play occasional serious male roles (such as Hamlet) in a Broadway theatre, the press was reluctant to acknowledge them; when these actresses were reviewed the response was negative.[98]

The same trends continued throughout the century. By the late 1890s, few women played male dramatic roles even in more popular forms of entertainment (although burlesque still occasionally employed breeches performers, and women—especially "Walking Ladies"—still played boys on occasion) and those who approached serious male characters met with harsh criticism. An anonymous review of Marie Prescott's Hamlet in 1892 illustrates the critical attitude toward breeches performers at the turn of the century. The critic writes:

> Marie Prescott indulged in a bit of eccentricity a few nights ago, which happily, was so little of a success, even of a curiosity, that she is not likely to repeat it. . . . She has had predecessors in this assumption of a masculine role by a woman in Anna Dickinson, who used to essay Hamlet, and Charlotte Cushman, who made a mild failure of Romeo. Miss Prescott wore a cloak in which she practically concealed the feminine characteristics of her figure, but her strut was mock-manly and her voice though deep enough was strained like that of a child pretending to be a man. And though her reading was fairly good there was a lack of virility in her every action that showed the folly of her innovation.[99]

Continued critical anxiety about female cross-dressing is evident in this review, as the writer takes obvious pleasure in Prescott's failure. Yet it is apparent that such fears were not aroused too often, as Prescott's Hamlet is perceived by this critic as eccentric, which suggests that the practice of breeches performance was very infrequent during the latter half of the century. Indeed, the critic feels compelled to contextualize the convention, mentioning two other actresses who also indulged a seemingly singular desire to play men. While Dickinson's Hamlet (which she performed in 1882) was indeed a "mild failure" (according to the press), Cushman's Romeo certainly was not. Significantly, this critic is either trying to rewrite history by refashioning public memories of Cushman's Romeo, which was unarguably the most successful breeches performance during the nineteenth century, or he/she simply does not remember (or never learned about) the incredible effect that this role had on both the English and the American public; both possible responses reinforce the fact that by the end of the nineteenth century, breeches performance had significantly declined.

This review also reiterates the influence that the "leg business" had on the breeches convention, for Prescott is reported to have worn a cloak in order to hide her "feminine characteristics." Prescott's attempt to avoid tights suggests that she deliberately sought to sever any ties with this "business," as any association with the sexualized breeches performer of the 1860s would jeopardize her chances of being perceived by the public (and evaluated by the press) as a serious artist. Despite her efforts to appear masculine, or at least unfeminine, her gait was considered "mock-manly" and her voice childlike. Both comments are revealing, considering the context of burlesque's subversive tendency towards masculine parody and the discourse of containment employed by critics throughout the century to infantilize the breeches performer by associating her with children.

In this age of Belasconian interior settings and realistic costumes and props, the breeches performer became simply an eccentricity, a "dim ghost." Forgotten were the days when actresses like Barnes and Fisher amazed audiences with their transformative talents and Lewis and Crampton impressed critics with their ability to convincingly play tragic Shakespearean villains. American critics, who confessed at midcentury to "being carried captive at [Cushman's] will" as she scaled the Capulet wall and worsted Tybalt in mortal combat, were now indifferent at best to such impersonations. As one late-century critic explained, "breeches parts" were burlesque roles, "peculiarly designed for women." Any other female attempts at male role playing were in "bad taste, and somewhat questionable in point of morality."[100] This critic's conclusion regarding the pointlessness of breeches performance is striking in its complete disregard for a practice that, despite its controversial nature, had once been a popular antebellum theatrical convention. By emphatically declaring breeches performance unnecessary and irrelevant, this critic constructed the ultimate discourse of containment—a statement that did not simply try to undermine the potential power in cross-dressed appropriations of masculinity through castigating, feminizing, infantilizing, or objectifying the breeches actress. Rather, this critic's assessment of breeches performance was much more direct: there was simply "no earthly need" for her presence on the American stage.

Conclusion ⚜

"A DOUBLET AND HOSE IN MY DISPOSITION"
Feminism, Lesbianism, and Late Century Breeches Performance

> ... [D]ost thou think,
> though I am caparison'd like a man,
> I have a doublet and hose in my disposition?
>
> —*As You Like It* [3.2.194]

DURING THE THEATRICAL SEASON OF 1893–1894, a New York ladies' club, the Professional Women's League, mounted an unusual production of *As You Like It*. Performed solely by women and conceived with the specific intent of putting unemployed actresses back to work, this benefit was produced in order to ameliorate financial difficulties engendered by the Panic of 1893. Not only was this event lucrative for the PWL and beneficial for its indigent members (participants were paid salaries throughout the entire—albeit brief—production period), but it was one of few traditional productions *ever* presented on the nineteenth-century American stage in which women comprised the entire cast. Indeed, the *Spirit of the*

Times remarked that *As You Like It* had "never before been acted exclusively by women."[1] Over 100 women appeared on the stage of Palmer's Theatre on November 21, 1893, the majority of them in male clothing. In addition to the all-female acting company, the director, the properties manager, the backstage crew, the orchestra and conductor, the house manager, and the ushers were all women. "Men only entered into the execution of this remarkable production in three very subordinate departments," claimed the *New York Herald:* "It was a man who sold tickets in the box office, another man who took tickets at the door, and behind the scenes the muscular fellows who usually shift the scenery for the regular performances at this theatre did the same duty for the women."[2]

Notwithstanding cynics who expressed doubt that this rendition would be taken seriously and anticipated instead "a travesty of the great play,"[3] the League's single matinee performance at Palmer's Theatre on November 21, 1893, was well received by the New York press and so popular with audiences that a longer six-day run was scheduled for the following late January/early February at the Garden Theatre in New York. Joseph Jefferson was reported to have said, "I never saw 'As You Like It' played as well in all its parts,"[4] and the *New York Dramatic Mirror* allowed that, "The presentation was earnest in everything, and as a whole it reflected great credit upon the management and upon those who took the parts."[5] Similarly, the *Herald* praised the League's "daring venture," allowing that "its success from an artistic standpoint appeared to be undisputed."[6]

It is curious that such an event could have enjoyed such critical and popular favor after the convention of breeches had (indirectly) been pronounced dead by New York critics and, with the exception of some burlesque performance, had almost completely vanished from the American stage. Yet, even more perplexing is the abrupt disappearance of breeches performance following the League's encore production at the Garden Theatre. Under what circumstances could breeches be allowed to momentarily thrive again on the New York stage, and what precipitated the convention's ultimate decline by 1900? A brief conclusionary investigation of the cross-dressed theatrics of the PWL provides answers to these questions and contributes to a more thorough understanding of the ways in which the breeches performer was perceived at the century's end. In many ways, turn-of-the-century critical interpretations of the cross-dressed actress followed patterns that had been established during the first half of the century, and specific discourses of containment, such as feminization, remained operative. In addition, new hegemonic strategies of containment were constructed to undermine the breeches performer, strategies that refashioned the Madonna/Whore dialectic, which for centuries had functioned as an ideological yardstick, categorizing the cross-dressed actress as either feminine or dangerously transgressive. Indeed, members of the Professional Women's League who performed in drag had more to contend with than the haunting shadow of the burlesque "low other"; late century breeches performance encountered a much more daunting specter (and one that ultimately put an end to its brief resurrection): the "sexual invert."

※ ※ ※

Unlike male theatrical organizations such as Booth's Player's Club, the PWL's history, politics, and artistic output have received almost no scholarly attention.[7] Founded in New York City in 1892, the League was created to offer relief to unemployed actresses, aid that other theatrical charitable organizations, such as Lester Wallack's Actor's Fund of America, failed to provide. Ironically, the PWL was originally conceived as an auxiliary to the Actor's Fund, yet, despite valuable promises of support offered by the Fund, founding members of the League felt that a separate organization should be created to "pursue their own specific benevolent objects among women of the profession." The PWL's primary aim was "to help women in trouble by loans of money, by advice and counsel, and by all other feasible means," yet it adopted a policy that eschewed simple acts of charity and instead empowered women to help themselves.[8]

A bazaar, a typewriting branch, and a theatrical dressmaking establishment were created by the ruling members and were designed to employ "needy young actresses, paying them for their services." In order not to expose the dire financial circumstances facing many of these women, other members of the club were also required to work, but without pay; only the executive committee knew the wage workers from the volunteers. The League proclaimed that the "star and the chorus girl will sew side by side . . . and every woman connected with the profession, from the most distinguished to the most humble, will be invited to enter the guild and to take some share in its work."[9] Despite the fact that most of the founders of the organization were white, upper- or middle-class women, the League did attempt to counter its elitism by instituting such equitable (and perhaps naive) regulations.

In addition to its social and philanthropic function, the PWL acted in many ways as a proto-feminist organization, sponsoring symposiums on "The Twentieth Century Woman"[10] and providing educational opportunities for its members. Every Wednesday afternoon a lecture would be given at the League's brownstone headquarters at 29 West Thirtieth Street, an establishment that also furnished classes in French, German, and fencing as well as new play readings by female playwrights. No male members were permitted to join this club, for its interests and events were entirely focused on women's issues. The League's quarters provided a forum where women could speak out and in some sense transcend certain oppressive Victorian social antitheses (between public and private, male and female, aggressive and passive, professional and domestic) that shaped and defined their lives. At one afternoon gathering, actress Maude Banks declared: "Women are only beginning to live. . . . Women have been content to be mothers. They have never had a voice in the world, and yet it is their world, and they have never paid their life's blood for its existence. The woman of the past is dead. The pretty bird that twittered to please its master is to be found only in books. . . . We are a crippled people and we have a right to a perfect freedom and to bring up a race perfect in poise, to whom living will be a joy."[11]

Banks was not the only actress figuratively to play Nora on Wednesday afternoons and express herself candidly concerning the rights of women. In a lecture entitled "Average Man Mentally Lazy," Ella Starr asked the rhetorical question: "Do men care for erudition in women?" League members were not quick to respond positively to this question, reported the *New York Dramatic Mirror,* whose critic added, "An unprejudiced observer might have exclaimed, in the words of the song 'Man, poor man!' Not a voice was raised in his favor and he was even personally excluded from listening to a discourse that might have resulted in reducing any exorbitant degree of self-esteem on his part."[12] Significantly, neither Banks nor Starr was among the more radical women within the League. Suffragettes, business women, female journalists, and scholars filled the rooms of the spacious brownstone, in addition to well-known theatrical women such as Mary Shaw, who according to Robert A. Schanke, would one day "use the theatre as a vehicle for her feminist ideas."[13] In addition to Shaw, members of the PWL included eminent "New Women" of the stage such as Minnie Maddern Fiske, Helena Modjeska, May Robson, Lotta Crabtree, and Fanny Janauschek, as well as early feminists/suffragettes like Marilene Palmer, Jane Cunningham Croly, and Kate Field.[14]

Despite their edifying (and somewhat singular) lecture series and their varied wage earning opportunities, the most significant project undertaken by the PWL in the early years of its existence involved mounting an elaborate—and extremely popular—production of *As You Like It*. Not only were additional performances scheduled to accommodate the crowds that overwhelmed the Palmer Theatre box office in November, but critics responded more positively to the breeches actress than they had in 60 years. Individual actresses were even reported to have passed as men onstage, a difficult task considering the context of cross-dressed performance in the late nineteenth century and its association since the 1860s with the "leg business." Members of the League (like Miss Prescott who performed Hamlet in 1892) made a conscious decision to eschew the traditional doublet and hose in favor of more concealing apparel, perhaps as a way of shattering destructive discourses constructed in the wake of Thompsonian burlesque. The *Mirror* wrote that, "In costume, the women will as far as possible avoid the effects of tights, affecting such cloakings as may be thought appropriate to the play."[15] A few critics were convinced by the disguise, proving that Rosalind/Ganymed was not the only boundary-crosser. The *Herald* critic noted, under a rubric reading "LOOKED AND

ACTED LIKE MEN," that "[t]he spectacular difference of sex was quite elusive. So cleverly did the majority of the women taking men's parts counterfeit the more rugged and less graceful speech and bearing of the men that very early in the play, the illusion, so far at least as the chief roles were concerned, was quite perfect." Marion Abbott, who played Charles the wrestler "looked every inch her part," while Maude Banks, who "in some respects made the greatest success of the evening as Orlando, was here, as always, a remarkably easy young gentleman."[16]

How does one explain this phenomenon in light of the supposed decline of breeches performance? An answer may lie in certain recuperative strategies employed by the New York press, who, despite laudatory comments concerning particular "manly" actresses, constructed a discourse of feminization (similar to certain rhetorical campaigns during the first half of the century) around the League and its performances to counter illusions of masculinity and contain any possible threat implied by their cross-dressing. The League, whose feminist bent was publicly recognized—since reports about its members and its activities were routinely disclosed by the press— may have seemed particularly suspect in their choice to appropriate male dress and behavior (and possibly male power) on such a grand scale.[17] By undermining the actresses' supposed masculinity with repeated references to their seemingly essential "womanhood," critical reviews succeeded in mitigating this threat. In addition, this feminization process also helped to, as Elizabeth Drorbaugh says, "shore up lax boundaries" within the sex-gender system, reversing the subversive effects of drag and reinforcing the "natural" gender binarism—as an emphasis on difference, in the wake of burgeoning medical studies in sexology, was paramount.[18]

As outlined earlier in this study, recent writings on cross-dressing rely heavily upon the theory that gender is a construct, a deliberately manufactured ideology whose machinations are exposed by the cross-dressed artist. Indeed, breeches performance, as I have argued throughout this book, did not simply function as an erotic entertainment for men but was used, on specific occasions, as a self-consciously subversive act that foregrounded the performative nature of gender. Drag renders the "natural" artificial (as Cushman's androgyne demonstrates), exposes gender's instability, and disrupts essentialist binaries. Evidence of what Butler calls gender's "contingency" may well be found in the drag performances of Arden, a place where gender distinctions become fluid and borders are easily crossed.[19] The PWL's performance of *As You Like It* perhaps emphasized the subversive potency of female-to-male drag, as most of the participants in the action joined Rosalind in *performing* masculinity. Yet, because these actresses supposedly never abandoned "the hidden woman's fear" [1.3.119] underneath their disguise, their performances perhaps implied that gender was as specious as their masquerade.

Such fanciful Greenworld gender-trekking found a less receptive audience upon the larger nineteenth-century American *social* stage, where the doctrine of separate spheres and its prescriptive codes surrounding masculinity and True Womanhood still held center despite late-century feminist calls for suffrage and other reforms. For while women such as Rosalind might have had the ability to challenge hegemonic categories by exposing gender constructions, their triumphs could only be temporary, as discussions in chapter 4 of Cushman's portrayal make clear. Both Arden and Ganymed are abandoned—despite their magical qualities and transformative powers—by Rosalind, who must hang up her doublet and hose in act 5 and forfeit all prerogative to Orlando. Thus the motives behind drag performance are found to be, as Whittier points out, "conventionally feminine," just as comprehension of Rosalind's wit necessitates knowledge of her disguise.[20]

The New York press depended upon such knowledge as well, for along with reports about particular actresses who "looked and acted like men," critics inserted constant reminders that the costume was, indeed, no more than a disguise, an illusion of masculinity played out within a definitively feminine environment. Every review of the "pretty comedy" made numerous references to this seemingly ubiquitous femininity.[21] Even the *Herald*, which was the one paper to praise the "spectacular difference of sex," shared in constructing this discourse. Critics made it clear that the audience entered into a feminine space from the minute they stepped into the theatre. The orchestra pit was described as "a veritable flower garden of new fall bonnets" and the ushers, arrayed in silk evening gowns, reportedly smiled as they "called out in shrill voices" for ticket stubs and kept the aisles clear of patrons by declaring, "'no gossip here.'"[22] Many performers were commended for their "truly masculine *style,*" yet critics made sure also to comment upon their "extraordinarily thin feminine voices," their "generous outlines," which were "essentially feminine" and, of course, their weakness. The *Herald* critic describes the events that followed the wrestling scene: "Four scarlet habited soldiers, quite ferocious with sweeping mustaches and Machiavillian [sic] chin whiskers, advanced haughtily and thrust their spear handles under the form of the wrestler. But when they came to lift him their feminine weakness was so apparent and they struggled so under the dead weight that the audience fairly shouted with laughter."[23] Even the illustrations that accompanied the *Herald*'s review accentuated the actresses' femininity. Regardless of the actresses' expressed desire to hide their bodies under capes and other less revealing costumes, these sketches seem to indicate that this goal was either not realized by the actresses or that the artist's rendition of them was deliberately crafted to showcase their "feminine" features.

A review from *Collier's Weekly* epitomizes such reductive critical efforts. After considering possible reasons for the League's absurd undertaking, the journalist concludes that the breeches performer who attempts Shakespeare (or any male role) is bound to fail in such a task, for "sublime" dramatic expression would lamentably become "ridiculous" if women assumed men's parts—the typical critical response to post-1869 traditional breeches performance. "Women can do most anything nowadays; but she [sic] cannot part with her birthright of fine feature, dainty limb and tuneful voice. She may swagger and even swear in small clothes and doublet, and throw herself about in all kinds of free-and-easy attitudes; but—well, she isn't a man for a' that."[24]

In addition to foregrounding repeatedly the transparency of the actresses' disguises, the New York press also described the PWL's performance as "singular," "unusual," "a theatrical curio," and "daring," while the play itself was called "uniquely poetic, fanciful, even fantastic in some of its refinements of human capriciousness and eccentricity."[25] By employing such language, critics furthered a discourse of containment in making allowances for this anomaly. Because the vehicle itself was viewed as fantastic or "unreal," the possibly transgressive display of one hundred cross-dressed—yet "feminine"—women was rendered innocuous; the entire project was a lark, unorthodox, an odd but benign bit of whimsy to entertain audiences and assuage the ill effects of a bitter and economically disastrous New York winter. The *Mirror* was especially aggressive on this front, stating that,

> There is a very femininity in the dreamy, vagarious, romantic atmosphere of the play that this performance illustrated and satisfyingly enhanced. This was because there was no bizarre attempt, either abstractly or concretely [to seriously convey manhood].... We have had at one time and another a woman essaying the part of Romeo or the role of Hamlet in incongruous environment.... Such things illustrate their own impossibility. This "As You Like It" was something wholly apart from all such efforts.[26]

These critical efforts at feminization were perhaps mirrored on a larger scale through associations cultivated by female club life. While PWL members might have been perceived as more subversive than most due to their cross-dressed histrionics, women's clubs in general operated within the paradigm of "Domestic Feminism." In her book, *The Clubwoman as Feminist: True Womanhood Redefined, 1868–1914*, Karen Blair argues that Domestic Feminism was the clubwoman's modus operandi. "Ladies" used their supposedly innate qualities of domesticity and morality to help them achieve rights within a public male arena.[27] Regardless, however, of any real strides that might have been made through such experiments in social housekeeping, gender was always—and necessarily—foregrounded, as "ladydom" insidiously countered, and therefore contained, the threat of potential freedoms. Such a compromised politic is evident in many of the PWL's proto-feminist lectures mentioned above, for while Shaw, for example, spoke of women as a "crippled people" with a right to "perfect freedom," she concluded her sentence by talking about bringing up a race "perfect in poise, to whom living will be a joy," thus reinforcing the idea that the principle "right" of the free woman is to shape a nation and affect change through the mothering of her offspring.

Club life was firmly grounded in ideological femininity—a mooring that buttressed critical efforts to legitimize the League's feminist leanings and displays of transvestism.[28] Every public report concerning the PWL's work, both before and beyond the footlights, was shaped by this discourse of femininity. The League's brownstone was "prettily furnished," and although its rooms were predominantly reserved for various business transactions, there still existed a "dainty feminine air about the place, distinguishing it from similar apartments ruled over by mere matter-of-fact men."[29] Offstage, members were similarly typed, cast as moral scions who were not simply ethically superior to men but to other women as well. The PWL actress/member stood at the pinnacle of feminine propriety: she was the apotheosis of True Womanhood. Referring to League members as "the guardians of the honor of the dramatic profession," one observer (known only by the initials A. P.) was so impressed by their "high purpose" that s/he sent a special letter to the editor of the *Dramatic Mirror* that was published in its weekly column, "The Woman's Page." A. P. illustrates the moral superiority of the PWL members, declaring:

> The theatrical profession is the only profession which is open to flippant intruders who have the power to degrade it. Therefore, the duty of the actress to her profession is two-fold. Not only does she owe it a life of spotless uprightness; she also owes it a carefulness, a prudence, a dignity in living so marked as to contradict the faintest seeming of moral laxity. In other words, the actress must be more prudent, more rigorous in observing social laws, and outward conventionalities than any other woman.... [T]he honor of her profession is in her keeping.[30]

Charged with such an ennobling responsibility, the women involved with the League may have appeared somewhat untouchable, their lofty moral purpose thus shielding them from critical barbs. Even cross-dressed PWL members were still benefitting their profession—literally. Because it was widely known that the proceeds from their production of *As You Like It* were going to help needy actresses, critics may have perceived their male disguise as less subversive. The *Spirit* reviewer remarked, "Such a performance for such a cause does not call for criticism. The Woman's League benefited by over $2,000, and that is the best justification for the reversal of the sexes."[31] By critically representing the PWL as a collection of moral icons, the press reinforced their femininity; their male dramatic roles did not make them the *head* of any theatrical house, but rather its *angel*.

Such seemingly urgent mandates regarding the rigid maintenance of femininity in the 1890s can be better understood in light of late century studies within the relatively embryonic field of sexology. First published in Germany in the 1870s and appearing in the United States within the decade, the findings of the sexologists necessitated this emphasis on difference, as sexuality and object choice were thought to be directly contingent on gender and its sartorial markings. The principal disseminator of ideas regarding "sexual inversion" in the 1880s was the German sexologist Richard von Krafft-Ebing, who theorized a symptomatic link between lesbianism, feminism, and cross-dressing. Smith-Rosenberg explains that Krafft-Ebing based his categorization of women as lesbians not on sexual practices but on social practices and physical attributes. A woman was judged to be lesbian if she eschewed True Womanhood, cross-dressed, and/or displayed other masculine bodily features. "[H]aving rooted social gender in biological sexuality, Krafft-Ebing then made dress analogous to gender. Only the abnormal woman would challenge conventional gender distinctions—and by her dress you would know her."[32]

Krafft-Ebing's theories surrounding the "mannish lesbian"[33] were widely recognized by American doctors, who repeatedly invoked him in late nineteenth-century medical journals. George Chauncey explains that prior to 1900, the American medical community theorized a direct parallel between the female sexual invert's social and sexual roles (via Krafft-Ebing): if a woman desired another woman sexually, she must be thinking and acting like a man, a phenomena that would be apparent through her propensity to dress like a man.[34] Many case studies involving cross-dressed female inverts were reported throughout the 1880s, such as Dr. P. M. Wise's report in 1883 concerning Lucy Anne Slater, alias Rev. Joseph Lobdell, who married a woman and moved to the wilds of upper New York State, where she became known as the "Female Hunter of Long Eddy." Slater is described by Wise as having a coarse voice and masculine features: "She was dressed in male attire throughout and declared herself to be a man."[35]

This connection between male-identified women and sexual inversion, as exemplified by Wise's case study, was repeatedly articulated in medical journals. In 1884, a review of a lecture on inversion was written up in *The Chicago Medical Journal and Examiner* by a doctor who identified himself by his initials, L. H. M. He discusses a female patient of Dr. James G. Kiernan (who delivered the lecture in Chicago), describing her as being of "neurotic ancestry" and possessing a face and cranium that were "asymmetrical." Her behavior had a similar "bent," suggests L. H. M., for she had "a fondness for male attire, and [felt] sexually attracted by some of her female friends."[36] In a paper Kiernan wrote for *The Medical Standard,* he details a case study involving a 35-year-old boarding school mistress. Kiernan describes the patient's history and states that as a child she had been fond of both male attire and of boys' games and activities. He added that as an adult this "perverse tendency was exceedingly obnoxious to her and she desired to be freed from it. In her voluptuous dreams she appeared to herself to be a man."[37]

Various other accounts, which represented cross-dressing as symptomatic of sexual inversion, were published throughout the 1880s and 1890s in American medical journals in addition to Krafft-Ebing's own writings, which were published in translation in the *Alienist and Neurologist* in 1888.[38] In an article entitled "Perversion of the Sexual Instinct," the German professor describes one of his female patients as having male features and short hair and wearing a man's hat and spectacles along with a "gentleman's cravat and a sort of coat of male cut." Krafft-Ebing continues, "She had coarse male features, a rough and rather deep voice, and, with the exception of the bosom and female contour of the pelvis, looked more like a man in woman's clothing than like a woman."[39] He hypothesized that his patient (who also was interested in male pastimes as a youth) developed an erotic love for women after an illness that she experienced in 1872, and, after 1874, "did not consider herself to be a woman." Krafft-Ebing further explained, "Her passion for women showed itself in tears, fits of jealousy, etc. While she was at the baths in 1874 a young woman fell in love with her, thinking she was a man in woman's clothing. When this young lady married Miss X [his patient] became very melancholy and complained of faithlessness."[40]

Yet, despite the notoriety gained by Krafft-Ebing and his American disciples within the medical profession, articles linking transvestism and inversion enjoyed a limited popular readership in the eighties and early nineties. Significantly, however, in 1892—the year before the League's first production—a scandalous murder case in Tennessee made national headlines, indoctrinating both inversion and transvestism into a broader public discourse. Smith-Rosenberg describes the Alice Mitchell/Freda Ward story as a *"cause celebre* [that] catapulted the discussion of lesbianism, until now quite a minor theme in the medical and asylum journals, into polite and influential family circles."[41] Alice Mitchell, a resident at a boarding school in Memphis and the daughter of a wealthy family, fell in love with her classmate Freda Ward. After making plans to elope to St. Louis where Mitchell would cross-dress and assume a male persona as Alvin J. Ward, their plot was detected and foiled by Ward's relatives. In what the court later termed to be a fit of insanity, Mitchell jumped from her carriage in January of 1892, accosted Ward, and slit her throat.

In her study of the Mitchell/Ward trial, Lisa Duggan remarks upon the themes of cross-dressing and cross-gender identification that permeated national press coverage. "Though there was no evidence reported of any sexual contact between Alice and Freda . . . there were indications in the news accounts that they recognized, played with, and eroticized a masculine/feminine difference between them."[42] New Yorkers would have been able to read about this case and its reports of inversion and cross-dressing/cross-gender identification, as both the *Times* and the *World* closely followed the story. Almost every article that was printed by the New

York press concerning the case portrayed Mitchell as a male-identified woman and as perverse; conversely, Ward was depicted as a feminine lady, an innocent victim. A report on the front page of the *New York Times* on January 29, 1892, discusses Mitchell as the aggressor in the relationship; it was she who proposed to Ward and who sent her fiancee an engagement ring.[43] Similarly, the *New York World* carried a story on the case the same day, entitled "Is Alice Mitchell Crazy?," which also presented Mitchell as masculine. "[A] slave to an abnormal passion," Mitchell was described as having no romantic interest in men, rather she was exclusively fond of women and took part in male pastimes such as rifle shooting and riding bareback.[44]

Furthermore, on January 31, the *Times* boldly detailed—in another front page article—the literal aspect of Mitchell's masculine tendencies as revealed through her proclivity towards cross-dressing. The reporter explained that Mitchell and her friend Lillie Johnson (later thought to be her accomplice) were spotted trailing Ward a few weeks after the engagement was broken off by Ward's older sister, who discovered some disturbing letters written by Mitchell to Ward and immediately dissolved the match. Ward and her sister (who had subsequently moved to Gold Dust, Tennessee) had been visiting in Memphis, where Mitchell still resided, but were planning to return home after a short stay. The *Times* commentator continued, "It also seems that it appeared in evidence that Miss Mitchell and Miss Johnson dressed themselves in men's clothes and went aboard the steamer Ora Lee on the Monday preceding the murder, when it was reported that the Misses Ward would take passage on the boat for home."[45]

New York medical journals also discussed the case and made note of Mitchell's desire to wear men's clothes. In an article entitled "Alice Mitchell of Memphis: A Case of Sexual Perversion or 'Urning' (A Paranoiac)," a Dr. Comstock stated, "[Mitchell] was to have been dressed as a man and take a bridegroom's part in the marriage ceremony."[46] All of the information that circulated about Mitchell's cross-dressing was probably based on the "Hypothetical Case" that was constructed by Mitchell's defense attorneys and was reprinted, as Duggan points out, by a Memphis paper. In the "Hypothetical Case," the story of Mitchell's plan to adopt a male identity as Alvin J. Ward is outlined. Duggan refers to this plan as a classic "passing strategy," a ruse occasionally employed throughout the nineteenth century by women who hoped that by cross-dressing, they might escape certain Victorian restrictions on love and work. As the "Case" reveals,

> Alice was to put on man's apparel, and have her hair trimmed by a barber like a man; was to get the license to marry, and Fred was to procure the Rev. . . . [or] a justice of the peace to marry them. The ceremony performed, they intended to leave for St. Louis. Alice was to continue to wear man's apparel, and meant to try and have a mustache, if it would please Fred. She was going out to work for Fred in men's clothes.[47]

While Duggan acknowledges that this "Case," as well as the newspaper articles that covered the story, were constructed and "designed to procure a particular medical opinion and a desired legal outcome," they were, nevertheless, based on information that had been issued by Mitchell herself. Mitchell deliberately embraced a male persona in order to effect a love relationship that supposedly consumed her. One particularly interesting aspect about this case, as noted by Duggan, involves the influence that cross-dressing had on public opinion. Mitchell and Ward's romantic friendship was thought to be innocuous by their schoolmates, headmistress, and by their families, until Mitchell's plans regarding her male disguise were discovered by Ward's sister. Their love was thought to be "abnormal" and "perverse" only after they decided to undertake a "passing strategy"; thus the link between transvestism and sexual inversion was reestablished. This case was subversive, Duggan implies, precisely because of this link that signaled Mitchell's break from Victorian womanhood. Duggan discusses Mitchell, "a cross-gender-identified lesbian," as contributing to a "new narrative-information," since she threatened social boundaries and gender binaries[48] by her decision to abandon them—just as all women (specifically members of the PWL) who strived to obtain rights and express themselves politically also threatened hegemonic stability and legitimacy.

The Mitchell/Ward case, and the national headlines it generated, publicly associated cross-dressing and displays of masculine behavior with inversion and brought the findings of the sexologists before a much larger—specifically New York—forum. This may, in part, explain the discourse of feminization generated by the New York press to counter any subversions possibly engendered through the League's cross-dressed theatrics. Since cross-dressing was indicative of inversion in the 1890s, and inversion was connected to feminism (or the adoption of male social roles—Krafft-Ebing thought that the female invert was actually a man trapped in a woman's body), the League's performance of *As You Like It* could be read as doubly transgressive considering the group's feminist tendencies. Given this context, critics may not have been able to ignore so many New Women making attempts to appropriate male behavior and dress in a play that sanctioned, perhaps even celebrated, gender boundary crossing. By constantly foregrounding the League's femininity in their reviews, the New York press eclipsed emerging popular images of the "mannish lesbian" as realized by Mitchell, and assured New York audiences that despite the fact that League members were "caparison'd like [men]," they did not have "a doublet and hose in [their] disposition."

Notwithstanding the press's recuperative discourse, the specter of lesbianism still loomed over the New York theatrical community and continued to haunt the breeches actress in particular. The Professional Women's League's 1893/94 drag productions were closely followed by an increasingly potent sexual discourse that proved more directly damning for theatrical women than subtler implications brought up by the Mitchell/Ward incident. What may have been perceived in 1892 as inconclusive media-generated associations between the actress, the feminist, the cross-dresser, and the lesbian or "invert," became direct indictments in the wake of sexologist Havelock Ellis's writings and Krafft-Ebing's later studies. In 1895—one year after the PWL's second run of *As You Like It*—Ellis published an article entitled "Sexual Inversion in Women" in the *Alienist*. While Ellis disagrees with Krafft-Ebing on many points and argues that transvestism is not *always* indicative of inversion, he echoes some of the German professor's ideas regarding cross-dressing, as he notes the "very pronounced tendency among sexually inverted women to adopt male attire when practicable." Ellis goes on to discuss the rise of feminism and the professional woman's inclination toward inversion. He writes, "[A] tendency develops for women to carry this independence still further and to find love where they find work."[49] Smith-Rosenberg explains the lethal effect these ideas had on the women's movement by turning the New Woman into a "sexual anomaly and a political pariah." Anywhere women gathered became suspect after Ellis's writings gained notoriety, she argues—including the women's club.[50]

The ramifications of Ellis's work hit theatrical club women especially hard, for two years later, Ellis revised his 1895 article to include specific information on the actress. "Great actresses from the eighteenth century onward have frequently been more or less correctly identified with homosexuality," declared Ellis, who went on to relate the story of the Tiller sisters, "two quintroons," who in his narrative, are portrayed as criminals in addition to being inverts—a common coupling in medical case studies. (Ellis went so far as to say that the majority of cases "in which homosexuality has led to crimes of violence . . . was among women.") According to Ellis, one of the sisters was an invert and sexually attracted to the other noninverted sister, who was eventually seduced by a man and moved away from the first sister. The inverted sister was "overcome by jealousy, broke into the apartment of the couple and shot the man dead."[51] This story illustrates Ellis's unsurprising conflation of "othered" traits: sex, sexuality, class (the Tillers acted in "cheap theatres"), and ethnicity—all of which contrast nicely to the Mitchell/Ward case. The inverted Tiller was not only a violent murderer, but a sexually "deviant" individual, a working-class woman, a quintroon, and an actress—qualities that seemed to make her crime a bit less shocking than Mitchell's, who was upper-middle-class and white.

Not only was sexual inversion among actresses conspicuously gendered by Ellis, but it also led to death. He writes, "The infatuation of young girls for actresses and other prominent women may occasionally lead to suicide." Ellis gives the specific example of a 19-year-old Philadelphia girl who dreamt of becoming prima donna Mary Garden's personal maid. When the girl realized her hopes were futile, she shot herself with a revolver.[52] Women like Miss Garden, Ellis implies, were inclined toward homosexuality, just like their admirers, for two reasons. Actresses cultivated a sexual interest among themselves by keeping such close quarters within theatres, and allegedly possessed a "general tendency for homosexuality," since inversion was supposedly "connected with dramatic aptitude." Ellis goes on to explain that:

> [P]assionate friendships among girls, from the most innocent to the most elaborate excursions in the direction of Lesbos, are extremely common in theatres, both among actresses and, even, more, among chorus—and ballet—girls. Here the pell mell of the dressing rooms, the wait of perhaps two hours between the performances *[sic]*, during which all the girls are cooped up, in a state of inaction and of excitement, in a few crowded dressing rooms, afford every opportunity for the growth of this particular kind of sentiment.[53]

Here again, Ellis associates inversion with working-class actresses such as the chorus and ballet girl—a sentiment that he seems to contradict elsewhere in his study by stating that lesbianism appears to be more prominent among the idle rich, for they possess both a "liberty of action" and a "much greater freedom from prejudices."[54] Such a statement would incriminate women like Alice Mitchell, as well as most members of the PWL.

Krafft-Ebing makes a similar connection between actresses and lesbianism in contemporaneous writings, claiming that "Uranism [inversion] may nearly always be suspected in females wearing their hair short, or who dress in the fashion of men, or pursue the sports and pastimes of their male acquaintances; also in opera singers and actresses who appear in male attire on the stage by preference."[55] While Krafft-Ebing comes to recognize the breeches performer as particularly suspect at the turn of the century, his formula for inversion remains the same: the woman who looks like a man and chooses to act like a man (onstage), must, indeed, also love like a (heterosexual) man. Unlike Ellis, however, Krafft-Ebing still focuses on the physical appearance and social behavior of the lesbian/actress as opposed to her sexual behavior.

Significantly, the *New York World* reported that Mitchell aspired to become an actress. The *World* published several letters in 1892 supposedly written by Mitchell (although they were signed Freda), in which she poses as an actress in order to dupe an unsuspecting pen pal. In these letters, Mitchell claims that she ran away to New York where she became a chorus girl but quickly added more weighty roles to her repertoire. Duggan suggests that women such as Mitchell (and male impersonator Annie Hindle) may have found safe harbor in the theatre, "an institution where collectivities of those with unconventional gender identifications and sexual lives could congregate relatively free from censure."[56] Yet, as we have seen, the breeches performer was either castigated, ignored, or contained in the late nineteenth/early twentieth century, and, as the writings of Krafft-Ebing demonstrate, those turn-of-the-century actresses who possessed unorthodox gender identities were categorized as sexual perverts. As the New York press's feminization campaign implies, gender identities were hegemonically defined and constructed within the theatre just as they were in society; neither actresses nor tabloid sensations were granted any sort of exonerating social immunity because of their work within the theatre. Like the late century theories of Ellis and Krafft-Ebing, the Mitchell/Ward case may also have conjured up associations in the popular mind between inversion, transvestism, *and* the actress. Indeed, early connections such as this one possibly influenced Ellis and Krafft-Ebing, who seemed to read the female theatrical transvestite as inverted because of her "dramatic aptitude," her marginal social behavior, and her physical appearance.

Such turn-of-the-century writings, directly linking inversion with the cross-dressed actress, and associations between the decline of breeches performance and the institutionalization of the "sexual invert," help to explain both the feminizing discourse of containment woven by the New York press around the PWL and the fact that the League never mounted another drag show after 1894—despite the extreme popularity of their rendition of *As You Like It*. The age of supposed innocence was over both for the New Woman and for the breeches performer, whose forays into manhood after midcentury (and on certain occasions prior to midcentury) were seldom regarded as innocuous. For just as the cast of the PWL's *As You Like It* could, after 1895, no longer escape the "instrumentality of the perverse," previous breeches performers' perceived subversions were subject to limiting discourses of containment—some of which were still operative at the turn of the century.

Indeed, the cross-dressed theatrics of the PWL serve as a fitting epilogue for explorations of transvestism and gender representation on the antebellum stage. Members of the cast of *As You Like It* were celebrated for their masculine portrayals only because they acted within a "dreamy, vagarious, and romantic atmosphere" that invoked a spirit of femininity that "satisfyingly enhanced" the transparency of their disguise. Like critical readings of Ellen Tree in 1837 ("She becomes not Ion, but Ion becomes Ellen Tree"), the New York press watched the characters on stage and *saw* the actress; her femininity was writ large upon the performance text as social renderings of serious breeches performance became unimaginable after burlesque indelibly marked the cross-dressed actress as female. While some members of the PWL cast reportedly attempted to "pass" as Cushman did (Charles the Wrestler "looked every inch her part"), creating a double image onstage—and/or within the mind of the critical reader—that exposed the stipulatory nature of gender, recuperative discourses were employed that successfully countered transcendent images. Yet despite various nineteenth-century containment strategies, contemporary students of cross-dressing can understand Cushman's androgyne, and other attempts at antebellum and Victorian transvestism, as a kind of theoretical paradox, a model that serves to enhance current discussions of gender performativity and that contributes to the deconstruction of hegemonic ideologies. Indeed, women's appropriation of male clothing—while eroticized and/or feminized in the late nineteenth century—did, on many occasions, function as a freedom suit, as Alice Mitchell/Alvin J. Ward hoped it would. By "wearing the breeches," the cross-dressed actress literally and figuratively performed a "benefit" for American women and enacted, on both a theatrical and a social stage, a liberating text that strained against the doctrine of separate spheres and worked to redefine TRUE Womanhood.

NOTES

INTRODUCTION

1. Samuel Pepys, *The Diary of Samuel Pepys* (London: Macmillan and Co., 1924), 181.
2. Richard Findlater, *The Player Queens* (New York: Taplinger Publishing Co., 1976), 83.
3. Our Lady Correspondent, "Theatricals in Boston," *Porter's Spirit of the Times* 93.4 (June 12, 1858): 229.
4. Tracy C. Davis, *Actresses as Working Women: Their Social Identity in Victorian Culture* (New York: Routledge, 1990), 112.
5. Barnard Hewitt, *Theatre U.S.A.: 1665–1957* (New York: McGraw-Hill, 1959), 133–134.
6. Ibid.
7. See Treva Rose Tumbleson, "Three Female Hamlets: Charlotte Cushman, Sarah Bernhardt, and Eva Le Galliene," (Ph.D. diss., University of Oregon, 1981), 95.
8. Letter from William Burton to Benjamin Webster, n.d., Harvard Theatre Collection. This letter is located in the Charlotte Cushman "Extra-Illustrated," vol. 4 no. 6. Although no date is written on this letter, it was almost definitely composed in 1844 since it was in this year that Cushman acquired letters from her former employees to take with her to London.
9. William Dunlap, *History of the American Theatre* (New York: Burt Franklin, 1963), 320.
10. Joseph Ireland, *Records of the New York Stage from 1750–1862*, 2 vols. (New York: T. H. Morrell, 1866), 1: 361.
11. Although Shakespeare's cross-dressed women (Rosalind, Imogen, Viola, Portia, and Julia) are frequently referred to as breeches roles by theatre historians, I believe it is more appropriate to label such

parts disguise roles. Charlene Edwards makes this distinction in her dissertation, "The Tradition for Breeches in the Three Centuries that Professional Actresses Have Played Male Roles on the English-Speaking Stage," diss., University of Denver, 1957.

12. Marjorie Garber, *Vested Interests: Cross-Dressing and Cultural Anxiety* (New York: Routledge, 1992), 184.

13. The concept of True Womanhood is one that will be discussed at length throughout the course of this study and implies a very specific type of woman. In her influential article "The Cult of True Womanhood," Barbara Welter explains that the term True Woman was repeatedly employed throughout the nineteenth century by authors who wrote about middle-class white women (women of color were never eligible for True Womanhood) and was a phrase that was used "as frequently as writers on religion mentioned God" (151).Welter points out that despite its constant invocation, this phrase was never defined and that the reader's understanding of it was simply assumed. Welter attempts to determine what the Victorians meant by True Womanhood and concludes that women were judged both publicly and privately according to their ability to embrace "four cardinal virtues—piety, purity, submissiveness and domesticity." Failure to abide by these virtues engendered both societal aspersion and personal disdain. See Welter, "The Cult of True Womanhood: 1820–1860," *American Quarterly* 18 (Summer 1966): 151–174.

14. For information on bifacial constructions of women (both within the theatre and society) see Lesley Ferris, *Acting Women: Images of Women in Theatre* (New York: New York University Press, 1989), x-xiv and Mary Poovey, *Uneven Developments: The Ideological Work of Gender in Mid-Victorian England* (Chicago: University of Chicago Press, 1988), 11.

15. The American theatre historian George Odell may also be included in this group, yet I have omitted him because he does not discuss breeches in any detail but merely reports on specific performances in which women assumed male roles. The image he constructs of the breeches performer does not necessarily reproduce dominant gender ideology by reinforcing her femininity or her sexual appeal; rather it is simply misogynistic. The actress in male disguise is repeatedly referred to as a "freak" or a "curiosity" and all of her attempts at male impersonation are perceived as a joke. Significantly, Odell published his history of the New York stage between 1928–1937, which was after the medical community had pathologized lesbianism and had

come out with many reports that argued that transvestism was symptomatic of lesbianism. See Odell's *Annals of the New York Stage*, vols. 1–19 (New York: Columbia University Press, 1928–1937). For more information about the relationship between breeches performance and lesbianism see my article entitled "A Doublet and Hose in My Disposition: Sexology and the Cross-Dressed Theatrics of the Professional Women's League," *Theatre History Studies* XV (1995):1–18. Sections of this article appear in the Conclusion.

16. See David Chesire, "Male Impersonators," *Saturday Book* 29 (1969): 245–256, and Lisa Merrill, *When Romeo Was a Woman: Charlotte Cushman and her Circle of Female Spectators* (Ann Arbor: University of Michigan Press, 1999), 111.

17. Dunlap and Ireland both reinforce the image of the breeches performer as undeniably feminine while Gilder gives special emphasis to the "easy display of the perfect leg." For examples see Dunlap, *History of the American Theatre*, 240; Ireland, *Records of the New York Stage*, 1:606, and Gilder, *Enter the Actress: The First Woman in the Theatre* (Boston: Houghton Mifflin, 1931), 270.

18. Hewitt, *Theatre U.S.A.*, 133.

19. Edwards, "The Tradition for Breeches," 9. Although Edwards's work serves to reinforce traditional views of the breeches performer as a sexual object, her dissertation provides an extremely thorough record of the convention from the seventeenth-century onward and presents future historians with an invaluable resource. In addition, her first appendix lists a majority of the breeches performers in the eighteenth and nineteenth centuries in both England and America, and includes the role they played and the date on which the role was performed.

20. Chesire, "Male Impersonation," 249.

21. Edwards, "The Tradition for Breeches," 5–6.

22. Jane Stedman and Peter Ackroyd also reify this connection between the actress and the boy/child. See Stedman, "From Dame to Woman: W. S. Gilbert and Theatrical Transvestism," *Suffer and Be Still: Women in the Victorian Age*, ed. Martha Vicinus (Bloomington: Indiana University Press, 1972), 21. Ackroyd draws the stronger comparison stating, "the male impersonator is never anything more than what she pretends to be: a feminine, noble mind in a boy's body. It is a peculiarly sentimental and therefore harmless reversal." Ackroyd implies that the cross-dressed actress's reversal is "harmless and sentimental" because it is, in fact, not a reversal: the

woman in male attire is "never more than what she pretends to be," a feminine boyish figure. He, like Edwards and Stedman, infantilizes the actress and implies that as a woman she could never be a man, only a boy, an imitation or a smaller non-threatening substitute for manhood. See Ackroyd, *Dressing Up: Transvestism and Drag: the History of an Obsession* (New York: Simon and Schuster, 1979), 102.

23. See Lesley Ferris, *Crossing the Stage: Controversies on Cross-Dressing* (New York: Routledge, 1993) and Laurence Senelick, *Gender in Performance: The Presentation of Difference in the Performing Arts* (Hanover, NH: University Press of New England, 1992). The essays in Ferris's book which specifically discuss cross-dressed female performance include: Jean Howard's "Cross-Dressing, the Theatre, and Gender Struggle in Early Modern England," Laurence Senelick's "Boys and Girls Together: Subcultural Origins of Glamour Drag and Male Impersonation on the Nineteenth-Century Stage," Lynn Garafola's "The Travesty Dancer in Nineteenth-Century Ballet," Drorbaugh's previously mentioned article on Stormé Delarverié, and Alisa Solomon's "It's Never too Late to Switch: Crossing Towards Power." In addition to these essays, J. S. Bratton's historiographical article "Irrational Dress" gives a summary of the recent theories and trends in women's theatrical cross-dressing. She discusses new scholarly interpretations of Vestris's career and remarks upon the strides being made by new studies on male impersonation. In addition, she briefly outlines the history of breeches performance, arguing that it was always a sexual institution and that this stereotypical assessment of the actress mitigated any subversive messages generated by her impersonation and therefore contained the threat of female usurpation. See Bratton, "Irrational Dress," in *The New Woman and her Sisters: Feminism and Theatre 1850–1914*, edited by Vivian Gardner and Susan Rutherford (Ann Arbor: University of Michigan Press, 1992): 77–82. See also Yvonne Shafer, "Women in Male Roles: Charlotte Cushman and Others," in *Women in the American Theatre*, ed. Helen Kirch Chinoy and Linda Walsh Jenkins (New York: Crown Publishers, 1981), 75.

24. See Anne Russell, "Gender, Passion, and Performance in Nineteenth-Century Women Romeos," *Essays in Theatre* 11.2 (May 1993):163. Faye Dudden's brief discussion of breeches performance occurs in her chapter on Cushman. See Dudden, *Women in the American Theatre: Actresses and Audiences* (New Haven: Yale University Press,

1994), 92–103. See also Kathy Fletcher, "Planche, Vestris, and the Transvestite Role: Sexuality and Gender in Victorian Popular Theatre," *Nineteenth Century Theatre* 15.1 (Summer 1987): 17. Fletcher argues very successfully that Vestris' theatrical transvestism mirrored her ability to enjoy masculine privileges off stage; the role of principal boy served as a symbol of gender transcendence and male power, and yet she simultaneously capitalized upon the sexual image which had been created for her to contain the threat of her onstage and offstage subversion.

25. See Beth H. Friedman-Romell, "Breaking the Code: Toward a Reception Theory of Theatrical Cross-Dressing in Eighteenth-Century London," *Theatre Journal* 47(1995): 459–479; Kristina Straub, *Sexual Suspects: Eighteenth-Century Players and Sexual Ideology* (Princeton: Princeton University Press, 1992), 127–150 and Robert A. Schanke and Kim Marra, eds. *Passing Performances: Queer Readings of Leading Players in American Theatre History* (Ann Arbor: University of Michigan Press, 1998). See also James Cain's queer treatment of medieval performance in "Putting on the Girls: Cross-Dressing as a Performative Strategy in the Twelfth-Century Latin Comedy Alda," *Theatre Survey* 38.1 (May 1997): 43–72.

    In addition to sources that discuss theatrical cross-dressing there have also been a number of books and articles written about non-theatrical crossdressing such as David Cressy's "Gender Trouble and Cross-Dressing in Early Modern England," *Journal of British Studies* 35 (October 1996): 438–465; Tania Modleski, "A Woman's Gotta Do . . . What a Man's Gotta Do? Cross-Dressing in the Western," *Signs: Journal of Women in Culture and Society* 22.3 (1997): 519–544, and Richard Ekins and Dave King, eds. *Blending Genders: Social Aspects of Cross-Dressing and Sex-Changing* (New York: Routledge, 1996).

26. Merrill discusses Cushman's ability to blur gender lines, perform gender (see also Faye Dudden who discusses this as well in her 1994 study) and communicate lesbian desire. In my fourth chapter (first published as an essay in Theatre Survey in 1996), I also discuss Cushman's active disruption of gender binaries, but focus less upon Cushman's sexuality and more upon perceptions of her as an androgynous or hermaphrodidical character. I theorize the construct of androgyne to analyze Romeo, her most popular breeches role.

27. See Renee M. Sentilles, "Performing Menken: Adah Isaacs Menken's American Odyssey," Ph.D. diss., College of William and Mary, 1997

and Marilyn Moses, "Lydia Thompson and the British Blondes in the United States," P.h.D. diss, University of Oregon, 1978, for the best studies of Menken and Thompson's careers. For the most recent and thorough treatment of burlesque see Robert Allen, *Horrible Prettiness: Burlesque and American Culture* (Chapel Hill: University of North Carolina Press, 1991); see Annemarie Bean, James V. Hatch and Brooks McNamara, eds. *Inside the Minstrel Mask: Readings in Nineteenth-Century Blackface Minstrelsy* (Hanover and London: Wesleyan University Press, 1996).

28. See Welter, "The Cult of True Womanhood," 151–174.
29. Joan Scott, *Gender and the Politics of History* (New York: Columbia University Press, 1988), 27. Carroll Smith Rosenberg's book *Disorderly Conduct: Visions of Gender in Victorian America* (New York: Oxford University Press, 1985) has also significantly influenced my thinking about the construction of femininity and masculinity in American society and culture.
30. Judith Butler, "Performative Acts and Gender Constitution: An Essay in Phenomenology and Feminist Theory," in *Performing Feminisms: Feminist Critical Theory and Theatre* ed. Sue-Ellen Case (Baltimore: John Hopkins University Press, 1990), 272–273. See also Butler, *Gender Trouble: Feminism and the Subversion of Identity* (New York: Routledge, 1990).
31. I have been most specifically influenced by the following two articles: Sandra Gilbert, "Costumes of the Mind: Transvestism as Metaphor in Modern Literature," *Critical Inquiry* (Winter 1980): 391–417 and Susan Gubar, "Blessings in Disguise: Cross-Dressing as Re-Dressing for Female Modernists," *Massachusetts Review* 22 (Autumn 1981): 479.
32. For information on the African Theatre see George A. Thompson Jr.'s *A Documentary History of the African Theatre* (Evanston: Northwestern University Press, 1998), 131, 140 and 228–229.

CHAPTER 1

1. William Wizard, "Theatrics," *Salmagundi* 1.6 (1807): 123. Emphasis in original.
2. "'The Soldier's Daughter,' and 'The Spoiled Child,'" *Theatrical Censor* 1.2 (December 1805): 12.

3. A good example of this association between dress and privilege lies in the constant references during the nineteenth century to "petticoat government," a term employed to denote women who tried to assume public responsibilities such as managing a business or theatre.
4. "Letters to Anthony Evergreen," *Salmagundi* 2.4 (Sept. 1807): 394–395.
5. With the exception of an occasional "Lady Correspondent" or blue-stocking columnist such as Pffafian Ada Clare (who wrote in the late 1850s/early 1860s), critics during the first half of the nineteenth century were male. Most male critics, however, were never identified with the exception of those recognized by the infrequent pseudonym or initial. Generally speaking, dramatic critics during the first half of the nineteenth century were literary men of letters, and/or journalists whose reporting duties included dramatic criticism among various other topics. In his dissertation, Vincent Angotti argues that William Coleman, editor of the *Evening Post* until 1829, "is one of the few known dramatic critics whose work can be definitively identified" [7]. Some of the most influential drama critics from the early part of the century include Washington Irving, Stephen Cullen Carpenter, and William Leggett. See Angotti, "American Dramatic Criticism, 1800–1830," diss., University of Kansas, 1967, 7.
6. "Newspaper Criticism," *Arcturus* 1.3 (Feb. 1841): 149.
7. See *New York Mirror* 3.18 (Dec. 26, 1825): 162; David Grimstead, *Melodrama Unveiled: American Theatre and Culture, 1800–1850* (Chicago: University of Chicago Press, 1968), 43–44 and *New York Mirror* 6.34 (Feb. 2, 1829): 271.
8. Oscar G. Brockett, *History of the Theatre,* 8th ed. (Boston: Allyn and Bacon, 1999), 126.
9. *Polyanthos* 1 (December 1805): 60.
10. Angotti, "American Dramatic Criticism,"127.
11. Grimstead, *Melodrama Unveiled,* 42.
12. Angotti, "American Dramatic Criticism," 24. Critics often complained about the tedium of having to repeatedly write about the same performers in the same roles. One critic for the *Albion* remarked, "It is not easy to write honestly without trenching upon the pride or interests of some candidate for the public favour, and if managers will not assiduously present to the public a succession of new pieces, it is not easy to write at all. We are tired—absolutely tired—with drawling about the character and merits of plays that

have been a century or less on the town." See *Albion* 5.45 (April 7, 1827): 344.
13. Tice Miller, *Bohemians and Critics: American Theatre Criticism in the Nineteenth Century* (Metuchen, N. J.: Scarecrow Press, Inc., 1981), 14.
14. Ibid., 15.
15. Ibid., 2.
16. "The Theatre," *Ladies's Port Folio* 1.5 (January 29, 1820): 35.
17. Rosemarie K. Bank, *Theatre Culture in America, 1825–1860* (New York: Cambridge University Press, 1997), 117.
18. Walt Whitman, "The Old Bowery," in *Complete Prose Works* (New York, 1914), 429.
19. Barnaby Bangbar, "New Theatre," *The Thespian Monitor* 1.1 (Nov. 25, 1809): 3.
20. Allen, *Horrible Prettiness*, 51. Newspaper reviews from the 1850s and 1860s suggest that men still comprised the majority of the audience.
21. Bank, *Theatre Culture in America*, 132–133.
22. Grimstead, *Melodrama Unveiled*, 62.
23. Allen, *Horrible Prettiness*, 58.
24. See Simon Williams, "The Actors: European Actors and the Star System in the American Theatre, 1752–1870," in *The Cambridge History of American Theatre, Volume One: Beginnings to 1870* Don B. Wilmeth and Christopher Bigsby eds. (New York: Cambridge University Press, 1998), 326.
25. Lawrence Levine, *Highbrow/Lowbrow: The Emergence of Cultural Hierarchy in America* (Cambridge: Harvard University Press, 1988), 68.
26. John H. Wilson, *All the King's Ladies: Actresses of the Restoration* (Chicago: University of Chicago Press, 1958), 20–21.
27. David Chesire argues that early English actresses played breeches roles in order to deliberately showcase their supple bodies. He asks, "What more obvious way for a suitably endowed actress to show that she had legs than to appear as a man?" See Chesire, "Male Impersonators," *Saturday Book* 29 (1969): 248.
28. Elizabeth Howe, *The First English Actresses: Women and Drama, 1660–1700* (Cambridge: Cambridge University Press, 1992), 56.
29. Straub, "Guilty Pleasures," 144.
30. Edwards, "The Tradition for Breeches," 63.
31. I have found no information to suggest that any breeches performers were associated with other early American players such as Anthony Aston, the Staggs, or the Murray/Kean company.

32. Philip Highfill Jr., "The British Background of the American Hallams," *Theatre Survey* 1.1 (1970): 24.
33. These roles include: Wildair, Captain Plume, Osric in *Hamlet* (Hamlet was not played by a woman until Sarah Siddons performed the role in 1775), Lothario in *The Fair Penitent*, Prince Edward and the Duke of York in *Richard the Third*, Captain Flash and Fribble in Garrick's *Miss in Her Teens*, and Damon in *Damon and Philida*.
34. Edwards records that Mrs. Lewis Hallam did play Hippolito in Davenant's *The Tempest* at the New Wells Theatre in London in 1745.
35. In her chapter in *The Cambridge History of American Theatre*, Mary Henderson notes that recent unpublished research by Peter Davis suggests that the Hallams arrived on a brig called The Sally and not on the smaller intercoastal sloop The Charming Sally. See Henderson, "Sceneography, Stagecraft, and Architecture in the American Theatre: Beginnings to 1870," in Wilmeth and Bigsby, pg. 422.
36. It is interesting to note that Isabella Hallam, who latter became famous as Mrs. Mattocks at Covent Garden, also played breeches roles on occasion in London. See Highfill, 26–27.
37. Highfill, "British Background," 26.
38. Robert Seilhamer, *The History of the American Theatre Before the Revolution* 3 vols. (New York: Benjamin Blom, 1968), 1: 117–119.
39. Miss Harding is, however, the first breeches performer for whom there exists any sort of critical examination.
40. Seilhamer, *History of the American Theatre*, 1: 136.
41. Ibid., 191.
42. One reason for the lack of text next to a male actor's name may have to do with the fact that actors rarely played melodramatic boys roles after 1800. My research indicates that none of the handicapped boy characters described above were played by young men or boys.
43. "Theatre Critique No. 5," *New York Evening Post* 14 Dec. 1801. Although the *Post* spells the actress's name Hodgekinson, this performer was probably France Brett Hodgkinson, the wife of actor John Hodgkinson. Dunlap reports that both were playing at the Park during this season and although he does not mention Mrs. Hodgkinson playing Theodore (rather he describes a Mrs. Powell in the role), it is likely that she was the performer discussed in the *Post* review. See Dunlap, *History of the American Theatre*, 146.
44. "A Biography of Mrs. Jones," *The Thespian Monitor* 1.1 (November 1809): 11.

45. Christine Stansell, *City of Women: Sex and Class in New York, 1789–1806* (New York: Alfred A. Knopf, 1986), 12.
46. Odell, *Annals of the New York Stage*, 1: 385.
47. *Thespian Mirror* 1.1 (December 28, 1805): 7.
48. *Thespian Mirror* 1.2 (Jan.4, 1806): 23.
49. Odell, *Annals of the New York Stage*, 1: 385.
50. William Wood, *Personal Recollections of the Stage* (Philadelphia: Henry Carey Baird Pub., 1855), 306.
51. "Thespian Register," *American Monthly Magazine and Critical Review* 1.1 (May 1817): 53.
52. "Thespian Register," *American Monthly Magazine and Critical Review* 1.2 (June 1817): 134, 136. Emphasis in the original.
53. "Thespian Register," *American Monthly Magazine and Critical Review* 1.4 (August 1817): 399. Critics disliked Barnes' Norval, which she presented for the first time on her benefit night in 1816. Although critics were displeased by this representation, it seems that audiences were much more forgiving, for Barnes' repeated her performance of Norval on three other occasions.
54. Odell, *Annals of the New York Stage*, 2: 456.
55. *The Mirror of Taste and Dramatic Censor* 3.1 (Jan. 1811): 62.
56. "Mr. Cain," *Theatrical Censor* 1.15 (March 1806): 134.
57. "The Drama," *The Spirit of the Times* 2.36 (June 6, 1833): 3. The critic for this journal describes the license allowed during the benefit. He writes, "It was an old adage in the theatrical world that an actor was allowed to make a fool of himself once in a season—for his own benefit—but in modern days, he is not satisfied with wearing the Cap and Bells himself, but insists on each of his friends bearing one of the tassels; for the real or imagined necessity for such variety of performances, causes every actor to moult his feathers so frequently that character is altogether lost sight of in the labour of dressing, and Othello and Iago become indistinguishable by any other attribute than complextion."
58. "The Drama," *The Albion* 5.36 (Feb. 17, 1827): 288. The *Albion* is a valuable source because the critic in this paper (during the first half of the century) often covers the entertainment at a variety of theatres including the Park, Bowery, La Fayette and the Chatham theatres. Many papers such as the New York *Mirror* and the *Spirit of the Times* only reported upon activity at the Park and reluctantly mentioned what was happening at the Bowery.
59. "The Drama," *The Albion* 5.39 (March 10, 1827): 312.

60. "Woman's Sphere," *The Lily* 2.4 (April 1850): 26.
61. "The Drama," *The New York Mirror and Ladies' Literary Gazette* 1.48 (June 26, 1824): 382.
62. *Spirit of the Times* 7.13 (May 13, 1837): 97.
63. Odell, *Annals of the New York Stage,* 3:300.
64. "The Drama," *The Albion* 6.12 (Sept. 1, 1827): 94.
65. "The Drama," *The Albion* 6.14 (Sept. 15, 1827): 112.
66. Ibid. In the December issue (6.28) of the *Albion,* Fisher is unreservedly praised as Norval and Shylock. While it is possible that the critic who earlier condemned her forays into such masculine territory, may have completely revised his opinion of this practice it is unlikely that he would have done so in three months. This notice, therefore, is most likely a puff since it is extreme in its enthusiasm even for Fisher and markedly different from the other entries written about her up until this date.
67. See William T. Price, *A Life of Charlotte Cushman* (New York: Brentano's, 1894), 124.
68. "National Theatre," *New York Mirror* 15.33 (Feb. 10, 1838): 262.
69. "Theatrical in Boston," *Spirit of the Times* 6.14 (May 21, 1836):106. While Lewis was popular in her own day, I have been unable to find more than a brief listing for her in any of the histories of the American stage. Additionally, it is impossible even to learn her first name, as she was referred to as Mrs. Henry Lewis in reviews and also in her obituaries. In his history of the New York stage, Brown gives a short bio of her. See T. A. Brown, *History of the New York Stage, 1836–1918* (New York: Dood Mead and Co., 1923).
70. "A Boston Boy in Gotham," *Spirit of the Times* 7.1 (Feb. 18, 1837): 1.
71. Alexander Saxton, "Blackface Minstrelsy and Jacksonian Ideology," *American Quarterly* 27:1 (1975): 27.
72. "Introduction," *Meanings for Manhood: Constructions of Masculinity in Victorian America,* ed. Mark C. Carnes and Clyde Griffen (Chicago: University of Chicago Press), 2. See also David G. Pugh, *Sons of Liberty: The Masculine Mind in Nineteenth-Century America* (Westport, Conn: Greenwood Press, 1983).
73. For ways in which Forrest's career was influenced by Jacksonian ideology see Mark E. Mallett, "'The Game of Politics': Edwin Forrest and the Jackson Democrats," *Journal of American Theatre and Drama* 5.2 (Spring 1993): 31–47.

74. While is it true that Norval was considered a youth and Hamlet a man, Norval was thought to be a manly youth by nineteenth century standards and a dangerous undertaking for breeches performers.
75. "Things Theatrical," *Spirit of the Times* 8.2 (Feb. 24, 38): 9.
76. "Things Theatrical, " *Spirit of the Times* 8.15 (May 26, 1838): 113.
77. See Sara M. Evans, *Born For Liberty: A History of Women in America* (New York: The Free Press, 1989); Mary P. Ryan, *Womanhood in America: From Colonial Times to the Present*, Third ed., (New York: Franklin Watts, 1983); and Carroll Smith-Rosenberg, *Disorderly Conduct: Visions of Gender in Victorian America* (New York: Oxford University Press, 1985).
78. Evans, *Born for Liberty*, 75.
79. Ryan, *Women in Public: Between Banners and Ballots, 1825–1880* (Baltimore: Johns Hopkins University Press, 1990), 134.
80. *New York Herald* 12 Sept. 1852. This quote also appears in Evans, *Born For Liberty*, 102.
81. *Spirit of the Times* 10.21 (July 25, 1840): 252.
82. See *New York Mirror*, May 6, 1837.
83. "Things Theatrical," *Spirit of the Times* 11.39 (November 27, 1841): 468.
84. George Vandenhoff, *Leaves from an Actor's Notebook: Anecdotes of the Green Room and the Stage* (London: T. W. Cooper and Co., 1860), 203.
85. "Things Theatrical," *Spirit of the Times* 15.49 (Jan. 31, 1846): 584.
86. "Things Theatrical," *Spirit of the Times* 19.45 (Dec. 29, 1849): 540.
87. "Things Theatrical," *Spirit of the Times* 21.36 (Oct. 25, 1851): 432.
88. "Drama," *The Albion* 10.48 (Nov. 29, 1851): 572.
89. "Things Theatrical," *Spirit of the Times* 27.40 (Nov. 14, 1857): 480. Merrill gives evidence of some critical response to Cushman's Wolsey. Unfortunately the three reviews that Merrill draws from are all unidentified clippings; thus it is difficult to profile New York critical sentiment regarding this portrayal. See Merrill, *When Romeo Was a Woman*, 134, 289.
90. "Things Theatrical," *Spirit of the Times* 28.49 (Jan. 15, 1859): 588.
91. "Things Theatrical," *Spirit of the Times* 15.3 (March 8, 1845): 20.
92. "Things Theatrical," *Spirit of the Times* 25.18 (June 16, 1855): 216.
93. "Things Theatrical," *Spirit of the Times* 21.13 (May 17, 1851): 156.
94. "Things Theatrical," *Spirit of the Times* 17.48 (Jan. 22, 1848): 572.
95. "Things Theatrical," *Spirit of the Times* 19.46 (Jan 5, 1850): 548.
96. Evans, *Born for Liberty*, 95.

97. "Woman, Considered a Domestic Animal, " *Spirit of the Times* 21.23 (July 26, 1851): 266.
98. This discourse is discussed by Allen in *Horrible Prettiness*, 16.
99. Olive Logan, *Apropos of Women and Theatre* (New York: Carleton Pub., 1869), 114.

CHAPTER 2

1. "Green Room Intelligence," *Spirit of the Times* 14.45 (January 1845): 540. This review came to the *Spirit* in a rather roundabout way: the *New Mirror* supposedly carried a story on the incident that was then picked up by the New Orleans *Picayune*. In this issue, the *Spirit* carries the story as found in the *Picayne*. Surprisingly, I found no mention of this incident in the *New Mirror* in any issue as far back as six months prior to this notice in the *Spirit*.
2. Ibid.
3. Ibid.
4. Ibid.
5. "Rights of Women," *The Christian Inquirer* 1.12 (Jan 2, 1847): 46.
6. Barbara Welter, "The Cult of True Womanhood: 1820–1860," *American Quarterly* (1966): 151–174.
7. "Rights of Women," *The Christian Inquirer* 1.12 (Jan 2, 1847): 46.
8. Ryan, *Women in Public*, 67.
9. Margaret Fuller, *Woman in the Nineteenth Century* (Reprint, New York: W.W. Norton and Co., 1971), 174.
10. *Broadway Journal* 1.9 (March 1, 1845): 130.
11. *Broadway Journal* 1.10 (March 8, 1845): 145.
12. Indeed, individuals who were referred to as "public women," or prostitutes, were regarded as unfeminine and inhuman: "Once deprived of the maternal crown of her femininity, the dangerous female lost her humanity as well; her most frequent label became 'the savage female.' ... She infested, polluted, defiled, repelled, and sickened." Ibid., 72.
13. Anna Cora Mowatt, *Autobiography of an Actress* (Boston: Ticknor, Reed and Fields, 1854), 139, 142. Emphasis is mine.
14. Ibid., 154.
15. *Arctus* 3.14 (January 1842): 152.
16. Tracy C. Davis, "Private Women and the Public Realm," *Theatre Survey* 35.1 (May 1994): 68.

17. In a lecture delivered to the Dunlap Society in 1889, the American tragedian Lawrence Barrett praised Cushman's "earnestness of nature," her ennobling "womanhood," and her purity. Similarly, the early women's rights sympathizer Mary Howitt, recognized in Cushman "an approach to our ideal of the greatly pure in art" and regarded her as "one of its noblest representatives," and the *Arctus* declared that by undertaking the management of a new theatre building in New York, Cushman might bring about "the purification of the Theatre." Even her African-American "maid," Sallie Mercer, remembered her as one worthy of intense reverence. Shortly after Cushman's death, Mercer wrote a letter to Dennis Alward, a grieving friend of the actress. Echoing his expressions of pain, she writes, "I understand what you miss in the loss of dear Miss Cushman, only those who have lived under the shelter of her angel's wings can know; and while she was here all was so different and while there was her smile to reward every little effort far beyond its worth." See Barrett, "Charlotte Cushman: A Lecture," (New York: The Dunlap Society, 1889), 15; Mary Howitt, "The Miss Cushmans," *The People's Journal* 1 (1847):30; "Miss Cushman's Theatre," *Arctus* 3.17 (April 1842): 388; Letter from Sallie Mercer to Dennis Alward, 26 December., 1884. Charlotte Cushman Box, Harvard Theatre Collection.
18. Davis, "Private Women," 68.
19. Helene Roberts, "The Exquisite Slave: The Role of Clothes in the Making of the Victorian Woman," *Signs* 2.3 (1977): 554–569; Lawrence Langner, *The Importance of Wearing Clothes* (New York: Hastings House, 1959), 51.
20. William Butler Yeats, "Adam's Curse," *W. B. Yeats: The Poems*, ed. Richard J. Finneran (New York: Macmillan, 1983), 80.
21. Roberts, "The Exquisite Slave," 556.
22. Sir James Mackintosh, *Woman As She Is and As She Should Be*, 2 vols. (London: James Cochrane and Co., 1835), 187.
23. *New Mirror* 2.10 (December 1843): 159. Apparently this fellow was not a frequent guest at the theatre!
24. An interesting example of how this principle played itself out in popular culture occurred immediately after the Civil War. A report about Barnum's American Museum in New York City noted a new addition to his collection of wax effigies. The notice read, "Among the latest additions to Barnum's 'wax figgers' is one of Jefferson Davis and them female clothes. The petticoats will stick to Jeff as

long as there is anything left of him to cling to." This excerpt was written on May 27, 1865, approximately two weeks after Davis was taken prisoner by the Union cavalry at Irwinsville, Georgia. With the war won, and the confederate president now under Union supervision, Barnum may have felt that the only way to communicate Davis' extreme loss was to represent him as a woman. Audiences who paid a dime to see Davis at Barnum's, would have read his costume as symbolic of utter devastation: the loss of the war and the confederacy metaphorically stripped him of his masculinity, his position was completely reversed or inverted. See the *New York Clipper* 13.7 (May 27, 1865): 54.
25. See Ann Russo and Cheris Kramarae, eds. *The Radical Women's Press of the 1850s* (New York: Routledge, 1991).
26. "Female Attire," *The Lily* 3.2 (February 1851): 13.
27. Susan J. Kleinberg, introduction to *The Life and Writings of Amelia Bloomer*, ed. D.C. Bloomer (1895; reprint, New York: Schocken Books, 1975), xii.
28. *The Lily* 3.1 (June 1851): 4.
29. Amelia Bloomer, "Mrs. Kemble and Her New Costume," *The Lily* 1.12 (Dec. 1849): 94.
30. William Nevin, "The Bloomer Dress," *The Ladies Wreath* 6 (1852): 252–253.
31. Bloomer, "Who are the Leaders?" *The Lily* 3.6 (June 1851): 45.
32. Odell, *Annals of the New York Stage,* 6: 178. For more information on the Bloomer Troupe see also pages 191, 194, 197, and 199.
33. See Jack W. McCullough, *Living Pictures on the New York Stage* (Ann Arbor: UMI Research Press, 1983).
34. Julie Wheelwright, *Amazons and Military Maids: Women Who Dressed As Men in the Pursuit of Life, Liberty and Happiness* (New York: Pandora, 1989), 51.
35. Loreta J. Velazquez, *The Woman in Battle: A Narrative of the Exploits, Adventures, and Travels of Madame Loreta Janeta Velazquez*, ed. C. J. Worthington (New York: Arno press, 1972), 130.
36. See Gubar, "Blessings in Disguise," 477–508.
37. Velazquez, *Woman in Battle,* 38, 55–56.
38. Vern and Bonnie Bullough, *Cross Dressing, Sex, and Gender* (Philadelphia: University of Pennsylvania Press, 1993), 134–135.
39. "Deborah Gannett," *Sharon Historical Society of Sharon, Massachusetts* No. 2, April, C. H. Hight, Boston, 1905, 192. As quoted in Wheelwright, 132.

40. Deborah Gannett, *An Address Delivered With Applause, At the Federal Street Theatre, Boston, 4 Successive Nights of the Different Plays, beginning March 22, 1802* (Dedham, Mass.: H. Mann,1802), 6.
41. Costumes did begin to change (at the request of the managers) during the 1860s due to the influence of burlesque and other types of popular entertainment. With the introduction of fleshlings in the early 1860s, costumes for burlesque and equestrian drama (pantomime was never popular in America) became much more revealing. However, costumes for legitimate performances seem to have stayed the same or to have changed in ways similar to the changes in male theatrical fashions. For visual evidence of the similarity between breeches costumes and male costumes see Odell, *Annals of the New York Stage,* Vol. 2, 454.
42. See Joseph Leach, *Bright Particular Star: The Life and Times of Charlotte Cushman* (New York: Yale University Press, 1970), 306; Merrill, *When Romeo was a Woman,* 131–132 and Shafer, "Women in Male Roles: Charlotte Cushman and Others," 78.
43. Vandenhoff, *Leaves from an Actor's Notebook,* 202.
44. A photograph of Cushman as Romeo is located at the Harvard Theatre Collection. The actress's matronly figure suggests that this picture was taken later in her career. For an illustration of Wheatley in his Romeo costume see Odell, *Annals of the New York Stage,* Vol. 4, 466.
45. For an illustration of Tree as Ion see Odell, *Annals of the New York Stage,* Vol. 4, 130.
46. See "Theatricals in Boston," *Spirit of the Times* 6.14 (May 21, 1836): 106. Visual evidence of her Tell can be found in Odell, *Annals of the New York Stage,* Vol. 4, 68.
47. Davis, *Actresses as Working Women,* 112.
48. Turner Wilcox, *Five Centuries of American Costume,* (New York: Scribner's, 1963), 141. Emphasis is mine. For an illustration of the male silhouette for 1831, see Wilcox, pg. 150.
49. See Odell, *Annals of the New York Stage,* Vol. 2, 310 and 502 for illustrations of Goldfinch and Belino in breeches and Vol. 6, 302 and 470 for photographs of Agnes Robertson as Bob Nettles (in trousers) and Fanny Herring in William's sailor suit.
50. *New York Mirror* 12.21 (November 22, 1843): 167.
51. Henry Milner, *Mazeppa or the Wild Horse of Tartary* (London: Thomas Hailes Lacy, 1870), 8. This play was adapted from Byron's poem and was written in 1830. It was first presented in 1831 with a

male actor and women did not begin playing Mazeppa with any sort of regularity until the 1850s. Because the performances of *Mazeppa* that I discuss took place in the 1860s, I have referred to the 1870 edition of the adaptation since it is most contemporary to my discussion. The original promptbook for the play can be found in the Readex Series of English and American plays. The title page reads, "As performed at the Royal Amphitheatre, Westminster Bridge under the Mangement of Messrs Ducrow and West, on Easter Monday, 1831." The costume description for the 1831 text matches the description printed in 1870 suggesting that the costume had not been changed as women began to assume the role.

52. *New York Clipper,* 14.5 (May 12, 1886): 38.
53. See Davis, *Actresses as Working Women,* 113.
54. *New York Mirror* 3.27 (January 27, 1827): 215.
55. *The Albion* 6.28 (December 22, 1827): 224. Emphasis is mine.
56. *The Albion* 6.29 (Dec., 29, 1827): 232. The *Abion* reports that Sharpe played feminine roles in New York from January through June. See volume 6 issues 31, 34, 35, 38, 42, 44 and volume 7.1 for 1828.
57. *Spirit of the Times* 1.26 (June 9, 1832): 3. It is important to remember that the critics who were reviewing actresses like Sharpe and Clifton saw themselves as the "guardians" of tradition; though the audiences seemed to have responded enthusiastically to the performances given by these women, the reviewers may have felt that it was their duty to police the boundaries of social decorum.
58. "The Editor's Easy Chair," *Harper's Magazine* 28 (December, 1863): 133.
59. "Theatricals in Boston," *Spirit of the Times* 6.14 (May 21, 1836): 106; *Spirit of the Times* 6.17 (May 11, 1836): 13.
60. *Spirit of the Times* 7.13 (May, 13, 1837): 97. While it appears that Lewis (like Cushman) was simply unique in her ability to convincingly impersonate masculinity, it is important to note that she was being reviewed during a decade when critics seemed to be more magnanimous. Critical commentaries briefly took on a much less condemnatory tone during the 1830s for reasons outlined in the previous chapter.
61. *Spirit of the Times* 8.20 (June 30, 1838): 153.
62. *Spirit of the Times* 15.47 (January 17, 1846): 560.
63. See Leach, *Bright Particular Star* (New Haven: Yale University Press, 1970) 306, 307 and Lisa Merrill, "Charlotte Cushman: American

Actress on the Vanguard of New Roles for Women," Ph.D. diss., New York University, 1985, pg. 79. In *When Romeo Was a Woman,* Merrill does discuss Cushman's success as Hamlet in Philadelphia and Washington but does not interrogate Cushman's performance of the Dane at length.

64. Tumbleson, "Three Female Hamlets," 120.
65. *New York Clipper* (Sept. 7, 1876): 38. The Congressmen's approval of Cushman's Hamlet in 1861 seems a bit problematic in that hegemonic opinion usually condemned such serious forays into masculinity. However, the Congressmen's desire to see the performance may have marked the difference between public opinion (since audiences generally responded favorably to the breeches performer) and the sentiment of the critic, who established himself as a moral watchdog. Additionally, Cushman had a Washington connection in William Seward, who was Lincoln's Secretary of State in 1861 and a good friend of the actress's. His influence might explain the Congressmen's desire to see Cushman perform Hamlet—especially if Seward knew how important this role was to her.
66. Charlotte Cushman, *Charlotte Cushman: Her Letters and Memories of Her Life,* ed. Emma Stebbins (Boston: Houghton, Osgood, and Company, 1879): 217.
67. Letter from Charlotte Cushman to William Henry Chippendale, September 20, 1849. Manuscript collection, Harvard Theatre Collection.
68. Gamaliel Bradford, *Biography of the Human Heart* (Boston: Houghton Mifflin Co., 1932), 115.
69. *Spirit of the Times* 19.42 (Dec. 8, 1849): 493.
70. Eleanor Ruggles, *Prince of Players* (W. W. Norton, 1953), 133.
71. Letter from Charlotte Cushman to Emma Crow, January 29, 1861. Letters of James and Annie Fields, 1837–1874. Schlessinger Library Collection.
72. Stebbins, *Charlotte Cushman,* 217.
73. The *Albion* critic remarked that in Forrest's hands "the melancholy Dane" appeared as an "enraged Titan," which suggests a much more macho interpretation of the role. See *Albion* Sept. 2, 1848.
74. Tumbleson, "Three Female Hamlets," 180, 183.
75. *Albion* 10.48 (November 29, 1851): 572.
76. Ibid.
77. Toril Moi, *Sexual Textual Politics: Feminist Literary Theory* (New York: Routledge, 1985), 133–134.

78. Tumbleson, "Three Female Hamlets," 160.
79. Ibid.
80. By discussing Cushman's sword as "phallus," I do not mean to imply that *she* anachronistically thought about her weapon in terms that were later articulated by post-Lacanian feminist scholars. Rather, by overlaying a Lacanian analysis of her use of the sword in this scene, I am trying to suggest that her stage business proves that she regarded her weapon as a symbol of male power and that she used it in a way that clearly expressed a protofeminist intent. Because, according to Lacanian theorists like Irigaray, women's "lack" of a phallus defined her marginal position within society, the creation of a simulated phallus—or male symbol of power—like Cushman's sword, perhaps signifies an attempt to claim some kind of subjectivity within representation.
81. Scott, *Gender and the Politics of History*, 26.
82. For a detailed investigation of female theatrical managers in the nineteenth century see Jane Kathleen Curry, *Nineteenth-Century American Women Theatre Managers* (Westport, CT: Greenwood Press, 1994).
83. Letter from S. A. E. Walton to Cushman, New York, 2 Nov. 1874. As quoted by Dudden, 77.
84. Leach, *Bright Particular Star*, 253.
85. Ibid., 265. See also Merrill, *When Romeo Was A Woman*, 173.
86. Cushman to William H. Seward, 4 Dec. 1861. William Seward Papers, University of Rochester Library, New York.
87. Ibid.
88. See Sarah Foose Parrott, "Networking in Italy: Charlotte Cushman and 'The White Marmorean Flock,'" *Women's Studies* 14.4 (1988): 317.
89. Letter from Charlotte Cushman to Mr. Grigg, n.d. Charlotte Cushman Manuscript Collection. Harvard Theatre Collection. Although this letter is undated it must have been written before 1844. Because she is thinking of going to England, it was probably not written before 1840 or 1841.
90. See Chapter 2 in Merrill, *When Romeo Was A Woman*, 15–51.
91. See Merrill, "Charlotte Cushman," 160.
92. John Coleman, *Fifty Years of An Actor's Life* (New York: James Pott and Co., 1904), 2: 361–362.
93. *Spirit of the Times* 21.25 (August 1851): 324. Emphasis is in the original.

94. Leach supplies additional proof of Cushman's off stage cross-dressing in his account of the actress's first meeting with Herman Melville. He suggests that Cushman boldly embraced a masculine image, an expression that mystified Melville. "The fact presented a paradox, a dilemma few Victorians easily understood. Why would any woman willingly make herself outlandish in a man's collar, cravat, and Wellington boots? Charlotte never explained, but the case had to do with her Boston honesty. If life onstage was a constant pretense, life offstage would be otherwise." Leach's statement, while cryptic, suggests a possible feminist and lesbian politic, a donning of male clothing as a "costume of freedom," an outfit that Gubar discusses in relation to the female modernist half a century later. See Leach, *Bright Particular Star*, 179–180.
95. George O. Willard, *History of the Providence Stage 1762–1891* (Providence: The Rhode Island News Co., 1891), 153.
96. Thomas Allston Brown, *History of the New York Stage, 1836–1918*, (New York: Dodd Mead and Co., 1923), 332.
97. Ibid.
98. Price, *A Life of Charlotte Cushman*, 120.
99. Willard, *History of the Providence Stage*, 153.
100. Tumbleson, "Three Female Hamlets," 84.
101. Brown, *History of the New York Stage*, 1: 333. While Brown is the only historian who writes about the incident in Crampton's life, he, unfortunately, does not discuss the result of Crampton's efforts to persuade Lincoln to free her son. For more information on Crampton see also the Extra-Illustrated Volume of Joseph Ireland, *Records of the New York Stage*, vol. II. XI # 77, Harvard Theatre Collection.
102. Wolf Mankowitz, *Mazeppa: The Lives, Loves and Legends of Adah Isaacs Menken* (New York, Stein and Day, 1982), 11. Sentilles argues that Menken's relaxed attitudes towards marriage may have resulted from her familiarity with *placage*, a form of sanctioned concubinage practiced between white men and quadroon women in antebellum Louisiana. According to Sentilles, Menken performed her public identity throughout her life and part of this enactment included a playing with race; Menken performed herself intermittently as a free woman of color.
103. See Chapter Four in Sentilles, "Performing Menken," 190–252.
104. As quoted by Mankowitz, *Mazeppa*, 38.
105. As quoted by Mankowitz, *Mazeppa*, 39.
106. Sentilles, "Performing Menken," 88.

107. Mankowitz, *Mazeppa*, 24.
108. Quotation printed in "The Play of the Period: The Blondes and Their Abusers." Broadside, n.d. Performing Arts Collection, New York Public Library. See Allen, *Horrible Prettiness*, 19. For the most thorough treatment of Thompson's American tour see Moses' dissertation.
109. As quoted by Allen, 20. Allen retells this story based on the account in broadside written by Henderson or Gordon.
110. "Women's Sphere," *The Lily* 2.4 (April 1850): 27. Emphasis in the original.
111. *The Cynick* 1.2 (Sep. 28, 1811): 16.
112. *Spirit of the Times* 1.1 (Dec., 10, 1831): 3.
113. Constance Rourke, *American Humor: A Study of the National Character* (New York: Harcourt, Brace and Co., 1931), 112–113. Lawrence Levine relates this story as well.
114. Grimstead, *Melodrama Unveiled*, 60.
115. *Theatrical Censor* 1.9 (Feb. 22, 1806): 63. Emphasis in the original.
116. See Grimstead, *Melodrama Unveiled*, 180.
117. *Albion* 6.14 (Sept. 15, 1827): 112.
118. *Albion* 6.16 (Sept. 29, 1827): 128.
119. *Spirit of the Times* 19.42 (Dec. 8, 1849): 540.
120. *Spirit of the Times* 20.35 (Oct. 19, 1850): 420.
121. "Miss Cushman," *Tallis's Dramatic Magazine and General Theatrical and Musical Review* (Feb. 1851): 102. Found in the Harvard Theatre Collection's *Extra-Illustrated Actresses and Actors of Great Britain and the United States,* vol 4. no. 6, ed. Brander Mathews and Laurence Hutton (New York: Cassell and Company, 1886). It is possible that critical responses during mid-century were influenced by new "realistic" stirrings within the theatre and that gender play seemed incongruous amid increasingly realistic plots, sets, props, and lighting techniques. Yet this does not seem to have been a factor that influenced American criticism until at least 1855 when the actress Matilda Heron was "hailed by many as the exponent of a new 'realism' in acting" according to Hewitt. Furthermore, although new realistic elements began to appear within the theatre, spectacle, melodrama, extravaganza, burlesque and specialty acting were still extremely popular and much more paradigmatic of American entertainment in the 1850s and 1860s; the new realistic mode did not begin to predominate until the 1870s—at which time, it did seemingly shape the way critics viewed the cross-dressed actress. See Hewitt, *Theatre U.S.A.*, 218–280.

122. Benjamin Brown French, *Witness to the Young Republic: A Yankee Journal*, ed. Donald B. Cole and John J. McDonough (Hanover: University Press of New England, 1989), 58.
123. "Thespian Register," *American Monthly Magazine and Critical Review* 1.4 (Aug. 1817): 398.
124. Significantly, the critic does allow that Barnes could have adequately presented a younger Norval, a boy of fifteen, for younger boys were considered effeminate by nineteenth-century standards and therefore unthreatening.
125. *Thespian Monitor and Dramatick Miscellany* 1.3 (Dec. 9, 1809): 49.
126. *Ladies Port Folio* 1.3 (Jan. 15, 1820): 19.
127. *Ladies Port Folio* 1.5 (Jan. 29, 1820): 35. Emphasis in the original.
128. *Spirit of the Times* 9.5 (April 6, 1839): 6.
129. *Spirit of the Times* 17.48 (Jan. 22, 1848): 512.
130. Some actresses, like Conway, who consistently played men's roles, seem to have been favored by audiences (if their performance record indicates success). Yet they were not getting jobs in the major New York houses but playing outside the city. Conway, for example, often played serious male parts at the Park Theatre in Brooklyn. Likewise, Menken's career started in Albany and proved a catalyst to her fame while Broadway theatres were still disregarding her.
131. Ironically, there seems to be some confusion on Vandenhoff's part as to who actually was the manager of the Walnut Street Theatre during this performance in April of 1843. In his book, Vandenhoff implies that E. A. Marshall was the manager at the time but Leach states that Cushman took her last bow as manager on July 10, 1843. Francis Wemyss also confirms this in his book by stating that "W. R. Blake relieved Miss Cushman at the Walnut the following season" meaning that she would have acted out her tenure as manager during the 1842–43 season. Vandenhoff is also mistaken about another point for he says that Cushman played Romeo for the first time on this occasion. This statement is incorrect. Cushman played Romeo at least five times before this performance with Vandenhoff, her first performance being in 1837. See Wemyss, *Twenty-Six Years of the Life of an Actor and Manager* (New York: Burgess Stringer and Co., 1847), 306.
132. Vandenhoff, *Leaves from an Actor's Notebook: Anecdotes of the Green Room and the Stage*, 203. While it is indeed true that Vandenhoff was acting in America when he made this statement, I am not trying to imply that Cushman was accepted as Romeo in Lon-

don and eschewed in America. On the contrary, Cushman was internationally renowned in this role. Breeches was a popular convention in both England and American during mid-century and with the exception of the lack of American interest in the pantomime and its Principal Boy, female theatrical transvestism was generally embraced by the theatre-going public at this particular time. It was not until the last decades of the nineteenth century that the convention began to change with the rise of the burlesque performer and the music hall's male impersonator.

133. Davis discusses feminist historical treatment of stage space as a function of gender. She quotes Nancy S. Reinhardt who charges that center stage is territory of male protagonists while "the sides, background, niches and balconies function as the inner domestic space where the woman are [sic] usually kept.... If as a character on the stage, she defies convention and invades the male central stage area, she is often exaggerated or distorted as 'an angel or a monster.'" See Davis, "Questions for a Feminist Methodology," 75.

CHAPTER 3

1. "Richmond Hill Theatre," *Spirit of the Times* 1.17 (April 7, 1832): 3.
2. See Dudden, *Women in the American Theatre*, 99.
3. Garber, *Vested Interests*, 165.
4. Edwards describes these types as, "the page ... the tiger (the boyish man's servant who at a sign from his master was supposed to jump or descend from their vehicle and accost any pretty woman passing by and get her name and address), the youthful brothers beset with misfortune, unfortunate gamins or street Arabs, the deaf mute, the blind boy, and, as in opera particularly, the love-sick youth in love with an older woman. See "The Tradition for Breeches," 5.
5. Clara Morris, *Life on the Stage: My Personal Experiences and Recollections* (New York: n.p., 1901): 59–60.
6. *Thespian Monitor and Dramatick Miscellany* 1.4 (Dec. 16, 1809): 64.
7. "Richmond Hill Theatre," *Spirit of the Times* 1.17 (April 7, 1832): 3.
8. Stebbins, *Charlotte Cushman*, 59.

9. See Price, *Charlotte Cushman*, 140; Merrill, "Charlotte Cushman," 118; and chapter 4.
10. "Things Theatrical," *Spirit of the Times* 17.39 (Nov. 20, 1847): 464.
11. "Richmond Hill Theatre," *Spirit of the Times* 1.10 (Feb. 18, 1832): 3.
12. *New York Mirror* 14.45 (May 6, 1837): 45.
13. According to the *OED*, the word "manner" may have referred to either one's behavior or one's outward bearing or deportment during the 1830s. Both meanings reinforce the idea that, as a woman, Cushman was well suited for juvenile roles. Anne Russell, in her article concerning "Gender, Passion, and Performance in Nineteenth-Century Women Romeos," confirms this desire on the part of early critics to establish an ideological kinship between the cross-dressed actress and the boy. She argues, "These writers see a natural equivalence between the immature juvenile and the woman, even when the woman is past youth. It is an extent to which 'femininity' and 'immaturity' were associated in much nineteenth-century discourse." See Russell, "Gender, Passion, and Performance," 159.
14. Mary Wollstonecraft, *A Vindication of the Rights of Women* (1792; rpt. New York: Prometheus Books, 1989), 11.
15. Ibid., 12. Although this book was published in the eighteenth century, it was still regarded as threatening by male critics well into the next century. Even theatrical journals denounced Wollstonecraft's feminist tract as a "singular and reprehensible book." The *Mirror of Taste and Dramatic Censor* charged that women must not adhere to Wollstonecraft's advice and eschew domestic duties and stereotypic concepts of womanhood, rather they must act as a "decent housewife" and attend to the home and children. "Women formed on the narrow unphilosophic plan here aimed at, would probably not reach that criterion of absolute perfection and equality sought after and expected by Mrs. Wollstonecraft; they perhaps would in some respects, come under the description of what she calls *domestic drudges*—but surely a more desirable state than being drudges to infamy and prostitution." See *Mirror of Taste and Dramatic Censor* 4.1 (July 1811): 102.
16. Wollstonecraft, *Vindication*, 43.
17. Elizabeth K. Helsinger, Robin Lauterbach Sheets, and William Veeder, *The Woman Question: Society and Literature in Britain and America, 1837–1883*, vol. 2 (Chicago: The University of Chicago Press, 1983), 4–5.

18. Beth Millstein and Jeanne Bodin, *We, the American Women: A Documentary History* (Chicago: Jermone S. Ozer, Publisher Inc., 1977), 110.
19. Helsinger, Sheets, and Veeder, *The Woman Question*, 91.
20. Philip Greven, *The Protestant Temperament: Patterns of Child-Rearing, Religious Experience, and the Self in Early America* (New York, Alfred A. Knopf, 1977), 282.
21. Greven, *Protestant Temperament*, 283.
22. Anthony Rotundo, "Boy Culture," *Meanings for Manhood*, 17.
23. Notably, the most recent *Official Boy Scout Handbook* mirrors such nineteenth century rhetoric in its campaign to teach boys to be obedient, pure, devout, and morally superior. Indeed, the "Scout Law" still charges boys to be: "trustworthy, loyal, helpful, friendly, courteous, kind, obedient, cheerful, thrifty, brave, clean, and reverent." In addition, the "Scout Oath" asks the scout to keep himself "physically strong, mentally awake, and morally straight." As in the nineteenth century, these qualities are outlined and *deliberately* gendered. Yet, all associations with the feminine world of domesticity are erased as boys are required to follow these guidelines so that they might cultivate qualities which "make men fine and great." The emphasis for the contemporary boy is on achieving the privileged state of manhood as the opening lines of the manual suggest: "Today you are an American boy. Before long you will be an American man." See William Hillcourt, *Official Boy Scout Handbook* (Printed by the Boys Scouts of America, 1979), 9, 31, 491.
24. "The Benevolent Boy," *The Lily* 2.2(Feb. 1850): 16.
25. "A Word to Boys," *The Lily* 2.3 (March 1850): 24.
26. As quoted in Greven, *The Protestant Temperament*, 39.
27. John S. C. Abbott, *The Mother at Home* (New York: The American Tract Society, 1833), 5.
28. *Godey's Ladies' Book* 19 (Oct. 1839): 184.
29. "The Fisher Boy," *Godey's Ladies' Book* 1 (Jan. 1830): 280.
30. Carroll Smith-Rosenberg, "Davy Crockett as Trickster: Pornography, Liminality, and Symbolic Inversion in Victorian America, " in *Disorderly Conduct*, 91–92.
31. William Diamond, *The Broken Sword: or, the Torrent of the Valley* (London: Thomas Lacy, 1850).
32. Diamond, *The Broken Sword*, 36.
33. Ibid., 15.
34. *American Monthly Magazine* 1.11 (June 1817): 134.

35. *New York Evening Post,* April 30, 1817, 2.
36. *New York Mirror* 9.49 (June 9, 1832): 391.
37. *New York Mirror* 1.12 (Oct. 18, 1823): 91.
38. *New York Mirror* 2.25 (Jan. 15, 1825): 199.
39. Thomas Holcroft, *Deaf and Dumb; or, The Orphan Protected* in *The London Stage: A Collection of the Most Reputed Tragedies, Comedies, Operas, Melo-dramas, Farces, and Interludes,* vol. 1 (London: G. Balne, 1825), 228–235.
40. Ibid., 230.
41. Ibid., 234.
42. Ibid., 232.
43. "Theatre Critique No. 5," *New York Evening Post,* Dec. 14, 1801, 3.
44. Celeste played Theodore at least three times, the first in early November of 1827, the second on November 12 of the same year and then again on March 4, 1828. She enacted Manuel on January 5, 1835, Florio on December 4, 1829, and Myrtillo sometime in 1828. Cushman also played the role of Theodore several times while she was a utility actress at the Park from 1837–1839.
45. *The Albion* 6.23 (Nov. 17, 1827): 484. Critics continued to praise Celeste for her boy roles while describing her in feminine terms. In 1835, upon Celeste's return to the Bowery Theatre, the *Albion* wrote, "Her talent and extraordinary versatility, with the beautiful series of pieces, (got up and written expressly for her) must ensure a succession of good houses. Her Arab boy in the French Spy, and Narrahmattah in Wisht-ton-wish are among the most beautiful creations of dramatic talent we have ever witnessed." It is especially interesting that such roles were "written expressly for her" as this suggests that playwrights were trying to fortify this association between immaturity and femininity. See *Albion* 3.13 (March 28, 1835): 104.
46. *The Albion* 7.24 (Nov. 15, 1828): 183.
47. J. B. Buckstone, *The Pet of the Petticoats* (New York: O. A. Roorbach, Jr., 1855).
48. Ibid., 7.
49. Ibid.
50. I am not trying to preclude the possibility for lesbian desire here; however, a woman on the early nineteenth-century stage was consistently read by male spectators/critics as heterosexual as there was no language or ontology to identify lesbian women until much later in the century. While issues of sexuality certainly may have compli-

cated readings of cross-gender performance prior to the 1890s when the findings of sexologists became more ubiquitous, it is safe to assume, I think, that the antebellum drama critic's gaze was largely heterocentric.

51. Buckstone, *Pet of the Petticoats*, 13.
52. Ibid., 18.
53. Ibid., 23.
54. Ibid., 43–44.
55. *The Thespian Mirror* 1.14 (May 31, 1806): 115.
56. Cushman played Paul on October 14, 1837; May 5 and 31, 1883; January 23 and 28 1839; October 23, 1839; and February 7, 1840.
57. "Things Theatrical," *Spirit of the Times* 6.9 (April 16, 1836): 65.
58. *Thespian Mirror* 1.12 (March 15, 1806): 98 and *Thespian Mirror* 1.1 (Dec. 28, 1805): 7; *American Monthly Magazine* 1.1 (May 1817): 53.
59. *The New York Mirror* 2.18 (Nov. 27, 1824): 142.
60. *New York Mirror* 2.42 (May 14, 1825): 330.
61. "Things Theatrical," *Spirit of the Times* 1.38 (Sept. 1, 1832): 2.
62. "Things Theatrical," *Spirit of the Times* 1.43 (October 6, 1832): 2.
63. "Things Theatrical," *Spirit of the Times* 25.6 (March 24, 1855): 72. I have not been able to establish life dates for either Miss Wheatley or Fanny Brown.
64. For a discussion of the innocence of nineteenth-century children see Greven's *The Protestant Temperament*.
65. Clara Fisher Maeder, *Autobiography of Clara Fisher Maeder* ed. Douglas Taylor(1897; rpt. by Burt Franklin, 1970), 6.
66. For more information on Master Betty see John Hanners, *"It was Play or Starve": Acting in the Nineteenth-Century American Popular Theatre* (Bowling Green, Ohio: Bowling Green State University Popular Press, 1993), 58.
67. Laurence Hutton, "Infant Phenomena of America," in *Curiosities of the American Stage* (New York: Harper and Brothers, Franklin Square, 1891), 230.
68. Maeder, *Autobiography*, 7.
69. Ibid., 42. Her performances as Shylock and Richard III occurred mainly during the early part of her career when she was playing in England.
70. *The Albion* 6.14 (Sept. 15, 1827): 112.
71. *The Albion* 6.16 (Sept. 29, 1827): 128.
72. *New York Mirror* 5.11 (Sept. 23, 1827): 88.

73. Maeder, *Autobiography*, 88.
74. Cushman, for example, began her career at the age of nineteen.
75. Maeder, *Autobiography*, 12. Many other parents of female infant stars also tried to perpetuate their childlike status. Nina Auerbach explains that Ellen Terry's father Ben lied to her about her age throughout her entire life. So convincingly did he assure his daughter of her supposed age, that Terry died thinking that she was one year younger than she actually was. Similarly, H. L. Bateman consistently told the press that his daughters, Ellen and Kate, were younger than they actually were so that their talents would be seen as being even more extraordinary. As Hanners points out, "In the best American Show-business tradition, the more their careers prospered, the younger became the 'official' ages of this sister act." See Auerbach, *Ellen Terry*, 31; and Hanners, *"It Was Play or Starve,"* 59.
76. *New York Mirror* 6.11 (Sept. 23, 1827): 88.
77. For more information on the child star see the chapter entitled "Infant Prodigies" in Hanner's previously cited work and G. R. MacMinn's chapter "Child Wonders" from *Theatre of the Golden Era in California* (Caldwell, Idaho: Caxton Printers, 1941), 447–469.
78. It is interesting that as more and more breeches actresses added Norval to their repertoires, his status changed from a young man to a boy.
79. "Things Theatrical," *Spirit of the Times* 8.24 (July 28, 1838): 185.
80. In discussing the construction of cultural "myths," I am relying upon the term as used by Roland Barthes. See Roland Barthes, "Myth Today," in *Mythologies* trans. Annette Lavers (New York: Hill and Wang, 1972).
81. Ackroyd, *Dressing Up*, 102.
82. Smith-Rosenberg, "Hearing Women's Words: A Feminist Reconstruction of History," in *Disorderly Conduct*, 18.
83. Ibid., 43.
84. Ibid., 39.
85. Peggy Phelan, "Crisscrossing Cultures," in *Crossing the Stage*, 156. The section on "seeing" and "reading" in this article first appeared in Phelan's "Feminist theory, poststructuralism, and performance," *The Drama Review* 32.1 (1988): 107–127. Phelan also makes a connection between immaturity and femininity in this article, stating, "The child is 'closer' to the woman than to the man" [157]. Addi-

tionally, it should be noted that Phelan's conception of the pre-Oedipal impulse is similar to Lacan's theory of the Imaginary.
86. Elizabeth Drorbaugh, "Sliding Scales: Notes on Storme DeLarverie and the Jewel Box Revue, the cross-dressed woman on the contemporary stage, and the invert," in *Crossing the Stage,* 130.
87. T. N. Talfourd, *Ion* (London: A. J. Valpy, 1835). Talfourd's piece is loosely based on Euripides' play.
88. *New York Mirror* 14.24 (Dec. 10, 1836): 190.
89. Talfourd, *Ion,* 10–11.
90. Ibid., 12.
91. Ibid., 44, 152.
92. *Albion* 4.51 (December 17, 1836): 407.
93. "Ion at the Park with Ellen Tree as Ion," *Albion* 5.5 (Feb. 4, 1837): 39.
94. *New York Mirror* 14.42 (April 15, 1837): 183.
95. "Lines to Miss Ellen Tree," *New York Mirror* 16.3 (July 14, 1838): 23.
96. "Things Theatrical," *Spirit of the Times* 6.51 (Feb. 4, 1837): 401.
97. "Things Theatrical," *Spirit of the Times* 6.52 (Feb. 11, 1837): 407.
98. Ibid.
99. William Shakespeare, *Romeo and Juliet* (New York: W. M. Taylor and Co., n.d.), v. This manuscript, which is presently housed at the Harvard Theatre Collection, was used by Cushman in performance and bears the date, written in her hand, March 5, 1852. Because it is based on Garrick's version (Cushman was a strong advocate of Shakespearean originals), it was probably not performed often. This copy seems to have been printed expressly for theatrical purposes as a quotation on the frontispiece reveals: "With stage business, cast of characters, costumes, relative positions, &c."
100. In her book *Acting Women,* Lesley Ferris discusses "the female Hamlet syndrome" by featuring a quote from an article in the *Village Voice* which focuses on cross-dressed Hamlets. Ferris quotes Ericka Munk: "Female Hamlets are usually undertaken to extend and show off the actress's range, not to look newly at revenge, princeliness, or misogynistic priggishness. Hamlet, stereotyped as a waffling neurotic prone to violent fits, is considered proper for women to enact, unlike Lear, Henry V, Caesar, Coriolanus, or Falstaff." See Ferris, *Acting Women,* 162 or Munk, "Drag: 2. Women." *The Village Voice* (March 12, 1985): 80–81.
101. Cushman Promptbook, v.

102. *New York Mirror* 8.12 (Sept. 25, 1830): 95.
103. Smith-Rosenberg, "The Hysterical Woman: Sex Roles and Role Conflict in Nineteenth-Century America," in *Disorderly Conduct*, 205.
104. Noah Ludlow, *Dramatic Life As I Have Found It* (St. Louis: G. I. Jones and Co., 1880), 316.
105. Brander Mathews and Laurence Hutton, eds. *Actors and Actresses of Great Britain and the United States*, vol. 4 (New York: Cassell and Co., 1886), 149.
106. *The Athenaeum* (Jan. 3, 1846): 19. It should be noted that while some critics interpreted Romeo as a boy, many others (such as George Vandenhoff) perceived him to be a young man. This was also the conception of the role favored by Cushman who attempted to play the lover in a manly fashion. Such a desire on Cushman's part to appear masculine is evidenced by the numerous reviews of her Romeo that both recognize and praise her manly efforts and her masculine style.
107. Straub, "Guilty Pleasures, " in *Body Guards*, 149–150.
108. *The Britannia* Jan. 3, 1846, 6.
109. Coleman, *Fifty Years*, 363.
110. Merrill, *When Romeo Was a Woman*, 124.
111. Nancy F. Cott, "Passionlessness: An Interpretation of Victorian Sexual Ideology, 1790–1850," in *A Heritage of Her Own*, ed. Nancy Cott and Elizabeth H. Plecks (New York: Simon and Schuster, 1979), 175. Although Nancy Cott's article deals only with American women (specifically eastern women), the concept of passionlessness seemed to also exist in England as the *Britannia* critic's remarks indicate. Although this critic refers to a specific performance of Cushman's in London, it is likely that she was regarded similarly in America considering the prevalence of the doctrine of passionlessness in the eastern United States.
112. Bruce McConachie, *Melodramatic Formations: American Theatre and Society, 1820–1870* (Iowa City: University of Iowa Press, 1992), 1.
113. In 1832 Noah wrote to Dunlap regarding the composition of *The Wandering Boys:* "In the year 1812, while in Charleston, Mr. Young requested me to write a piece for his wife's benefit. You remember her, no doubt; remarkable as she was for her personal beauty and amiable deportment, it would have been very ungallant to have refused, particularly as he requested that it should be a 'breeches part,'

to use a green-room term, though she was equally attractive in every character." See Dunlap, *History of the American Theatre*, 320.

114. Anon, *The Wandering Boys; or the Castle of Olival* (New York: Samuel French, 1860). The above plot summary was based on the "Acting Edition" of the play. Although the author is listed as "Anon" many sources attribute the play to Noah including Dunlap who published the letter that Noah wrote to him about the play in his *History of the American Theatre*. While McConachie's analysis of the play is informative, his version of the plot often differs from the above text. For example, McConachie states that Paul and Justin are the grandsons of the Count as opposed to their sons. Because his source for the text comes from the Readex Series (composed of nineteenth-century American acting editions), his departures from the standard version perhaps indicate an alternative acting edition.
115. McConachie, *Melodramatic Formations*, 33.
116. Ibid., 38.
117. Ibid., 40.
118. Ibid., 48.
119. Ibid., 46.
120. Anon, *The Wandering Boys*, 25.
121. Garber, *Vested Interests*, 165.
122. Ibid., 175.
123. Garber, *Vested Interests*, 184.
124. Anthony Rotundo, "Boy Culture," *Meanings for Manhood*, 15.
125. Ibid., 19.
126. Ibid., 29.

CHAPTER 4

1. As I noted in the "Introduction," this chapter was initially published as an article in *Theatre Survey* in 1996. While others have discussed Cushman's performance of gender as Romeo (Faye Dudden and most recently Lisa Merrill), and thus share some of my conclusions about gender performance (Dudden argued in 1994, albeit briefly, that Cushman disrupted gender binaries as Romeo and that her lesbianism influenced her performance), I discuss her theoretical position as androgyne (as I did in 1996) and Merrill focuses upon Cushman as a sapphic Romeo.

For specific information on Cushman as Romeo see: Susan S. Cole, "Charlotte Cushman as Romeo," *Southern Theatre* 24 (1981): 3–10; Faye Dudden, "Female Ambition: Charlotte Cushman Seizes the Stage," in *Women in the American Theatre* (New Haven: Yale University Press 1994), 92–100; Lisa Merrill, "Charlotte Cushman: American Actress on the Vanguard of New Roles for Women," (Ph.D. diss., New York University, 1984), 105–118; Merrill, *When Romeo Was a Woman*, 111–131; Elisabeth M. Puknat, "Romeo was a Lady: Charlotte Cushman's London Triumph," *Theatre Annual* 9 (1951): 59–69; Russell, "Gender, Passion, and Performance in Nineteenth-Century Women Romeos," 153–166. The following sources also contain material on Cushman's Romeo: Emma Stebbins ed., *Charlotte Cushman: Her Letters and Memories of Her Life* (Boston: Houghton, Osgood, and Company, 1879), 58–64; Joseph Leach, *Bright Particular Star: The Life and Times of Charlotte Cushman* (New Haven: Yale University Press, 1970), 169–180; William T. Price, *A Life of Charlotte Cushman* (New York: Brentanos, 1894), 137–143; Edwards, "The Tradition for Breeches," 185–189; Shafer, "Women in Male Roles," 74–81.
2. Russell, "Gender, Passion and Performance," 153.
3. Price, *A Life,* 120.
4. "Charlotte Cushman in London," *Spirit of the Times* 15.14 (May 1845): 154; "Things Theatrical," *Spirit of the Times* 19.34 (October 1849): 408. The *Spirit* provides just one example of the press's perception of Cushman as manly; there are many.
5. Charles H. Shattuck, *Shakespeare on the American Stage: From the Hallams to Edwin Booth* (Washington: Folger Shakespeare Library, 1976), 2:22.
6. J. A. Simpson and E. S. C. Weiner, eds. *Oxford English Dictionary,* second edition, vols. 1 and 7 (Oxford: Clarendon Press, 1989), 452, 168.
7. See *Salmagundi* 2.4 (Sept. 19, 1807): 395.
8. Although Romeo (even Cushman's Romeo) was sometimes regarded as a youth by critics during the first half of the nineteenth century—as Ludlow and Hutton's remarks prove—Cushman's Romeo was almost always interpreted as a young man. While Cushman never explicitly stated her thoughts about the character's age, records of her performance indicate that she conceived of Romeo as a young man rather than a boy. Her passions were reported to have been fervent and sophisticated and her sword play was skillfully executed. Moreover, reviews of Cushman in this role repeatedly referred to her

Romeo as masculine and manly as opposed to youthful, weak, and delicate. Indeed, Vandenhoff states in 1843 that "Romeo requires a man to feel his passion." Cushman's interpretation of Hamlet was aggressively masculine and, while the characters are very different, it is possible that she approached the role of Romeo similarly. For though he is a young man, Romeo is the principal male representative for his family on the streets of Verona where the feuding takes place; additionally, he takes on the responsibility of marriage throughout the course of the play. That Romeo considered himself a man (or at least a young man) is perhaps evidenced by the fact that Tybalt's reference to Romeo as "Boy" in Act III.i is meant as an incendiary comment.

9. John Coleman, *Fifty Years of an Actor's Life* 2 vols. (New York: James Pott and Co., 1904) 2: 363.
10. Quoted by Parrott in "Networking in Italy," 317.
11. Letter from William Burton to Benjamin Webster, n.d., Harvard Theatre Collection. This letter is located in the Charlotte Cushman "Extra-Illustrated," vol.4 no. 6.
12. As quoted in Clara Erskine Clement's, *Charlotte Cushman* (Boston: James R. Osgood and Co., 1882), 39.
13. Ibid., 37.
14. J. M. W., "First Impressions of Miss Cushman's Romeo," *People's Journal* 2 (1847): 118.
15. *The Observer* (March 2, 1845): 3.
16. Ibid.
17. As quoted in *Charlotte Cushman her Letters and Memories of Her Life,* Stebbins, 54.
18. Although Cushman arrived in New York on September 1, 1849, she purposely delayed her New York engagement on account of the recent Astor Place Riot. Cushman was aware that audiences often associated her with Macready (both because he was her acting mentor and because she resembled him in appearance and style) and decided to postpone her New York engagement at the Astor Place until tempers had eased regarding the affair. Instead, Cushman went immediately to Boston, continued on to Philadelphia, went back to Boston, and then proceeded on a tour of the southern states. It was not until May of the following year that Cushman appeared for a long engagement in New York.
19. *Spirit of the Times* 20.14 (May 18, 1850): 156. The critic calls Tree Miss Kean in reference to her husband Charles Kean. Regardless of

their marital status, actresses were often referred to as Miss—a prefix which both sanctified and inspired public interest because it suggested that an actress was still "available." Fisher, for example, was said to have declined in popularity after she married Maeder.

20. Ibid.
21. *New York Herald,* May 14, 1850. Cushman's portrayal of Rosalind also differed greatly from another English actress, Helen Faucit, the most celebrated Rosalind during the mid-nineteenth century. Cushman, when "caparison'd like a man" (3.2.195), appropriated a masculine persona unlike Faucit who never lost touch with the "hidden woman's fear" (1.3.119) underneath a deliberately transparent disguise. Faucit reflected, "No one can study this part without seeing that, through the guise of the brilliant-witted boy, Shakespeare meant the charm of the high-hearted woman, strong, tender, delicate, to make itself felt. . . . The actress will, in my opinion, fail signally in her task, who shall not suggest all this" [14]. Shattuck also remarks on Cushman's innovative interpretation in regards to her delivery of specific lines from the script. As Shattuck explains, Cushman "avoided that coy squeamishness which other Victorian Rosalinds affected when they had to speak certain naughty words" [1:92]. See Helen Faucit, *On Some of Shakespeare's Women* (London: printed for private circulation, 1885) and Shattuck, *Shakespeare on the American Stage.*
22. Quoted in Stebbins, *Charlotte Cushman,* 63.
23. *Athenaeum,* January 3, 1846, 19.
24. Lloyd's *Weekly Messenger* as quoted by Price, 135; *London Times,* December 30, 1845, 5; *The Britannia,* January 3, 1846, 6.
25. It is important to point out that the American press did not dedicate a great deal of attention to *any* of Cushman's dramatic efforts before she achieved international success in 1845. While many of the papers carried brief statements about her work or passing mentions of her performances, she rarely received a full review. Cushman was considered a highly competent actress but because she had not yet reached star status, dramatic critics reserved their column space in the late thirties and early forties for Fanny Kemble, Celeste, Forrest and Macready.
26. See, for example, "Things Theatrical" *Spirit of the Times* 15.49 (Jan. 31, 1846): 584. This issue reprints the review of Cushman's Romeo from the *London Times.*

27. *Spirit of the Times* 20.14 (May 18, 1850): 156; *Spirit of the Times* 20.35 (October 19, 1850): 420.
28. "Astor Place Theatre," *The Albion* 9.20 (May 18, 1850): 236. Emphasis in the original.
29. *The New York Herald,* May 14, 1850; *New York Herald* Oct. 15, 1850.
30. *New York Herald,* Oct. 15, 1850.
31. *The Albion* 35.43 (Oct. 24, 1857): 512.
32. *Porter's Spirit of the Times* 4.15 (June 12, 1858): 229.
33. J. W. M., "First Impressions of Miss Cushman's Romeo," *The People's Journal* 1 (1847): 118. Emphasis added.
34. Quoted in Stebbins, *Charlotte Cushman,* 63.
35. *The Albion* 35.43 (October 24, 1857): 512.
36. *New York Herald,* Oct. 15, 1850.
37. *London Times,* December 30, 1845, 5. Russell writes of a similar situation in Ellen Tree's performance of Romeo. Although certain reviewers had "a divided mind" as they watched Tree's similarly convincing enactment of the young Montague, "Tree's continuing and stable presence as a woman' is also stressed by Victorian theatrical convention." Russell describes how Tree was escorted before the audience for her curtain call, thus reinforcing the actresses need for male direction. See Russell, "Gender, Passion and Performance," 161.
38. Phyllis Rackin, "Androgyny, Mimesis, and the Marriage of the Boy Heroine on the English Renaissance Stage," *Speaking of Gender,* ed. Elaine Showalter (New York: Routledge, 1989), 113. I should point out that while I find Rackin's ideas concerning transcendence and monstrosity helpful in terms of their contribution to my theory of the double image, I disagree with her ultimate conclusions about the androgyne. Rackin argues that this figure "refuses to choose between actor and character or between male and female but instead insists on the ambiguities" [124]. My theory of the double image works against this idea of an ambiguous or blurred persona. Rather, the androgyne as I conceive it, is a double figure who embodies the potential to switch between genders, to be either one or the other.
39. Smith-Rosenberg, *Disorderly Conduct,* 98.
40. Judith Butler, *Gender Trouble: Feminism and the Subversion of Identity* (New York: Routledge, 1990), 137–138. Emphasis is Butler's.

41. Judith Butler, "Performative Acts and Gender Constitution: An Essay in Phenomenology and Feminist Theory," in *Performing Feminisms: Feminist Critical Theory and Theatre*, ed. Sue-Ellen Case (Baltimore: Johns Hopkins University Press, 1990), 270–271.
42. Vandenhoff, *Leaves from an Actor's Notebook*, 202–203.
43. Smith-Rosenberg, *Disorderly Conduct*, 290–291. In her chapter entitled "The New Woman as Androgyne: Social Disorder and Gender Crisis, 1870–1936," Smith-Rosenberg discusses the New Woman's appropriation of a politico-sexual language created by male physicians in the late nineteenth century in order to contain the threat of women's entrance into institutions of higher education. The New Woman adopted terms like "Mannish Lesbian" and "intermediate sex" in an attempt to exercise male power and "demand a role beyond conventional gender restraints" [40]. Smith-Rosenberg employs theories surrounding the trickster figure to better interpret the endeavors of the New Woman in this respect. Thus the term trickster is used to explain the New Woman or female modernist as Androgyne. For example, Woolf's Orlando is described as a "joyous androgyne" who glories "in androgyny, the confusion of categories, the options that extend beyond social proprieties" [289]. Orlando is also described by Smith-Rosenberg as "a trickster par excellence" [291]. These terms are used in conjunction with one another because they complement and explain one another. It is in this manner that I have employed them in an attempt to illuminate Cushman's Romeo.
44. "Our Lady Correspondent," *Porter's Spirit of the Times* 4.15 (June 12, 1858): 229; *Athenaeum*, Jan. 3, 1846, 19; *New York Herald*, May 10, 1852.
45. Smith-Rosenberg, *Disorderly Conduct*, 293.
46. In placing Rosalind's name in quotation marks to make a distinction between the character and the disguise put on by Ganymed, I am borrowing a convention used by Michael Shapiro in his recent book *Gender in Play on the Shakespearean Stage: Boy Heroines and Female Pages* (Ann Arbor: University of Michigan Press, 1994).
47. Catherine Belsey, "Disrupting Sexual Difference: Meaning and Gender in the Comedies," *Alternative Shakespeares*, ed. John Drakakis (New York: Methuen, 1985), 180.
48. Ibid.
49. Regardless of her musings about gender instability, Belsey does not consider the androgyne (with its double image) as a possible alter-

native identity to take the place of unstable representations of male and/or female.
50. Ibid. It is important to note here that the version of *As You Like It* which Cushman used was Macready's reformed version which included the Epilogue. In his attempts to restore the text to its original form, Macready returned the Epilogue to the play.
51. Ibid., 183.
52. Julia Kristeva, "Women's Time," *Signs* 7.1 (August 1981): 34–35.
53. Ibid., 34.
54. Belsey, "Disrupting Sexual Difference," 189, 190.
55. Gayle Whittier, "The Sublime Androgyne Motif in Three Shakespearean Works," *Journal of Medieval and Renaissance Studies* 19, no. 2 (1989): 188.
56. Garber, *Vested Interests,* 16. Russell also invokes Garber and makes the very good point that while Garber "sees most instances of cross-dressing as complicated" she inexplicably dismisses Cushman's potential to inspire category crisis. Garber, Russell explains, does not regard the nineteenth century female theatrical transvestite as significantly anomalous, a point which both Russell and I find debatable.
57. *Athenaeum,* Jan. 3, 1846, 19.
58. J. M. W., *People's Journal,* 118.
59. As quoted by Leach, *Bright Particular Star,* 178.
60. Dutton Cook, *Hours with the Players,* vol. 2 (London: Chatto and Windus, 1881), 196.
61. Weston Marston, *Our Recent Actors,* vol.2 (London: Sampson Low, Marston, Searle and Rivington, 1888), 77.
62. Coleman, *Fifty Years of an Actor's Life,* 302.
63. *Albion* 35.43 (Oct. 24, 1857): 512.
64. Russell, "Gender, Passion, and Performance," 157.
65. In addition to reinserting the information concerning Rosaline, Cushman also depicted Romeo's death in the proper fashion (dying before Juliet wakes from her drugged state), restored Lady Montague's character, returned Mercutio's Queen Mab speech to its proper place in the text, and reinstituted the reconciliation scene between the Montagues and the Capulets in Act V.iii. See George C. Odell, *Shakespeare from Betterton to Irving* (New York: Benjamin Blom, 1963), 2: 271–272.
66. *London Times,* December 30, 1845, 5.
67. Charlotte Cushman promptbook, *Romeo and Juliet* (New York: W. M. Taylor and Co., 1852): v. Harvard Theatre Collection. This

promptbook bears a handwritten note, stating that it was used in performance on March 5, 1852—seven years after Cushman's debut as Romeo at the Haymarket. Although I have been unable to locate Cushman's promptbook for the 1845–46 run at the Haymaket, one can be relatively certain that the Garrick-based 1852 promptbook is strikingly different from the original which Cushman is reported to have restored in 1845. Shattuck states that, "beginning about with Macready in the late 1830s and after, Phelps in the 1840s and after, and others of the 'restorers,' the usual practice was to eschew the acting editions with their petrified 'errors' and to work from a 'true text,' using sheets from one or another well-printed, good paper, multi-volume complete *Works.*'" See Shattuck, *The Shakespeare Promptbooks: A Descriptive Catalog* (Urbana: University of Illinois Press, 1965), 8.

The fact that versions of the play like the 1852 promptbook were still in use after Cushman attempted to reform the text can be explained through the triumph of theatrical pragmatism. Cushman's need to work overwhelmed her desire to be celebrated as a textual reformer and when managers and audiences wanted to see Garrick's version, Cushman responded by performing this adaptation. This can be evidenced by an undated letter which Cushman wrote to Benjamin Webster, the manager of the Princess Theatre in London. She writes: "Your brother wrote me a note this morning saying that your stage manager had informed you of my preference for the acting 'Romeo and Juliet.' Understand from me pray, that I am *thoroughly prepared to do whatever you wish,* I found that when the gentlemen now expressing in no very measured terms [the] displeasure . . . this *original text* was giving them, the stage manager informed them that it was all stuff and nonsense doing it in the way proposed . . . I am quite prepared to act Romeo in any way that *shall please you.*" Cushman manuscript collection, Harvard Theatre Collection. Emphasis is Cushman's.

68. As quoted in Price, *A Life*, 137.
69. *London Times,* December 30, 1845, 5.
70. Marianne Novy, "Violence, Love, and Gender in *Romeo and Juliet*" in *Romeo and Juliet: Critical Essays,* ed. John F. Andrews (New York: Garland Publishing, Inc., 1993), 361–362.
71. Whittier, "The Sublime Androgyne," 193.
72. Butler, *Gender Trouble,* 25.
73. Novy, "Violence, Love, and Gender," 365.
74. Whittier, "The Sublime Androgyne," 194–195.

75. Vandenhoff, *Leaves From an Actor's Notebook*, 202.
76. Coleman, *Fifty Years*, 2: 363.
77. From "First Impressions of Miss Cushman's Romeo," *The People's Journal* 1 (1847): 118.
78. George Fletcher, *Studies of Shakespeare* (London: Longman, Brown, Green, and Longmans, 1847), 380. Although he never mentions Cushman by name, it is certain that Fletcher is referring to her performance at the Haymarket because he says he will discuss the production which was "on the boards of one of the patent theatres of London, in the following December, 1845." There was no other production of *Romeo and Juliet* at either the Covent Garden or the Drury Lane at this time, therefore, it is evident that Fletcher is remarking upon Cushman's run at the Haymarket.
79. Ibid.
80. Ibid., 382.
81. Erroll Sherson, *Lost London Theatre's of the Nineteenth Century* (London: Constable and Co., 1932), 128.
82. Butler, "Performative Acts and Gender Constitution," 270.
83. Jewsbury published her novel one year after Fletcher's scathing account of Cushman's Romeo appeared in print, which suggests that she may have been directly responding to his critiques of her friend's performance. Yet, Coleman and Vandenhoff published their attacks after Jewsbury's book came out, which indicates that Jewsbury recognized the potential threat that Cushman presented (perhaps after she became familiar with Fletcher's review) and commented satirically about the potential for further critical anxiety.
84. Geraldine Jewsbury, *The Half Sisters* (London: Chapman and Hall, 1848), 2:22–24.
85. Merrill, *When Romeo Was a Woman*, 57–58. See also Nancy F. Cott, "Passionlessness: An Interpretation of Victorian Sexual Ideology, 1790–1850," in *A Heritage of Her Own*, Nancy F. Cott and Elizabeth H. Plecks, ed. (New York: Simon and Schuster, 1979), 162–181.
86. Ellen Donkin, "Mrs. Siddons Looks Back in Anger: Feminist Historiography for Eighteenth-Century British Theater," in *Critical Theory and Performance*, ed. Janelle G. Reinelt and Joseph R. Roach, 276–290 (Ann Arbor: University of Michigan Press, 1992), 278. Emphasis is Donkin's.
87. Weston Marston, *Our Recent Actors*, vol. 2 (London: Sampson Low, Marston, Searle and Rivington, 1888) 2:76.

88. Price, *A Life*, 120.
89. Ibid., 141.
90. After discovering that her former business agent Louis Harlan embezzled the interest due her on almost seventy thousand dollars, Cushman, with the advice of her financial agent Wayland Crow, made all future business decisions herself. See Leach, *Bright Particular Star*, 279.
91. As quoted by Stebbins, *Charlotte Cushman*, 12.
92. Ibid.
93. Ibid., 16.
94. Coleman, *Fifty Years*, 2: 309. Emphasis added. It is interesting that Cushman uses the term "actor"—now often used in a non - gender specific manner—to describe herself in an age when terminology reflected strict gender prescriptions. A woman was a lady, an "angel of the house," a True Woman—a female performer was an actress.
95. Leach, *Bright Particular Star*, 210.
96. Recent studies discuss Cushman's lesbianism at length. See Merrill's book length study on this subject, *When Romeo Was a Woman* ; also Lillian Faderman, *Surpassing the Love of Men* (New York: William Morrow and Co., 1981), 220–226.
97. Faderman, *Surpassing the Love of Men*, 156. See also Smith-Rosenberg, "The Female World of Love and Ritual: Relations Between Women in Nineteenth-Century America," in *Disorderly Conduct*.
98. Coleman, *Fifty Years*, 1:310.
99. In an interview conducted by LaSalle Corbell Pickett towards the end of Cushman's life, the actress was asked if Lady Macbeth had been her favorite role. She replied, "No; I preferred Romeo to all others. He has such a varied career and so many different emotions, and each one is so tensely felt, that nearly all the facets of emotional life are presented. Then it gave me a chance to fight a real duel, which is always a triumph for a woman." See Pickett, *Across My Path* (New York: Brentano's, 1916), 21.
100. Coleman, *Fifty Years*, 1:363; Marston, *Our Recent Actors*, 75–76.
101. As quoted in Price, *A Life*, 132; *London Times*, December 30, 1845, 5.
102. *New York Herald*, Oct. 15, 1850.
103. *New York Daily News*, Nov. 10, 1860.
104. *New York Herald*, Nov. 10, 1860.
105. *The Spirit of the Times* 21.27 (August 1851): 324.
106. Coleman, *Fifty Years*, 2:361–362; Leach, *Bright Particular Star*, 179–180.

107. The photographs of Cushman with a cravat appear in the Harvard Theatre Collection's extra-Illustrated volume of Mathews and Hutton's *Actors and Actresses of Great Britain and the United States,* vol. 4 (New York: Cassell and Company, 1886).
108. Pickett, *Across My Path,* 22.

CHAPTER 5

1. *Albion* 38.44 (Nov. 3, 1860): 523.
2. Dudden, *Women in the American Theatre,* 143.
3. *Albion* 38.5 (Feb. 4, 1860): 55.
4. Wood, *Personal Recollections of the Stage,* 69. Emphasis in the original.
5. Hutton, *Curiosities of the American Stage,* 322.
6. "Hamlet at Haverly's Fifth Avenue Theatre," *New York Herald,* March 21, 1882. This clipping is from the Harvard Theatre Collection's file entitled "Women as Hamlet; Miscellaneous," drawer 7, folder 33. This file contains numerous articles about actresses who attempted to play men and, according to the press, failed miserably. Breeches performers such as Anna Dickinson, Marie Prescott, and Mrs. Bandmann Palmer were castigated by critics who found their attempts at serious male characters absurd.
7. See Shafer, "Women in Male Roles," 81 and Edwards, "The Tradition for Breeches," 13. Realism did not, however, significantly contribute to the decline of non-legitimate breeches performance since cross-dressed actresses involved in spectacles like Keene's the *Seven Sons* (which was, like her *Seven Sisters,* "A Grand Operatic Spectacular, Diabolical, Musical, Terpsichorean, Farcical Burletta, in Three Acts")—the most popular theatrical genre between 1850–1870—were not bound by the same realistic conventions that affected actresses playing Sam Willoughby and even Hamlet.
8. Ferris, *Acting Women,* 162.
9. Ibid.
10. "Past Stage Favorites: Remembrances of Jenny Lind, Cushman, and Menken," clipping from a New York newspaper, 1891. Adah Isaacs Menken clipping file, Harvard Theatre Collection.
11. "Hamlet at Haverly's Fifth Avenue Theatre," *New York Herald* 21 March 1882. Clipping from the Harvard Theatre Collection's "Women as Hamlet" file: drawer 7, folder 33.

12. Price, *Charlotte Cushman*, 119.
13. William Winter, *Shakespeare on Stage* (New York: Moffat, Yard and Co., 1911), 437.
14. The eighteenth-century dramatic critic and playwright, Samuel Johnson argued against prescriptive neoclassical "rules of drama" such as the unities of time, place and action. Johnson maintained that since audiences were always aware of the convention of the theatre, strict ideas governing supposedly natural settings and actions were unnecessary. See Johnson, "Preface to the Plays of William Shakespeare," in Bernard Dukore's *Dramatic Theory and Criticism: Greeks to Grotowski* (New York: Hold, Rinehart and Winston, 1974), 414.
15. Russell, "Gender, Passion, and Performance," 156.
16. Dudden, *Women in the American Theatre*, 155–156.
17. Benjamin McArthur, *Actors and American Culture, 1880–1920* (Philadelphia: Temple University Press, 1984), 24. McArthur attributes the elimination of the benefit system to Lester Wallack's Actor's Fund of America. The institutionalization of this fund changed the way benefits were allocated and reorganized the ways in which profit was handled. For a discussion of this innovation, see McArthur, 95.
18. *Albion* 38.16 (April 21, 1860): 187.
19. *New York Clipper* 10.25 (Oct. 4, 1862): 198; *New York Clipper* 11.41 (Jan. 23, 1864): 323.
20. While Merrill does cite a few unidentified clippings that praise Cushman's Wolsey, most of the reviews temper their praise by acknowledging that they initially expressed doubt over her success, by suggesting that her triumph came by imitating Macready's style, by reminding the reader that she is both the "only living actress who could undertake such a character" and also "intensely feminine," or by couching their favorable comments in the discourse of True Womanhood (Cushman was "calm" and possessed a "quiet manner and sedate deportment"). See Merrill, *When Romeo Was A Woman*, 134–135.
21. *Albion* 41.40 (October 3, 1863): 475.
22. *Albion* 41. 48 (Dec. 5, 1863): 583.
23. *New York Dramatic Mirror*, Jan. 19, 1892, 3.
24. *Spirit of the Times* 120.12 (December 13, 1890): 808; *Spirit of the Times*, March 12, 1892, 318; *New York Times*, Nov. 10, 1891, 5.
25. *New York Clipper* 12.5 (May 14, 1864): 38. Unlike legitimate breeches actresses, who often had difficulty acquiring costumes, women who played Mazeppa could easily purchase fleshlings in the

Bowery. An advertisement in the *Clipper* reads: "THEATRICAL AND EQUESTRIAN: Hosiery and Tights, A Large Assortment on Hand And All Sizes and Qualities Made to Order, By A. Rankin and Co., 96 Bowery." See *New York Clipper* 10.8 (June 7, 1862).

26. While breeches performers became increasingly objectified in the 1860s as new breakthroughs in technology engendered copious celebrity photographs, it should be noted that many Mazeppas were not altering their costumes at all; many actresses simply wore the costume as described in the text of the play—a costume which was originally envisioned for a male actor. The process of sexualization, therefore, occurred chiefly through critical rhetoric. As drama critics became more interested in reporting on women's sexual allure, fleshlings became more revealing.
27. Dudden, *Women in the American Theatre*, 160–161.
28. Hewitt, *Theatre U.S.A.*, 120.
29. Allen, *Horrible Prettiness*, 89.
30. Dudden, *Women in the American Theatre*, 116.
31. See Chapter Three in McCullough, *Living Pictures on the New York Stage;* also Allen, *Horrible Prettiness*, 93; Dudden, *Women in the American Theatre*, 116–118.
32. I find Allen's three-part explanation regarding the feminization of the stage helpful, yet I should note that my discussion of equestrian melodrama is significantly different from his. While Allen describes Menken's career and its contribution to the rise of what he calls "feminine spectacle," he mentions it simply as an antecedent to burlesque. However, I see Menken's career as seminal because she spawned so many imitators and initiated a craze for the adoption of fleshlings and equestrian melodramatic roles in the 1860s. In effect, she began an entertainment industry—at least within lowbrow theatres—which influenced the way other breeches performers were perceived by the press and by the public.
33. *Israelite* 5.6 (Aug. 13, 1858): 45.
34. See Allen Lesser's *Enchanting Rebel: The Secret of Adah Isaacs Menken* (Philadelphia: Ruttle, Shaw and Wetherill, 1947), 29–40.
35. Allen reports that Menken appeared as Mazeppa at New York's Broadway Theatre on June 13, 1861 but this is incorrect. Menken was on tour in Pittsburgh and Milwaukee at this time and did not make her New York debut in Mazeppa until June of 1862. This engagement was played at the New Bowery, an east end theatre that was considerably less reputable than the Broadway theatre.

36. Louis Adler, "Adah Isaacs Menken in *Mazeppa*," in *Women in American Theatre*, ed. Helen Krich Chinoy and Linda Walsh Jenkins (New York: Theatre Communications Group, 1981), 83.
37. *Wilkes' Spirit of the Times*, Feb. 18, 1860. Sentilles explains that this paper had a vested interest in denying the marriage between Heenan and Menken since George Wilkes, the editor of the paper, was also responsible for making Heenan famous and for continuing to promote his career in London.
38. See Sentilles "Performing Menken" for a copy of Menken's suicide note (pg. 313–314).
39. "Ada Isaacs Menken, the Wife of John C. Heenan," *The New York Illustrated News*, March 31, 1860. This four-part article was featured throughout March and April, beginning on March 17 and concluding on April 14. It is especially interesting that this story directly preceded Menken's extreme success in Albany. A copy of this article appears in the Allen Lesser Collection at the American Jewish Archives.
40. See Menken's "Shylock," *Israelite* 4.13 (Oct. 2, 1857): 101 and "The Jew in Parliament," *Israelite* 5.9 (Sept. 3, 1858): 65. For information regarding Menken's essay on Mortara, see Lesser, *Enchanting Rebel*, 37.
41. Lesser, *Enchanting Rebel*, 37.
42. Sentilles, "Performing Menken," 127.
43. Further evidence of the press's anxiety over Menken appears in an article written for the *New York Daily Tribune*. Menken gave a public lecture/poetry reading that took her outside her sphere as she was not performing a dramatic character but a woman wronged. The critic who reported on the event called her a "female appologist" and urged her to return to the drawing room rather than pursue a putlic career as an actress. See "An Evening with the Poets: the Position of Miss Adah Isaacs Menken," *New York Daily Tribune*, August 21, 1860.
44. *New York Clipper* 7.49 (March 24, 1860): 390. Much of my information on equestrian breeches performers comes from the *Clipper*, New York's most popular theatrical trade paper during the mid-nineteenth century. While my research for this chapter comes from six different papers (the *New York Times, New York Clipper, New York Tribune, New York Illustrated News, Spirit,* and the *Albion)*, the *Clipper* is the only paper which repeatedly covered activity at the Bowery and other East Side theatres where most of the eques-

trian performances took place. The *Albion,* which at this time reported only on activity in "highbrow" theatres, does not even mention Menken until her second New York engagement as Mazeppa in 1866.
45. Herring specialized in breeches roles, performing them almost exclusively. She was a member of the Bowery's stock company throughout the 1860s and played over forty-four breeches roles during her career, including Mose the Bowery b'hoy in *A Glance at New York.* See Edwards, "Tradition for Breeches," 354.
46. *New York Clipper* 10.9 (June 14, 1862): 60.
47. *New York Clipper* 10.10 (June 21, 1862): 78.
48. For a review of Menken as Cheerly see the *Israelite* 4.13 (October 2, 1857): 101; Dudden discusses her Camille on pg. 160.; and Sentilles notes that Menken told her friend Daly that she preferred weightier roles. See "Performing Menken," 188.
49. Dudden, *Women in the American Theatre,* 160.
50. Both Hewitt and Dudden briefly mention the Civil War's affect on the theatre. Hewitt states, "The outbreak of the Civil War had only a brief depressing effect upon the theatre. After that it boomed, as apparently always in wartime." He goes on to imply that while Shakespearean tragedians such as Booth became popular during the war, the public mainly supported variety entertainment. Dudden points out the success of Keene's productions during wartime; the *Seven Sisters,* for example, featured war tableaus such as the attack on Ft. Sumner and incorporated popular songs such as "Dixie." She also explains that Concert Saloons did a great deal of business during the war as they "were quite popular with soldiers passing through town." See Hewitt, *Theatre U.S.A.,* 187, and Dudden, *Women in the American Theatre,* 142–143.
51. Allen, *Horrible Prettiness,* 73–75. More information about concert saloons is forthcoming in a new study by Brooks McNamara.
52. *New York Clipper* 10.10 (June 21, 1862): 78. Emphasis in the original.
53. *New York Clipper* 11.31 (Nov. 14, 1863): 243.
54. *New York Clipper* (February 3, 1866): 342.
55. *New York Clipper* 11.31 (Nov. 14, 1863): 243.
56. *New York Clipper* 11.32 (Nov. 21, 1863): 251.
57. *New York Clipper* 11.40 (Jan., 16 1864): 316.
58. *New York Clipper* 11.32 (Nov. 21, 1863): 251.
59. *New York Clipper* 11.40 (Jan. 16, 1864): 315.

60. *New York Clipper* 12.5 (May 14, 1864): 38.
61. *New York Clipper* 11.43 (Feb. 6, 1864): 339.
62. *New York Tribune*, Dec. 1, 1862.
63. Allen, *Horrible Prettiness*, 26.
64. Lesser, *Enchanting Rebel*, 174.
65. Christine Stansell argues that in the Bowery, nineteenth-century gender prescriptions (based on a middle-class ideal) were less strict. She writes, "The rise of the Bowery was inseparable from the growth of working-class consciousness between 1830 and 1860. In this context, the rough version of republican ideology that the Bowery Boys inherited—the celebration of the virtues of manual labor and physical prowess, the virile patriotism, the truculence toward outside authority—promoted a change in republican views of women." As working women, Bowery Gals were more independent and visible within the public arena. As Stansell points out, "the possibilities of the Bowery Gal would continue, throughout the rest of the nineteenth century, to pose an alternative mode of feminine self-realization to the bourgeois ideal of truth womanhood." These more relaxed conceptions of womanhood might explain why Bowery audiences were more accepting of women who "wore the breeches." See Stansell, *City of Women*, 95, 100.
66. *New York Tribune*, May 1, 1866.
67. *New York Express*, May 1, 1866; *New York World*, May 1, 1866. These quotes also appear in the *New York Clipper* 14.5 (May 12, 1866): 38.
68. *New York Clipper* 14.5 (May 12, 1866): 38.
69. Ibid.
70. Ibid.
71. Lesser, *Enchanting Rebel*, 175.
72. *Albion* 44.18 (May 5, 1866): 211.
73. Allen, *Horrible Prettiness*, 101.
74. See Allen's discussion of Thompson's influence throughout *Horrible Prettiness* and Dudden on Thompson, 164–171. See also Marilyn A. Moses, "Lydia Thompson and the 'British Blondes' in the United States," Ph.D. diss., University of Oregon, 1978.
75. *New York Times*, Oct. 1, 1868, 6.
76. Allen, *Horrible Prettiness*, 16.
77. Notably, photographs of Thompson do not suggest that her costume ever became as revealing as the equestrian fleshling. Her tunics did get a few inches shorter as her American career progressed. Similarly,

her costumes were drawn in at the waist and were cut slightly lower than the standard breeches tunic.
78. As quoted by Allen, 134. Notably, Howells makes the same observation about burlesque that the *New York Times* critic made after witnessing Thompson's Ixion. Howells, however, is disturbed by an anomaly that the *Times* critic does not even acknowledge.
79. Richard Grant White, "The Age of Burlesque," *The Galaxy* 3.2 (August 1869): 256.
80. Ibid., 259.
81. Ibid., 260.
82. *The Polyanthos* 4.3 (March 1807): 282. While the critic in this journal refers to the actress as "Mrs. Poe," this would have been Eliza Poe, the mother of Edgar Allan Poe, as her biographer Geddeth Smith mentions that she played Little Pickle in addition to other breeches parts. See Smith's *The Brief Career of Eliza Poe* (London: Associate University Presses, 1988), 50.
83. *American Monthly Magazine and Critical Review* 1.4 (June 23, 1817): 399.
84. Logan's feminism is discussed by both Allen and Dudden. Allen argues that Logan found burlesque to be the antithesis of the campaign for women's advancement because the display of a sexualized body furthered women's entrapment within matrimony and hindered their independence. Dudden claims that Logan's feminism was "decidedly economic"; Logan felt that it was important for women to establish themselves as independent financial agents within the marketplace. By selling sexual pleasure, actresses involved in the leg business sacrificed their dignity and their autonomy by perpetuating a subjugating system of representation and employment. See Allen, *Horrible Prettiness*, 122–127, and Dudden, *Women in the American Theatre*, 171–175.
85. Logan, *Apropos of Women and Theatre*, 114, 128. My discussion of Logan focuses on two chapters of this book: "About the Leg Business" and "About Nudity in Theatres." Both of these chapters appeared as previous articles in *The Galaxy* and *Packard's Monthly*. Allen and Dudden both discuss Logan too, but I should point out that neither of them analyzes her treatment of "Mazeppas," nor do they mention Logan's direct association between burlesque and breeches performance.
86. Allen, *Horrible Prettiness*, 124.
87. Logan, *Apropos*, 115.

88. Ibid., 114.
89. Ibid., 116.
90. Ibid. In a letter written to the editor of the *Chicago Times* on February 10, 1870, Lydia Thompson recounts similar reasons for her work within the leg business. "I . . . appear in the class of entertainment that is most remunerative. The public taste has deposed the legitimate business and elevated burlesque in its place. The most profitable seasons of the legitimate drama in their returns fall far short of a burlesque entertainment." As quoted in Moses, "Lydia Thompson and the British Blondes," 127.
91. *Albion* 45.22 (June 1, 1867): 259.
92. I have established six breeches roles in Vestvali's personal repertoire: Romeo, performed for the first time in 1857; Charles Quint in *Ernani* in October, 1857; Orpheus in *Bel-Demonio,* performed on May 25, 1863; Angelo in the opera bearing the same name, performed on May 16, 1864; Philip Beaufort in *A Marriage Certificate* on Sept. 26, 1867 at the Brooklyn Academy of Music; and Gamea (play unknown) at the Academy of Music on Sept. 24, 1867.
93. Logan, *Apropos,* 115.
94. Ibid., 143. This quote was actually phrased by Logan as a question that managers would ask a prospective actress. Logan unmistakenly implies, however, that those who did comply were *choosing* to display themselves in exiguous attire. Exploitation is not an issue that Logan even considers, which is curious considering her self-proclaimed feminism.
95. "Reply to Olive Logan's Letter on the Theatrical Profession," *New York Times,* May 30, 1869, 5.
96. Ibid.
97. By December of 1868, the *Albion* was already reporting on the incredible impact that Lydia Thompson's troupe had made on the New York theatrical scene. While *Ixion* was still at Wood's, most of the major houses in New York had started doing burlesques. In his chapter entitled "The Institutionalization of Burlesque," Allen discusses the "dozens of burlesque troupes" that infiltrated New York after Thompson's arrival. See Allen *Horrible Prettiness,* 159–193.
98. Alice Marriott stared as Hamlet in the spring of 1869 at Wood's Broadway Theatre. The *Times* commented, "The lady had disappointed public expectation. Her appearance was prefaced by the publication of voluminous opinions of the English Press, given probably when the actress was much younger; at all events, when she was

much better,—and in no particular have her performances at Wood's Museum reached more than respectable mediocrity." *New York Times,* April 17, 1869.
99. Anonymous clipping, "Women Who Played Hamlet" file, Harvard Theatre Collection, 18 Jan., 1892.
100. "Some Female Hamlets," *Boston Herald,* Oct. 30, 1893.

CONCLUSION

1. *Spirit of the Times* 12 (Nov. 25, 1893): 604.
2. "Women Players Win Applause," *New York Herald,* Nov. 22, 1893, 9.
3. "The League Performance," *New York Dramatic Mirror,* Dec. 2, 1893, 2.
4. "Women Players Win Applause," *New York Herald,* Nov. 22, 1893, 9.
5. "The League Performance," *New York Dramatic Mirror,* Dec. 2, 1893, 2.
6. "Women Players Win Applause," *New York Herald,* Nov. 22, 1893, 9.
7. I have found only four secondary sources that mention the Professional Women's League: Benjamin McArthur's article "Theatrical Clubs of the Nineteenth Century: Tradition Versus Assimilation in the Acting Community," *Theatre Survey* 23.2 (Nov. 1982): 197–212; McArthur's book *Actors and American Culture, 1880–1920* (Philadelphia: Temple University Press, 1984), 75; Yvonne Shafer's previously cited article on Cushman, "Women in Male Roles: Charlotte Cushman and Others," in *Women in American Theatre*; and Charles Shattuck's *Shakespeare on the American Stage* (Washington: Folger Books, 1987), 2:97–99. In his article, McArthur devotes only one paragraph to women's clubs (he discusses ten men's clubs), half of this paragraph focuses on the PWL. Similarly McArthur's book has a brief paragraph about the League as does Shattuck's study. Shaffer's article contains one sentence about the League's performance of *As You Like It* which states that Cushman played Orlando. This statement is obviously erroneous since Cushman died in 1876, the League was founded in 1892, and Maude Banks played Orlando in both 1893 and 1894 productions.

While scholarship on the PWL is scanty, women's theatrical clubs in general have been almost completely ignored; in addition to the PWL such clubs include: the Twelfth Night Club and the Gamut Club (located in New York) and the Charlotte Cushman Club (located in Philadelphia). The Charlotte Cushman Club was originally founded by Mary Shaw and still exists today.

8. "The Women's Association," *New York Dramatic Mirror*, Dec. 17, 1892, 3.
9. Ibid.
10. "Professional Women's League: Twentieth Century Woman," *New York Times*, April 4, 1894, 2.
11. Ibid.
12. Ella Starr, "Average Man Mentally Lazy," *New York Times*, April 18, 1894, 2.
13. Robert A. Schanke, "Mary Shaw: A Fighting Champion," in *Women in the American Theatre* ed. Chinoy and Jenkins (New York: Theatre Communications Group, 1987), 98.
14. "The Women's Association," *New York Dramatic Mirror*, Dec. 17, 1892, 3.
15. "The League Performance," *New York Dramatic Mirror*, Nov. 18, 1893, 18.
16. "Women Players Win Applause," *New York Herald*, Nov. 22, 1893, 9.
17. While some of the PWL's more overtly feminist statements, such as those found in the 1894 papers of Banks and Starr, were not made until later in the League's history, the group was recognized from the very beginning as a protofeminist organization because of its membership, its mission, and its deliberate break with the Actor's Fund.
18. Drorbaugh, "Sliding Scales," 126.
19. Smith-Rosenberg, *Disorderly Conduct*, 293.
20. Whittier, "The Sublime Androgyne," 188.
21. "Women Players Win Applause," *New York Herald*, Nov. 22, 1893, 9.
22. Ibid.
23. Ibid.
24. "Shakespeare and Opera in Pantalettes," *Collier's Weekly* 12.18 (Feb. 1894): 3.
25. "Women in As You Like It," *New York Dramatic Mirror*, Feb. 10, 1894, 2.
26. Ibid.

27. Karen J. Blair, *The Clubwoman as Feminist: True Womanhood Redefined, 1868–1914* (New York: Holmes and Meier Pub., 1980). The term "Domestic Feminism" was coined by Daniel Scott Smith in 1974. I would argue that the PWL's feminism was in reality considerably less "domestic" than that of other women's clubs although it may have been perceived similarly.
28. Laurence Senelick also discusses this tendency towards feminization in his article regarding male impersonation on the nineteenth-century popular stage. Women such as Annie Hindle and Ella Wesner, who in the 1870s won favor for their "raucous depictions of loose-living dudes," were replaced in the 1890s by male impersonators who were markedly less butch. Equipped with soprano voices and a "principal-boy approach," impersonators like Bessie Bonehill and Vesta Tilley appealed to "the more genteel culture of the 1890s," a culture which would not tolerate the masculine efforts applauded in the 1870s. See Senelick, "The Evolution of the Male Impersonator on the Nineteenth-Century Popular Stage," *Essays in Theatre* 1.1 (1982): 39–40.
29. "The Professional Women's League," *New York Dramatic Mirror,* May 20, 1893, 12.
30. "The Woman's Page: Some Words About the League," *New York Dramatic Mirror,* July 1, 1893, 12.
31. *Spirit of the Times* 12 (Nov. 25, 1893): 604.
32. Smith-Rosenberg, *Disorderly Conduct,* 271–272.
33. In a recent article, Lisa Duggan briefly discusses the historical debate over the meaning of the "mannish lesbian." Duggan argues that some scholars see the "mannish lesbian" as a deliberately constructed figure, created by anti-feminist sexologists who strategically cultivated such distorted images of independent women in order to dissuade eager New Women from unorthodox professional ambitions and love interests. On the other hand, the "mannish lesbian" might have been a narrative engendered by lesbians who sought to carve out new social and romantic possibilities for themselves. See Duggan, "The Trials of Alice Mitchell: Sensationalism, Sexology, and the Lesbian Subject in Turn-of-the-Century America," *Signs* (Summer 1993): 792.
34. George Chauncey Jr., "From Sexual Inversion to Homosexuality: Medicine and The Changing Conceptualization of Female Deviance," *Salmagundi* 58–59(Fall 1982/Winter 1983): 119.

35. P. M. Wise, "Case of Sexual Perversion," *Alienist and Neurologist* 4 (1883): 87. Women had successfully passed as men (offstage) throughout American history, fighting in the Revolutionary and Civil Wars, and working at male jobs within the public sphere. It was not until the sexologist's reports were issued that such behavior was labeled "perverse." For information on non-theatrical female cross-dressing in America see: "'She Even Chewed Tobacco': A Pictorial Narrative of Passing Women in America" by the San Francisco Lesbian and Gay History Project in *Hidden From History: Reclaiming the Gay and Lesbian Past*, ed. Martin Duberman, Martha Vicinus, and George Chauncey Jr. (New York: Meridan Press, 1989), 183–195; Vern and Bonnie Bullough, *Cross Dressing, Sex and Gender* (Philadelphia: University of Pennsylvania Press, 1993); and Julie Wheelwright, *Amazons and Military Maids: Women Who Dressed as Men in the Pursuit of Life, Liberty, and Happiness* (London: Pandora, 1989).
36. *The Chicago Medical Journal and Examiner* 48.3 (March 1884): 263–264.
37. James G. Kiernan, "Sexual Perversion and the Whitechapel Murders," *The Medical Standard* 3 (1888): 170.
38. See for example: *The Medical Record: A Weekly Journal of Medicine and Surgery* 26.3 (July 1884): 70; *The Medical Standard* 13.1 (January 1893): 16; *Alienist and Neurologist* 13 (1892): 554–557; and *The New York Medical Times* 20 (1892–93): 170–173.
39. Prof. Von Krafft-Ebing, "Perversion of the Sexual Instinct," *Alienist and Neurologist* 9 (1888): 580.
40. Ibid., 581.
41. Smith-Rosenberg, *Disorderly Conduct*, 273.
42. Duggan, "The Trials of Alice Mitchell," 799.
43. "Jealousy the Motive," *New York Times*, Jan. 29, 1892, 1.
44. "Is Alice Mitchell Crazy?" *New York World*, Jan. 29, 1892, 8.
45. "Memphis Murder Case," *New York Times*, Jan. 31, 1892, 1.
46. T. Griswold Comstock, "Alice Mitchell of Memphis: A Case Sexual Perversion or 'Urning' (A Paranoiac)," *New York Medical Times* 20 (1892–1893): 170.
47. "Sane or Insane? Is She Cruel Murderess or Irresponsible Lunatic?" *Memphis Commercial*, July 19, 1892, 1. As quoted by Duggen in "The Trials of Alice Mitchell," 797.
48. Although Mitchell adopted a passing strategy, a tactic which seems only to reinforce gender polarities, she still acted as a woman trying

to play a male societal role. Because her plan was discovered and exposed before she was allowed to act it out, her decision to *pose* as a man or to *perform* gender publicly could be seen to threaten sacred Victorian notions of difference.
49. Havelock Ellis, "Sexual Inversion in Women," *Alienist and Neurologist* 16 (1895): 156.
50. Smith-Rosenberg, *Disorderly Conduct,* 280.
51. Havelock Ellis and John Addington Symonds, *Sexual Inversion* (London: Wilson and Macmillan, 1897), 197, 200, 201.
52. Ibid., 203.
53. Ibid., 215.
54. Ibid.
55. Richard von Krafft-Ebing, *Psychopathia Sexualis* trans. F. J. Rebman (Brooklyn: Physicians and Surgeons Book Co., 1908), 334. This study was first published in Stuttgart in 1886. For a discussion of this passage see also, Smith-Rosenberg, 271.
56. Duggen, "Trials of Alice Mitchell," 803.

Appendix

EIGHTEENTH-CENTURY AMERICAN BREECHES PERFORMANCE

*THE FOLLOWING LIST HAS BEEN COMPRISED FROM INFORMATION made available by the following scholars: Dunlap, Edwards, Ireland, Odell, Seilhamer, Shattuck and Wilmeth and Bigsby. While this list establishes certain patterns/trends in eighteenth-century breeches performance, it is intended as a sampling and is by no means exhaustive.

1759—June 29   Nancy Hallam plays the Duke of York in *Richard III* at the Southstreet Theatre in Philadelphia.
1759—Oct. 26   Nancy Hallam plays Fleance in *Macbeth*.
1759—Dec. 1   Nancy Hallam plays Fleance at a benefit for Mr. Allyn.
1766—Dec. 5   Miss Dowthwaite plays the Duke of York at the Southwark Theatre with the American Company.
1767—March 14 Miss Dowthwaite plays a page in *Love Makes a Man* at the Southwark Theatre.
1767—March 30 Miss Dowthwaite plays Fleance at the Southwark Theatre.
1767—Summer   The John Street Theatre is built in New York City for the Hallam-Douglass company; the Storer sisters (Ann, Fanny, and Maria) join this company.
1768—Feb. 25   Mrs. Wall plays Prince John from *Henry IV, Part 1* at the John Street Theatre. (Edwards records this as the first breeches performance in America.)

1768—Feb. 11	Maria Storer plays a page in *The Orphan* at the John Street Theatre.
1768—March 3	Maria Storer plays Fleance and Captain Flash from *Miss in Her Teens* at the John Street Theatre.
1768—April 8	Mrs. Osborne plays Damon in *Damon and Phillida* in Williamsburg, Virginia.
1768—May 2	The Storer sisters have a benefit at the John Street Theatre. Maria Storer plays the Duke of York in *Richard III* and Fribble in *Miss in Her Teens*, and Fanny Storer plays Prince Edward in *Richard III* and Captain Flash in *Miss in her Teens*.
1768—May 18	Mrs. Osborne plays Sir Harry Wildair in *The Recruiting Officer* and the First Courtier in *The Miller of Mansfield* in Williamsburg, Virginia for her benefit.
1768—June 3	Mrs. Osborne as Macheath and Ranger in *The Suspicious Husband* for Mr. Burdett's benefit.
1768—Oct.	Maria Storer plays Prince Arthur and Mrs. Harman plays Prince Henry in *King John* in Philadelphia. (They repeated these roles on Jan 9, 1769 at the John Street Theatre.)
1769—March 30	Maria Storer plays Fribble for her benefit at the Southwark Theatre.
1769—May 1, 4	Mrs. Osborne plays Hal in *Henry VI, Part 1* in Annapolis with the New American Company.
1769—May 11	Maria Storer plays Fribble in a joint benefit with John Henry and her sister Ann.
1770–1790s	There is a paucity of information on breeches performance during this twenty year period; indeed no breeches performer of serious note emerges until the 1790s when Miss Harding begins playing various boy roles at the John Street Theatre and becomes the first actress to perform multiple breeches roles. While the Revolutionary War certainly affected theatre production and thus breeches performance during this time period, this is an area that requires further research.
1794—March 14	Mrs. West plays Lucilius in *Julius Caesar* at the John Street Theatre.
1795—Jan. 14	Miss Harding plays Fleance at the John Street Theatre.
1795—Feb. 23	Miss Harding plays the Page in *The Purse* at the John Street Theatre.

1796—April 18   Miss Harding plays the son of William Tell in *The Archers* at the John Street Theatre.
1796—Oct. 7   Miss Harding plays the Prince of Wales.
1798—March 2   Miss Harding plays Prince Arthur in *King John* at the Park Theatre.
1800—Aug. 25   Miss Hogg plays the Boy in *Five Thousand a Year* at Mt. Vernon Gardens.
1800—Dec. 24   Mrs. Hodgkinson plays Sir Edward Bloomly in *Cheap Living* at the Park.

BIBLIOGRAPHY

BOOKS

Abbott, John S. C. *The Mother at Home.* New York: The American Tract Society, 1833.

Ackroyd, Peter. *Dressing Up: Transvestism and Drag: the History of an Obsession.* New York: Simon and Schuster, 1979.

Alger, William Rounseville. *Life of Edwin Forrest, the American Tragedian.* 2 vols. New York, 1877.

Allen, Robert. *Horrible Prettiness: Burlesque and American Culture.* Chapel Hill: University of North Carolina Press, 1991.

Auerbach, Nina. *Ellen Terry: Player in Her Time.* New York: W. W. Norton, 1987.

Bank, Rosemarie K. *Theatre Culture in America, 1825–1860.* New York: Cambridge University Press, 1997.

Barthes, Roland. *Mythologies.* Translated by Annette Lavers. New York: Hill and Wang, 1972.

Bean, Annemarie, James V. Hatch, and Brooks McNamara, eds. *Inside the Minstrel Mask: Readings in Nineteenth-Century Blackface Minstrelsy.* Hanover and London: Wesleyan University Press, 1996.

Blair, Karen J. *The Clubwoman as Feminist: True Womanhood Redefined, 1868–1914.* New York: Holmes and Meier Pub., 1980.

Bradford, Gamaliel. *Biography of the Human Heart.* Boston: Houghton Mifflin Co., 1932.

Brockett, Oscar. *History of the Theatre.* 8th ed. Boston: Allyn and Bacon, 1999.

Brown, Thomas Allston. *History of the New York Stage, 1836–1918.* New York: Dood Mead and Co., 1923.

Bullough, Vern and Bonnie. *Cross Dressing, Sex, and Gender.* Philadelphia: University of Pennsylvania Press, 1993.

Butler, Judith. *Gender Trouble: Feminism and the Subversion of Identity.* New York: Routledge, 1990.

Carnes, David G. and Cylde Griffen eds. *Meanings for Manhood: Constructions of Masculinity in Victorian America.* Chicago: University of Chicago Press, 1991.

Clement, Clara Erskine. *Charlotte Cushman.* Boston: James R. Osgood and Co., 1882.

Coleman, John. *Fifty Years of An Actor's Life.* 2 vols. New York: James Pott and Co., 1904.

Cook, Dutton. *Hours with the Players.* 2 vols. London: Chatto and Windus, 1881.

Curry, Jane Kathleen. *Nineteenth-Century American Women Theatre Managers.* Westport, Conn.: Greenwood Press, 1994.
Davis, Tracy C. *Actresses as Working Women: Their Social Identity in Victorian Culture.* New York: Routledge, 1990.
Dolan, Jill. *The Feminist Spectator as Critic.* Ann Arbor: The University of Michigan Press, 1991.
Dudden, Faye. *Women in the American Theatre: Actresses and Audiences.* New Haven: Yale University Press, 1994.
Dukore, Bernard. *Dramatic Theory and Criticism: Greeks to Grotowski.* New York: Hold, Rinehart and Winston, 1974.
Dunlap, William. *History of the American Theatre.* New York: Burt Franklin, 1963. (Originally published in New York by J. Oram in 1797.)
Ellis, Havelock and John Addington Symonds. *Sexual Inversion.* London: Wilson and Macmillan, 1897.
Elkins, Richard and Dave King. eds. *Blending Genders: Social Aspects of Cross-Dressing and Sex-Changing.* New York: Routledge, 1996.
Evans, Sara M. *Born For Liberty: A History of Women in America.* New York: The Free Press, 1989.
Faderman, Lillian. *Surpassing the Love of Men.* New York: William and Morrow, 1981.
Falk, Bernard. *The Naked Lady.* London: Hutchinson Press, 1952.
Faucit, Helen. *On Some of Shakespeare's Women.* London: printed for private circulation, 1885.
Ferris, Lesley. *Acting Women: Images of Women in Theatre.* New York: New York University Press, 1989.
———. ed. *Crossing the Stage: Controversies on Cross-Dressing.* New York: Routledge, 1993.
Findlater, Richard. *The Player Queens.* New York: Taplinger Publishing, 1976.
Fletcher, George. *Studies of Shakespeare.* London: Longman, Brown, Green, and Longmans, 1847.
French, Benjamin Brown. *Witness to the Young Republic: A Yankee Journal.* Edited by Donald B. Cole and John J. McDonough. Hanover: University Press of New England, 1989.
Fuller, Margaret. *Woman in the Nineteenth Century.* 1845; Reprint, New York: W. W. Norton and Co., 1971.
Gannett, Deborah. *An Address Delivered With Applause, At the Federal Street Theatre, Boston, 4 Successive Nights of the Different Plays, beginning March 22, 1802.* Dedham, Mass.: H. Mann,1802.
Garber, Marjorie. *Vested Interests: Cross-Dressing and Cultural Anxiety.* New York: Routledge, 1992.
Gilder, Rosamond. *Enter the Actress: The First Woman in the Theatre.* Boston: Houghton Mifflin, 1931.
Greven, Philip. *The Protestant Temperament: Patterns of Child-Rearing, Religious Experience, and the Self in Early America.* New York, Alfred A. Knopf, 1977.
Grimstead, David. *Melodrama Unveiled: American Theatre and Culture, 1800–1850.* Chicago: University of Chicago Press, 1968.
Hanners, John. *"It was Play or Starve": Acting in the Nineteenth-Century American Popular Theatre.* Bowling Green, Ohio: Bowling Green State University Popular Press, 1993.

Hartnoll, Phyllis. ed. *The Oxford Companion to the Theatre*. New York: Oxford University Press, 1983.
Helsinger, Elizabeth K., Robin Lauterbach Sheets, and William Veeder. *The Woman Question: Society and Literature in Britain and America, 1837–1883*. Vol. 2. Chicago: The University of Chicago Press, 1983.
Hewitt, Barnard. *Theatre U.S.A.: 1665–1957*. New York: McGraw-Hill, 1959.
Hillcourt, William. *Official Boy Scout Handbook*. Printed by the Boys Scouts of America, 1979.
Howe, Elizabeth. *The First English Actresses: Women and Drama, 1660–1700*. Cambridge: Cambridge University Press, 1992.
Hutton, Lawrence. *Curiosities of the American Stage*. New York: Harper and Brothers, Franklin Square, 1891.
Ireland, Joseph. *Records of the New York Stage from 1750–1862*. 2 vols. New York: T. H. Morrell, 1866.
Jewsbury, Geraldine. *The Half Sisters*. London: Chapman and Hall, 1848.
Johnson, Claudia. *American Actress: Perspective on the Nineteenth Century*. Chicago: Nelson-Hall, 1984.
Krafft-Ebing, Richard von. *Psychopathia Sexualis*. translated by F. J. Rebman. Brooklyn: Physicians and Surgeons Book Co., 1908.
Langner, Lawrence. *The Importance of Wearing Clothes*. New York: Hastings House, 1959.
Laver, James. *Clothes*. New York: Horizon Press, 1953.
Lesser, Allen. *Enchanting Rebel: The Secret of Adah Isaacs Menken*. Philadelphia: Ruttle, Shaw and Wetherill, 1947.
Levine, Lawrence. *Highbrow/Lowbrow: The Emergence of Cultural Hierarchy in America*. Cambridge: Harvard University Press, 1988.
Logan, Olive. *Apropos of Women and Theatre*. New York: Carleton Pub., 1869.
Ludlow, Noah. *Dramatic Life As I Have Found It*. St. Louis: G. I. Jones and Co., 1880.
Mackintosh, Sir James. *Woman As She Is, and As She Should Be*. 2 vols. London: James Cochrane and Co., 1835.
MacMinn. G. R. *Theatre of the Golden Era in California*. Caldwell, Idaho: Caxton Printers, 1941.
Maeder, Clara Fisher. *Autobiography of Clara Fisher Maeder*. Edited by Douglas Taylor. 1897; rpt. by Burt Franklin, 1970.
Mankowitz, Wolf. *Mazeppa: The Lives, Loves and Legends of Adah Isaacs Menken*. New York, Stein and Day, 1982.
Marston, Weston. *Our Recent Actors*. Vol. 2. London: Sampson Low, Marston, Searle and Rivington, 1888.
Mathews, Brander and Laurence Hutton, eds. *Actors and Actresses of Great Britain and the United States*. Vol. 4. New York: Cassell and Co., 1886.
McArthur, Benjamin. *Actors and American Culture, 1880–1920*. Philadelphia: Temple University Press, 1984.
McConachie, Bruce. *Melodramatic Formations: American Theatre and Society, 1820–1870*. Iowa City: University of Iowa Press, 1992.
———. and Thomas Postlewait, eds. *Interpreting the Theatrical Past: Essays on the Historiography of Performance*. Iowa City: University of Iowa Press, 1989.
McCullough, Jack W. *Living Pictures on the New York Stage*. Ann Arbor: UMI Research Press, 1983.

Merrill, Lisa. *When Romeo Was a Woman: Charlotte Cushman and her Circle of Female Spectators*. Ann Arbor: University of Michigan Press, 1999.

Miller, Tice. *Bohemians and Critics: American Theatre Criticism in the Nineteenth Century*. Metuchen, N. J.: Scarecrow Press, Inc., 1981.

Millstein, Beth and Jeanne Bodin. *We, the American Women: A Documentary History*. Chicago: Jermone S. Ozer, Publisher Inc., 1977.

Moi, Toril. *Sexual Textual Politics: Feminist Literary Theory*. New York: Routledge, 1985.

Morris, Clara. *Life on the Stage: My Personal Experiences and Recollections*. New York: 1901.

Mowatt, Anna Cora. *Autobiography of an Actress*. Boston: Ticknor, Reed and Fields, 1854.

Murdoch, James E. *The Stage; or Recollections of Actors and Acting*. New York: Benjamin Blom, 1880.

Odell, George. *Annals of the New York Stage*. Vols. 1–19. New York: Columbia University Press, 1928–1937.

———. *Shakespeare from Betterton to Irving*. New York: Benjamin Blom, 1963.

Pepys, Samuel. *The Diary of Samuel Pepys*. London: Macmillan and Co., 1924.

Phelps, H. P. *Players of A Century: A Record of the Albany Stage*. New York: 1880, rpt.; Benjamin Blom, 1972.

Pickett, LaSalle Corbell. *Across My Path*. New York: Brentano's, 1916.

Poovey, Mary. *Uneven Developments: The Ideological Work of Gender in Mid-Victorian England*. Chicago: University of Chicago Press, 1988.

Price, William T. *A Life of Charlotte Cushman*. New York: Brentano's, 1894.

Pugh, David G. *Sons of Liberty: The Masculine Mind in Nineteenth-Century America*. Westport, Conn: Greenwood Press, 1983.

Rable, George. *Civil Wars: Women and the Crisis of Southern Nationalism*. Urbana: University of Illinois Press, 1991.

Rourke, Constance. *American Humor: A Study of the National Character*. New York: 1935.

Ruggles, Eleanor. *Prince of Players*. New York: W. W. Norton, 1953.

Russo, Ann and Cheris Kramarae, eds. *The Radical Women's Press of the 1850s*. New York: Routledge, 1991.

Ryan, Mary P. *Womanhood in America: From Colonial Times to the Present*. 3rd ed. New York: Franklin Watts, 1983.

———. *Women in Public: Between Banners and Ballots, 1825–1880*. Baltimore: Johns Hopkins University Press, 1990.

Schanke, Robert A. and Kim Marra, eds. *Passing Performances: Queer Readings of Leading Players in American Theatre History*. Ann Arbor: University of Michigan Press, 1998.

Scott, Joan. *Gender and the Politics of History*. New York: Columbia University Press, 1988.

Senelick, Laurence, ed. *Gender in Performance: The Presentation of Difference in the Performing Arts*. Hanover, N. H.: University Press of New England, 1992.

Seilhamer, Robert. *The History of the American Theatre Before the Revolution*. 3 vols. New York: Benjamin Blom, 1968.

Shapiro, Michael. *Gender in Play on the Shakespearean Stage: Boy Heroines and Female Pages.* Ann Arbor: University of Michigan Press, 1994.
Shattuck, Charles H. *Shakespeare on the American Stage: From the Hallams to Edwin Booth.* Washington: Folger Shakespeare Library, 1976.
———. *The Shakespeare Promptbooks: A Descriptive Catalog.* Urbana: University of Illinois Press, 1965.
Sherson, Erroll. *Lost London Theatres of the Nineteenth Century.* London: Constable and Co., 1932.
Smith, Geddeth. *The Brief Career of Eliza Poe.* Rutherford: Fairleigh Dickinson University Press, 1988.
Smith-Rosenberg, Carroll. *Disorderly Conduct: Visions of Gender in Victorian America.* New York: Oxford University Press, 1985.
Stansell, Christine. *City of Women: Sex and Class in New York, 1789–1808.* New York: Alfred A. Knopf, 1986.
Stebbins, Emma. ed. *Charlotte Cushman: Her Letters and Memories of Her Life.* Boston: Houghton, Osgood, and Company, 1879.
Straub, Kristina. *Sexual Suspects: Eighteenth-Century Players and Sexual Ideology.* Princeton: Princeton University Press, 1992.
Thompson, George A. Jr. *A Documentary History of the African Theatre.* Evanston: Northwestern University Press, 1998.
Vandenhoff, George. *Leaves from an Actor's Notebook: Anecdotes of the Green Room and the Stage.* London: T. W. Cooper and Co., 1860.
Velazquez, Loreta J. *The Woman in Battle: A Narrative of the Exploits, Adventures, and Travels of Madame Loreta Janeta Velazquez.* Edited by C. J. Worthington. New York: Arno Press, 1972.
Wemyss, Francis. *Twenty-Six Years of the Life of an Actor and Manager.* New York: Burgess Stringer and Co., 1847.
Wheelwright, Julie. *Amazons and Military Maids: Women Who Dressed As Men in the Pursuit of Life, Liberty and Happiness.* New York: Pandora, 1989.
Whitman, Walt. *Complete Prose Works.* New York, 1914.
Wilcox, Turner. *Five Centuries of American Costume.* New York: Charles Scribner's Son's, 1963.
Willard, George O. *History of the Providence Stage 1762–1891.* Providence: The Rhode Island News Co., 1891.
Wilmeth, Don and Christopher Bigsby eds., *The Cambridge History of American Theatre, Volume One: Beginnings to 1870.* New York: Cambridge University Press, 1997.
Wilson, John H. *All the King's Ladies: Actresses of the Restoration.* Chicago: University of Chicago Press, 1958.
Winter, William. *Shakespeare on Stage.* New York: Moffat, Yard and Co., 1911.
Wollstonecraft, Mary. *A Vindication of the Rights of Women.* 1792; rpt. New York: Prometheus Books, 1989.
Wood, William. *Personal Recollections of the Stage.* Philadelphia: Henry Carey Baird Pub., 1855.
Yeats, William Butler. *W. B. Yeats: The Poems.* Edited by Richard J. Finneran, New York: Macmillan, 1983.

ARTICLES

"Adah Isaacs Menken, the Wife of John C. Heenan," *The New York Illustrated News*, March 31, 1860.

Adler, Louis. "Adah Isaacs Menken in *Mazeppa*." In *Women in American Theatre*, edited by Helen Krich Chinoy and Linda Walsh Jenkins, 81–87. New York: Theatre Communications Group, 1987.

Bangbar, Barnaby. "New Theatre." *The Thespian Monitor* 1.1 (Nov. 25, 1809): 3.

Bank, Rosemarie. "Mrs. Trollope Visits the Theatre: Cultural Diplomacy and Historical Appropriation." *Journal of American Drama and Theatre* 5.3 (Fall 1993): 16–27.

Barrett, Lawrence. "Charlotte Cushman: A Lecture." New York: The Dunlap Society, 1889.

Belsey, Catherine. "Disrupting Sexual Difference: Meaning and Gender in the Comedies." In *Alternative Shakespeares*, edited by John Drakakis, 166–190. New York: Methuen, 1985.

"The Benevolent Boy." *The Lily* 2.2 (Feb. 1850): 16.

"A Biography of Mrs. Jones." *The Thespian Monitor* 1.1 (November 1809): 11.

Bloomer, Ameilia. "Mrs. Kemble and Her New Costume." *The Lily* 1.12 (Dec. 1849): 94.

———. "Women's Dress." *The Lily* 3.3 (March 1851): 17.

———. "Who are the Leaders?" *The Lily* 3.6 (June 1851): 45.

———. "Our Dress." *The Lily* 3.4 (April 1851): 30.

"A Boston Boy in Gotham," *Spirit of the Times* 7.1 (Feb. 18, 1837): 1.

Bratton, J. S. "Irrational Dress." In *The New Woman and her Sisters: Feminism and Theatre 1850–1914*, edited by Vivian Gardner and Susan Rutherford, 77–82. Ann Arbor: University of Michigan Press, 1992.

Butler, Judith. "Performative Acts and Gender Constitution: An Essay in Phenomenology and Feminist Theory." In *Performing Feminisms: Feminist Critical Theory and Theatre*, edited by Sue-Ellen Case, 270–282. Baltimore: Johns Hopkins University Press, 1990.

Cain, James. "Putting on the Girls: Cross-Dressing as a Performative Strategy in the Twelfth-Century Latin Comedy Alda." *Theatre Survey* 38.1 (May 1997): 43–72.

"Charlotte Cushman in London." *Spirit of the Times* 15.14 (May 1845): 154.

Chauncey, George Jr. "From Sexual Inversion to Homosexuality: Medicine and the Changing Conception of Female Deviance." *Salmagundi* 58–59 (Fall 1982-Winter 1983): 114–146.

Chesire, David. "Male Impersonators." *Saturday Book* 29 (1969): 245–256.

Cole, Susan S. "Charlotte Cushman as Romeo." *Southern Theatre* 24 (1981): 3–10.

Cott, Nancy F. "Passionlessness: An Interpretation of Victorian Sexual Ideology, 1790–1850." In *A Heritage of Her Own*, edited by Nancy Cott and Elizabeth H. Plecks, 162–181. New York: Simon and Schuster, 1979.

Cressy, David. "Gender Trouble and Cross-Dressing in Early Modern Europe." *Journal of British Studies* 35 (October 1996): 438–465.

Davis, Tracy C. "Private Women and the Public Realm." *Theatre Survey* 35.1 (May 1994): 65–71.

———. "Questions for a Feminist Methodology in Theatre History." In *Interpreting the Theatrical Past: Essays on the Historiography of Performance*, edited by Bruce McConachie and Thomas Postlewait, 59–81. Iowa City: University of Iowa Press, 1989.

Donkin, Ellen. "Mrs. Siddons Looks Back in Anger: Feminist Historiography for Eighteenth-Century British Theater." In *Critical Theory and Performance*, edited by Janelle G. Reinelt and Joseph R. Roach, 276–290. Ann Arbor: University of Michigan Press, 1992.

Drorbaugh, Elizabeth. "Sliding Scales: Notes on Storme Delarverie and the Jewel Box Revue, the cross-dressed woman on the contemporary stage, and the invert." In *Crossing the Stage: Controversies on Cross-Dressing*, edited by Lesley Ferris, 120–143. New York: Routledge, 1993.

Duggan, Lisa. "The Trials of Alice Mitchell: Sensationalism, Sexology, and the Lesbian Subject in Turn-of-the-Century America." *Signs* (Summer 1993): 791–814.

Edmonds, Jill. "Princess Hamlet." In *The New Woman and Her Sisters*, edited by Vivian Gardner and Susan Rutherford, 59–76. Ann Arbor: University of Michigan Press, 1992.

Elliot, C. W. "One Woman's Work." *The Galaxy* 7.2 (Feb. 1869): 220–229.

"Female Attire." *The Lily* 3.2 (February 1851): 13.

Fletcher, Kathy. "Planche, Vestris, and the Transvestite Role: Sexuality and Gender in Victorian Popular Theatre." *Nineteenth Century Theatre* 15.1 (Summer 1987): 9–33.

"The Fisher Boy." *Godey's Ladies' Book* 1 (Jan. 1830): 280.

Friedman-Romell, Beth H. "Breaking the Code: Toward a Reception Theory of Theatrical Cross-Dressing in Eighteenth-Century London." *Theatre Journal* 47 (1995): 459–479.

Gilbert, Sandra. "Costumes of the Mind: Transvestism as Metaphor in Modern Literature." *Critical Inquiry* (Winter 1980): 391–417.

Gubar, Susan. "Blessings in Disguise: Cross-Dressing as Re-Dressing for Female Modernists." *Massachusetts Review* 22 (Autumn 1981): 477–508.

"Hamlet at Haverly's Fifth Avenue Theatre." *New York Herald*, March 21, 1882.

Highfill, Philip Jr. "The British Background of the American Hallams." *Theatre Survey* 1.1 (1970): 1–35.

Howitt, Mary. "The Miss Cushmans." *The People's Journal* 1 (1847): 30–48.

J. M. W. "First Impressions of Miss Cushman's Romeo." *The People's Journal* 2 (1847): 118.

Kleinberg, Susan J. Introduction to *The Life and Writings of Amelia Bloomer*, edited by D. C. Bloomer, i-xii. 1895; rprt, New York: Schocken Books, 1975.

Kristeva, Julia. "Women's Time." *Signs* 7.1 (August 1981): 13–35.

"Letters to Anthony Evergreen." *Salmagundi* 2.4 (Sept. 1807): 394–395.

Mallett, Mark E. "'The Game of Politics': Edwin Forrest and the Jackson Democrats." *Journal of American Theatre and Drama* 5.2 (Spring 1993): 31–47.

McArthur, Benjamin. "Theatrical Clubs of the Nineteenth Century: Tradition Versus Assimilation in the Acting Community." *Theatre Survey* 23.2 (Nov. 1982): 197–212.

Menken, Adah Isaacs. "Shylock." *Israelite* 4.13 (Oct. 2, 1857): 101.

———. "The Jew in Parliament." *Israelite* 5.9 (Sept. 3, 1858): 65.

"Miss Cushman's Theatre." *Arcturus* 3.17 (April 1842): 388.

Modleski, Tania. "A Woman's Gotta Do . . . What a Man's Gotta Do? Cross-Dressing in the Western." *Signs* 22.3 (1997): 519–544.

Mullenix, Elizabeth Reitz. "A Doublet and Hose in My Disposition: Sexology and the Cross-Dressed Theatrics of the Professional Women's League." *Theatre History Studies* 15 (1995): 1–18.

Munk, Erica. "Drag: 2. Women." *The Village Voice* (March 12, 1985): 80–81.

Nevin, William. "The Bloomer Dress." *The Ladies Wreath* 6 (1852): 247–255.

"Newspaper Criticism." *Arcturus* 1.3 (Feb. 1841): 149.

Novy, Marianne. "Violence, Love, and Gender in *Romeo and Juliet.*" In *Romeo and Juliet: Critical Essays,* edited by John F. Andrews. New York: Garland Publishing, Inc., 1993.

"Our Lady Correspondent. Theatricals in Boston". *Porter's Spirit of the Times* 93.4 (June 12, 1858): 229.

Parrott, Sarah Foose. "Networking in Italy: Charlotte Cushman and 'The White Marmorean Flock.'" *Women's Studies* 14.4 (1988): 334–344.

Phelan, Peggy. "Crisscrossing Cultures." In *Crossing the Stage,* edited by Lesley Ferris, 155–170. New York: Routledge, 1993.

———. "Feminist Theory, Poststructuralism, and Performance." *The Drama Review* 32.1 (1988): 107–127.

Puknat, Elisabeth M. "Romeo was a Lady: Charlotte Cushman's London Triumph." *Theatre Annual* 9 (1951): 59–69.

Rackin, Phyllis. "Androgyny, Mimesis, and the Marriage of the Boy Heroine on the English Renaissance Stage." In *Speaking of Gender,* edited by Elaine Showalter, 113–133. New York: Routledge, 1989.

"Reply to Olive Logan's Letter on the Theatrical Profession." *New York Times,* May 30, 1869, 5.

Roberts, Helene. "The Exquisite Slave: The Role of Clothes in the Making of the Victorian Woman." *Signs* 2.3 (1977): 554–569.

Rotundo, E. Anthony. "Boy Culture: Middle-Class Boyhood in Nineteenth-Century America." In *Meanings for Manhood: Constructions of Masculinity in Victorian America,* edited by David G. Carnes and Cylde Griffen, 14–33. Chicago: University of Chicago Press, 1991.

Russell, Anne. "Gender, Passion, and Performance in Nineteenth-Century Women Romeos." *Essays in Theatre* 11.2 (May 1993): 153–166.

San Francisco Lesbian and Gay History Project. "'She Even Chewed Tobacco': A Pictorial Narrative of Passing Women in America." In *Hidden From History: Reclaiming the Gay and Lesbian Past,* edited by Martin Duberman, Martha Vicinus, and George Chauncey Jr., 183–195. New York: Meridan Press, 1989.

Saxton, Alexander. "Blackface Minstrelsy and Jacksonian Ideology." *American Quarterly* 27:1 (1975): 3–28.

Schanke, Robert A. "Mary Shaw: A Fighting Champion." In *Women in the American Theatre,* edited by Chinoy and Jenkins. New York: Theatre Communications Group, 1987.

Scott, Joan. "Gender: A Useful Category of Analysis." *American Historical Review* 91.5 (October 1985): 1053–1075.

Senelick, Laurence. "The Evolution of the Male Impersonator on the Nineteenth-Century Stage." *Essays in Theatre* 1.1 (1982): 30–44.

———. "Boys and Girls Together: Subcultural origins of glamour drag and male impersonation on the nineteenth-century stage." In *Crossing the Stage*, edited by Lesley Ferris, 80–95. New York: Routledge, 1993.

Shafer, Yvonne. "Women in Male Roles: Charlotte Cushman and Others." In *Women in the American Theatre*, edited by Helen Kirch Chinoy and Linda Walsh Jenkins, 74–81. New York: Crown Publishers, 1981.

"'The Soldier's Daughter,' and 'The Spoiled Child.'" *Theatrical Censor* 1.2 (December 1805): 12.

"Some Female Hamlets." *Boston Herald*, Oct. 30, 1893.

Stedman, Jane. "From Dame to Woman: W. S. Gilbert and Theatrical Transvestism." In *Suffer and Be Still: Women in the Victorian Age*, edited by Martha Vicinus. Bloomington: Indiana University Press, 1972.

Straub, Kristina. "The Guilty Pleasure of Female Theatrical Cross-Dressing and the Autobiography of Charlotte Charke." In *Body Guards: The Cultural Politics of Gender Ambiguity*, edited by Julian Epstein and Kristina Straub, 142–166. New York: Routledge, 1991.

"The Theatre," *Ladies' Port Folio* 1.5 (January 29, 1820): 35.

"Theatre Critique No. 5," *New York Evening Post*, Dec. 14, 1801.

Welter, Barbara. "The Cult of True Womanhood: 1820–1860." *American Quarterly* 18 (Summer 1966): 151–174.

White, Richard Grant. "The Age of Burlesque." *The Galaxy* 3.2 (August 1869): 256–266.

Whittier, Gayle. "The Sublime Androgyne Motif in Three Shakespearean Works." *Journal of Medieval and Renaissance Studies* 19. 2 (1989): 185–210.

Wizard, William. "Theatrics." *Salmagundi* 1.6 (1807): 123.

"Woman, Considered a Domestic Animal." *Spirit of the Times* 21.23 (July 26, 1851): 266.

"Woman's Sphere." *The Lily* 2.4 (April 1850): 26.

"A Word to Boys." *The Lily* 2.3 (March 1850): 24.

J. M. W. "First Impressions of Miss Cushman's Romeo." *The People's Journal* 2 (1847): 118–119.

NEWSPAPERS AND PERIODICALS

Albion, 1823–1869.
Alienist and Neurologist, 1883.
American Israelite, 1857–1859.
American Monthly Magazine and Critical Review, 1817–1818.
Arcturus, 1841–1842.
Athenaeum, 1846.
The Britannia, 1846.
Broadway Journal, 1845–1846.
The Chicago Medical Journal and Examiner, 1884.
The Christian Inquirer, 1847.
Collier's Weekly, 1894.
The Cynick, 1811.

Godey's Ladies' Book, 1830–1839.
Harper's Magazine, 1863.
Ladies' Port Folio, 1820.
The Ladies Wreath, 1852.
The Lily, 1849–1852.
Lloyd's Weekly Messenger, 1846.
London Times, 1845–1846.
The Medical Record: A Weekly Journal of Medicine and Surgery, 1884.
The Medical Standard, 1888.
Mirror of Taste and Dramatic Censor, 1810–1811.
New Mirror, 1843–1845.
New York Clipper, 1853–1869.
New York Daily News, 1860.
New York Daily Tribune, 1866.
New York Dramatic Mirror, 1893–1894.
New York Express, 1866.
New York Herald, 1852–1860.
New York Evening Post, 1801–1817.
New York Illustrated News, 1860.
The New York Literary Gazette, 1839.
The New York Medical Times, 1892–1893.
New York Mirror, 1823–1841.
New York Times, 1860–1893.
New York Tribune, 1862–1866.
New York World, 1866.
The Observer, 1846.
Polyanthos, 1805–1807.
Porter's Spirit of the Times, 1858.
Salmagundi, 1807
The Spirit of the Times, 1831–1861, 1893.
Theatrical Censor, 1805–1806.
Thespian Mirror, 1806.
Thespian Monitor and Dramatick Miscellany, 1809.
Wilkes' Spirit of the Times, 1859–1860.

DISSERTATIONS

Angotti, Vince. American Dramatic Criticism, 1800–1830. Ph.D. diss., University of Kansas, 1967.

Edwards, Charlene. The Tradition for Breeches in the Three Centuries that Professional Actresses Have Played Male Roles on the English-Speaking Stage. Ph.D. diss., University of Denver, 1957.

Merrill, Lisa. Charlotte Cushman: American Actress on the Vanguard of New Roles for Women. Ph.D. diss., New York University, 1984.

Morgan, Kathleen A. Of Stars and Standards: Actress-Managers of Philadelphia and New York, 1855–1880. Ph.D. diss., University of Illinois, 1983.

Moses, Marilyn. Lydia Thompson and the British Blondes in the United States. P.h.D. diss, University of Oregon, 1978.
Renee M. Sentilles. Performing Menken: Adah Isaacs Menken's American Odyssey. Ph.D. diss., College of William and Mary, 1997.
Tumbleson, Treva Rose. Three Female Hamlets: Charlotte Cushman, Sarah Bernhardt, and Eva Le Galliene. Ph.D. diss., University of Oregon, 1981.
Whitehead, Barbara. Fancy's Show Box: Performance in the Republic, 1790–1866. Ph.D. diss., University of Chicago, 1976.
Young, Liz. Border States and Counterfeit Confederates: Cross-Dressing and the Fictions of Civil War Narrative. Ph.D. diss., University of California at Berkley, 1994.

UNPUBLISHED MATERIAL

Burton, William. Letter to Benjamin Webster. Charlotte Cushman "Extra-Illustrated," vol. 4 no. 6. Harvard Theatre Collection.
Cushman, Charlotte. Letter to William Henry Chippendale, September 20, 1849. Charlotte Cushman Manuscript Collection. Harvard Theatre Collection.
———. Letter to Emma Crow, January 29, 1861. Letters of James and Annie Fields, 1837–1874. Schlessinger Library Collection.
———. Letter to Mr. Grigg, n.d. Charlotte Cushman Manuscript Collection. Harvard Theatre Collection.
———. Letter to William H. Seward, 4 Dec. 1861. William Seward Papers. University of Rochester Library, New York.
Mercer, Sallie. Letter to Dennis Alward, 26 December 1884. Charlotte Cushman Box. Harvard Theatre Collection.

DRAMATIC LITERATURE

Anon. (also Noah Mordecai) *The Wandering Boys; or the Castle of Olival*. New York: Samuel French, 1860.
Buckstone, J. B. *The Pet of the Petticoats*. New York: O. A. Roorbach, Jr., 1855.
Diamond, William. *The Broken Sword: or, the Torrent of the Valley*. London: Thomas Lacy, 1850.
Holcroft, Thomas. *Deaf and Dumb; or, The Orphan Protected*. In *The London Stage: A Collection of the Most Reputed Tragedies, Comedies, Operas, Melodramas, Farces, and Interludes*, 228–235. vol. 1. London: G. Balne, 1825.
Milner, Henry. *Mazeppa or the Wild Horse of Tartary*. Adapted from the poem by Byron. London: Thomas Hailes Lacy, 1870.
Talfourd, T. N. *Ion*. London: A. J. Valpy, 1835.
Shakespeare, William. *As You Like It*. Edited by G. Blakemore Evans. Boston: Houghton Mifflin Co., 1974.
Shakespeare, William. *Romeo and Juliet*. New York: W. M. Taylor and Co., n.d.

Index

Abbe De L'eppe or The Dumb Made Eloquent (by Thomas Holcroft, also known as *Deaf and Dumb, or, The Orphan Protected*), 147
Ackroyd, Peter, 160
Actor's Fund of America (Lester Wallack), 283
African Theatre (also African Grove Theatre), 14
Aladdin *(Aladdin)*, 43, 85
Allen, Robert, 29, 245–246, 254, 266–269
Almanzor and Almahide, or the Conquest of Granada (Dryden), 32
androgyne, *see* gender
Angotti, Vincent, 24
antebellum gender ideology, *see* gender
As You Like It (Shakespeare), 281–282, 285–289, 296, 300
Astor Place Riot, 30–31
audiences, 27–31, 259, 260

Bangbar, Barnaby, 29
Bank, Rosemarie, 28–29
Barnes, Mary, 28, 41, 43, 122–123
 as Hamlet, 122
 as Myrtillo, 144–145
 as Norval, 120–122
Barnes-McLain, Noreen, 10
Barnum, P. T., 272–273, 314–315n24
Barrington, John, 35
Beckett, Gilbert Abbott á, 208
Belino, Count *(The Devil's Bridge)*, 15, 51, 90–91, 93
Belsey, Catherine, 202–204, 206

benefits, 36, 44–45, 237–238
Black-Eyed Susan (by Douglas Jerrold), 87
Blair, Karen, 289
Bloomer, Amelia, 67–81
Bloomer Troupe, 83
bloomers, *see* clothing, nineteenth-century
Booth, Edwin, 85
Bowery Theatre, 22, 28–29, 54
boy culture, 182–183
boys (women as), *see* cross-dressed actress
Bradford, Gamaliel, 97
breeches performer, *see* cross-dressed actress
Broken Sword, The (or The Torrent of the Valley by William Diamond), 40, 43–44, 141–146
Buford, Harry T., *see* Velazquez, Loreta Janeta
Burton, William E., 5
Butler, Judith, 12, 200, 216

Carnes, Mark C., 54
Celeste, 118–120, 147
Charke, Charlotte, 34
Chatham Theatre, 28
Chauncey, George, 291
child stars, 48, 63, 154–159
 see Fisher, Clara
 see West, William Henry
 see Payne, John Howard
Cibber, Colly, 34
Cinderella, 72
Civil War, 83, 108, 345n50, 111

INDEX

Clifton, Miss, 94
Clive, Kitty, 1
Coleman, John, 105–106, 188, 215, 217, 222, 226, 228
Colin *(Nature and Philosophy)*, 43, 153
   Miss Johnson as, 153–154
clothing, nineteenth-century, 77–90
   Bloomers, 67, 79–83
   costumes of the breeches performer, 86–89, 143, 242–244
Company of Comedians from London, *see* Hallam troupe
Constant Couple, The (by George Farquhar), 1
Cook, Dutton, 208
Cooper, Thomas A., 43, 123
Cott, Nancy, 174–175, 220
Covent Garden Theatre, 34
Crampton, Charlotte, 62–63, 106–108
critics/criticism, 22–27
cross-dressed actress
   as boy, 8, 39–40, *see* Chapter 3 (127–183)
   as feminine, 148, 150–151, 153, 163–171
   as sexual object, 7–8, 32, 242–277
   as subversive, 51, 71–126, also 185–230
   decline of breeches performance, 231–280
   disguise role vs. breeches role, 6, 31
   drag, 9, 12, 82, 268
   male impersonator, 5
   origins of, 31–38
   "passing," 189–199
   Principal Boy, 46
   transvestite, 6, 180–183
   trends after 1869, 277–280
   Trickster, 201, 220
Cushman, Charlotte, 2, 5, 16–17, 49, 51, 59–62, 65–66, 85, 103, 105, 117–118, 123
   as Androgyne, *see* Chapter 4 (185–230)
   as bread winner, 104
   as Cardinal Wolsey, 239–240
   as Claude Melnotte, 96
   as Hamlet, 96–102
   as model for Bianca Pazzi in *The Half Sisters*, 218–220
   as offstage cross-dresser, 106, 183, 228–229
   as Paul the Pet, 148–149, 152–153
   as Romeo, 105, 124, 131–132 (illustration), 134–135, 171–175, 185–186, 189,192, 193 (illustration), 194–198, 201, 207, 211, 214–217
   as Rosalind, 190–192, 202–206, 334n21
   lesbianism, 224–228
Cushman, Susan, 104
   as Juliet, 192

Darley, Mrs., 40
Davenport, Jean, 56
Davis, Tracy C., 3, 77
Deaf and Dumb; or, The Orphan Protected, 145, 147
   see Abbe De L'Eppe or The Dumb Made Eloquent
decline of breeches, *see* cross-dressed actress
Dickinson, Anna, 278
discourses of containment, 160–180
disguise role vs. breeches role, *see* cross-dressed actress
Donkin, Ellen, 220–221
Douglass, David, 35–36
Dowthwaite, Miss, 37
drag, *see* cross-dressed actress
Drorbaugh, Elizabeth, 162, 286
Drury Lane Theatre, 34
Dryden, John, 32
Dudden, Faye, 10, 238, 245–246
Duggan, Lisa, 293–295, 299
Duke's House, *see* Lincoln's Inn Fields Theatre
Dunlap, William, 5, 7, 24, 39

Edwards, Charlene, 7–9, 237, 277
Ellis, Havelock, 296–299
Evans, Sara, 57, 67
Evergreen, Anthony, 21

Faderman, Lillian, 226
Farquhar, George, 1, 35
Ferris, Lesley, 9, 234
Fielding, Henry, 35
Fisher, Clara, 47–51, 156–158, 178
    as Goldfinch, 116–117
    as Norval, 117
Fisher, Kate, 89
    as Mazeppa, 239
Fletcher, George, 215–217
Forrest, Edwin, 30, 95, 99
Friedman-Romell, Beth H., 10
Fuller, Margaret, 75–76

Gannett, Dorothy Sampson, 84–85
Garber, Marjorie, 6, 130, 180–181
Garcia, Signorina, 91
Garden Theatre, 282
Garrick, David, 210
Gay, Tony *(A Trip to Chinatown* by Charles Hoyt), 241
gender
    androgyne, 199–230
    antebellum gender ideology, 29, 47, 74–77, 114, 116
    performance of, 12, 84, 90, 100, 179, 286–287
    True Womanhood, 7, 11, 75, 77–78, 100, 105, 108, 116, 138, 140, 199, 218, 222, 250, 287, 291, 300, 302n13
    women compared to children, 134–140
Gilbert, Sandra, 12
Gilder, Rosamond, 7
Goldfinch *(The Road to Ruin), see* Clara Fisher
Gray, Hannah, 84
Greven, Philip, 138
Griffen, Clyde, 52
Grimstead, David, 26, 30, 115
Grow, Willie *(A Trip to Chinatown* by Charles Hoyt), 241
Gubar, Susan, 12, 84
Gwynn, Nell, 32

The Half Sisters (by Geraldine Jewsbury), 218–220

    see Cushman, Charlotte as model for Bianca Pazzi
Hallam troupe (Company of Commedians from London), 34–35
    Adam, 36
    Lewis, 34–36
    Mrs. Lewis, 35–36
    Nancy (Anne), 35–36
    William, 35
Hamlet, 28, 56
    Barnes as, 122
    Cushman as, 61, 96–102
    Dickinson as, 278
    Prescott as, 278
Harding, Miss, 37–38
Hayes, Matilda, 225
Haymarket Theatre, 60, 185
Helsinger, Elizabeth K., 137
Herring, Fanny, 252–253
Hewitt, Barnard, 3–4, 8
Highfill, Philip Jr., 34–35
Hodekinson, Mrs., 39–41
Home, John, 40
Hosmer, Harriett, 103
Howe, Elizabeth, 32
Howells, William Dean, 268
Hudson, Leo, 89, 255, 271–273
    as Mazeppa, 255, 256 (Illustration), 257

Ion (Ion; or The Foundling of Argos by T. N. Talfourd)
    Shaw-Hamblin as, 133
    Tree as, 163–171 (Illustration, 168)
Ireland, Joseph, 7
Irving, Washington, 19
Ixion; or The Man at the Wheel, see Thompson, Lydia

J. M. W., 196–197
Johnson, Miss, 14
    as Colin, 153–154
Johnson, Samuel, 27
Jones, Mrs., 41–42
Julio, Count (also known as Theodore; in *Deaf and Dumb)*, 145–146

Keene, Laura, 231
Kemble, Fanny, 80, 109
Knowles, Sheridan, 192, 197, 215, 227
Krafft-Ebing, Richard von, 291–293, 296, 298–299
Kristeva, Julia, 204–205

Lacan, Jacques, 101, 162, 319n80
Ladies' Port Folio, 27
lesbians/lesbianism, 105–106, 174–175, 224–228, 291–300,
Lesser, Allen, 260
Levine, Lawrence, 31
Lewis, Mrs. Henry, 52–56
  as Richard III, 95
Licensing Act of 1737, 35
Lincoln's Inn Fields Theatre, 1
lines of business, 46–47
Little Pickle *(Little Pickle; or The Spoil'd Child),* 40, 42
living pictures (tableaux vivants), 245–246, 258
Logan, Olive, 17, 237 267, 270–277
Luppino, Miss, 141

Macheath, Captain *(The Beggar's Opera* by John Gay), 231
Mackintosh, James, 78
male gaze, 221
Macready, William Charles, 30, 60, 99, 189, 190, 194, 207, 208
male impersonator, *see* cross-dressed actress
Marra, Kim, 10
Marston, John Westland, 227
"Master" Betty, *see* William Henry West
Mazeppa *(Mazeppa; or The Wild Horse of Tartary* by Henry Milner), 67, 242, 273
  Fisher, Kate as, 239
  Hudson, Leo as, 255–257
  Menken, Adah Isaacs as, 68, 88–89, 244 (Illustration), 253, 255, 261-264
  Vance, Kate as, 242, 257
McConachie, Bruce, 175–178, 181
Melnotte, Claude *(The Lady of Lyons* by Edward Bulwer-Lytton), 96

melodrama, 16, 26, 27
  equestrian, 242–264, 277
Melville, Herman, 228
Menken, Adah Isaacs, 10–11, 17, 69, 246–253, 260, 270–271
  as French Spy, 243 (Illustration)
  as Jack Sheppard, 247, 253
  as Mazeppa, 68, 88–89, 244 (Illustration), 248, 253, 255, 261-264
  as offstage cross-dresser
  as sex object, 251
  as William, 88
  in Dayton, Ohio, 247
  Jewish heritage, 110, 248
  patriotism, 111
Merrill, Lisa, 10, 104, 174, 220, 225, 227
Mitchell/Ward Trial, 293–297, 300
Morris, Clara, 131
Morrow, Lee Allen, 10
Mowatt, Anna Cora, 76–77
Mulvey, Laura, 221
Munk, Erica, 234
Myrtillo *(The Broken Sword* by William Diamond), 40, 43, 44, 141–145
  Barnes as, 144–147

Nature and Philosophy, 43, 127, 153
Nevin, William, 80
New Theatre, 34
New Wells Theatre (in Goodman's Fields), 34
Niblo's Garden, 266
Noah, Mordecai, 5–6, 331n114
Norval *(Douglas* by John Home), 40, 44
  Barnes as, 120–122
  Fisher as, 117
  Payne, John Howard as, 121
Novy, Marianne, 212

Odell, George, 42, 44, 302n15
Oldmixon, Mrs., 40
Olympic Theatre, 71- 72
origins of breeches performance, *see* cross-dressed actress

Osborne, Mrs., 37
Othello *(Othello* by Shakespeare), 19

Palmer's Theatre, 282
Park Theatre, 28, 39, 60
"passing," *see* cross-dressed actress
Paul *(The Pet of the Petticoats* by J. B. Buckstone), 148–153
  Cushman as, 148–149, 152–153
Paul and Justin *(The Wandering Boys* by Mordecai Noah, also anonymous), 6, 176–180, 181
Paul and Alexis; or The Orphas of the Rhine, see *The Wandering Boys*
Payne, John Howard, 42, 48, 121–122
Pearlman, Mr., 51, 91, 93
performance of gender, *see* gender
Pepys, Samuel, 1
Pet of the Petticoats, The (J. B. Buckstone), 148–153
Peter Pan *(Peter Pan* by J. M. Barrie), 180–181
Pickett, LaSalle Corbell, 229
Prescott, Marie (as Hamlet), 278
Price, William, 223, 235
Principal Boy, *see* cross-dressed actress
Professional Women's League, 281–285, 287–290, 295–296, 298–300
Provok'd Husband, The, 34

Rackin, Phyllis, 199
Recruiting Officer, The (George Farquhar), 35
Revolutionary War, 84
Richard III *(Richard III* by Shakespeare), 14, 35, 47, 48, 53, 56
  Lewis, Mrs. Henry as, 95
  Tree, Ellen, 96
Richmond Hill Theatre, 43, 127, 128
Romeo *(Romeo and Juliet* by Shakespeare)
  Cushman as, 60, 66, 85, 105, 124, 131, 132 (Illustration), 134–135, 171–175, 185–186, 189, 192, 193 (Illustration), 194–198, 201, 207, 211, 214–217
Romeo and Juliet (Shakespeare), 211–214

Rosalind *(As You Like It* by Shakespeare), 285, 287
  Cushman as, 190–192, 202–206, 334n21
  Tree as, 169, 191
Rotundo, Anthony, 182
Rourke, Constance, 114
Russell, Anne, 10, 159, 186, 209, 238
Russell, Mrs., 127–128, 134
  as Julian, 128, 131
Ryan, Mary, 57–58, 75

Saxton, Alexander, 54
Schanke, Robert A., 10
Scott, Joan, 12, 90, 102
Seilhamer, George, 35
Senelick, Laurence, 5, 9
Sentilles, Renée, 11, 110, 251
sexology, 291–293, 296–299
Sharpe, Mrs., 15, 51, 90–94
Shaw, Miss, 14
Shaw-Hamblin, Eliza Trewar, 56
  as Ion, 133
Sheets, Robin Lautebach, 137
Sheppard, Jack, *see* Herring, Fanny and Menken, Adah Isaacs
Shurtleff, Robert, 84
Smith-Rosenberg, Carroll, 12, 57, 160–161, 176, 297
Smock Alley Theatre, 34
Southwark Theatre, 37
Spirit of the Times, 15, 19, 59
Spoil'd Child, The see *Little Pickle*
Stallybrass, Peter, 260
Stansell, Christine, 41
Stebbins, Emma, 96, 98, 103, 131, 225
Storer, Maria, 37
Straub, Kristina, 10, 12, 16, 34, 174
Swisshelm, Mrs., 80

Talbot, Mary Ann, 84
Taylor, Mary, 71–73
Tempest, The (Charles Gayler's rendition), 254
Theodore (also known as Count Julio in *Deaf and Dumb/Abbe De L'Eppe),* 145–147

Thompson, Lydia, 10, 17, 69, 111–112, 269
  as Ixion, 265–267, 270
Thompsonian Burlesque, 13, 69, 264–277
Timm, Sarah, 15, 71–73
Tom and Jerry, 14
Townley, Lady *(The Provok'd Husband),* 34
transvestite, *see* cross-dressed actress
Tree, Ellen, 16
  as Ion, 163–171 (Illustration, 168)
  as Richard III, 96
  as Rosalind, 169, 191
Trollop, Clarinda, 21
Trollope, Frances, 28
True Womanhood, *see* gender
Tumbleson, Treva Rose, 96

Vance, Kate, 89
  as Mazeppa, 242–243, 257, 258
Vandenhoff, George, 19, 124, 214, 216- 217
Veeder, William, 137
Velazquez, Loreta Janeta, 83
Verbruggen, Susan, 32
Vestvali, Felicja, 271, 273

Walen, Denise A., 10
Wales, Prince of *(Richard III),* 36
Wall, Mrs., 35
Walnut Street Theatre, 214, 322n131
Wandering Boys, The (Mordecai Noah or Anonymous), 6, 175–181

"wearing the breeches," 4, 9, 11, 20, 21, 92, 102–113
Webster, Benjamin, 5
Welch, Miss S., 14
West, William Henry, 48, 156
White, Allon, 260
White, Richard Grant, 268–269
Whitman, Walt, 22, 29
Whittier, Gayle, 206
Wildair, Sir Harry *(The Constant Couple),* 1
William *(Black-Eyed Susan),* 87, 242
Willoughby, Sam *(Ticket-of-Leave Man* by Tom Taylor), 241
Wilson, J. H., 31
Winter, William ("Mercutio"), 235, 240, 261–264
Wizard, William, *see* Irving, Washington
Woffington, Peg, 1, 5, 33–34
Wollstonecraft, Mary, 135–136
Wolsey, Cardinal, 61
  Cushman as, 239, 240
women compared to children, *see* gender
Women's Right's Movement, 57- 58, 66, 136–137
Wood, William, 233
Wood's Broadway Theatre, 265
Worry, Roderick, 21
Wright, Fanny, 58, 75

Yeats, William Butler, 78
York, Duke of *(Richard III),* 35–37